Christopher R. Seitz
Theology in Conflict

Christopher R. Seitz

Theology · in Conflict

Reactions to the Exile in the Book of Jeremiah

Walter de Gruyter · Berlin · New York
1989

Beiheft zur Zeitschrift für die alttestamentliche Wissenschaft

Herausgegeben von Otto Kaiser

176

Printed on acid free paper
(ageing resistent — pH 7, neutral)

Library of Congress Cataloging-in-Publication Data

Seitz, Christopher R.
  Theology in conflict : reactions to the Exile in the book of
Jeremiah / Christopher R. Seitz.
  p.   cm. — (Beiheft zur Zeitschrift für die
alttestamentliche Wissenschaft ; 176)
  Abridgement of thesis (Ph. D.) — Yale University, 1986.
  Bibliography: p.
  Includes indexes.
  ISBN 0-89925-303-2 (U.S. : alk. paper)
  1. Jews—History—953—586 B. C. 2. Jews—History—Babylo-
nian captivity, 598—515 B. C. 3. Bible. O. T. Jeremiah—Theology.
I. Title. II. Series: Beihefte zur Zeitschrift für die alttestamentliche
Wissenschaft ; 176.
BS410.Z5 vol. 176
[DS121.6]
221.6 s—dc19
[221.9'5]   89-1293
                                                         CIP

CIP-Kurztitelaufnahme der Deutschen Bibliothek

Seitz, Christopher R.:
Theology in conflict : reactions to the exile in the Book of Jeremiah
/ Christopher R. Seitz. — Berlin ; New York : de Gruyter, 1989
  (Beiheft zur Zeitschrift für die alttestamentliche Wissenschaft ;
  176)
  Zugl.: New Haven, Yale Univ., Diss., 1986
  ISBN 3-11-011223-X
NE: Zeitschrift für die alttestamentliche Wissenschaft / Beiheft

ISSN: 0934-2575

to
Thomas Comstock Seitz
Janet Reese Seitz
טוֹב יַנְחִיל בְּנֵי־בָנִים

Preface

This study of conflict in the exilic period is a shortened version of a dissertation submitted in 1986 to Yale University for the degree of Doctor of Philosophy. It is a broad-based study which examines history, sociology, and the biblical literature relevant for the period, including Ezekiel, 2 Kings 24—25, and especially the Book of Jeremiah.

I would like to thank my dissertation director, Professor Robert R. Wilson, and my colleagues at Yale Divinity School, Professors Brevard S. Childs and Robert Lansing Hicks, for their support and encouragement. Mr. Donald J. Westblade provided invaluable technical assistance with preparation of the final manuscript. Ms. Corrine L. Patton prepared the index.

I wish to express my deep appreciation to the Frederick W. Hilles Publication Fund of Yale University for their generous financial assistance with publication expenses. The Episcopal Church Foundation and Lutheran Theological Seminary at Philadelphia provided further support.

Finally I would like to thank Professor Dr. Otto Kaiser and Walter de Gruyter & Co., publishers, for accepting my manuscript in this series.

This book is dedicated to my parents in gratitude for their faith and and love of life.

New Haven, 1 January 1989   Christopher R. Seitz

Table of Contents

Chapter One
The Nature of the Problem

Debate persists among exegetes over the correct procedure for critical interpretation of the Book of Jeremiah. Problem areas include the selection and execution of a literary critical method which recognizes the diversity of formal types of literature in the book (poetic speech; biographical narrative; historical report; auto-biographical account; "formal prose"; poetic lament).[1] The Book of Jeremiah is a rich panoply of differing literary forms, unique among the other prophetic books. Herein lies the problem. The question of overall narrative coherence is a vexed one; a satisfactory explanation for the origins and development of the diverse oral and literary forms is equally problematic.

Material arguments have been brought to bear based upon evidence from outside the book to help adjudicate matters related to correct literary approach.[2] But these arguments have likewise proven tricky. For example,

---

[1] Compare the studies of Helga Weippert and William Holladay with those of Winfried Thiel and Ernest Nicholson: H. Weippert, *Die Prosareden des Jeremiabuches* (Berlin/New York: Walter de Gruyter, 1973); W. L. Holladay, "Prototype and Copies: A New Approach to the Poetry-Prose Problem in the Book of Jeremiah," *JBL* 79 (1960) 351—67; "The Background of Jeremiah's Self-Understanding: Moses, Samuel, and Psalm 22," *JBL* 83 (1964) 153—64; "The Recovery of Poetic Passages of Jeremiah," *JBL* 85 (1966) 401—35; "A Fresh Look at 'Source B' and 'Source C' in Jeremiah," *VT* 25 (1975) 394—412; "The Identification of Two Scrolls of Jeremiah," *VT* 30 (1980) 452—67; "The Year of Jeremiah's Preaching," *Int* 37 (1983) 146—59; W. Thiel, *Die deuteronomistische Redaktion von Jeremia 1—25* (WMANT 41; Neukirchen-Vluyn: Neukirchener, 1973); *Die deuteronomistische Redaktion von Jeremia 26—45* (WMANT 52; Neukirchen-Vluyn: Neukirchener, 1981); E. W. Nicholson, *Preaching to the Exiles: A Study of the Prose Tradition of the Book of Jeremiah* (New York: Schocken, 1970). See also the careful study of the problem by William McKane, "Relations Between Poetry and Prose in the Book of Jeremiah with Special Reference to Jeremiah III 6—11 and XII 14—17," *VTSup* 28 (1980) 220—37.

[2] G. Hölscher, *Die Propheten: Untersuchungen zur Religionsgeschichte Israels* (Leipzig: J. C. Hinrichs'sche, 1914) esp. 379—405; John Skinner, "Jeremiah and Deuteronomy," in *Prophecy and Religion: Studies in the Life of Jeremiah* (Cambridge: At the University Press, 1922) 89—107; O. Eissfeldt, *Einleitung in das Alte Testament* (Tübingen: J. C. B. Mohr, 1934) esp. 16—18 and 389—441; J. P. Hyatt, "Jeremiah and Deuteronomy," *JNES* 1 (1942) 156—73; H. H. Rowley, "The Prophet Jeremiah and the Book of Deuteronomy," in *Studies in Old Testament Prophecy Presented to T. H. Robinson* (Edingburgh: T. & T. Clark, 1950) 157—74; H. Cazelles, "Jérémie et le Deutéronome," *RSR* 38 (1951) 5—36; J. Bright, "The Date of the Prose Sermons of Jeremiah," *JBL* 70 (1951) 15—35; J. W. Miller, *Das Verhältnis Jeremias und Hesekiels sprachlich und theologisch untersucht* (Assen: Royal VanGorcum, 1955); A. Weiser, *The Old Testament: Its Formation and Development* (New York: Association Press, 1966) 217—8; C. Rietzschel, *Das Problem der Urrolle: Ein Beitrag*

turning to theories which compare prose-types from Jeremiah with prose-types from Deuteronomy only begs much broader — and more difficult — questions as to the origins, development, date, and provenance of the complex Deuteronomic and Deuteronomistic phenomena. This is true precisely at the moment one grants an essential correctness to arguments in support of their common origin. Those who reject a common origin must still supply reasonable explanations for the striking similarity between Jeremiah and Deuteronomistic literary forms — involving date-lowering, different religio-historical conclusions, alternative proposals for Jeremiah's affiliation to deuteronomic(istic) thought and sociological milieu, and the like. But the outcome is essentially the same. Turning to Deuteronomism for aid in interpreting Jeremiah, even if on the right track, is tantamount to entering a war to win a battle.[3]

Rather than move within the orbit of these traditional approaches, this study will seek instead to broaden the base of the socio-historical inquiry and alter the sequence of investigation. Literary, form, and redaction critical approaches all share a common assumption about proper approach to Jeremiah: one interprets the book by beginning with the literary phenomenon of Jeremiah. This was well and good when the method was conceived and as it moved through its various permutations: from source, to form, to tradition, to redaction critical emphasis.[4] (We leave to the side so-called rhetorical analysis.) But increasingly, as the method developed and reached a level of sophistication, it became impossible to assume a neutrality with respect to religio-historical conclusions. These conclusions involved matters as diverse as the influence of Deuteronomy, mentioned above, but also the Reform of Josiah,[5] the date of the prophet's call,[6] the impact of the

---

zur Redaktionsgeschichte des Jeremiabuches (Gütersloh: Gerd Mohn, 1966); E. Würthwein, "Die Josianische Reform und das Deuteronomium," *ZTK* 73 (1976) 395—423.

[3] For this reason, Karl-Friedrich Pohlmann has attempted to avoid appeal to Deuteronomism in his own redaction-critical study, *Studien zum Jeremiabuch: Ein Beitrag zur Frage nach der Entstehung des Jeremiabuches* (FRLANT 118; Göttingen: Vandenhoeck & Ruprecht, 1978).

[4] This evolution can be plotted through the works of B. Duhm (*Das Buch Jeremia* [KHC 11; Tübingen/Leipzig: J. C. B. Mohr, 1901]) and S. Mowinckel (*Zur Komposition des Buches Jeremia* [Kristiania: Jacob Dybwad, 1914]); W. Rudolph (*Jeremia* [HAT 12; Tübingen: J. C. B. Mohr, 1947], J. P. Hyatt ("The Deuteronomic Edition of Jeremiah," in *Vanderbilt Studies in the Humanities* 1 [1951] 71—95), and T. H. Robinson ("Baruch's Roll," *ZAW* 42 [1924] 209—21); S. Mowinckel (*Prophecy and Tradition* [Oslo: Jacob Dybwad, 1946]), G. Wanke (*Untersuchungen zur sogenannten Baruchschrift* [BZAW 122: Berlin/New York: Walter de Gruyter, 1973]), and C. Rietzschel *(Das Problem der Urrolle)* W. Thiel *(Die deuteronomistische Redaktion)* and K.-F. Pohlmann *(Studien zum Jeremiabuch).*

[5] J. Skinner, "In the Wake of the Reform," in *Prophecy and Religion,* 108—37; H. H. Rowley, "The Early Prophecies of Jeremiah in Their Setting," *BJRL* 45 (1962) 198—234.

[6] C. F. Whitley, "The Date of Jeremiah's Call," *VT* 14 (1964) 467—83; J. P. Hyatt, "The Beginning of Jeremiah's Prophecy," *ZAW* 78 (1966) 204—14; T. Overholt, "Some

exile,[7] Jeremiah's relationship to the cult,[8] and many others. The religio-historical world outside the strict literary phenomenon of Jeremiah was gradually outfitted with a wide range of diachronic data and assumptions.

For those who have worked with the Jeremiah scholarship produced in this century, it is impossible to engage a strict literary analysis of the text without at the same time developing certain expectations about the religio-historical outcome of this analysis. This is not said as a negative judgment. To a certain degree early (ninteenth-century) claims for objectivity and neutrality were simply more valid, seen now with hindsight. For the whole gathering accumulation of possible religio-historical conclusions had yet to make its influence known. There was a rightful claim to neutrality that could emerge in the naive spirit of the day: the "first naivete" of early historical-critical optimism. But as solutions to fixed problems encountered in traditional literary approaches were compounded, it would become inevitable that the informed interpreter was moving within a large but reasonably closed circle. How could one develop a literary method without knowing ahead of time what religio-historical conclusions would follow from it?

In an attempt to avoid this stalemate, the first object of scrutiny for this study will be the socio-historical world from which the literary product, the canonical Jeremiah, emerged. Only then will we take up literary analysis as such, from a perspective informed principally by this preparatory, self-consciously diachronic analysis.

From the outset, however, we will work with one general piece of information from the literary world of Jeremiah. This is the conviction that the Jeremiah traditions reflect to a greater degree than other prophetic books a situation of conflict. Many have noted this conflict as evidenced in the prophetic personality itself.[9] Jeremiah is a man in conflict — in conflict with God, himself, and especially the community in which he lives and to whom he must address a difficult word. This type of conflict

---

Reflections on the Date of Jeremiah's Call," *CBQ* 33 (1971) 165—84. W. L. Holladay, "A Coherent Chronology of Jeremiah's Early Career," in *Le Livre de Jérémie: Le Prophète et son milieu. Les oracles et leur transmission* (Pierre-Maurice Bogaert, ed; BETL 54; Leuven: Leuven University, 1981) 58—73.

[7] Nicholson, *Preaching to the Exiles;* Pohlmann, *Studien zum Jeremiabuch;* E. Janssen, *Juda in der Exilszeit: Ein Beitrag zur Frage der Entstehung des Judenthums* (Göttingen: Vandenhoeck & Ruprecht, 1956).

[8] H. G. Reventlow, *Liturgie und das prophetische Ich bei Jeremia* (Gütersloh: Gütersloher Verlagshaus Gerd Mohn, 1963); C. Rietzschel, *Das Problem der Urrolle;* A. R. Johnson, *The Cultic Prophet in Ancient Israel* (2nd ed; Cardiff: University of Wales, 1962).

[9] J. Skinner, "Individual Religion — The Inner Life of Jeremiah," in *Prophecy and Religion*, 201—30; H. Kremers, "Leidensgemeinschaft mit Gott im Alten Testament: Eine Untersuchung der 'biographischen' Berichte im Jeremiabuch," *EvTh* 13 (1953) 122—40. Further: J. Crenshaw, *Prophetic Conflict: Its Effect Upon Israelite Religion* (BZAW 124; Berlin/New York: Walter de Gruyter, 1971).

is significant in the Book of Jeremiah; it is in no small measure related to the fact that Jeremiah is the prophet who delivers a divine word regarding a judgment he himself must witness and whose outcome he must personally share. The Jeremiah traditions, be they close historical accounting or distant redactional reminiscence, describe the prophet as a man in conflict living in times of conflict.

The conflict within the man Jeremiah is an interesting subject, but ultimately a frustating one since psychological concerns do not form an integral part of the traditions which have grown up around him. It is, therefore, the second of these conflict factors which is of interest to this study. The central observation that the Book of Jeremiah has its roots in a time of conflict is more capable of testing and detailed exploration.

There are several further matters which make investigation into the Book of Jeremiah from this angle particularly compelling. When one speaks of the "Exile" in both general and more technical discussion, the assumption is that the "Exile" refers to life in deportation following the "Fall" of Jerusalem, the destruction of the temple, and the specific trans-ference of Judahite populations to Babylon in the year 587 B. C. (there is scholarly debate about the exact date). Now this description of events is accurate, but it simplifies matters considerably. Approximately a decade prior to this "Exile", there were widespread incursions into Judah and the capital, which resulted in the death of one king, the deportation of another, the appointment of a puppet ruler, and the transfer of significant portions of the population to Babylon. In neither of these historical instances was the prophet himself deported. He remained prophetic spokesman in Judah following the "Exile" of 597 B. C., and was active in the decade following, at which time another community and prophetic voice, Ezekiel, was in existence in Babylon. Neither was he deported in 587 B. C., but formed an integral part of the post-587 community, under the leadership of Gedaliah, prior to his final removal to Egypt several years later. The relatively simple staging, Assault/Fall/Exile, does not do justice to the complexity of the situation, nor the potential for conflict inherent within it.[10]

When we return to the present impasse over proper literary approach, it is to be noted that this description of conflict and complexity in the actual historical situation is not derived from some one controversial literary critical analysis of the extant traditions. A simple, straightforward

---

[10] C. R. Seitz, "The Crisis of Interpretation over the Meaning and Purpose of the Exile: A Redactional Study of Jeremiah XXI—XLIII," *VT* 35 (1985) 78—97; P. R. Ackroyd, "Historians and Prophets," *SEA* 33 (1968) 18—25; Ackroyd, *Exile and Restoration* (Philadelphia: Westminster, 1968) esp. 57; A. Malamat, "Jeremiah and the Last Two Kings of Judah," *PEQ* 83 (1951) 81—7; Malamat, "The Twilight of Judah in the Egyptian-Babylonian Maelstrom," *VTSup* 28 (1974) 123—45.

reading of the Jeremiah narratives, the Book of Ezekiel, and 2 Kings 24—25 would confirm this description of affairs. What stands out is that this was a time of unprecedented conflict: within the community in Judah prior to 597; within the respective communities in Babylon and Judah after 597 and 587; and especially between these two geographically separated communities after 597. Again, it must be stressed that this description of affairs sums up the general picture we get from the biblical account, without recourse to any specific literary critical approach. Put another way, all levels of tradition, regardless of where and when they are diachronically located, breathe the same spirit of conflict.[11]

This moves us to the central thesis of this study, and one that can be developed only after careful socio-historical groundwork has been laid. Indeed, the task of providing an accurate, comprehensive description of social, religious, civil, and theological conflict in the years leading up to the "exiles" will represent a major part of our labors. The thesis then to be argued is that conflict over the theological evaluation of judgment and exile, both in 597 and 587, gave rise to one distinct level of tradition in the present Book of Jeremiah: the exilic, or Golah-redaction.[12] This redactional level extends throughout the present text but is most notable in chapters 21—45. Its theological burden is that Jeremiah's word of judgment, spoken prior to 597, remains in effect and forms the base-line of God's ongoing dealings with sinful Judah. In short, there can be no life in the land after 597 which is not under false illusions, and which does not stand under God's ultimate judgment. God spoke this word through his prophet Jeremiah early and often. It remained in unaltered effect. Only those already exiled could be sure that judgment had fallen. As such, they alone could properly hear a divine word regarding restoration.

Over against this redactional position lies both the stock of original prophetic speech from the pre-597 period (with which the Golah redaction sees itself in continuity) and post-597 pronouncements from the prophet, most of them contained within a new prose format. We also, however, begin to see a level of tradition *about* Jeremiah, consciously developed by others in scribal circles close to the prophet.[13] The theological positions represented in this Scribal Chronicle are less fixed, more open to ongoing history and changing social factors, and more complex in respect of

---

[11] This is as true for the historically cautious (Duhm; Pohlmann; Thiel) as for the historically optimistic (Bright; Weippert; Holladay).

[12] See the work of Pohlmann *(Studien zum Jeremiabuch)* and Seitz ("Crisis of Interpretation").

[13] See J. Muilenburg, "Baruch the Scribe," in *Proclamation and Presence. Old Testament Essays in Honour of Gwynne Henton Davies* (J. I. Durham and J. R. Porter, eds; London: SCM, 1970) 215—38; M. Weinfeld, *Deuteronomy and the Deuteronomic School* (Oxford: University, 1972); N. Lohfink, "Die Gattung der 'Historischen Kurzgeschichte' in den letzten Jahren von Juda und in der Zeit des Babylonischen Exils," *ZAW* 90 (1978) 319—47.

Jeremiah's assessment of life in the land, for king and people, and life in exile (in both the post-597 and post-587 periods).

These two levels of traditions, Scribal Chronicle and Golah Redaction, exist side-by-side in the present canonical text. Our task will be to isolate them, describe their literary shape and theological burden, their provenance, interrelationships, and approximate time of development. In so plotting these tradition levels we also hope to say something about the peculiar shape the present book has taken, a shape that seems to aggressively defy description. However one accounts for it diachronically, the radical divergence between Greek and Massoretic Jeremiahs stands as an early testimony to this defiance.

By proceeding far more self-consciously with socio-historical analysis before moving to literary analysis, we hope to isolate one feature they both have in common: theological conflict. Then we can return to the task of literary analysis with some informed clue as to why the book has the peculiar literary complexity and final shape it has.

One final note. The reader should be alerted that the impact the exile has had on the Book of Jeremiah is wide-ranging and complex. Moreover, this impact cannot be isolated in the narrow context of Jeremiah alone, even though this is our primary interest. A wider perspective is demanded because many sources are available at this period in history which reflect the influence of the exile. Chief among these sources are the biblical books Ezekiel and 2 Kings. Both have their own unique interpretive problems. This is particularly true of 2 Kings, whose correct critical interpretation involves the larger questions of the development and composition of the Deuteronomistic History (DtrH). It is necessary to examine in detail the accounts of 2 Kings 24 and 25, and to evaluate their respective witnesses to the exile, before correlating these witnesses with Jeremiah. In this evaluation a fresh analysis of 2 Kings 24 and 25 — pivotal chapters for a description of the redactional development of the DtrH — will be undertaken. In sum, this study of reactions to the exile in the Book of Jeremiah necessarily involves a broad look at the biblical literature which also emerged in this period and which likewise reflects differing attitudes toward Israel's exile.

Chapter Two
Judahite Society and Kingship Prior to the Exile

INTRODUCTION

It shall be argued in the chapters which follow (Three and Four) that secondary development of Jeremiah tradition took place within the context of a conflict over the interpretation of the Exile. As distinct from previous attempts to understand the growth of the book, it will be shown that this particular conflict gave rise to secondary expansion and organization of tradition associated with the prophet Jeremiah. Such a thesis seeks to account for a variety of factors not successfully clarified in earlier source and tradition-critical models. Chief among these factors is the actual motivation behind development of new literary levels in the text. This development is not primarily concerned with preservative matters, and is therefore neither archival (positive) nor obscurantistic (negative). Rather, it represents a serious theological interpretation of Israel's past (Fall of Judah), present (Exile), and future (Restoration), developed on the basis of received traditions from the prophet Jeremiah. When this central theological focus is correctly recognized, several other factors related to secondary levels of tradition fall into place: provenance (Babylonian Exile), date (upon reception of the primary tradition, in the post-597 years), and complexity of the literary material (representing distinct forms, language, and organization).

If this proposed model of conflict is to explain both the literary peculiarities in the present text and also account for the book's internal development, such a conflict must be rooted in actual historical events. In other words, a model based upon a theory of conflict is useless for explaining the *literary* growth of the book unless there is clear evidence that such a conflict did in fact take place on the *historical* plane. In the sections to follow (Chapters Three and Four), it will be shown how the Exilic Redaction blunted the force of certain original Jeremiah proclamation expressing hope for the continued existence of a remnant community in Judah. This redactional effort has been carried out on the literary level by means of specific editorial shifts, refinements, and supplementation. Literary analysis of the Jeremiah tradition will be on much firmer ground if it is first established that an actual conflict did occur between those in the land and those in exile during the period of transmission and interpretation of Jeremiah tradition. Consequently, the present chapter is dedicated to an investigation of those historical, sociological, and religious factors which played an important role in the period leading up to the Exile.

I. SOCIO/HISTORICAL STUDY OF THE EXILIC PERIOD: GENERAL OBSERVATIONS

The existence of multiple sources is a mixed blessing for the biblical historian. Multiple sources mean increased information, but frequently this information is self-contradictory.[1] A rich array of prophetic (Jeremiah + Lamentations, Ezekiel) and historical (2 Kings, Chronicles, Ezra/Nehemiah) narratives are available for documenting conflict in the exilic period. All in all, they present a fairly uniform picture of events leading up to the Fall of Jerusalem and the Exile. In this instance, it is fortunate that the sources are both extensive and in rough agreement over the major events, principal figures, and pertinent dates of the period.[2] The modern historian must approach the biblical sources with a degree of circumspection. The Old Testament, including those narratives which most closely approximate "historical chronicle," is at all points self-consciously theocentric, selective about what it chooses to report, and only occasionally concerned with the kind of historical and sociological information of importance for the modern historian. Often in biblical narratives such information remains incidental to a larger theological point of focus. Insofar as it assists in the telling of the story and the movement toward a theological statement this information is included, functioning like stage props in a play. But this fact should not be overstressed. In other places, the biblical narratives pay a remarkable degree of attention to details which are otherwise unrelated to a bald theological pronouncement. Such is the case with the accounts which describe events in the period of the Exile. In comparison with other biblical narratives these accounts display a remarkable interest in certain specific historical, sociological, and religious features.

Two examples illustrate this point. In the space of sixteen chapters in the Book of Jeremiah (primarily Chs 20—45 and 51—52) over fifty individuals are introduced. Most often the patronymic, place of origin (if Jerusalem is not assumed), and professional status of each is supplied (see Chart One).

---

[1] See the pertinent comments of E. Thiele, who has devoted a book-length study to the chronological problems related to Israelite kingship (*The Mysterious Numbers of the Hebrew Kings: A Reconstruction of the Chronology of the Kingdoms of Israel and Judah* [Grand Rapids: Eerdmans/Paternoster, 1965]). Thiele notes, "The more details (the biblical scholar) has found in his record, the greater have been his perplexities . . ." (7).

[2] This rough agreement exists even granting discrepencies which have resulted from the employment of different systems of dating (accession/nonaccession year reckoning; Tishri-Tishri/Nisan-Nisan calendrics).

Chart One

Figures Identified in the Book of Jeremiah

1. Pashhur the priest, son of Immer (20:1)
2. Pashhur, son of Malchiah (21:1; 38:1)
3. Zephaniah the priest, son of Maaseiah (21:1; 29:25; 37:3)
4. Uriah, son of Shemaiah, from Kiriath-jearim (26:20)
5. Elnathan, son of Achbor (26:22)
6. Ahikam, son of Shaphan (26:24)
7. Hananiah, son of Azzur, the prophet from Gibeon (28:1)
8. Elasah, son of Shaphan (29:3)
9. Gemariah, son of Hilkiah (29:3)
10. Ahab, son of Kolaiah (29:21)
11. Zedekiah, son of Maaseiah (29:21)
12. Shemaiah of Nehelam (29:24)
13. Jehoiada the priest (29:26)
14. Hanamel, son of Shallum, Jeremiah's uncle (32:7)
15. Baruch, son of Neriah, son of Mahseiah (32:12; 36:4; 43:3)
16. Jaazaniah, son of Jeremiah, son of Habazziniah (35:3)
17. Hanan, son of Igdaliah, the man of God (35:4)
18. Maaseiah, son of Shallum, the doorkeeper (35:4)
19. Jonadab, son of Rechab (35:14)
20. Gemariah, son of Shaphan, the secretary (36:10)
21. Micaiah, son of Gemariah, son of Shaphan (36:11)
22. The princes: Elishama the secretary (36:12),
23. Delaiah, son of Shemaiah (36:12),
24. Zedekiah, son of Hananiah (36:12)
25. Jehudi, son of Nethaniah, son of Shelemiah, son of Cushi (36:14)
26. Jerahmeel, the king's son (36:26)
27. Seraiah, son of Azriel (36:26)
28. Shelemiah, son of Abdeel (36:26)
29. Jehucal, son of Shelemiah (37:3; 38:1)
30. Irijah, son of Shelemiah, son of Hananiah, a sentry (37:13)
31. Jonathan, the secretary (37:15)
32. Shephatiah, son of Mattan (38:1)
33. Gedaliah, son of Pashhur (38:1)
34. Malciah, the king's son (38:6)
35. Ebed-melech, the Ethiopian, an officer (38:7)
36. Princes of Nebuchadnezzar: Nergal-sharezer (39:3),
37. Sam-gar-nebo (39:3),
38. Sarsechim (39:3),
39. Nergal-sharezer the Rabmag (39:3)
40. Nebuzaradan, captain of the guard (39:9)

41. Gedaliah, son of Ahikam, son of Shaphan (chs 39—43)
42. Ishmael, son of Nethaniah, son of Elishama, of the royal family (40:8 ff.)
43. Johanon, son of Kareah (chs 40—43)
44. Seraiah, son of Tanhumeth (40:8)
45. the sons of Ephai, the Netophathite (40:8)
46. Jezaniah, the son of the Maachithite (40:8)
47. Azariah, son of Hoshaiah (43:2)
48. Seraiah, son of Neriah, the quartermaster (51:59)
49. Hamutal, daughter of Jeremiah of Libnah (52:1)
50. Seraiah, the chief priest (52:24)
51. Zephaniah, the second priest (52:24)

Chart Two

Various Offices Identified in the Book of Jeremiah

1. 20:1   "chief officer" (*pāqîd nāgîd*)
2. 24:1   "princes of Judah" (*śārê yĕhûdāh*)
3. 24:1   "craftsmen" and "smiths" (*heḥārāš, hammasgēr*)
4. 27:20 "all the nobles of Judah and Jerusalem" (*kol-ḥōrê yĕhûdāh*)
5. 29:1   "the elders of the exiles" (*ziqĕnê haggôlāh*)
6. 29:2   "the queen mother" (*haggĕbîrāh*)
7. 29:2   "the eunuchs" (*hassārîsîm*)
8. 29:8   "your diviners" (*qōsĕmêkem*)
9. 33:18 "levitical priests" (*hakkōhănîm halĕwiyyim*)
10. 34:19 "the people of the land" (*'am hā'āreṣ*)
11. 35:4   "keeper of the threshold" (*šōmēr hassap*)
12. 36:10 "the secretary" (*hassōpēr*)
13. 37:13 "a sentry" (*ba'al pĕqidut*)
14. 37:21 "the guard" (*hammaṭṭārāh*)
15. 39:3   "the Rabsaris" (*rab-sārîs*)
16. 39:3   "the Rabmag" (*rab-māg*)
17. 39:9   "the captain of the guard" (*rab-ṭabbāḥîm*)
18. 39:13 "the chief officers" (*rabbê*)
19. 40.5   "appointed governor" (*'ăšer hipqîd*)
20. 40:7   "captains of the forces" (*śārê haḥăyālîm*)
21. 41:1   "the royal family" (*mizzera' hammĕlûkāh*)
22. 41.10 "the daughters of the king" (*bĕnôt hammelek*)
23. 51:59 "the quartermaster" (*śar mĕnûḥāh*)
24. 52:15 "the artisans" (*hā'āmôn*)
25. 52:24 "the chief priest" (*kōhēn hārō'š*)
26. 52:24 "the second priest" (*kōhēn hammišneh*)

27. 52:25 "an officer in command" (*sārîs 'ăšer-hāyāh pāqîd*)
28. 52:25 "the king's council" (*mērō'ê pĕnê-hammelek*)
29. 52:25 "secretary of the commander of the army" (*sōpēr śar haṣṣābā'*)

Apart from the well-known figures of prophet and king, a wide variety of other governmental, religious, and military officials appear on the scene (Chart Two).[3] The specificity with which they are introduced militates against seeing them as stock or invented characters, of no particular consequence for the reader. Furthermore, this specificity is a feature particularly striking in the Book of Jeremiah. In comparison with other pre-exilic prophetic witnesses (Isaiah, Zephaniah, Hosea, Amos, Micah) one does not usually see such attention to detail.[4] Here it is interesting to compare Jeremiah with Ezekiel. Like Jeremiah (which supplies a plethora of dated and specifically located oracles), the Book of Ezekiel is concerned to tell the reader precisely when a certain word from Yahweh went forth through the prophet to the people (Chart Three).[5] This specificity argues against a lack of concern for historical background on the author's part, presumably because these features were important not only for the compiler of the oracles, but also for the audience to whom they were addressed. One might expect such specificity in Israel's historical chronicles; the fact that it occurs within these prophetic books is striking and demands further study. Earlier critics noted the special quality of prose narratives in the Book of Jeremiah and argued that they were derived from historical or biographical sources ("B" and "C"). Though such assignment is questionable, the unique quality of these narratives, concerned as they are with a raft of historical features, had been rightly recognized.

---

[3] J. Muilenburg aptly notes: "The canvas upon which the scribe (Baruch) portrays the events of the prophet's career is crowded with many *dramatis personae*. Kings, princes, priests, prophets, scribes, and others appear upon the stage . . ." ("Baruch the Scribe," *Proclamation and Presence: Old Testament Essays in Honour of Gwynne Henton Davies* [John I. Durham and J. R. Porter, eds; London: SCM, 1970] 234).

[4] Brief historical notices often appear in the superscriptions to the prophetic material (so Micah, Amos, Hosea, Isaiah, Zephaniah; extremely brief for Nahum and lacking for Habakkuk, Obadiah, and Joel). The historical significance of "two years before the earthquake" (Amos 1:2), even if intended by the author, is all but lost to us. Although Isaiah 40—55 can be critically separated from the oracles of Isaiah who writes in Exile, these chapters do not emphasize their Babylonian provenance or the details peculiar to that setting, even though they can be critically recovered. But more important is the relative lack of interest in the kind of historical, biographical, and sociological details which does come to the fore in Jeremiah and Ezekiel.

[5] Noted recently by Robert R. Wilson ("Prophecy in Crisis: The Call of Ezekiel," *Int* 38 [1984] 117—30). For a critical assessment of these dates, see K. S. Freedy and D. B. Redford, "The Dates in Ezekiel in Relationship to Biblical, Babylonian, and Egyptian Sources," *JAOS* 90 (1970) 462—79.

Chart Three

Specifically Dated Passages in the Book of Ezekiel

1. 30th year, 4th month, 5th day of the month (1:1)
2. 5th day of the month, 5th year of Jehoiachin's exile (1:2)
3. at the end of 7 days (3:16)
4. 6th year, 6th month, 5th day (8:1)
5. 7th year, 5th month, 10th day (20:1)
6. 9th year, 10th month, 10th day (24:1)
7. 11th year, 1st day of the month (26:1)
8. 10th year, 10th month, 12th day (29:1)
9. 27th year, 1st month, 1st day of the month (29:17)
10. 11th year, 1st month, 7th day of the month (30:20)
11. 11th year, 3rd month, 1st day of the month (31:1)
12. 12th year, 12th month, 1st day of the month (32:1)
13. 12th year, 1st month, 15th day (32:17)
14. 12th year, 10th month, 5th day of the month (33:21)
15. 25th year of our exile (40:1)

Specifically Dated Passages in the Book of Jeremiah

1. 13th year of Josiah (1:2)
2. 11th year, 5th month of Zedekiah (1:3)
3. cross reference to 37:1 (21:1)
4. Jehoahaz (22:11)
5. Jehoiakim (22:18)
6. Jehoiachin (22:24)
7. After Nebuchadnezzar had exiled Jeconiah (24:1)
8. 4th year of Jehoiakim = 1st year of Nebuchadnezzar (25:1)
9. Beginning of the reign of Jehoiakim (26:1)
10. Beginning of the reign of Zedekiah (MT 27:1)
11. Beginning of the reign of Zedekiah, 5th month, 4th year (28:1)
12. In that same year, in the 7th month (28:17)
13. date assumed from 28:17 (29:1)
14. 10th year of Zedekiah = 18th year of Nebuchadnezzar (32:1)
15. When only Lachish and Azekah were left (34:1,7)
16. In the days of Jehoiakim (35:1)
17. 4th year of Jehoiakim (36:1)
18. 5th year of Jehoiakim, 9th month (36:9)
19. Army of Pharaoh had come out of Egypt (37:1−5)
20. 9th year of Zedekiah, 10th month (39:1)
21. 11th year of Zedekiah, 4th month, 9th day (39:2)
22. [11th year], 7th month (41:1)
23. 9th year, 10th month, 10th day (52:4)

24. [11th year], 4th month, 9th day (52:6)
25. [11th year], 5th month, 10th day = Nebuchadnezzar's 19th year (52:12)
26. 7th year of Nebuchadnezzar (52:28)
27. 18th year of Nebuchadnezzar (52:29)
28. 23rd year of Nebuchadnezzar (52:30)
29. 37th year of Jehoiachin's exile, 12th month, 25th day (52:31)

A. *Introduction*

Old Testament prophetic and historical narratives provide an interesting glimpse into the historical/political situation of the wider Ancient Near East, especially from the rise of the Neo-Assyrian empire in the eighth-century through its decline and collapse in the sixth. In the earlier period, the Philistines generally and a number of smaller states specifically pose the chief threat to Israel, a threat which the biblical texts portray primarily as religious in nature (Deut 7:1—26). The full emergence of Israel as a national entity during the reign of Solomon also witnesses to the gradual emergence of larger and more powerful external political forces, chiefly Assyria and Egypt. In the early period, Israel must contend with an enemy which is physically close at hand, as she seeks to set up a stable political system and establish herself as the people of Yahweh, holding what the biblical texts insist are unique religious convictions (Josh 24:1—28). The physical proximity of the enemy is consistently emphasized, as Israel attempts to occupy territory she views as the gracious gift of Yahweh and the sign of her election, but which the indigenous population, with its own religious, cultural, and political convictions, views as home.[6] The power and constant threat of larger external nations is quite well known, and this power is described in almost mythopoetic terms. But a sense of the distance of these nations is both a reality and a blessing for which Israel as a liberated people is to give thanks. In objective historical/political terms, these larger external powers are not dormant. Israel is simply occupied with a threat much closer at hand, both after the calling forth from Mesopotamia, the exodus from Egypt, and particularly during the period of the settlement.

The rise of the Neo-Assyrian empire, bent upon total domination of the Levant, changed all this.[7] Nations once depicted as stationary and

---

[6] The distinction between Israelites as such (worshippers of Yahweh) and the indigenous population can be overdrawn (Deut 7:1 ff.; Joshua 1—12). At other points the texts are clearer about the difficulty of establishing precise distinctions (Josh 24:15; Judges 1—2; Hosea).

[7] J. Bright states, "The truth is that the entire history of Israel through the first five hundred years of her existence as a people had been spun out in a great power vacuum; no empire had existed that had been in a position to trouble her deeply and permanently. After the middle of the eighth century, this was to never be the case again" (*History,* 267). This is the point of the distinction between internal threats during the early period as contrasted with the period of the divided kingdom during which external threats predominated.

distant, though powerful, become much more directly involved in the region of Palestine. Nearly all modern histories of Israel devote a substantial section to the period of Assyrian domination.[8] Not only is such domination attested in the wider history and literature of the ancient Near East, a major part of the Old Testament likewise witnesses to the power and increasing threat of the Assyrian foe.

This threat is most keenly felt in the Northern Kingdom (Samaria), in part due to her physical proximity to the kingdoms of Syria and Assyria. Testimony to the might of these nations is provided in a number of biblical passages (Hazael and Ben-Hadad of Syria: 1 Kgs 20:1—22:40; 2 Kgs 13:1—9; Rezin: 2 Kgs 16:5—9; Isa 7:1—17; Shalmeneser and Sargon: 2 Kgs 17:1—41).[9] This threat also extends at several important times to the

[8] Note William W. Hallo's choice for the title of his thorough historical survey of this important period: "From Qarqar to Carchemish," *BA* 23 (1960). These important dates (853—605 B. C.) mark the limits of Assyrian domination over the ANE in general, including the kingdoms of Israel and Judah. Apart from the broader historical treatments of Bright, Noth, and Herrmann, see Herbert Donner's contribution to *Israelite and Judaean History* ("The Separate States of Israel and Judah," 381—434) and the pertinent sections of *The World History of the Jewish People* (Jerusalem: Massada, 1979) by H. Reviv and I. Eph'al, Vol. IV, Part 1, 180—204. On specific features of Assyria's political and religious influence over Israel and the debate over the extent of that influence, see the recent studies of: Hermann Spieckermann, *Juda in der Sargonidenzeit* (Göttingen: Vandenhoeck & Ruprecht, 1982); Morton Cogan, *Imperialism and Religion: Assyria, Judah and Israel in the Eighth and Seventh Centuries B. C. E.* (SBLDS 19; Missoula: Scholars, 1974); John William McKay, *Religion in Judah under the Assyrians 732—609 B. C.* (SBT 26; Napierville, Illinois: Alec R. Allenson, 1973); and further, G. W. Ahlström, *Royal Administration and National Religion in Ancient Palestine* (Leiden: E. J. Brill, 1982). More specialized articles on this period include: Hayim Tadmor, "The Campaigns of Sargon II of Assur: A Chronological Historical Study," *JCS* 12 (1958) 22—40, 77—91; "Assyria and the West: The Ninth Century and its Aftermath," in *Unity and Diversity: Essays in the History, Literature, and Religion of the Ancient Near East* (Hans Goedicke and J. J. M. Roberts, eds; Baltimore and London: John Hopkins, 1975) 36—48; Bustenay Oded, "Observations on Methods of Assyrian Rule in Transjordan after the Palestinian Campaign of Tiglath-Pileser III," *JNES* 29 (1970) 177—86; Benedikt Otzen, "Israel under the Assyrians: Reflections on Imperial Policy in Palestine," *ASTI* 11 (1977/78) 96—110; Carl D. Evans, "Judah's Foreign Policy from Hezekiah to Josiah," in *Scripture in Context: Essays on the Comparative Method* (Carl D. Evans, William W. Hallo, John B. White, eds; Pittsburgh Theological Seminary Monograph Series 34; Pittsburgh: Pickwick, 1980) 157—78 and in *Scripture in Context II: More Essays on the Comparative Method* (William W. Hallo, James C. Moyer, Leo G. Perdue, eds; Winona Lake, Indiana: Eisenbrauns, 1983) articles by Stephan Stohlmann ("The Judaean Exile after 701 B.C.E.," 147—75) and Richard Nelson, ("*Realpolitik* in Judah," 177—89). An exceptionally fine historical sketch of this period can also be obtained from H. J. Katzenstein's *A History of Tyre* (The Schocken Institute for Jewish Research of the Jewish Theological Seminary of America; Jerusalem: Goldberg's, 1973).

[9] Note for instance the journey of Amos, a southern prophet, to the Northern Kingdom during this period. One might well conjecture about Amos' knowledge of the rise of the Neo-Assyrian empire, spear-headed by Tiglath-Pileser III (745—727), and his role vis-à-vis Israel/Judah (as does Gerhard von Rad, *Old Testament Theology* [2 Vols; New York: Harper & Row, 1965] 2.133—4).

Southern Kingdom as well (2 Kgs 18:1—25:26; Isa 5:26—30; 7:1—8:15; 10:5—11, 27d—32; 36:1—37:38).[10] Internal political confusion and decay within the Northern Kingdom is also well documented in the Books of Kings (1 Kgs 15:25—16:34; the reign of Ahab and the Elijah/Elisha narratives in 1 Kgs 17:1—2 Kgs 10:36), seen particularly in the decadence and instability of the dynastic system and the early, wholesale destruction of the state itself (2 Kgs 17:1—41).

Although Judah cannot be pictured in comfortable isolation during this period, the historical reports of the Deuteronomistic History depict a relatively stable political system, seen for example in the maintenance of one (Davidic) dynasty throughout the period of Assyrian hegemony (and beyond). When Judah's kings are harshly evaluated by the Dtr Historian, it is consistently for religious omissions (failure to abolish the high-places). The standard evaluations of the Historian have a political as well as a religious dimension (the cultic reform and political expansion of Josiah). It would be fair to conclude that for the time when both kingdoms were intact, the picture which emerges in the Dtr History is one of a Judah never as directly threatened, militarily or politically, as her neighbor to the north.[11]

The situation changes radically after the death of Josiah (609). Assyrian influence had reached its zenith in the Southern Kingdom during the reign of Manasseh.[12] Whatever buffer the Northern Kingdom once provided from direct Assyrian influence vanished when, after the rebellion of vassal-king Hoshea, Shalmeneser V invaded the northern capital and executed the notorius Assyrian plan of deportation and resettlement.[13] At

---

[10] On the significance of the Assyrian empire in relationship to the redaction of the book of Isaiah, see Hermann Barth's dissertation, "Israel und die Assyrerreiche in den Nichtjesajanischen Texten des Protojesajabuches. Eine Untersuchung zur produktiven Neuinterpretation der Jesajaüberlieferung," (Hamburg, 1974). Now published as, *Die Jesaja-Worte in der Josiazeit. Israel und Assur als Thema einer produktiven Neuinterpretation der Jesajaüberlieferung* (WMANT 48; Neukirchen: Neukirchener-Vluyn, 1978).

[11] Mention might be made of the Assyrian crisis of 701, which did have a profound affect on Judah. The Northern Kingdom, it is to be noted, had already fallen by this time and therefore provided no appreciable buffer to the forces of Sennacherib (see Hayes & Miller, 436).

[12] There is a scholarly impasse over the nature of that influence, viz, whether it was primarily political or religious (see the work of Spieckermann, Cogan and McKay cited above). All would acknowledge that the Assyrian empire was an awesome force under the leadership of Esarhaddon and Assurbanipal. The important element, stressed by Cogan, is that despite this fact, Judah remained a vassal and not a province, in this strict sense.

[13] Stage three of a well-organized system of empire building: 1) tribute and vassalage; 2) puppet kingship; 3) population resettlement (adopted by H. Donner in Hayes & Miller, 418—9). Cogan seems to prefer a two-tiered system: vassal and province. Although these two labels could be applied to Judah and Israel, respectively, for a period in the history of both and highlight an important distinction between them, the three-stage system more accurately reflects events as they have been recorded in the biblical and extra-biblical sources.

that point, the Assyrian province of *Samerina* included villages just north of Jerusalem. Even earlier Judah had consigned herself to vassal-status as a result of Ahaz' appeal to Tiglath-Pileser III for assistance against the Syro-Ephraimitic alliance of Pekah and Rezin (2 Kgs 16:7 ff.). She then recovered a bit during the reign of Hezekiah, though major hopes for independence were fueled largely by the fact that, following the death of Sargon II, Assyria was occupied with threats from the Twenty-fifth (Nubian) dynasty in Egypt.[14] Despite the debate over the precise circumstances of Sennacherib's campaign to Judah and siege of Jerusalem, we know that any sustained push for independence in the Southern Kingdom was halted (2 Kgs 18:13—16; *ANET*, 288).[15] Under the vigorous leadership of Esarhaddon, the Assyrian empire succeeded in establishing its dominion over virtually the entire known world. In the wake of Esarhaddon's victorious compaign to Thebes (No-Amon), Manasseh remained a loyal if not relatively insignificant vassal in this now gargantuan and somewhat unwieldy Assyrian empire.[16] The death of Esarhaddon only led to his replacement by an equally capable monarch, his son Assurbanipal, who promptly quashed initial rebellions in Egypt and coerced a pliant leadership out of this area in the persons of Necho and his son Psammetichus, the last vestiges of the Twenty-fifth dynasty having been eliminated.[17]

---

[14] Also, the resurgence of Elamite and neo-Babylonian forces, and the rebellion of Luli (Eloulaios), king of Sidon, the strongest ruler in Hattiland (*ANET*, 287). See B. Oded, "Hezekiah's Rebellion and Sennacherib's Campaign against Judah," in Hayes & Miller, 446 ff.; Katzenstein, *Tyre,* Chapter X, esp. 244 ff.; Israel Eph'al, "Assyrian Domination in Palestine," *The World History of the Jewish People,* IV/1.276—80.

[15] For an excellent discussion of the options for interpretation, see B. S. Childs, *Isaiah and the Assyrian Crisis* (SBT 2.3; Napierville, Illinois: A. R. Allenson, 1967). Most recently: R. E. Clements, *Isaiah and the Deliverance of Jerusalem* (JSOTSS 13; Sheffield: JSOT Press, 1980).

[16] 2 Chronicles 33:11—16 hints at a rebellion of Manasseh, but there is no evidence to support this in the Assyrian annals, which depict him as a loyal vassal. See Donner's full discussion in Hayes & Miller, 434. Also Eduard Nielsen, "Political Conditions and Cultural Developments in Israel and Judah during the reign of Manasseh," *The Fourth World Congress of Jewish Studies* (1967). For an alternative view, see Morton Cogan (*Imperialism,* 67—70).

[17] On the relationship between Assyria and Egypt during the waning years of the empire, and on the possibility of greater cooperation between Psammetichus and the Assyrians, see the recent studies by Anthony Spalinger: "Esarhaddon and Egypt: An Analysis of the First Invasion of Egypt," *Or* 43 (1974) 2945—326; "Assurbanipal and Egypt: A Source Study," *JAOS* 94 (1974) 316—28; "Psammetichus, King of Egypt: I" and "Psammetichus, King of Egypt: II," in *The Journal of the American Research Center in Egypt* 13 (1976) 133—47 and 15 (1978) 49—55; "Egypt and Babylonia: A Survey c. 620 B. C.—550 B. C.," *Studien zur altägyptischen Kultur* 5 (1977) 221—44. These update earlier treatments by P. G. Elgood (*Later Dynasties of Egypt* [Oxford: Basil Blackwell, 1951]); Sir Alan Gardiner (*Egypt of the Pharaohs: An Introduction* [Oxford: At the Clarendon Press, 1961]); Mary Giles (*Pharaonic Policies and Administration* [The James Sprunt Studies in History and Political Science, Chapel Hill, 1959]); Friedrich Karl Kienitz (*Die politische*

Much has been written on the reform of Josiah and the political dimensions of that reform. Particular attention has been paid to the success of Josiah's attempts at expansion and the possible re-establishment of the former kingdom of David. A complete treatment of this subject stands outside the scope of this study. What is important to note in considering the resurgence of Judah under Josiah's leadership, however, is that hopes for expansion occurred within the context of a rapidly disintegrating Assyrain empire.[18] It took a mere twenty years for this massive military, judicial and administrative superstructure to collapse, most likely under its own sheer weight.[19] However important Josiah's reform was in the final analysis of the Dtr Historian (2 Kgs 22—23), this same historian knows the ultimate fate of the Kingdom of Judah, despite eleventh-hour attempts at expansion and reformation (2 Kgs 23:26—27).

In recent years, the historical period stretching from the death of Josiah to the destruction of Jerusalem, as it is related in the final chapters of the Books of Kings, has been relegated by scholars to the status of monotonous addendum. The popular version of this theory argues that the final chapters of 2 Kings form a postlude to the primary literary strand of the Dtr History (Deuteronomy through 2 Kings): the so-called Dtr 1. This document (Dtr 1) purportedly tells the history of Israel up to and in glorious support of the reign of Josiah, the new Davidid who truly fulfilled the messianic expectations originally promulgated in the Nathan Oracle (2 Sam 7:12—16). When he was tragically slain at Megiddo (so the theory continues) trying to intercept the rebellious Necho II, and hopes associated with his kingship were dashed, the Dtr 1 was brought to an ignominious close (see 2 Kgs 23:29—30). The chapters which conclude the History (24—25), then, are viewed as a supplement whose intent is to explain the failure of Josiah's Reform and the ultimate judgment of Judah as based upon the overwhelming sins of Manasseh — sins which could not be countered, despite the pious intentions of Josiah. Whatever the flaws in such a theory, one consequence has been a serious failure to evaluate this important period on its own merits.[20] With so much emphasis being placed

---

Geschichte Ägyptens vom 7. bis zum 4. Jahrhundert vor der Zeitwende [Berlin: Akademie-Verlag, 1953]); and K. A. Kitchen (*The Third Intermediate Period in Egypt* [1100—650 B. C.] [Warminster: Aris & Phillips, 1973]).

[18] See the brief article by F. M. Cross and D. N. Freedman: "Josiah's Revolt against Assyria," *JNES* 12 (1953) 56—8.

[19] For a review of the historical circumstances and a description of the many factors involved, see H. W. F. Saggs, *The Greatness that was Babylon* (New York: Hawthorn, 1962).

[20] Negative assessments of 'Dtr 2' are more frequent in recent studies than in the pilot version of Frank Moore Cross, *Canaanite Myth and Hebrew Epic* (Cambridge: Harvard, 1973) 274—89. Recent adaptations include those of Richard Nelson (*The Double Redaction of the Deuteronomistic History* [JSOTSS 18; Sheffield: JSOT Press, 1981]) and Richard Elliot Friedman (*The Exile and Biblical Narrative* [HSM 22; Chico, California: Scholars, 1981] and "From Egypt to Egypt: Dtr 1 and Dtr 2," in *Traditions in Transformation* [B.

upon the reign of King Josiah, its adherents are forced to view the period following his death as one of dashed hopes and resignation, during which the "subtheme" of Manasseh's sins is generated to account for the final judgment of 587.[21]

The years following the death of Josiah until the Fall of Jerusalem mark a completely unique period in the history of Judah. Throughout the historical period sketched above, Judah was either fortunate enough to avoid direct entanglements with the larger external powers or, when involvement was inescapable, to fare reasonably well. One result was that a single dynastic system withstood all internal and external challenges right up to the end.[22] The instability of the Northern Kingdom, however one measures this, resulted in its destruction by the Assyrians in the year 721 and an ongoing process of resettlement (2 Kgs 17:24 ff.; Ezra 4:2).[23] Judah was to remain intact for another century and a half. During the reign of Hezekiah, Judah attempted to forestall Assyrian dominance by establishing a treaty-alliance with Egypt and actually sided with her in a later rebellion which included Ashdod, Ekron and Gaza (Isa 36—39).[24] She did not, however, jeopardize her situation to the extent that the Northern Kingdom had a short time earlier. Usually, a judicious policy of vassalage insured a relatively stable internal situation and the avoidance of harsher measures.

Halpern, J. D. Levenson, eds; Winona Lake: Eisenbrauns, 1981] 167—92). Nelson describes the contribution of the Exilic Editor (Dtr 2) as "dry and colorless," "woodenly imitative," marked by a "rubber-stamp character" (36—41). See the full treatment of 2 Kgs 24 and 25 in Chapter Three.

[21] There has been too great an emphasis on the reign of Josiah as the fulfillment of messianic expectations. A false dichotomy is set up between "unconditional promises" to David of a "never-ending kingdom" (Friedman, "Egypt to Egypt," 169) and "thematic" explanations for the failure of these promises. In the end, such a theory pushes its adherents into odd agreement with Noth, who saw the *entire* History as a picture of irretrievable doom, since the theoretical Dtr 2 becomes the representative of such a position. These studies also tend to ignore or reduce the significance of the History's final word, the report of Jehoiachin's release, in their insistence that Dtr 2 is concerned only with the finality of God's judgment and the end of the Davidic Promises. Compare studies by Klaus Baltzer ("Das Ende des Staates Juda und die Messias-Frage" in *Studien zu alttestamentlichen Überlieferungen* [FS Gerhard von Rad; R. Rendtorff and K. Koch, eds; Neukirchen: Neukirchener, 1961] 33—43) and Erich Zenger ("Die deuteronomistische Interpretation der Rehabilierung Jojachins," *BZ* 12 [1968] 16—30). The position of von Rad (*Theology, ad loc*) and Wolff ("The Kerygma of the Deuteronomistic Historical Work," in *The Vitality of Old Testament Traditions* [Atlanta: John Knox, 1978] 83—100) is more balanced. See the detailed discussion in Chapter Three below.

[22] Tomoo Ishida, *The Royal Dynasties in Ancient Israel* (BZAW 142; Berlin/New York: Walter de Gruyter, 1977) 150—70; J. A. Soggin, *Das Königtum in Israel* (BZAW 104; Berlin: Alfred Töpelmann, 1967) 105.

[23] Cogan, *Imperialism,* 101.

[24] I. Eph'al, "Assyrian Dominion in Palestine," 276—280; Tadmor, "Campaigns of Sargon II," 83—4; H. Reviv, "The History of Judah from Hezekiah to Josiah," *The World History of the Jewish People,* IV/1.196—99.

But in these last years, the larger ANE political situation changed, and the effect this had on internal affairs in Judah (military, governmental, religious) was enormous. The massive empire of Assyria began to erode. Egypt and Babylon vied both for their independence and for a share in Assyria's former glory. As Abraham Malamat has accurately termed it, Judah found herself caught in an "Egyptian-Babylonian Maelstrom."[25] This state of affairs would lead to her eventual demise. But it also meant persistent interference from these two nations in her internal affairs during the brief period before that demise, more so than at any earlier point.

Discussion will doubtless continue over the circumstances surrounding the composition of the Dtr History. Yet it should be obvious that, no matter how one assesses the significance of this twenty-year period for the compiler of the History, *it plays a most central role in the book of Jeremiah*. For although Jeremiah's prophetic career actually began in 626, many years before the death of King Josiah (609), compared with what is known about his actual life and preaching after 609, these earliest years are the most difficult to reconstruct. It is precisely this silence which has given rise to proposals on a number of interesting topics: Jeremiah's attitude toward King Josiah, his reform, the "book of the law" and/or Deuteronomy, the cult, temple heirarchy, and even Josiah's death at Megiddo (especially if such strong hopes were attached to his kingship).[26] Within the oracles which most likely emerged prior to the death of Josiah (Chs 1—19), there is a complete lack of concern for these topics, despite the intrigue they hold for modern scholarship.

Upon entering the exilic period, the situation is quite different. While strictly speaking Josiah plays no active role in the book of Jeremiah, a number of narratives include his successors as key *dramatis personae*. From Chapter 20 to the end of the book, attention is focussed on the historical period *after* the death of Josiah. It is also here that one confronts such a large number of specifically identified figures and an interesting barrage of details. Only by closely examining these narratives and the final chapters of the Books of Kings can we fully appreciate the distinctiveness of this historical period and its importance, not merely as a hurried prelude to the Fall of Jerusalem, but as the time when attitudes and responses to God's punishment, the Exile and Restoration were emerging and beginning to receive consistent formulation.

One final note: a considerable literature has been generated on the topic of chronology for this period — more so than for any other period in Israel's history. This is due to the many different sources, biblical

---

[25] A. Malamat, "The Twilight of Judah in the Egyptian-Babylonian Maelstrom," *VTSup* 28 (1974) 123—45.

[26] The relative silence of the book of Jeremiah over the person of Josiah is almost as deafening as the absolute silence over Jeremiah in the Book of Kings.

(Jeremiah, 2 Kings, Ezekiel, Lamentations, Obadiah, Chronicles, 2 Esdras) and extrabiblical, available to the historian. There is a debate over how to properly construct a chronological framework which can accommodate all these disparate sources and the synchronisms they themselves periodically attempt. This debate focuses on prior governing features: when the new-year began, whether fractional years are included in the king's tally, shifts in either procedure, and the like.[27] Having weighed the evidence, it does not appear that the debate *per se* is a critical factor in this treatment of Jeremiah. Therefore, for the purpose of the historical survey to follow and in order to avoid unnecessary entanglements, the most generally accepted chronological system has been adopted. Discussion of controversial dates will be taken up when pertinent to the larger thesis.

B. Historical Background

The death of a king was a highly charged event in the Ancient Near East. It often had ramifications extending beyond the mundane realm to that of the cosmos itself. The extent to which this was also true in Israel is open to debate.[28] For the purpose of our study, one fact that is to be noted is the contrast between dynastic principles in the Northern Kingdom and in Judah. In the former, no one single dynastic system obtained, and nine usurpers arose one after another in the two centuries of its foreshortened existence.[29] But for about 350 years, Judah was ruled by a single dynasty: the House of David.

As sketched above, this contrast was at least partly due to the threat posed to the Northern Kingdom by the more physically proximate Syrian and Assyrian empires. The biblical texts themselves also clarify the distinctiveness of dynastic kingship in the south as deriving from Yahweh's special choice of David (2 Sam 7:13—16; 1 Kgs 9:5). This fact ought not be underestimated, since it contributed to whatever stability Judah experienced during the period under discussion. Threats, both internal and external, arose on specific occasions in the south. These have been recorded by the Dtr Historian.[30] The clearest example is Judah's political maneu-

---

[27] See especially, Edwin Thiele, "The Chronology of the Kings of Judah and Israel," *JNES* 3 (1944) 137—86; K. S. Freedy and D. B. Redford, "The Dates in Ezekiel in Relation to Biblical, Babylonian, and Egyptian Sources," *JAOS* 90 (1970) 462—85. For a general discussion of the present state of the problem, see the appendix on Chronology in Hayes & Miller, 678 ff.

[28] See the lucid summary by Walter Zimmerli of recent shifts in interpretation: "The History of Israelite Religion," in *Tradition and Interpretation: Essays by Members of the Society for Old Testament Study* (G. W. Anderson, ed; Oxford: Clarendon, 1979) 351—9.

[29] See Ishida, "The Problems at the Passing of the Royal Throne," *Royal Dynasties,* 151—82.

[30] Not only did King Ahaz make appeal for military aid to the great Assyrian monarch, Tiglath-Pileser. After travelling to Assyria to pay tribute, he apparently returned with blue-prints for a new altar (2 Kgs 16:10—16). For a full treatment, see McKay (*Religion,* 5—12) and Cogan (*Imperialism,* 66).

vering after the death of Sargon II, which resulted in the hasty campaign of Sennacherib to the area and the widespread destruction of all major cities in the countryside surrounding Jerusalem.[31]

In reviewing this historical period, one factor is worthy of note. Despite the severity of reprisals in Sennacherib's campaign, no internal changes are wrought by the Assyrian empire in Judah's governing body. It may even be this fact which is viewed as primary in the miraculous deliverance recorded in Isaiah 36—38.[32] Assyria remains at stage-one of her usual administrative policy; put another way, Hezekiah is not replaced by a puppet-king and Sennacherib returns to Ninevah. That such an action was a live option is evidenced by Tiglath-Pileser's treatment of Rayṣin of Aram-Damascus in 732.[33] Pekah of Israel had avoided similar treatment at the time only by falling victim to pro-Assyrian forces in his own realm. And in any case, Hoshea was installed as vassal king in his stead, tribute was paid, and Galilee and the area east of the Jordan were annexed and established as Assyrian provinces (*Magidu* and *Gal'azu*).

No such radical internal changes in Jerusalem's governing system are recorded in either the biblical or Assyrian records. Hezekiah is "shut up like a bird in a cage," the countryside is ravaged, and tribute is sent by personal messenger to Assyria (*ANET*, 288). Since the Assyrian monarch had returned to his own country and the city and temple were not destroyed, the nearness of the approach, not its success, and the miraculousness of Yahweh's deliverance are what receive emphasis in the biblical text (Isa 37:22—38; Micah 1:9; Hos 1:7). Silence in the annals for Sennacherib's reign about the actual capture of Jerusalem confirms this.[34] God had defended Jerusalem "for his own sake and for the sake of his servant David" (2 Kgs 19:34). Hezekiah remained king and died a peaceful death a full fifteen years later. Though his successor, Manasseh, is excoriated by the Dtr Historian for the re-introduction of syncretistic religious practices done away with by Hezekiah (2 Kgs 21:1—10) and possible capitulation to Assyrian religious influences,[35] he succeeds to the throne by virtue of the fact that he is the son of Hezekiah. No

---

[31] Eph'al, "Assyrian Dominion," 277—80; Clements; *Isaiah,* 55—60.

[32] Clements, *Isaiah,* 60—63.

[33] More relevant: Sennacherib's treatment of Ṣidqa, rebellious king of Ashkelon, in this same campaign. See Eph'al, "Assyrian Dominion," 278. Ṣidqa is exiled with his whole household and replaced by Sarruludari, son of the former king. Luli, king of Tyre, "fled far overseas" (Cyprus) in this campaign (*ANET*, 287); Sennacherib installed Ethba'al (*Tuba'alu*) in his stead (Katzenstein, *Tyre,* 248 ff.).

[34] If there is any tension in the biblical account, it is over the nature of the report in 2 Kgs 19:35 ff. See Clements, *Isaiah, 20.*

[35] See the debate between Spieckermann and Cogan over this issue in the works cited above (note 8).

interference by Assyria in the Judahite monarchy is recorded or presupposed.[36]

The period following the death of Josiah stands in utter contrast to this. One might assume a significant threat to the dynastic system with the violent treatment of Amon and the intervention of the *am hā'areṣ (2 Kgs 21:19−26), but such acivity becomes standard practice from the death of Josiah to the Fall of Judah. The difficulties which attend the succession of Amon only foreshadow the uneven circumstances surrounding the accession of Judah's last four monarchs: Jehoahaz, Jehoiachim, Jehoiachin, Zedekiah. While frequent external threats to the Northern Kingdom are attested during the entire period of her existence with occasional threats to Judah's political stability after the death of Josiah, external and internal disruptions are the normal state of affairs in the Southern Kingdom until its collapse. In order to do full justice to the complexity of the historical situation in the period during which Jeremiah functioned as a prophet (particularly in his latter years), it is crucial that the broader international situation is kept firmly in view. In particular, it is important to recall the specific historical/political circumstances confronting the Northern Kingdom,[37] if we are to succeed in gaining better perspective on the final days of Judah's existence. We see that it is really only during this brief 20 year period prior to the Fall of Jerusalem that Judah's internal and external political situation closely resembled that of her neighbor to the north, before Israel's own demise at the hands of another enemy in 721 B. C.

C. Judah in the "Egyptian-Babylonian Maelstrom"

Although the chronicling of the history of Judah's monarchs in the first twenty-one chapters of the Book of Second Kings could hardly be termed dull, in comparison with what is found in the last four chapters (and esp. chapters 24−25) this earlier reporting is methodically predictable. For excitement in these ealier chapters, one would do better to turn to the reports of the activities of the northern kings.[38]

---

[36] A quote from Clements is instructive here: "From the Old Testament side, it was Jerusalem's escape from the destruction that had been inflicted upon so many other cities of *Israel* and Judah, and so many other nations, that drew attention to the singular nature of the city's having been spared ... God had defended his own reputation and honour in protecting Jerusalem, and he had displayed the unique importance which he attached *to the dynasty of David*" (62−63). (The underscoring is mine). What is to be stressed is that (1) it was in contrast to the fate Judah knew had befallen Israel and her kings that Jerusalem's deliverance was especially noteworthy, and (2) this deliverance included as well the Davidic dynasty. No puppet king is installed by Sennacherib.

[37] Many of which issued from her own peculiar understanding of kingship (Ishida, *Kingship*, 172).

[38] Or go to 2 Chronicles.

This is not the case with the last four chapters of the Deuteronomistic History, nor is excitement in Judah during this period merely the result of silence in Samaria. Now two powerful nations (Egypt and Babylonia) are quite actively involved in internal dynastic affairs (name changes; dynastic interference; murder; imprisonment; deportation; execution). The throne changes hands rapidly (4 times in twelve years), dramatically (Josiah killed at Megiddo; Zedekiah blinded), and in ways unpredictable (grandson Jehoiachin ruling before uncle Zedekiah; Jehoahaz before elder brother Jehoiakim). Judahite loyalties to external powers shift no less than six times during this brief period. Internal circumstances involve people and groups heretofore unremarkable (the "people of the land"; the "queen mother"; various royal, religious, and administrative officers, including Gedaliah as "governor" and the assassin Ishmael of the "royal family"). The whole Dtr History then draws to a close with a report from the place of Exile, Babylon itself, returning to a king who had been deported years earlier (Jehoiachin). All in all, these final chapters make for engaging reading, unique among accounts of the larger Dtr History. Collating this information with the extra-bliblical evidence and the narratives from Jeremiah, Lamentations, and Ezekiel, a fairly clear picture of Judah's final years emerges. The prophet Jeremiah is not only active during this period; it is also these years which are most fully related in the present text of Jeremiah. Furthermore, it is during this period that a crisis over the interpretation of the Exile was beginning have an effect both on the message of Jeremiah and also on those who would ultimately give the final form of that message its final literary shape.

A quick glance at the two pages of Chart Four (following) illustrates the sharp contrast between the period prior to the assassination of Amon and that which follows up to the Fall of Jerusalem. The first page shows the limited extent to which the Assyrian Empire played a role in the territory of Judah prior to the reign of Hezekiah, and the relative stability that obtained. Note as well that during this period the place of origin of the mother of the ruling Judahite monarch was, in most cases, Jerusalem or the neighboring Judahite countryside. The two exceptions to this pattern resulted in disturbances in the otherwise peaceful circumstances of the Southern Kingdom. By contrast, note on the second page the variety of places from which the "Queen Mother" came following the reign of Manasseh (Jotbah, Bozkath, Libnah, Rumah, Jerusalem). On two occasions, her place of origin was as far away as Galilee. Most significantly, interference from Babylon and Egypt is not only recorded, it dominates the biblical record. The frequent appearance of the "people of the land" is also to be observed. Is there any significance in these uneven events for the person and message of Jeremiah? This question must ultimately be faced. First, an overview of relevant historical events is provided.

Chart Four

Kingship in Judah
Solomon to Manasseh (961 — 642 B. C.)

Judahite King	Queen Mother/Place of Origin	Disruptions
Solomon	Bathsheba	
Abijah	Maacah (I 15:2) of Jerusalem	
Asa	Maacah (I 15:10) of Jerusalem	
Jehoshaphat	Azubah (I 22:42) of Jerusalem	
Jehoram/Joram		
Ahaziah	Athaliah (II 8:26) of Israel	External (II 9:27 ff.)
Athaliah		Internal (II 11:1) ʿam hāʾāreṣ (II 11:17 ff.)
Jehoah	Zibiah (II 12:1) of Beersheba	Internal (II 12:20 ff.)
Amaziah	Jehoiaddin (II 14:2) of Jerusalem	
Azariah/Uzziah	Jecoliah (II 15:2) of Jerusalem	ʿam hāʾāreṣ (II 15:5)
Jotham	Jerusha (II 15:33) of Jerusalem (?)	
Ahaz		
Hezekiah	Abi (II 18:2) of Jerusalem (?)	Assyria (II 18 — 19)
Manasseh	Hephzibah (II 21:1) of Jerusalem (?)	Internal (II 21)

Chart Four

Kingship in Judah
Amon to Zedekiah (642 — 587 B. C.)

Judahite King	Queen Mother/Place of Origin	Disruptions
Amon	Meshullemeth (II 21:19) Jotbah (Galilee)	Internal: ʿam hāʾāreṣ (21:23 ff.)
Josiah	Jedidah (II 22:1) Bozkath (Judah)	Egypt (II 23:29 ff.) ʿam hāʾāreṣ (II 23:30)

Jehoahaz	Hamutal (II 23:31) Libnah (Judah)	Egypt: Imprisonment & Deportation (II 23:33 ff.)
Eliakim/ Jehoiakim	Zebidah (II 23:36) Rumah (Galilee)	Egypt: Throne & Name Change Taxation of ʿam hāʾāreṣ Babylon: Vassal and Rebel (II 23:34 ff.)
Jehoiachin	Nehushta (II 24:8) Jerusalem	Deported with Royal Family to Babylon (II 24:14 ff.)
Mattaniah/ Zedekiah	Hamutal (II 24:18) Libnah (Judah)	Babylon: Throne & Name Change Blinded, Sons Killed, Deported (II 25:1–7)
Jehoiachin		Babylon: Re-instated as King? (II 25:27 ff.)

Chart Four: Observations

1. Most internal and external disruption occurs from the reign of Amon until the Fall of Jerusalem.

2. Prior to this period, the normal place of origin for the Queen Mother is Jerusalem.

3. The exceptions give rise to the following observations:
   (a) Athaliah is not only from the Northern Kingdom, she attempts to seize power in a manner unfamiliar in Judah, though less so in Samaria (cf. Jezebel); (b) she is ousted by what appear to be internal and external coalitions, made up of priests (Jerusalemite) and "the people of the land"; (c) when the "people of the land" get involved in the passing of the throne, the Davidid's mother may come from outside Jerusalem (Jehoash; Josiah; Jehoahaz); (d) note that internal rebellions occur (by the royal servants) when the Queen Mother is *not* from Jerusalem (Athaliah; Jehoash; Amon).

4a. The chief concern of the "people of the land" would appear to be the sustaining of Davidic rule against all internal and external threats; the place of origin of the Queen Mother may be decisive; the "people of the land" may favor a non-Jerusalemite in the instances in which they act (Jehoash; Josiah; Jehoahaz).

4b. This may lead to retaliation from internal forces who resent non-Jerusalemite rule (Jehoash; Amon; taxation of the "people of the land": under Jehoiakim, an Egyptian puppet).

5. External powers (Babylon and Egypt) may exploit internal tensions by installing a king whose origins are non-Jerusalemite:

(a) Jehoahaz, who garners strong support from the "people of the land", is imprisoned and deported by the Egyptians; (b) he is replaced by Eliakim (whose name is changed to Jehoiakim) whose Queen Mother is from Rumah (Egyptian-controlled territory) and who levies a tax against the "land" and the "people of the land"; (c) after the deportation of Jehoiachin (Jehoiakim dies), the Babylonians install his uncle Mattaniah (brother of Jehoiakim, name changed to Zedekiah) from Libnah, probably Babylonian territory.

6. The following observations are also relevant:

(a) Jehoiakim's son, Jehoiachin, reigns before his brother, Mattaniah (Zedekiah), although Jehoiachin (Coniah) is 3 years younger; (b) both Zedekiah and Jehoahaz have the same mother, Hamutal from Libnah; Jehoiachin's Queen Mother is a Jerusalemite; is he considered a less-threatening candidate than Zedekiah, who may have had support from the "people of the land", as did his older brother Jehoahaz, and who may have been prone to rebellion (II 24:20)? (c) Jehoahaz, placed in power by the ʿam-hāʾāreṣ, is selected over his *older* brother, Jehoiakim; while the principle of primogeniture is not slavishly followed in Judah, it is the assumed practice; departure from it is rare and, in this case, significant; (d) this may have to do with the "queen-mother-factor" since Hamutal is from the region of Libnah and is described as a "lioness" in Ezekiel 19; if she represented the interest of the landed nobility and the "people of the land", then Jehoahaz' selection might have had to do with the nationalistic ardor of "people of the land" and their particular anti-Egyptian fervor (note Jehoahaz' rough treatment at their hands).

7. It may be worth concluding with the general observation that at no point in Judah's long history does she face the kind of sustained internal and external disruption that she does from the reign of Amon to the Fall of Jerusalem in 587.

1. General Background: Judahite Society After the Fall of Samaria

The reason for disarray in the Kingdom of Judah during her final years is the swift disintegration of the Assyrian Empire.[39] This disintegration gives rise to takeover attempts by both the Neo-Babylonians (2 Kings 24—25) and the Egyptians (2 Kgs 23:29—35) who seek to inherit and

---

[39] Initially it looked like a good time for Judahite independence. See Hayes & Miller, 466—69; F. M. Cross & D. N. Freedman, "Josiah's Revolt Against Assyria," *JNES* 12 (1953) 56—58.

consolidate the empire established by the Assyrians. As usual, Israel stands
in a sticky geographical position. But other factors also aggravate Judah's
attempts to maintain a peaceful existence within her territory; one can get
a limited glimpse at these factors in the spotty yet indispensible reports of
the biblical record.

First, with the Fall of Samaria in 721 Judah found herself in an
unprecedented situation. Samaria's collapse brought the intermittent Assyrian foe quite close to her own borders. Attempts at sustaining peace
or even reasserting hegemony over her former northern holdings meant
dealing with this much closer and powerful force. Even though relations
with her northern neighbor, Israel, had been far from ideal, they were still
preferable to relations with hostile foreign powers bent upon dominating
the region.

Actually the northern territory of Samaria, after the Fall of the capital
in 721 B. C., contained a mixed population located in four provinces,
Duru, Magidu, Gal'azu, and *Samerina,* the territory closest to Judah. That
loyal Israelites were among their number is not to be doubted, the
exaggerated tone of 2 Kgs 17:6, 18, 24 notwithstanding.[40] Within the
biblical record, compare reports from 2 Kgs 23:15—20 (even stronger, 2
Chronicles 30—31, 34:33), Jeremiah 30—31, and 40, which assume without
need for clarification that a northern remnant continued to exist and often
formed the center of hopes for restoration and reincorporation.[41] What is
new is the extent to which the Northern Kingdom feels the proximity of
her Assyrian overlord. By immediate extension the same would hold true
for Judah. Any attempts at reincorporation by the tiny Judahite kingdom
would have to take this overlord or any new usurper into account (2 Kgs
23:29 ff.).

The collapse of the Northern Kingdom had other effects on Judah
and her own internal constitution. One could successfully chart the relative
stability of Judahite society during the period from David's kingship to
that of Hezekiah, in contrast with Samaria's situation. But with the Fall
of Samaria in 721, perceptible cracks in this stability begin to appear,
especially during the reign of Hezekiah's successor Manasseh.[42] Judahite

---

[40] This chapter of 2 Kings seems to imply that the whole territory was emptied of its native
population (see a similar move, with similar difficulties, in Jer 43:5—7 and 2 Chr 36:21).
For an historical analysis, see Cogan's summary in *Imperialism,* 98 ff.; also, compare Alt's
essay, "Die Rolle Samarias bei der Entstehung des Judenthums," in *Kleine Schriften* II,
316—337, and E. Nielsen, "Political Conditions and Cultural Developments in Israel and
Judah during the reign of Manasseh," *The Fourth World Congress of Jewish Studies, Papers.*
(Jerusalem, 1967) 1.103—6.

[41] See Nah 2:2; Jer 31:20; Ezek 37:22 ff.; Zech 10:6,7; also, David C. Greenwood, "On the
Jewish Hope for a Restored Northern Kingdom," *ZAW* 88 (1976) 376—385.

[42] Many cracks occurred even during the reign of Hezekiah. Merely recall the boastful
report of the Assyrian Annals for Sennacherib, relating the conquest of 46 "strong cities"

society undergoes certain irreversable transformations due to Samaria's Fall and the incorporation of new, non-Israelite populations into her territory. It is certain that this fact affected the complexion of Judahite society, as refugees from the Northern Kingdom fled south in a manner unprecedented in the United Kingdom's history.[43] Furthermore, there seems to be excellent evidence of major population shifts within the territory of Judah itself following Sennacherib's 701 invasion.[44] While it is possible to attribute disarray in Judah to the collapse of the Assyrian Empire, Judahite society had already begun to experience upheavals due to the influx of new, northern populations, as well as changes within her own internal makeup.

It would be an overstatement to term Anathoth (Jer 1:1) a northern city.[45] The fact, however, that a non-Jerusalemite prophet gets the hearing he does in Jerusalem, and indeed that he chooses to direct his oracles to the population of this city and region rather than his own more limited area, is not the consequence of a new kind of prophetic enthusiasm. It is tied to the fact of the Northern Kingdom's collapse and, more importantly, to the overall transference of population to the area.[46] Recall the stormy reception the southern prophet Amos received at the northern shrine Bethel (Amos 7:13). Jeremiah is not told to return north and earn his bread there, since this is no longer a realistic option. The real point of comparison is this: the composition of the population Jeremiah addressed

---

in the kingdom of Judah (*ANET,* 288). In addition to the studies of Cogan, McKay, and Spieckermann, see Carl Evans, "Judah's Foreign Policy from Hezekiah to Josiah," *Scripture in Context II,* 157—178 and especially the essay by Stephen Stohlmann in the same volume "The Judaean Exile of 701 B. C. E." Also: H. Reviv, "The History of Judah from Hezekiah to Josiah," *The World History of the Jewish People* IV/1.191—204.

[43] In addition to familiar treatments of population movements toward the south during this period (of levites, deuteronomists, etc., as in E. W. Nicholson, *Deuteronomy and Tradition,* 94, and A. Alt "Die Heimat des Deuteronomiums"), see now M. Broshi, "The Expansion of Jerusalem in the Reigns of Hezekiah and Manasseh," *IEJ* 24 (1975) 21—26. Broshi states: "the evidence makes it clear that Jerusalem at about 700 B. C. had mushroomed, historically speaking, overnight ... During the quarter millenium after King Solomon's reign, the city changed very little, but around 700 B. C. it increased to three or four times its former size" (23). He concludes: "In our opinion the growth was due to two waves of mass immigration, one from the northern kingdom of Israel after 721 B. C., and the other from the Judaean provinces ceded by Sennacherib to the Philistines after 701 B. C." (25).

[44] See the stimulating article by Stephen Stohlmann, "The Judaean Exile of 701 B. C. E.," in *Scripture in Context II: More Essays on the Comparative Method* (William W. Hallo, James C. Moyer, Leo G. Perdue, eds; Eisenbrauns: Winona Lake, Indiana, 1983) 147—175. Stohlmann's findings will be discussed more fully in the section of the "People of the Land" below.

[45] Anathoth is located in the territory of Benjamin, less than 10 kilometers north of Jerusalem.

[46] The province of *Samerina* was just as close for Jeremiah as Jerusalem, but his migration south is far more the pattern in this period than the exception.

in Jerusalem and its environs was quite different, more displaced and heterogeneous than that addressed by Amos and Bethel. Much military, political, and theological water had gone under the bridge in the time that separated these two prophets. Judahite society is fractured due to the collapse of the Northern Kingdom and strains on her own territory, composite due to shifts in population, and theologically more complex, given the legacy of varying prophetic traditions (Amos, Hosea, Micah, Isaiah, Nahum, Zephaniah) recognized as authoritative by the community addressed by the prophet Jeremiah.

Taking these various factors into account is important for understanding (1) the new role of the "people of the land" in Judahite monarchy and society, (2) the shifting place of origin of the Queen Mother and royal family, (3) the irregularities evidenced in Judah's dynastic system during this period, (4) the precise historical circumstances in which the prophet Jeremiah worked, and (5) the theological correspondences between the message of Jeremiah and other Israelite prophets of the period. With regard to this last factor, it is more likely that Jeremiah's message will resemble the prophetic message of a Micah or a Zephaniah than an Isaiah, given the fact of his non-Jerusalemite background. Note, for example, Jeremiah's avoidance of a theme given clear prominence in the message of his predecessor, Isaiah, concerning the inviolability of Zion.[47]

Beyond this disagreement, however, it is possible to find points of similarity in the message of the pre-exilic prophets on the subject of punishment, exile and deportation. All of them live in close proximity to the fact of foreign dominance and the threat or reality of "plague, pestilence and famine."[48] Deportation and exile are not just experiences for the groups of Judahites who were carried off to Babylon in 597 and 587, or who opted to journey to Egypt in 583. In addition to the 721 Assyrian deportation of substantial portions of the northern population, the biblical and extrabiblical evidence also indicates sizeable deportations of the Judahite population in the year 701 and widespread disturbances in the region due to Sennacherib's invasion. Where it is crucial to tie down Jeremiah's "remnant theology" as a backdrop for chs 21–45, the closest resources for comparison are to be found among the pre-exilic prophets (Micah, Isaiah, Zephaniah, Nahum and Habakkuk) who likewise must treat, in varying degrees of detail: the subject of God's punishment at the

---

[47] Whether or not this is Isaiah's own message or that of traditionists who develop his message (see R. E. Clements, *Isaiah and the Deliverance of Jerusalem*) is an important question. However, in either case it is still clear that traditions concerning the inviolability of Zion pre-dated Jeremiah and were certainly known to Jerusalemites of his day. In fact, the Assyrian redaction of Isaiah, which again pre-dates Jeremiah, probably developed this theme in light of Jerusalem's miraculous deliverance in 701.

[48] See the discussion in Chapter Four following.

hands of a foreign enemy, the threat of deportation, and the concept of a future beyond punishment (Remnant).

In order to comprehend the message of the prophet Jeremiah one cannot lose sight of the nature and complexity of Judahite society for this period. Out of the particular profile of Judahite society at this period a conflict emerged over (1) the nature of Yahweh's punishment through the "foe from the north," (2) the role of exile and deportation in that punishment, (3) the composition of a remnant within both the northern and southern and *Golah* communities, and (4) the interpretation of Jeremiah's message in light of the specific unfolding of historical events of the exilic period.[49]

D. Shifting Political Allegiances, Judah, 712–640 B. C.

1. Hezekiah

It is significant that Judah failed to intervene in the final struggle of the Northern Kingdom. Nor did Judah take part in the great uprising against Sargon II west of the Euphrates, led by Hamath, in which Samaria participated. Very quickly, however, with the demise of the Northern Kingdom, Judah's policy would have to change. In 712 B.C., when Sargon's *turtanu* conquered Ashdod (Isa 20:1), Hezekiah demonstrated greater sympathy toward the Philistine citystates than previously because of his own concern to maintain political independence from the Assyrians. This same desire for independence from Assyria, given new impetus when Sargon II died in battle in 705, led to later alliances with Ṣidqa, king of Ashkelon, and with Shebitku, second king of the 25th Egyptian (Nubian) dynasty (Isa 18:1; 31:1). Contact was also made with Merodach-baladan (*Marduk-apla-iddina*, prince of the Chaldean tribe) who sent envoys to Jerusalem to strengthen his position vis-à-vis the Assyrians.[50] Hezekiah and Ṣidqa together exerted pressure on the neighboring political units to join their coalition.[51] According to the prisms of Sennacherib, Hezekiah encouraged "the officials, the politicians, and the people of Ekron" to rebel against their king, Padi, who was then imprisoned in Jerusalem (*ANET*, 287).[52] In all of these actions Hezekiah was heartened by the

---

[49] See Chapter Four.

[50] Against the biblical record, the Neo-Babylonian envoy pre-dated Sennacherib's invasion. See J. Gray, *1 & 2 Kings,* (Philadelphia: Westminster, 1970) 300–7; J. A. Brinkman, "Merodach-Baladan II," *Studies Presented to A. L. Oppenheim* (Chicago: Oriental Institute, 1964) 31–3.

[51] H. Reviv, "The History of Judah," 196.

[52] This entry may obliquely reveal significant details concerning social stratification in Judahite society, at least as registered in Assyrian documents. Luckenbill's publication of the Oriental Institute Prism reads here, "the officials (^{lu}*šakkanakê*^{pl}), nobles (^{lu}*rubûtê*^{pl}) and people (*nišê*^{pl}) of Ekron" (ii-73) (*The Analysis of Sennacherib* [Chicago: University of Chicago Press, 1924] 31). More on this below.

example of Luli, king of Tyre and Sidon, the strongest ruler in Phoenecia, who had successfully rebelled against Assyria upon the death of Sargon II.

As the historical record shows, Assyria moved quickly and effectively to crush these uprisings.[53] Only the fact of Jerusalem's miraculous deliverance stands out in an otherwise grim picture of total devastation throughout Judah. It is astounding that Judah maintained vassal status, Hezekiah remained king, and the whole region was not made an Assyrian province. In stark contrast is the fate of Ṣidqa, partner in the coalition, who was deposed and taken captive by Sennacherib. A new ruler (Sharuludari) was then installed in his place. Sennacherib reports that the nobles of Ekron who had turned over their king, Padi, to Hezekiah, appealed to the Egyptians for aid. These same Egyptians were routed at Eltekeh, Ekron was captured, and the rebellious nobles executed.[54] Luli, king of Tyre, fled for his life to Cyprus and was replaced by Ethbaal. In stark contrast to these events, Jerusalem's deliverance was extraordinary.

Noting this fact, and bracketing for a moment the complexities involved in reconstructing Sennacherib's campaign to Judah, one striking point is the contrast between the fate of the Judahite countryside surrounding Jerusalem and the capital city itself. There has been a sustained debate about the precise number of cities besieged and the number of citizens deported (lit, "driven out"); but even if one claims exaggerated figures, the contrast is only diminished and not done away with. In a recent treatment of the subject, Stohlmann argues that the figures reported by Sennacherib are only relative overstatements and are essentially accurate.[55] He is quite successful, moreover, in showing that the verbs used in the annals ("drive out," "counting and considering them as booty") refer not to actual deportation, but only the first stage of deportation, that is, the reckoning of prisoners and spoil.[56] Deportations undoubtably occurred. But the figure 200,150 given in the annals represents the total population of the towns captured, "reckoned at the time of their capture for future deportation" (156). That the entire number were not deported

---

[53] Hayes & Miller, 448—51.

[54] "I made Padi, their king, come from Jerusalem and set him up as their lord on the throne, imposing upon him the tribute due to me as overlord" (*ANET*, 288).

[55] Stephan Stohlmann, "The Judean Exile of 701 B. C. E.," *Scripture in Context II*, 160.

[56] Compare the usual series, concerning the cities of Sidqa of Askelon (ii—72), "I besieged (*al-me*), I conquered (*akšud*), I carried their spoils away (*aš-lu-la šal-la-su-un*)" or again concerning the cities of Eltekeh and Timnah (iii-7), "I besieged, I conquered, I carried away their spoil" with the expressions in series concerning the 46 "strong cities" of Hezekiah (iii-23), "I besieged (*al-me*), I conquered (*akšud*)" and then (iii-24), "200,150 people (*nišê[pl]*)" (iii-26—27) "I drove out of their midst (*kir-bi-šu-un ú-še-ṣa-am-ma*) and counted as spoil (*šal-la-tiš am-nu*)." The actual verb for deportation (*ašlu*) is missing in this series. (Citations from Luckenbill's *OIP* Text, 31—33).

is shown by the fact that there is no evidence of significant Assyrian resettlement in the area.

Stohlmann, in examining the count of "46 of his strong cities, walled forts, and countless small villages in their vicinity," reasons that this number includes more than Judahite cities (Lachish, Libnah); it also includes walled cities in the territory of Philistia previously conquered by Hezekiah (2 Kgs 18:8). Of the number of citizens reckoned as spoil but not deported, some resettled in their previous regions if these had not been turned over to the Philistines. Others were handed directly over to their Philistine overlords. Of this latter group, some fled as refugees to Jerusalem and her environs. In making his population estimates, Broshi reckoned that Jerusalem's major westward expansion at this period was due both to the influx of refugees from the Northern Kingdom, as well as population shifts resulting from Sennacherib's 701 campaign.[57] Broshi notes other population increases in the Judahite hills, Negev and southern desert at about the same time, that is, territory uncontrolled by Philistine overlords. Recall that in his annals, Sennacherib boasted of plundering Judean towns and giving them to "Mitinti, king of Ashdod, Padi, king of Ekron, and Sillibel, king of Gaza" (*ANET*, 288). In contrast to the fate of Jerusalem, her king and inhabitants, the Judahite population experienced actual deportation, or the first phases of deportation, vassalage to Philistia and neighboring states, perilous resettlement, and/or further resettlement. In this sense, the treatment of the Judahite population was not altogether different from that of the Northern Kingdom just 20 years earlier. The only difference was the outcome: certain Judahite territory, though ravaged, maintained whatever political independence was possible for vassal-states. The Northern Kingdom had been turned into an Assyrian province. In contrast, however, to the fate of both of these regions, Jerusalem was left virtually untouched, a fact which quickly developed a significance all its own (Isa 37:5−7, 33−37). Moving into the period of Jeremiah little more than 75 years away, it is important to try to determine the extent to which the memory and outcome of these events still had an important effect on Judahite society and the message of the prophet who faced a new threat of deportation and resettlement at the hands of another "foe from the north."

2. Manasseh

If the time for overthrow of the Assyrians had been miscalculated by Hezekiah and his fellow-conspirators, it was never as seriously considered by his successor Manasseh. The decision of the biblical historian to see

---

[57] "The Expansion of Jerusalem," 25 (see note 43 for full citation).

Manasseh's reign as the nadir of the dynastic enterprise in Israel may be extreme. What is clear is that Manasseh ruled during a time of unrivalled Assyrian strength, under the leadership of Esarhaddon (681–669) and Assurbanipal (668–627). For most of Manasseh's 55-year reign, Assyrian military designs were targeted on Egypt and the Arab tribes. Judah and her neighboring states had had enough of rebellion due to the treatment they received at the hands of Sennacherib. This fact made further Assyrian expansion to the south possible. Assyrian annals depict Manasseh as a loyal vassal who collected taxes, remitted annual tribute, and provided military assistance. Esarhaddon tells of Manasseh's transporting timber to Ninevah, together with other loyal vassals (12 kings of Hatti, including the kings of Tyre, Edom, Moab, Gaza, Ashkelon, Ammon, Ashdod). Assurbanipal mentions Manasseh's accompanying him on his first military campaign (667) to Egypt/Nubia, when Tirhakah had once again incited local rulers to rebel (*ANET*, 294).[58] Nearby Lachish was an Assyrian garrison throughout Manasseh's reign.[59] According to cuneiform tablets found at Gezer, Assyrian officials were also in the region during the years 651–649, and probably earlier.[60]

The report of Manasseh's rebellion in 2 Chr 33:11–16 is difficult to square with the overall picture of Manasseh the servile king: it is therefore often attributed to the *tendenz* of the Chronicler. Assyrian annals do mention rebellions by Sidon (677) and Tyre (668/7), as well as the more serious revolt by Psammetichus I of Egypt (Sais) and Gyges of Lydia in 655. Furthermore, Assurbanipal had to stay in Babylon in the years 652–648 to put down the rebellion of his brother Samas-sum-ukin. It is possible to link a rebellion on Manasseh's part to these other waves of unrest, and, more specifically, to picture his imprisonment in southern Mesopotamia no later than 648. Assurbanipal's rather lenient treatment of Manasseh and other rulers in the west can be explained by his preoccupation with the dangers he was beginning to face on his eastern border.[61] Those who place his rebellion earlier do so on the strength of a fragmentary inscription of Esarhaddon which seems to belong to the context of his return from Egypt in 671.[62] During this campaign, reprisals were made against the

---

[58] For a discussion of these texts, see Carl Evans' "Foreign Policy," 167–8; H. Reviv, "The History of Judah," 200.

[59] M. Elat, "The Political Status of the Kingdom of Judah within the Assyrian Empire in the 7th Century B. C. E.," *Investigations at Lachish V* (Tel Aviv: Gateway, 1975) 61–70.

[60] Kurt Galling, "Assyrische und persische Präfekten in Geser," *PJB* 31 (1935) 76; for a more general discussion of the *šaknu* official, see R. A. Henshaw, "The Office of Šaknu in Neo-Assyrian Times," *JAOS* 87 (1967) 517–24 and 88 (1968) 461–82.

[61] These included the king of Tyre, Necho I, and Psammetichus I. See Hayes & Miller, *History*, 455.

[62] Evans, "Foreign Policy," 167; M. Cogan, *Imperialism*, 69 (citing the pertinent material from R. Borger, *Die Inschriften Asarhaddons Königs von Assyrien* [AfO Beiheft 9; Graz: Weidner, 1956]).

rulers of Hatti who had conspired against Esarhaddon with Tirhakah of Egypt. Manasseh may quite likely have been among them. Once Manasseh had sworn to maintain his vassalage he was allowed to return to Jerusalem.[63] At either this time or the later date, Manasseh began to fortify the capital city (2 Chr 33:14). It is not clear whether this move is to be interpreted as a pro-Assyrian action meant to strenghten Assyria's southern flank against the advance of Psammetichus I, or be viewed as preparation for further attempts at independence.

In conclusion, it is possible to see a kernel of historicity in the Chronicler's account. It is not clear whether the rebellion of Manasseh should be placed during the reign of Esarhaddon or later in the period of Assurbanipal. Some feel Manasseh was a more loyal vassal at the beginning of his reign,[64] others at the close.[65] This important disagreement aside, the overall thrust of the biblical record is on the *relative* loyalty of Manasseh to Assyrian overlordship, especially given the duration of his reign. But the overall stability of the Assyrian empire began to show signs of erosion more than a decade before the end of Assurbanipal's long reign. Although Memphis was captured by Esarhaddon in 671 and Thebes by Assurbanipal in 663, under the subsequent leadership of Psammetichus I (657—654) Egypt was again able to take an increasingly hostile position against Assyria.[66] Rebellions in the east (Babylon, Elam, Arab tribes) and invasions from the north (nomadic, perhaps Scythian) also meant a serious challenge to Assyria's dominance. They also kept Assyria occupied in such a way

---

[63] R. Frankena, "The Vassal Treaties of Esarhaddon and the Dating of Deuteronomy," *OTS* 14 (1965) 122—54; D. J. Wiseman, "The Vassal Treaties of Esarhaddon," *Iraq* 20 (1958) 1—99.

[64] Reviv, "The History of Judah," 201.

[65] Evans, "Foreign Policy," 169.

[66] Anthony Spalinger, in a series of articles, has argued for a much more balanced view of relationships between Assyria and Egypt for this period, minimizing Assyria's punitive role during the reigns of both Esarhaddon and Assurbanipal, and urging that the real enemy of both Assyria and Egypt be seen as the Kushites ("Assurbanipal and Egypt: A Source Study," *JAOS* 94 [1974] 316—28; "Esarhaddon and Egypt: An Analysis of the First Invasion of Egypt," *Or 43* [1974] 295—326; "Psammetichus, King of Egypt: I," *Journal of the American Research Center in Egypt* 13 [1976] 133—47; "Psammetichus, King of Egypt: II," *JARCE* 15 [1978] 49—57). Even if relationships within Egypt are seen as more co-operative than heretofore ("To the Saites, Kush was far more dangerous than Assyria," *JARCE* 13, 142), Assyria was still the invading conqueror and Egypt (Saite) the vassal. Spalinger succeeds in making understandable the rapprochment that occurs between these two at a later period, when both are allied against the Neo-Babylonians (Carchemish, 609 B. C., and earlier [Wiseman, 19]). But this rapprochment is preceded by a period during which Egypt rapidly expands into Palestine, under the leadership of the same Psammetichus, probably as early as the 630's. It would be wrong to see this as "anti-Assyrian" activity in the strict sense, since "Assyrian influence had diminished to such a degree by 628 B. C. as to render such a policy superfluous" ("Psammetichus: II," 52. See also M. Cogan, *Imperialism,* 70—1). Nevertheless, it may have appeared this way to a Judahite citizen or King Josiah. See the discussion following.

that she could contemplate no serious intervention in Judahite internal affairs after 640 B. C.[67]

Before moving to the reign of Amon it is important to comment briefly on Judah's internal situation. To say that Manasseh's relationship to external powers was relatively stable (and negatively evaluated) for the majority of his long reign is not to suggest that this stability was reflected in internal circumstances.[68] There has been a recent scholarly tendency to downplay Assyria's direct role in coercing adherence from vassal-states to her own religious beliefs and practices. This line of approach is best represented in the studies of McKay and Cogan.[69]

There is an important implication of such a view. Since the historicity of the biblical accounts, specifically their reports of syncretistic practices during the reigns of Ahaz and Manasseh, is not being called into question,[70] then the responsibility for such actions must be shifted internally. Moreover, while it may be the tendency of the Dtr Historian in these accounts to fasten primary responsibility for Judah's cultic sins on the single figure of the king, consistent with his understanding of the rights and obligations of Israelite kingship (see Deut 17:14—20), it is clear that the burden must also be borne by larger groups within the Judahite population. In other words, the sequence of obedience/disobedience running from Ahaz to Hezekiah to Manasseh to Josiah reflects more than the alternating pious and impious imposition of kingly wishes on a population. Rather, this sequence discloses a fundamental struggle within Judahite society itself to deal with more direct Assyrian presence and influence.

There has already been sufficient cause to note the extent to which Judahite society underwent significant changes prior to Manasseh's reign, with the influx of displaced populations from the Northern Kingdom in 721, and major resettlements of population within Judah after 701. Both groups had firsthand experience with the threat of deportation, harsh resettlement, and just general Assyrian oppression. Within both of their ranks, but also among the inhabitants of Jerusalem, there was bound to be significant disagreement over the nature and extent of capitulation to Assyrian overlordship, including its cultic aspects.

Attempts have been made to be much more specific about which groups aligned themselves in which ways.[71] This often means pitting the prophets Isaiah, Zephaniah, and Jeremiah (together with their support groups) and perhaps the Jerusalem temple-priests[72] against the members

---

[67] Cogan, *Imperialism,* 71.

[68] See only 2 Kgs 21:3—4.

[69] See note 8 above for full citation.

[70] Cogan only attempts further clarifications, *Imperialism,* 72—3.

[71] E. Nielsen, "Political Conditions"; Morton Smith, *Palestinian Parties and Politics that Shaped the Old Testament* (New York: Columbia University Press, 1971) esp. 45—48.

[72] Nielsen, "Political Conditions," 106.

of the royal court, most leaders and princes, the priests of Baal and other Judahite circles in close contact with Assyrian administration. Sharp distinctions such as these may overstate the evidence. At the same time, the categories "Yahweh-alone" or "not Yahweh-alone" are too abstract and far too difficult to attach to specific groups that can in fact be isolated in Judahite society at this period.[73] Furthermore, because Assyrian influence in Judah ranges over a fairly substantial period (most of the 7th century), each specific biblical account must be treated on its own, as relevant only for the period it describes.

By the time of Zephaniah, for example, Assyrian influence had spread through both city and country in such a way that one does not see in his prophecies a picture of tragic, enforced Assyrianism or virulent religious opposition, but one of advanced assimilation.[74] Alternatively, at no point during the period of Assyrian overlordship is it clear that having direct contact with Assyrian administration, in rural areas, led to greater assimilation of Assyrian culture.[75] As a matter of fact, greater contact could just as easily lead to greater resentment and stiffer rejection of Assyrian ways. Zephaniah directs oracles of restoration to the "humble of the land" (1:3; 3:12) who seek righteousness, not to the "inhabitants of Jerusalem," among whom are numbered officials and the king's sons (1:8), idolotrous priests, and those who swear by Milcom (1:4—6). Rural populations who have directly experienced Assyrian overlordship would also be those most anxious for reform and the casting off of foreign rule (see Zeph 2:3—4).

3. Amon

The vagueness of the biblical accounts concerning rebellion or shifting political allegiances for the long reign of Manasseh is probably indicative of the fact that only mild permutations can be noted in an otherwise submissive stance toward the Assyrians.[76] It would be a mistake to term Manasseh "pro-Assyrian," since this label suggests a degree of choice in political alignment he probably never had. This is precisely why permu-

---

[73] These are the labels used by M. Smith in *Palestinian Parties*. See also now, "Jewish Religious Life," *The Cambridge History of Judaism: The Persian Period* (Vol 1; W. D. Davies and Louis Finkelstein, eds; Cambridge: University Press, 1984) 222 ff.

[74] Cogan (*Imperialism*, 95) states: "In a word, the diminutive Judahite state was buffeted on all sides by cultural patterns dominant in the Assyrian empire." In Zephaniah there is reference to "foreign attire" (1:8), foreign speech (3:9), and even "the remnant" of Baal (1:4), suggesting long-standing syncretism.

[75] See Nielsen, "Political Conditions," 105,6.

[76] Nielsen ("Political Conditions," 104) makes note of the fact that Manasseh is no military figure. On the lack of prophetic activity during his reign, he also remarks: ". . . the prophets of Israel and Judah were called into action chiefly in periods of political crisis . . . During the 55 years of the reign of Manasseh, when the Assyrians dominated the world, an independent Judaean policy was simply precluded" (105).

tations (from remaining a reluctant vassal, with occasional attempts at rebellion, to faithful allegiance, with more direct involvement in the Assyrian cause) and no aggressive policy shifts, occurred. At any event, more decidely pro- and anti-Assyrian factions surfaced at Manasseh's death. They were probably gathering momentum for some time. This is suggested by the terse entry at 2 Kgs 21:16: "Moreover, Manasseh shed much innocent blood, till he filled Jerusalem from one end to another." This reference points to some form of internal disruption, possibly political in nature.

Equally cryptic are the circumstances surrounding the conspiracy against Amon, mentioned briefly at 2 Kgs 21:23, "And the servants of Amon conspired against him, and killed the king in his house." The aftermath of these events is also unclear: "But the people of the land slew all those who had conspired against King Amon, and the people of the land made Josiah his son king in his stead" (21:24). The summary information on the reign of Amon supplied by the Dtr Historian is customarily brief. It suggests that he followed the same general religious policy as had his father, continuity stressed in the repetition of the expression that he did "like his father" (2 Kgs 21:20—21). It is tempting to assume that his political alignments were also identical to those of his father (viz, cautious vassalage to Assyria). There is no compelling reason to think otherwise. But what else can be gleaned from this brief account?

First of all, the facts of conspiracy and assassination are themselves striking, given the relative political and military calm reported by the Dtr Historian for the reign of Manasseh. Ironically, these grim events anticipate the sanguinary days that lie ahead for the Judahite monarchy. Up to this time, radical internal disturbances are rare in Jerusalem, though not entirely unattested. Between the years 842 and 769, conspiracy and assassination hit three successive Judahite kings (Ahaziah, Joash, Amaziah). Yet this was brought on in part by the disruptive activities of the northerner, Athaliah, and her doubtless unpopular interference in the Judahite monarchy (2 Kgs 11:1). At both this earlier time and now, the "people of the land" play a role in stabilizing the Davidic dynasty (2 Kgs 11:14—20).

Second, it is to be noted that Amon was only 22 years old when he succeeded his father, who was 67 when he died (the longest reign and second oldest king in Judah's history).[77] This means Amon was not even born until Manasseh was 45, making it unlikely that he was the first-born or eldest surviving son.[78] The succession of Amon, as over against other

---

[77] See the helpful chart and discussion in T. Ishida, *Royal Dynasties*, 153 ff.

[78] Ishida states, "with the exception of Solomon, Manasseh, Amon and Zedekiah, all the kings were born when their father's ages were between eleven and twenty-four, that is, around twenty" (155). Also see his remarks in " 'The People of the Land' and the Political Crisis in Judah," *Annual of the Japanese Biblical Institute* 1 (1975) 35—6.

older candidates, suggests some sort of court or domestic intrigue not
related by the Dtr Historian. As Ishida has pointed out in his analysis of
Judahite kingship, though the principle of primogeniture is only "fundamental and not decisive," when it is abrogated, quite frequently it is stated
"how and why the irregular succession took place."[79] For the reign of
Amon, such information is lacking upon his succession, but it can be
inferred from his short reign and his assassination that problems occurred
at the passing of the throne.

Furthermore, it is somewhat unusual that Manasseh did not appoint
a co-regent prior to his death, given his advanced age. Was the appointment
of a co-regent avoided in order to maintain internal stability? The appointing of a co-regent would have inevitably led to new political alignments
and realignments, either at odds with or consistent with Manasseh's own
policies.[80] Yet attempts to forestall tangible political conflict, if such did
occur, may have in fact encouraged the forming of factions within the
royal court. The Dtr Historian reports some kind of bloody conflict
among the inhabitants of Jerusalem during Manasseh's long reign (2 Kgs
21:16; 24:4). Given the specific historical circumstances for the period,
including the decline of Assyrian hegemony over the region and renewed
Egyptian ascendency under Psammetichus I, it is most likely that these
factions disputed Judah's stance vis-à-vis Egypt and Assyria.

Given these political events, which will be discussed more fully below,
many scholars have seen behind the conspiracy and death of Amon a clash
between pro-Assyrian and pro-Egyptian factions.[81] Malamat has argued
that Amon was assassinated by an anti-Assyrian party. Then, in his view,
a counter-revolution ensued by the "people of the land" who were afraid
of Assyrian reprisals. He has also argued that some form of Egyptian
instigation lay behind the coup. Ishida has refined this position a bit by
seeking the grounds for political conflict between pro- and anti-Assyrian
factions earlier, prior to the succession of Amon. He also avoids labelling
the "people of the land" either pro-Assyrian or pro-Egyptian. The dispute
between these factions centered on the question of continuity or severence
with Assyrian overlordship. Considering the fact of Amon's young age

---

[79] "Political Crisis," 25, n. 1.

[80] See the remarks of J. Gray (*I & II Kings* [2nd ed; Philadelphia: Westminster, 1970] 711)
concerning Manasseh's failure to appoint a co-regent: "The failure of Manasseh to
appoint a co-regent in spite of his age . . . is a significant token of the status of Judah
as a vassal kingdom of Assyria. So careful were the rulers of Assyria that there should
be no ruler round whom national resistance might rally . . .". See as well the remarks of
Ishida, *Dynasties*, 170.

[81] See, for example, two brief articles by Abraham Malamat: "The Historical Background
of the Assassination of Amon, King of Judah," *IEJ* 3 (1953) 26–29; "Josiah's Bid for
Armageddon. The Background of the Judean-Egyptian Encounter in 609 B. C.," *JANES*
5 [*The Gaster Festschrift*] (1973) 270–73. In the 1973 study, Malamat concludes "the *'am
hā'āreṣ* appears to have been a steadfastly anti-Egyptian faction" (271).

and assuming that elder sons were on the scene, Ishida concludes: "The former (pro-Assyrian party) backed Manasseh's rule and Amon's succession, while the latter (pro-Egyptian) tried to overthrow the pro-Assyrian regime by supporting Amon's elder brothers under Egyptian instigation."[82]

Ishida's is a reasonable conjecture. There is no direct evidence of elder brothers playing a role; but it would be highly unusual for Manasseh, who was 45 at the time of Amon's birth, not to have fathered other sons prior to Amon.[83] In addition, there is the unfortunately brief but clear reference to "sons of the king" in Zephaniah 1:8, who are indicted for foreign ways. Are these the surviving sons of Manasseh (i.e., Amon's older brothers), or the sons of Amon (i.e., the brothers of Josiah)? The latter makes some sense if the traditional date of Zephaniah is accepted (i.e., in Josiah's early years).[84] But the former need not be excluded.

It is possible to envision both groups as involved, since *bny hmlk* may be a general term for *bt hmlk* "king's house" (so LXX). Josiah, it is to be remembered, was placed on the throne when he was only 8 years old. This means that both his uncles and brothers could have been on the scene. This in turn suggests the possibility of long-standing disagreement between political factions within Judah. It is reasonable, then, to infer from the Kings' account of Amon's reign that conflict over the nature and extent of capitulation to Assyrian rule existed within the capital and royal house. Though such a conflict would come to a head at the passing of the throne, it had probably begun to gather momentum years earlier. In many respects, it would better fit the historical circumstances around the time of Amon's birth. Even by 640 B.C., direct Assyrian influence in the region had dwindled.

It should be noted that objections to this picture of internal political posturing have been registered by those who see no significant Assyrian presence in the region from 640 B.C. on.[85] However, a clear distinction should be made between military/political influence in the region,[86] and cultural influence, which obtains well into the period of Joshiah, as is

---

[82] Ishida, "Political Crises," 36. See also Ihromi, "Die Königinmutter und der ʿamm hāʾāreẓ im Reich Judah," *VT* 24 (1974) 423 ff.

[83] Compare, for example, other kings the vinage of Manasseh (Ishida, *Royal Dynasties,* 153—4). David was 50 when Solomon was born; he had a good many sons before this (at a minimum, see 2 Sam 3:2—5; 5:13—16).

[84] See, for example, the arguments of Wilhelm Rudolph (*Micha-Nahum-Habakuk-Zephanja* [KAT 13; Gütersloh: Gütersloher Verlagshaus Gerd Mohn, 1975] 255 ff.) for a pre-reformation (622 B.C.) date.

[85] Cogan, *Imperialism,* 70—71.

[86] This is well attested for the majority of Manasseh's long reign. It would have had a direct impact on the designation of a successor.

acknowledged by Cogan (*Imperialism*, 95). Both factors suggest that political factions had begun to form at this period.

A further consideration has been obliquely raised by the findings of
Anthony Spalinger.[87] Spalinger, as noted above, has underscored the
cordiality and cooperation that existed between Psammetichus I and Assurbanipal, thus forcing us to adjust the traditional picture of Egypt and
Assyria as arch-enemies. In so doing, Spalinger shows how the rapprochment that later evolved between them was not as artificial, or as forced
on the part of the anxious Egyptians under Necho II, as one might have
expected. But such a view also has implications for the way in which one
views internal politics within Judah. At one point, supporting Cogan's
view on diminishing Assyrian influence in Judah for the period under
discussion, Spalinger concludes that "active anti-Egyptian or anti-Assyrian
policy" did not exist in Judah, at least during the early years (632 B. C.)
of Josiah. His reading of the relationship between Assyria and Egypt, not
only for the reign of Assurbanipal but also for Esarhaddon, points to the
unlikelihood of such factions having existed earlier.

Spalinger's work is helpful in correcting the larger ANE picture of
the relationship between these two super-powers, but as the picture relates
to Judah, it must be accepted with the following proviso: the relationship
between Egypt and Assyria, cordial or otherwise, can only indirectly
inform us about *Judah's* own internal situation and stance, as a vassal,
toward them both. The biblical narratives from the reign of Hezekiah (2
Kgs 18—19) describe the clear perception, from Judah's side, that Assyria
and Egypt are two distinct choices in a dangerous game of political and
military alignment. The invasion of Egypt by Esarhaddon (671 B. C.)
occurs not long after these events, in the second decade of Manasseh's
reign. The destruction of Thebes (No-Amon) has a definite impact on the
Judahite populace (Nahum 3:8—10). The larger point is that pro-Assyrian
and pro-Egyptian factions, at least within the royal court, probably existed
well into Manasseh's long reign. And furthermore, even if the overly
punitive picture of Assyria in Egypt is put in better perspective by seeing
them cooperating with the Egyptians against the Kushites (*Kusu*), they are
nevertheless *foreign invaders* in Egypt. From the Judahite perspective, this
would mean continued vassalage under Egypt or Assyria in a manner not
unfamiliar, or the slim possibility of independence.

All this underscores the probability that political factions existed
within Judah throughout the reign of Manasseh and up to the coronation
of Amon. Furthermore, it is likely that at the time of Amon's succession
several contenders for the throne existed and that these had certain stated
political alignments or support groups who did. Who backed Amon and
why, is unclear. The texts record that he ruled for 2 short years and that

---

[87] See note 66 above.

he was assassinated by "his servants" (2 Kgs 21:23). They then report that the "people of the land" placed an eight-year old monarch on the throne. From the data available to us, it is likely that other options were possible, including one of Amon's own brothers seizing power. But the 'am hā'āreṣ intervene to place young Josiah on the throne. Does this suggest a conscious political choice on their part, or a nationalistic rejection of the kind of political maneuvering attempted by the assassins? Both of these options have been suggested.[88]

This brings us to the third major factor in the events surrounding the assassination of Amon: the role of the "people of the land." Though it would perhaps be helpful to isolate the problem of their role only as it relates to the events of 642—640 B. C., the "people of the land" put in frequent appearances in the affairs of the Judahite monarchy. Therefore, before it is possible to enquire about their specific role in this or in subsequent affairs in Jerusalem, certain basic questions must be answered concerning their identity and function. It is all the more important to turn to the question of definition at this point since the "people of the land" continue to play an intermittent, unfortunately cryptic role right up to the Fall of Jerusalem.

E. Excursus: The "People of the Land"

Attempts to define the expression "people of the land," which appears over 60 times in the Old Testament, have ranged far and wide in this century. Against a backdrop in which no technical meaning was assigned to the term,[89] Judge Sulzberger pressed for the most extensive and inventive description essayed. He argued that the 'am hā'āreṣ were nothing less than an ancient Hebrew Parliament, complete with upper and lower houses.[90] Others interpreted the expression as meaning only the "rural inhabitants" of a given territory, though in fact these inhabitants might be contrasted with other sociologically and geographically distinct units.[91] Some have argued that the 'am hā'āreṣ (AH) were the "landed nobility" or "leaders/owners of the land"[92]; others, that they were in fact the

---

[88] Compare, for example, Malamat and Ishida.
[89] A general definition was the broader population apart from the ruling classes. E. Klamroth (Die jüdischen Exultanten in Babylon [Leipzig, 1912] 99—101) considered the 'am hā'āreṣ "die Volksmenge."
[90] The Am Ha-aretz: The Ancient Hebrew Parliament (Philadelphia, 1909) and "The Polity of the Ancient Hebrews," JQR 3 (1912—13) 1—81.
[91] R. Gordis, "Sectional Rivalry in the Kingdom of Judah," JQR 25 (1934/5) 237—59. (Gordis also has a review and critique of Sulzberger's proposal, 256—9).
[92] S. Daiches, "The Meaning of עם הארץ in the Old Testament," JTS 30 (1929) 245—9; Max Weber, Das antike Judentum (Tübingen, 1931) 30 ff.

proletariat.[93] Partial consensus was achieved in the 1936 monograph of
Ernst Würthwein devoted exclusively to the subject, *Der ʿamm haʾareẓ im
Alten Testament,* yet in part because of the rather broad definition settled
upon: "die zu einem bestimmten territorium gehörige Vollbürgerschaft."
In this definition, he is followed by both Martin Noth and Roland de
Vaux.[94]

In an attempt to do justice to the wider variety of contexts in which
the term occurs[95] a certain specificity for the context presently under
scrutiny was sacrificed. Recent studies, focused on the *AH* in the limited
range of texts provided by Kings, Jeremiah and Ezekiel, have been more
successful in bringing some precision to the term.[96] E. W. Nicholson
obliquely assisted the move toward restricting the scope of inquiry by
offering the kind of counsel of despair which results when one tries to
force a definition out of the fuller range and variety of texts in which the
term appears.[97] S. Talmon greatly aided the cause for more precision by
differentiating between approaches which take their departure from etym-
ological considerations (all the pre-Würthwein studies) and those which
understand that "the specific meaning of a word will be decided on its
context" (72). He thereby allowed the sensitive reader to hold to a more
general meaning of the term *AH* (such as is found in the Pentateuch or
post-exilic texts). Yet he also recognized a more restricted sense of the
phrase, e. g., "a technical term which can be applied only to a specific
entity in the Judaean body politic" (73). In this more technical use, the
word never refers to the citizens of the Northern Kingdom (a fact with

---

[93] A. Menes, *Die vorexilischen Gesetze Israels im Zusammenhang seiner kulturgeschichtlichen
Entwicklung* (BZAW 50; Berlin, 1928) 70 ff.; K. Galling, "Die israelitische Staatsverfassung
in ihrer vorderorientalischen Umwelt," *AO* 28 (1929) 23.

[94] Ernst Würthwein, *Der ʿamm haʾareẓ im Alten Testament* (BWANT 4; Stuttgart, 1936). M.
Noth, "Gott, König, Volk im Alten Testament," *ZThK* 47 (1950) 181; R. de Vaux,
Ancient Israel: Social Institutions (New York: McGraw-Hill, 1965) 1.70—72; See also,
Marvin H. Pope, "ʿAm Haʾareẓ," *IDB,* 1.106—7.

[95] For non-Israelites in Gen 23:12—13; 42:6; Nu 14:9; Ex 5:5 [Sam]; in general Israelite
settings, Lv 4:27; 20:2—4; specifically associated with the phenomenon of kingship in
Judah, in 2 Kgs, Jer, Ezek; in post-exilic [plural] forms; and further, in rabbinic texts,
as a term of opprobrium.

[96] Shemaryahu Talmon, "The Judaean *ʿam hāʾareṣ* in Historical Perspective, *The Fourth
World Congress of Jewish Studies, Papers* (Jerusalem, 1967) 1.71—76; Hayim Tadmor, "'The
People' and the Kingship in Ancient Israel: The Role of Political Institutions in the
Biblical Period," *Journal of World History* 11 (1968) 46—68; Tomoo Ishida, "'The People
of the Land' and the Political Crises in Judah," *Annual of the Japanese Biblical Institute* 1
(1975) 23—38; J. Alberto Soggin, "Der judäische *ʿam haʾareṣ* und das Königtum in
Juda," *VT* 13 (1963) 187—95; Ihromi, "Die Königinmutter und der ʿamm haʾareẓ im
Reich Juda," *VT* 24 (1974) 421—9.

[97] "The Meaning of the Expression עם הארץ in the Old Testament," *JSS* 10 (1965) 59—66.
He concludes that the expression "has no fixed and rigid meaning but is used in a purely
general and fluid manner and varies in meaning from context to context" (66).

its own significance). It appears most often in contexts dealing with Judahite monarchy, more specifically on occasions when the uninterrupted succession of Davidic kings is called into question. A further observation is that explicit references to the *AH* are spread over a period from about the middle of the ninth century to the beginning of the sixth. Again, the preponderance of references are related to (a) the turbulent period between 842 and 769, when 3 successive kings (Ahaziah, Joash, and Amaziah) and one usurper (Athaliah) are assassinated, or (b) the period from Amon's brief reign to the Fall of Jerusalem, periods, it should be stressed, in which significant external political disruptions led to major internal disturbances in Jerusalem.

Both Talmon and Ishida have made the observation that the *AH* seem to intervene to counteract the imminent threat to the Davidic dynasty at the passing of the throne.[98] Talmon goes even further to conclude that the essential identity and function of the "people of the land" involves "the de facto championing of the house of David" (75). Attempts to define them sociologically (poor, landed) or socio-politically (Hebrew Parliament, "leaders of the land") founder, for the *AH* are an *ad hoc* instrument of action and not a permanent instrument of deliberation (contra, Sulzberger).[99] As such, they can often appear in open opposition to royal courtiers, who may have political aspirations beyond mere maintenance of the Davidic dynasty.

Talmon and Ishida have done much good in (1) limiting the scope of inquiry to texts in Jeremiah, Ezekiel, and Kings, for in all three there is a specific setting and limited time-frame; (2) stressing the role of the *AH* vis-à-vis the Davidic dynasty, for they are always depicted in this context; (3) arguing for a technical meaning for the term which distinguishes the *AH* from the royal house (including servants, courtiers, and militia) from priests, prophets and scribes, and even from like-sounding groups, such as the *'am yĕhûdāh,* "the people of Judah" (2 Kgs 14:21).[100] For the purpose of this investigation, it will be worthwhile to take another look at the relevant texts in 2 Kings, Jeremiah, and Ezekiel to see if other factors exist which would help tie down the meaning of the expression *AH* and the role and function of the "people of the land" within Judahite society for this period. Certain fundamental observations made by Talmon and Ishida will receive more thorough analysis.

---

98   Talmon, "Judaean *'am ha'areṣ,*" 74; Ishida, "Political Crises," 31.
99   Talmon concludes: the "people of the land" lack "any *de jure* circumscription in the political framework of the Judaean kingdom. Accordingly the *AH* can not be defined in terms of a constitutional-legal nature" (75).
100 Ishida and Talmon disagree as to just how discrete these two groups are ("Political Crisis," 33; Judaean *'am ha'areṣ,*" 74).

While the expression "people of the land" appears to point to a general meaning, "the rural inhabitants of Judah," Talmon has correctly questioned whether the *AH* refers to the *whole* citizenry of Judah or even representatives of the same. In the broader use of the term in the OT, a general meaning appears to be the obvious sense, denoting the larger population of any given country or political unit (e. g., Hittites, Egyptians, Canaanites).[101] If one transfers this general sense to the narrower context of Judah, the "people of the land" would then be roughly equivalent to the "people of Judah" or representatives of the same. Studies which do not take the term in this wider sense, but only as a more limited body of representatives, have been troubled by lack of convincing evidence as to how this body functioned and was constituted.[102] Talmon is himself critical of "institutionalizing tendencies" in biblical research, but it requires a highly nuanced description of the *AH* to provide them with some definition in the "Judaean body politic" and still keep them distinct from the general Judahite population. In his reading, the *AH* is not a deliberative body, or an otherwise "constitutionally circumscribed institution." At the same time he claims for them a residence(s) in Jerusalem (76) and can describe them as a coherent sociological phenomenon, loyal to the Davidic house, having gained entrance to the capital at the early stages of the Davidic monarchy.

Talmon makes an important observation about silence concerning the *AH* in the sources prior to the revolt of Athaliah. He claims, however, that during this period the *AH* was simply dormant, keeping "a watchful eye on the affairs of the realm" (74). Another possibility is that though the rural population played an important role in David's early rise to power (e. g., at Hebron), the *AH* as found in 2 Kings are not identical in role or function to these early monarchial supporters. Nor are they even directly descended from them. Rather, the "people of the land" emerge at two key periods in the later history of Judah because of other important developments within the capital and countryside. These developments will be taken up for discussion shortly.

In the context of remarks about the more restricted activity and location of the *AH,* Talmon makes the observation that "the concentration of all its actions is within the city of Jerusalem" (75). When one reads the relevant passages closely, it is striking that the *AH,* in terms of the locus of its activity, does act as though it was a group within the capital city distinguishable from the larger rural population of Judah. The *AH* can

---

[101] With this general sense, one hears of a ʿam hāʾareṣ at Byblos and a niše māti — people of the land — in Assyria.

[102] Gordis ("Sectional Rivalry," 257) rightly points out that if the *AH* were in fact a kind of representative Hebrew parliament, why do they make an appearance so irregularly? Would one not have expected them at the coronation of every Judahite monarch?

also be distinguished from selected inhabitants of Jerusalem, including the royal court and other key individuals. In an attempt to find some ground between these two groups (city and country) and yet grant some relationship between the *AH* and them both, Talmon struck the kind of nuanced balance that he did. Yet if, as argued, there is not sufficient evidence to show that the *AH* is the kind of ad hoc, non-institutional, yet sociologically distinct action group with loyalties to David that Talmon urges, then who were they? Let us return to the previous scholarly conclusions again.

1. Those who argued that the *AH* were a deliberative body accurately noted that often they act within Jerusalem proper (2 Kgs 11:14,19,20; 21:24; 23:30) and seem to be a limited body of some kind (2 Kgs 15:5; 25:19), at least in so far as it is difficult to conceive of them as the *whole* population of Judah (21:24; 23:30). It was therefore reasoned that their proximity to the royal house and clear influence in dynastic affairs was due to the fact that they were an institutional, permanent, deliberative instrument, representative, perhaps, of the whole Judahite population, yet not identical with them.

2. Those who have seen in the *AH* the whole rural population of Judah have accurately noted the contrast between city inhabitants and the *AH*. In the lists in which they appear, they seem distinguishable from specific groups of people who are inhabitants of Jerusalem (2 Kgs 24:14; Jer 1:18; 34:19; 37:2; 44:21), including "princes," "mighty men of valor," "craftsmen and smiths," "kings, princes, priests," "princes of Judah, princes of Jerusalem [an interesting distinction], eunuchs," "servants."[103] Most argue, therefore, that *ʿam hāʾāreṣ* and *ʿam yĕhûdāh* are in fact synonymous expressions (de Vaux, Würthwein, Noth).

3. The third group, troubled by the overly institutional profile for the *AH* suggested by the first group, and yet unwilling to see the "people of the land" as strictly equivalent to the rural population, have sought a more subtle understanding of the term, based upon a closer reading of the texts, especially as found in Kings. Talmon is representative of this view, since he claims the actual *raison d'être* of the "people of the land" is functional, e. g., related to their support of the Davidic dynasty. Ishida's view is more cautious, and if anything he leans toward group 2.

It is to be said on behalf of the third group that they have been sensitive to the *role and function* of the "people of the land" vis-à-vis the phenomenon of monarchy in Judah, in which the dynastic enterprise depends upon the support of given power groups within the realm, rather than upon prophetic affirmation or veto, as in the north.[104] Yet function alone is not determinative of their identity. This perspective stands out because of the nature of the biblical reports, which emphasize significant interventions made by the "people of the land."

---

[103] As a matter of clarification, the distinction between city and "people of the land" should not be overdrawn in the case of 2 Kgs 11:20, as though the "people of the land" rejoiced at the same time the capital was sullen/quiet (so Alt, Würthwein, Gordis); *hāʿîr šāqēṭâ* should be simply rendered "the city became peaceful," that is, after the rebellion was over.

[104] H. Tadmor, "'The People' and the Kingship in Ancient Israel," 64—7.

There are several other problems with an overly functional under-standing of the *AH* focused only on their relationship to the Davidic monarchy. Other groups can also display loyalty to the dynastic enterprise, including royal courtiers, priests and prophets, apart from the "people of the land." Moreover, during the period of recurrent assassinations from 842—769 B. C., in which the royal family is destroyed by Athaliah (11:1), Joash is slain by his servants (12:21), and Amaziah is killed in a conspiracy, the role of the *AH* in assuring continuity within the Davidic line is only clearly attested for the succession of Joash (2 Kgs 11:13—20). When the same king Joash is later slain by his servants, no mention is made of the *AH* in the succession of Amaziah (12:20—21); perhaps the same servants were responsible for his succession. Neither is the *AH* explicitly mentioned in 14:19—22, at the conspiracy against Amaziah.[105]

It seems more likely that the group mentioned here, the "people of Judah," points to the wider population of Judah, distinct from Jerusalem. It does not therefore include royal officials. At the same time, it is not directly equivalent to the "people of the land," who tend to act in greater proximity to the capital and, as will be shown, have a distinct profile over against the wider population of Judah. In this specific instance, note that the conspiracy against Amaziah forced him out of the capital into the region around Lachish, e. g., in the Judahite countryside. It is there that he is slain. It is for this reason that mention is made of the *'am yĕhûdāh*, since the coup took place in the rural territory of Judah and not in proximity to the capital. Note too the concluding reference to Azariah's building of Elath and its restoration to Judah. This otherwise innocuous reference should be construed as an act of gratitude on Azariah's part toward those same Judahites (*'am yĕhûdāh*) who helped place him on the throne.

Ishida rejects the nuanced definition of the *AH* proposed by Talmon. He argues that "it is difficult to deduce from those passages (in Kings) any specific political role assigned to 'the people of the land' in that period" (33). He is correct to note that no reports exist of their activities prior to the revolt of Athaliah. Furthermore, there is "virtually no infor-mation at all on the political activity of 'the people of the land' during the two hundred year period from Athaliah's overthrow to Josiah's en-thronement."[106] So while Ishida is sensitive to the specific political role played by the *AH,* he sees no fixed political stance consistently taken by them. Their actions are too sporadic. They may intervene in conflicts in

---

[105] With Ishida and against Talmon, it is not possible to see the *'am yĕhûdāh* as directly equivalent to the *'am hā'āreṣ*. Ishida argues that the former is a more comprehensive term, including officials in Jerusalem ("Political Crises," 33); cf. Talmon, "Judaean *'am ha'areṣ*," 74.
[106] Ishida, "Political Crises," 33.

Jerusalem, but are not necessarily the instigators of such conflict. Having determined in a more cautious way the nature of the "people of the land's" activities, Ishida concludes that the "expression 'people of the land' is used simply as a synonym for 'the people of Judah' under monarchic rule" (33).

In basic agreement with Ishida, it is difficult to say anything definitive about consistent political stances taken by the *AH*.[107]. However, their role vis-à-vis the Davidic dynasty cannot be ignored. It should be stressed that they play the kind of role they do in Judah's dynastic affairs because of certain features inherent in the southern system. In the Judahite dynastic system, in contrast with the situation in the north, the one factor open for negotiation at the succession of the Davidid was the *specific choice of son*.[108] While in the Judahite system, in contrast to the Ephraimite one, "an ideology of sanctity surrounded its founder and emanated to all his successors,"[109] the principle of primogeniture was not so rigidly maintained that it was never rescinded under any conditions. Consequently, Judah often found herself in a position not wholly unlike that which obtained in Samaria, insofar as questions about continuance of a given dynasty (Davidic) were not done away with but only restricted to the crucial decision as to which of several sons should reign. It is precisely because of this fact that conspiracy and *coup d'état* frequently occur in Judah. Yet the system never experiences the kind of breakdown noteworthy in Samaria, due to the relative stability of the Davidic line (the closest thing being the usurpation of Athaliah).

What the biblical evidence suggests is that occasions arose on which there were problems at the passing of the throne in Judah. On such occasions, the "people of the land" intervene to exercise their own choice in designating a successor. This is the one consistent feature which helps move toward greater definition. On all occasions when they act, they place a new ruler on the throne (2 Kgs 11:13–20; 21:24; 23:30). Furthermore, in all cases the choice is not foregone, since the evidence suggests there were several options possible.

This can be illustrated at a number of points. Though Josiah was only eight when placed on the throne by the *AH,* it is likely that by this age he had surviving brothers.[110] Furthermore, the brothers of young Amon may have played some role in political factions prior to his succession, if not in his assassination itself. Mention is not made of them in 2 Kings, and the conspiracy is attributed to his "servants." However, they are probably among the *bny hmlk* referred to in Zeph 1:8, a text from

---

[107] Contrast, for example, the view of A. Malamat: ". . . the *ʿam hāʾāreṣ* appears to have been a steadfastly anti-Egyptian faction" ("Josiah's Bid for Armageddon," 271).

[108] Ihromi, "Königinmutter," 425.

[109] Tadmor, "'The People' and the Kingship," 62.

[110] See discussion above, Section D. 3.

Josiah's early period. It is noteworthy that these "sons of the king" and not the king himself, as one might expect, are the ones indicted by the prophet Zephaniah, along with other court officials (*śārîm*). The situation is much clearer in the case of Shallum/Jehoahaz. He had an older brother, Eliakim/Jehoiakim, as well as a younger brother, Mattaniah/Zedekiah. These brothers both succeed him at a later point, Zedekiah following his nephew Jehoiachin. In other words, a conscious choice to undo the principle of primogeniture was exercised in order to place this particular son of Josiah on the throne after his father's sudden death at 39 at Megiddo (2 Kgs 23:30b: "and the *AH* took [*wayyiqqaḥ*] Jehoahaz, anointed [*wayyim-šēḥû*] him, and made him king in his father's stead"). In the case of Joash, he was the only choice precisely because Athaliah had destroyed "all the royal family" (11:1) except him (2 Kgs 11:2: "Jehoasheba ... stole him away from the king's sons [*bny hmlk*] who were about to be slain"). In all of these cases, it is to be observed, the previous king died unexpectedly and at a relatively early age (Ahaziah, 23; Amon, 24; Josiah, 39), probably before a successor had been designated. The *AH* intervene to exercise their choice in designating the successor.

Before turning to the question as to *why* the particular choice was made as it was by the *AH*, it should be noted that the "people of the land" are not the only ones involved at the passing of the throne. It is the "inhabitants of Jerusalem" (2 Chr 22:1) who place the youngest son Ahazaiah on the throne (2 Chr 21:17); after the assassination of Amaziah in Lachish, "the people of Judah" place Azariah, just 16 at the time, on the throne (2 Kgs 14:21). Again, in these instances, the preceding king had died unexpectedly. Fortunately, records also exist of cases when the king, prior to his death, exercises his own choice in designating a successor:

> Rehoboam loved Maacah the daughter of Absalom above all his wives and concubines (he took eighteen wives and sixty concubines, and had twenty-eight sons and sixty daughters); and Rehoboam appointed Abijah the son of Maacah as chief prince among his brothers, for he intended to make him king (2 Chr 11:21–22).[111]

The longest and most famous account of court intrigue focused on the designation of a successor also involves the Judahite Kindom: the so-called "Succession Narrative" of 2 Samuel 7 through 1 Kings 2. David appoints his young son Solomon only after a lengthy contest which centered on two distinct groups: Joab and Abiathar in support of Adonijah (eldest surviving son after Absalom, 1 Kgs 1:6), and Zadok, Benaiah and Nathan supporting Solomon. But the decisive figures in this contest, as in the case of Abijah related in 2 Chr 11:21–22, were Haggith and

---

[111] Even though the possibility cannot be ruled out of exaggeration from the Chronicler intended to denigrate Rehoboam over against Solomon (normally considered the monarch with a penchant for wives), this does not affect inquiry into the general principle under discussion.

Bathsheba, the respective mothers of Adonijah and Solomon (see 1 Kgs 1:11 ff.).

What is clear in these narratives is the extent to which the principle of primogeniture, while at times assumed,[112] was nevertheless open to challenge. This was particularly true if the king had died unexpectedly or without naming a successor. But these same narratives also make clear that the king, even when alive, was not the only one who influenced the designation of a successor. Ishida can therefore conclude that the selection of a successor to the throne of Judah "was determined by a variety of factors."[113] These included (1) designation by the king of the first-born or eldest surviving son, or (2) appointment of a younger son under the influence of the queen mother. However, when the king died without designating an heir,

> the successor was determined by such elements as a commander of the army like Abner, a chief priest like Jehoiada, the "inhabitants of Jerusalem", the ruling class of Samaria, the "people of the land" of Judah, or the "people of Judah", compromising the inhabitants of Jerusalem and the people of the land. Moreover, foreign conquerors could depose one king and install another as they pleased (*Royal Dynasties*, 169—70).

Despite the variety of elements influencing the selection of a successor, in the narratives in 2 Kings in which the *ʿam hāʾāreṣ* appear, the convergence of several important factors can be noted. In all cases, the previous king had died unexpectedly (Josiah) or by assassination (Amon) or in battle and intrigue (Amaziah). It is likely that no successor had been named in these instances. In the case of Amaziah, the Queen Mother herself attempted to seize power by eliminating the "sons of the king" (11:2); Jehoash was only 7 when he was placed in power (2 Kgs 12:1). Amon was only 22 when he was assassinated and so surely had not named the 8-year old Josiah successor. Josiah had three sons, aged 25, 23 and 8, and since the eldest did not succeed him when he died unexpectedly at Meggido, he too had probably not named a successor; he was only 39 at the time.

Looking more closely at the choices made by the *AH*, another consistent feature appears which may help define their role and function within Judahite society. The mother of Jehoash, only 7 when he was placed in power, was Zibiah from Beersheba (2 Kgs 12:1). Up to this point, the usual place of origin for the Queen Mother was Jerusalem (see Chart Four), the significant exceptions being Jezebel and Athaliah. The mother of Josiah, only 8 when he was placed in power, was Jedidah from Bozkath, also in Judah (2 Kgs 22:1). When Josiah was killed at Megiddo and the *AH* intervened to place a successor on the throne, there were at

---

[112] "But he (Jehoshaphat) gave the kingdom to Jehoram, because he was the first-born (*habbĕkôr*)" (2 Chr 21:3).

[113] *Royal Dynasties*, 169.

least three known choices: the mother of the eldest, Jehoiakim, was Zebidah from Rumah in Galilee, while the mother of both Jehoahaz and Zedekiah (23 and 8 respectively) was Hamutal from Libnah, in Judah (2 Kgs 23:31; 24:18). It is significant that when the "people of the land" intervene to choose (*lqḥ*) a successor, they bypass the elder Jehoiakim in order to place Jehoahaz, whose mother is from Judah, on the throne.[114] In the previous two cases, the king selected was not even 10 years old when he succeeded to the throne, thereby shifting primary responsibility to others — notably the *AH* or the mother of the king, both of whom would be able to exercise clear influence over the young king. In other words, in those situations where the selection of a successor had not been made, and the "people of the land" take some direct action, they have a consistent preference for sons whose "queen mother" is from the Judahite countryside, and this in opposition to the principle of primogeniture.

It should also be noted at his juncture that Amon's "queen mother" did not come from either Jerusalem or Judah, but from Jotbah in Galilee. Certainly at this time Jotbah was in Assyrian controlled territory. As such, it is all the more likely that he was backed by a faction within the capital which was, at a minimum, not virulently anti-Assyrian. Whether or not such a support group was "pro-Assyrian" is a more complex question, since it raises broader issues about the extent to which such explicit posturing was possible. However, when one looks at the pieces of the puzzle which are available, including the fact of Amon's very short tenure and assassination, it appears that his selection was a controversial one. Given the state of flux of Egyptian and Assyrian military influence in the region, it is likely that other contenders for the throne looked more promising than Amon. It could be that a horizontal move, promoting one of Amon's brothers, was considered by the servants who assassinated him. The likelihood of this is increased given Amon's young age, his Galileen parentage, and the strong possibility of older brothers (see discussion above). What occurs instead is the swift intervention of the "people of the land" who place the 8-year old son, Josiah, in power. Josiah's mother is from Bozkath, in the territory of Judah. It appears as though another piece of the puzzle links the activity of the "people of the land" with concern for maintenance of the Davidic line, and for selections in which the mother of the king comes from the Judahite countryside. In order to confirm such a thesis, a word needs to be said about the role and function of the "Queen Mother" within Judahite society.

---

[114] Jehoiakim's father in law, Pedaiah, is from Rumah. At the time of Jehoiakim's succession, Rumah was in Egyptian-controlled territory. At the time of his birth (635 B. C.), it was still held by the Assyrians as part of the province of *Magidu*. Gray (*I & II Kings,* 755) infers that the name Pedaiah ("Yahweh has redeemed") "possibly indicates that his family had been spared in deportations under Tiglath-Pileser III (734 B. C.), when the grandfather of Pedaiah, whose name he bore, was born."

1. Excursus: The "Queen Mother" in Judahite Society

While it is an interesting subject in its own right, a complete treatment of the role of the so-called Queen Mother in Israelite society cannot be justified in this more restricted look at 7th century Judahite society. Furthermore, a competent literature on the topic as an independent subject already exists.[115] For our purposes, however, it will be helpful to review some of the pertinent material, since several scholars have recognized the subtle yet important relationship between "the people of the land" and the mother of the king.[116] That is to say, when the people of the land took part in the selection of a new king, as in the cases noted above, the queen mother came from the provinces and not from Jerusalem. This further suggests some loyalty between the people of the land and populations outside of Jerusalem. This will need to be probed further in a moment.

The general view on the Queen Mother is as follows: she was the mother of the reigning king who held "a significant official political position superseded only by that of the king himself."[117] It has been argued that the title *gĕbîrāh*, "Principal Lady," was conferred upon her at her son's designation or accession, and that she retained it for life.[118] This latter privilege, it is argued, is illustrated by the fact that when Maacah, the mother of Abijah, outlived her son, she remained *gĕbîrāh* during the reign of his successor, and her grandson, Asa (1 Kgs 15:9,13). It has also been conjectured that while in almost all cases the Dtr Historian supplies the name of the mother of the king, it cannot be assumed that in every case this is, in fact, the real mother of the king. In the case just mentioned, Maacah is called the mother of Asa (1 Kgs 15:10,13) when she is clearly his grandmother. It has been inferred from this that "the mother of the king" reported may not be the real mother, but the *gĕbîrāh*.[119] Some assume the office to have existed only in Judah.[120] Some link it to the *hieros gamos*

---

[115] Georg Molin, "Die Stellung der Gĕbira im Staate Juda," *TZ* 10 (1954) 161—75; Herbert Donner, "Art und Herkunft des Amtes der Königinmutter im Alten Testament," *FS Johannes Friedrich zum 65. Geburtstag am 27. August Gewidmet* (R. von Kienele et al, eds; Heidelberg: Carl Winter, 1959) 105—45. Most recently, Niels-Erik Andreasen, "The Role of the Queen Mother in Israelite Society," *CBQ* 45 (1983) 179—94. See also, G. W. Ahlström, *Aspects of Syncretism in Israelite Religion* (Lund: Gleerup, 1963) 57—88; further, Samuel Terrien, "The Omphalos Myth and Hebrew Religion," *VT* 20 (1970) 315—38.

[116] Ihromi, "Die Königinmutter," 425—9; Ishida, *Royal Dynasties*, 158—9; Andreasen, "Queen Mother," 191—2.

[117] Andreasen, "Queen Mother," 180. See also Donner, Molin, and the commentaries.

[118] Ishida, *Royal Dynasties*, 156.

[119] Ishida, *Royal Dynasties*, 156.

[120] Donner is of this opinion, since he sees the office of Queen Mother related to dynastic systems ("Königinmutter," 106—7).

ritual, though the evidence for this in Judah is not overwhelming.[121] Some
seek its point of origin in Hittite culture, where there was a distinct office
and title (*Tawannanna*) for the Queen Mother.[122] Others look to a variety
of ANE cultures for a description of the office, including Egypt, Mari,
Assyria (the *um-šarri*), Syria-Palestine, Ugarit, Arabia, and even Ebla.[123]
In these cultures, her office was independent of the king, enabling her to
retain it after his death and even act as regent, or to oppose him over
various religious, economic, military and political issues. It would, therefore, be reasonable to assume that some such office existed in Judah and
Israel.

Despite the attractiveness of the theory, the biblical evidence does
not warrant a view of the mother of the king in Judahite society directly
comparable to that of the Queen Mother in other ANE cultures. That the
mother of the reigning king could wield considerable power and influence
is undeniably proven by the lengthy accounts of the activities of Bathsheba,
Athaliah, and, in the Northern Kingdom, Jezebel. It should be noted in
Bathsheba's case, however, that she plays no decisive role whatsoever
during Solomon's reign, when she would technically have held the office
of *gĕbîrāh* according to regnant theories. Rather her influence is demonstrated prior to Solomon's accession, as David's consort/wife. Moreover,
during Solomon's reign she is referred to as "mother of the king" (1 Kgs
2:19) and never as *gĕbîrāh*. But the telling objection to an institutional
profile for the "queen mother" is the sparcity of evidence suggesting that
there was an actual *office* of Queen Mother, in which the mother of the
king had the title *gĕbîrāh* bestowed upon her. First of all, the word *gĕbîrāh*
only appears 15 times in the entire Old Testament, and in the majority of
these instances the references have nothing to do with kingship, queenship,
or the royal house (Gen 16:4,8−9; 2 Kgs 5:3; Ps 123:2; Pr 30:23; Isa 24:2;
47:5,7); they are simply general terms for "mistress" or "principal lady."
In one instance (1 Kgs 11:19), the term *gĕbîrāh* is applied not to the
monarch's mother, but to his wife, i. e., the queen. Actually, this reference,
along with the more general uses of the term, suggests that the term
gĕbîrāh means exactly what it says, "principal lady," with no explicitly
institutional overtones.

The only evidence encouraging such a (institutional) theory coalesces
around the single account of Maacah, mother of Abijam (1 Kgs 15:1 ff.).
1 Kgs 15:13 reports that on account of her involvement in foreign cults
Maacah was "removed" from being "principal lady" (*wayĕsirehā miggĕbîrāh*);
furthermore, because she is listed as "mother" of both Abijam (1 Kgs
15:2) and his son Asa (15:10), it is supposed that she had held the formal

---

[121] Ahlström, *Aspects,* 75 ff.

[122] The problem here is determining Hittite influence in Judah. Molin, "Gebira," 172−5;
Donner, "Königinmutter," 123−30. See also, A. A. Kampman, "Tawannannas, Der Titel
der hethietischen Königin," *JEOL* 2 (1939−42) 432−42.

[123] See Andreasen (183) for a bibliographic resume; also, Ishida, *Royal Dynasties,* 155−6.

office *gĕbîrāh* over two successive reigns, therefore seemingly independent of the king in question. Another hypothesis is developed from this, specifically, that the name of the king's mother listed in these introductory formulae is that of the Great Lady and not, as one would expect, the king's real mother. This is established by a complex argument *e silentio,* namely, that the reason no queen-mother is named in several places (Jehoram, 2 Kgs 8:16—19; Ahaz, 2 Kgs 16:1—2) is that the mother in question had already died, thereby leaving the office of Great Lady vacant; the theory implies that the Dtr Historian would have supplied the name of the mother even if she were dead, but not if the point of including her name was to show who held the actual office of Great Lady.[124]

This last theory is overly subtle. Two factors may account for why the name of the king's mother is withheld in the case of the Judahite kings Jehoram/Joram (8:18) and Ahaz (16:2). It is possible, as Gray and others suggest, that the king's mother was in fact dead, though this need not have been the case prior to the king's accession. But it does not follow from this that her name was omitted because she did not fill the office of Great Lady. Indeed, if the office were as formal as implied, and if it could be filled by one other than the uterine mother of the king, why did this not happen and why has the name of the woman filling the position not been supplied in the biblical text? This, it has been argued, was precisely what occurred during the reign of Asa, when according to some the Great Lady was not the uterine mother but the grandmother of Asa. It is just as likely that, whether the mother of the king was dead or not, she simply was not remembered as having played any significant role during the king's reign.

This leads to the second factor. In the case of Jehoram, his mother was probably not named since she was overshadowed by his own wife, who *is* named in the introductory formula (2 Kgs 8:18), the well-known Athaliah. The same thing would be true of another king whose mother is not listed, King David, precisely because his well-known wife Bathsheba and not his mother played the more significant role in affairs of the realm. Finally, this was also likely the case during the reign of Asa, since his grandmother Maacah played such a notable (negative) role in narratives supplied by the Dtr Historian (1 Kgs 15:13). That she was called *gĕbîrāh* only indicates that she was the "principal lady" in the realm at this period, in distinction to Asa's own mother or other ladies in the harem. But it seems to expect too much of the infrequently used term *gĕbîrāh* (unfortu-

---

[124] J. Gray (*I & II Kings,* 534), following Šanda (*Die Bücher der Könige* [Münster, 1912]), states regarding the non-mention of the mother of Jehoram: "Šanda makes the feasible suggestion that she was dead before Jehoram's accession, which supports the view that the point in mentioning the king's mother was that on his accession she became head of the harem and first lady of the land with the official status of *haggebīrā.*"

nately translated "queen mother" at 15:13 by RSV) to conclude from this that she held a formal office of some kind. That she is called "mother" in 1 Kgs 15:10 means nothing more than that she was his grandmother.[125].

It would seem therefore that the name of the woman listed in the introductory formulae for Judahite kings is provided (1) simply because she was the uterine mother of the king, or (2) because she was a lady of note in the realm, closely related to the reigning king, who played a decisive enough role to have been remembered in the historical notices; or, as is most often the case, both (1) and (2). When the mother of the king is not mentioned she may have been dead, but the evidence is inconclusive. Certainly the name was not withheld because the office of Great Lady was vacant. Rather, she was overshadowed by a woman in the realm who was more influential (Bathsheba, Athaliah). This is precisely why, in the two instances just mentioned when the name of the mother of the king is not given, some extended narrative exists concerning another powerful woman in the realm.

Niels-Erik Andreasen, employing a cultural-anthropological approach, has argued that the office of Queen Mother in Judah was that of "Lady Counsellor," and that it was held by the mother of the king after the time of childbearing. Fertility, then, was insured by younger women in the royal harem; wisdom and counsel, by the gĕbîrāh.[126] Andreasen's theory has relatively little to say about the explicitly governmental/institutional role of the Queen Mother within the Judahite realm. This is its strength. That the mother of the king, especially after her childbearing years, had an influential position in the harem and could use her power in affairs of state is quite plausible. This also explains how another senior lady, not necessarily the mother of the king but perhaps his wife (Bathsheba, Athaliah), might also exercise significant influence. But that there was a formal office of Great Lady, which was ceremonially bestowed upon the queen-mother in a manner similiar to that of the king at his accession, is simply not demonstrated by the biblical evidence.

2. The "People of the Land" (Conclusion)

Returning to the question of the role and identity of the "people of the land," it can be concluded from the sparse data that the selection of king, when his predecessor had died without naming a successor, could go to the "people of the land." In turn, their choice was influenced by the mother of the king. Looking at the instances in which the *AH* choose

---

[125] In the same way that "daughter" may mean "female descendent" or "granddaughter," as in 2 Kgs 8:26. See also the use of the terms "father/fathers" in the evaluation of kings in the Dtr History.

[126] "Queen Mother," 186.

to intervene, the mother of the king would have played an important role in at least two of the cases (Jehoash, Josiah) for the obvious reason that the king-designate was still quite young and not able to govern independently. The same was particularly true in the case of all of Judah's last four kings, none of whom was older than 25 upon ascending to the throne and all of whom ascended under highly volatile circumstances. To pick up, however, from the discussion concerning the role of the queen mother, it is to be noted that in all of these same instances the mother of the king never plays any active or significant role in the narratives supplied by the Dtr Historian.[127] So it seems that the decisive factor was not the actual *person* of the queen-mother. Rather, the significant factor in these actions of the "people of the land" in the affairs of the monarchy is the *place of origin* of the queen-mother (and by extension, that of her son). In all cases, the king placed in power is from the Judahite provinces, as distinct either from Jerusalem or northern districts. This important piece of information, supplied with a certain inadvertence by the Historian, may lend some further assistance in tying down the identity of the "people of the land." Having set out the important background considerations, this question can now be addressed.

Based upon a close reading of the biblical evidence, several clear conclusions can be drawn about the *function* of the "people of the land" in relationship to Judahite monarchy, at least on the occasions in which they act. An important observation of Talmon concerning the *AH* has already been mentioned; namely, that its actions are often concentrated within Jerusalem's city limits. This fact seemed to complicate a simple identification of the "people of the land" with the whole rural population or even the "people of Judah." It is necessary to examine the biblical accounts more closely in order to test this further.

The "people of the land" appear on numerous distinct occasions in the narratives of 2 Kings, as has been noted. Moreover, they seem to be a distinct group, separate from various other sociological groups (priests, prophets, king and royal officials) as well as more generally depicted bodies (inhabitants of Jerusalem). They are active in the overthrow and slaying of Athaliah (2 Kgs 11:14,18,20); they are said to be governed by the co-regent Jotham instead of his leprous father Azariah (2 Kgs 15:5); their ritual offerings are distinct from those of the king (2 Kgs 16:15); they kill the slayers of Amon and place the boy-king Josiah in power (2 Kgs 21:24); they take Jehoahaz and make him king when Josiah is killed at Megiddo (2 Kgs 23:30); they are taxed by his successor Jehoiakim (23:35); they are mentioned along with other groups, including princes,

---

[127] Contrast the earlier exploits of Athaliah, Bathsheba, or even Maacah. The Dtr Historian has much to say about the reign of Josiah, but his mother, Jedidah from Bozkath, has no role whatsoever in these accounts.

men of valour, craftsmen and smiths, mother, wives and officials of the
king, all of whom are carried off in the 597 deportation (24:14); they are
said to be without food because of a famine in the city (25:3); finally, 60
of their number, along with certain clergy and military personnel also
from the city, are tried and put to death at Riblah by Nebuchadnezzar
(25:21). It is striking that on all of these occasions, some more clearly than
others, the *AH* are described as though their normal place of activity is
inside the confines of Jerusalem — a fact which would be difficult to square
with a definition of the "people of the land" as primarily rural inhabitants.
Therefore it is important to look at several of the places where the *AH*
seem most likely to be a group within Jerusalem. Rather than move
chronologically, analysis will begin with those texts which clearly show
the *AH* active within Jerusalem; then those in which the situation is not
so clear will be examined. [128]

2 Kings 25:1—3

It is the 11th year of Zedekiah. The city has been under siege for
over a year. It is recorded that the famine was so harsh *in the city* that
there was no food for the "people of the land" (*wayyeḥĕzaq hārāʿāb bāʿîr
wĕlōʾ-hāyāh leḥem lĕʿam hāʾāreṣ*). Sensing a problem with this text if one
settles on a definition of the *AH* as a rural population only, Gordis
reasons: "If taken in its traditional (sic) sense, the verse is a meaningless
tautology. By recognizing *ʿam hāʾāreṣ* as meaning 'country inhabitants' it
takes on a new significance, in describing the famine which affected not
merely Jerusalem, but the rural districts as well" (Gordis, "Sectional
Rivalry," 243). The first problem with such an interpretation is its general
logic, given the larger perspective of the account, which is clearly focused

---

[128] There are certain clear literary and historical problems with Chs. 24—25 of 2 Kings that
will not be addressed at this point. A discussion of these problems follows below, and
in Chapter Three. Anticipating remarks there, the problems involve (1) the abundance
of both specific and oblique references to deportations from Judah which are difficult
to bring into coordination (Dan 1:1; Ezek 1:2; Jer 13:19; 27:19—20, cf. 2 Kgs 24:13;
Lam 4:20) and (2) the clearly divergent records of deportations themselves, as to both
the numbers and the dates (Jer 52:28—30; 39:1—10; 2 Kgs 24:10—16; 25:8—12,18—21).
But an even greater problem has to do with the present literary juxtaposition of chs. 24
and 25 in 2 Kings. In their present form, they are meant to describe a two-stage set of
events: ch. 24 reports the surrender of the king and the deportation of 10,000 in 597;
ch. 25 reports the actual fall of the city eleven years later. The problem has to do with
the tone of finality expressed in ch. 24, as though stage-one were in fact the only (final)
stage. Critics assume that certain details within this chapter (the large number of deportees;
the spoilation of the temple) are either anachronistic or proleptic, being transferred from
events of 587. But the motivation behind such a re-arrangement has not been adequately
explained. However, for the purpose of investigating the identity of the "people of the
land" as they appear in both chs. 24 and 25, the literary and historical problems can be
momentarily set aside.

on events not in Judah but in a besieged city. The second problem is
more obvious. In a state of siege, there would not only be a shortage of
food for the people outside the city; there would be little of anything else,
since they would have been in close quarters with Babylonian troops for
over a year, if not prisoners.[129] And in any case, the relationship between
famine in the city and lack of food in the country is less than obvious,
unless the "people of the land" were inside the city itself. The one question
that must still be pursued is whether Jerusalem was the actual place of
residence for the "people of the land" or simply the place to which they
had fled previously from the countryside for safety.

2 Kings 25:18–21

This brief entry tells of the execution of certain leaders who remained
in the city, among them "sixty men of the people of the land" (v. 19). The
problem here may be the appearance of the niphal participle at the end of
v. 19 (*hannimṣĕʾîm*), insofar as it would imply that the city was not the
normal place for the *ʿam hāʾāreṣ* to be rounded up; therefore, the author
specifically states, "sixty men of the people of the land *who where found in
the city*." Again, Gordis prefers this interpretation: "It seems that the
presence of the *ʿam hāʾāreṣ* in Jerusalem was highly unusual, and probably
the result of war, when all the nation's available manpower, and other
resources, were concentrated in the city. This confirms the reading of *ʿam
hāʾāreṣ* (as 'country inhabitants') considerably" (244). Strictly speaking,
Gordis here contradicts his own view as stated above, where he maintained
that the rural inhabitants and resources were still outside of Jerusalem. In
the space of just 15 verses and very little time, they are now to be found
concentrated within the city. But apart from this, it is clear that he
understands the participle "were found" to indicate the transfer of the
"rural inhabitants" to the city.

It should only be noted that the same verb in the niphal (v. 19a) is
used to describe five of the king's council (if not all of those mentioned,
depending on the exact referent intended) who also "were found in the
city" (*ʾăšer nimṣĕʾû bāʿîr*). Clearly the king's counsellors (and if they are
also meant, the two priests and a military officer) were inhabitants of
Jerusalem. What is also striking here is the inclusion of "the secretary
commander of the army who mustered the people of the land" (*hassōpēr
śar haṣṣābāʾ hammaṣĕbbiʾ ʾet-ʿam hāʾāreṣ*); not only is it clear that the "people
of the land" are a distinct entity, they are also included among the

---

[129] Of modern commentaries, Gray in *I & II Kings* (1970) remarks: "The famine in the city
was intensified by the fact that for two harvest seasons the Babylonians had been in the
land eating up the crop, and latterly by their circumvallation had prevented any produce
from reaching the city" (764–65). This is the obvious sense of the verse.

Jerusalemite population. As with the larger account of the Dtr Historian in Ch. 25 up to this point, the focus remains on activities within Jerusalem (the besieging of Jerusalem; the burning of houses and the breaking down of the city walls; the exiling of people who were left in the city), the exception being the report of the flight of Zedekiah, his sentencing in Babylonian-controlled Riblah, and the slaying of his sons. Within the narrative logic of the Kings' account of the Fall of Jerusalem (see for comparison Jer 39:1—10 and Jer 52:1—30), the final deporting of city inhabitants is reported in 25:11. There has been no mention of rural deportations up to this point in Ch. 25. When the "poorest of the land" (*middallat hā'āreṣ*) are mentioned in v. 12, they are left behind as farmers; given the decidedly Jerusalem-oriented perspective of the wider account, these "poorest of the land" could quite plausibly have been "poorest of the people of the land" sent from the city to farm the land in the immediate environs. This is more difficult to determine. But what is clear in the flow of the narrative is that the Babylonians considered this their final act regarding Jerusalem's citizenry. What follows in vv. 13—17 concerns temple valuables. Therefore the force of the participles in vv. 18—21, concerning both the men of the king's council and sixty of the "people of the land," suggests that they were "discovered" in the city, "found out" so to speak, after the major deportations had already taken place — not that they had just recently moved there from the countryside. As such, they are brought out by Nebuzaradan to Riblah and slain.

In this sense, the final notice concerning deportations (v. 21b) should more accurately read "And Jerusalem was taken into exile out of its land," given the specific focus of Ch. 25. Judah is the more expansive term, and it is used no doubt for this reason. Again, from the Jerusalem-oriented perspective of the narrative, the fall of the capital city was tantamount to the loss of the whole region. Moreover, given the wider scope of events, the Fall of Jerusalem was the final chapter in the Fall of Judah, which, though it is not chronicled in Ch. 25, is understood as already accomplished by the time the siege began (v. 1). Use of the term "Judah" at this point in the narrative (v. 21) is not without problems, however, since the next unit (vv. 22—26) begins for the first time to describe activities not in Jerusalem but in the countryside: namely, the appointment of Gedaliah as governor over both rural populations and refugees from Jerusalem. The phrasing of v. 22 ("And over the people who remained in the land of Judah . . .") suggests that a population is being referred to distinct from the "people of the land" mentioned above.

In conclusion, the narrative perspective of Ch. 25 is decidely Jerusalemite, and mention of the "people of the land" in these narratives suggests that they too could be conceived of together with other groups as inhabitants of Jerusalem.

2 Kings 24:10—17

The surrender of Judah occurred sometime in the autumn or winter of 603 B. C.[130] What appears in 2 Kings 24 is an account of the later surrender of Jehoiachin, in 597 B. C. The fate of his father Jehoiakim remains a mystery.[131] Again, the focus of the Dtr Historian falls on Jerusalem, the capital city. Jehoiakim had rebelled in the winter of 601, probably due to Babylonian reverses in an ambitious but premature campaign against Egypt. Nebuchadnezzar remained in Babylon to rehabilitate his chariot corps in 600/599, and could only take punitive action against Jehoiakim in the person of the Aramaens, Moabites, and Ammonites (2 Kgs 24:2). This action was probably directed more at Judah than the capital city. But by the time Nebuchadnezzar puts in a personal appearance (winter of 598/7), the target is Jerusalem itself: "And in the seventh month, the king of Akkad mustered his troops, marched to the Hatti Land, and encamped against the city of Judah (i. e., Jerusalem); on the second day of the month of Adar he seized the city and captured the king" (*ANET,* 564). This is also the general perspective of the biblical account (vv. 10—17).

Along with Jehoiachin and the royal entourage (v. 12) are deported military personnel and what appears to be a kind of corps of engineers (RSV: craftsmen and smiths).[132] The numbers are somewhat confusing, as two sets seem to be given (avoiding for a moment the quite different record of Jer 52:28—30). The first figure given in v. 14 (10,000) may refer to the total number of deportees, or those counted for deportation; the second reckoning (v. 16) may simply be a more specific listing, giving the precise number of military personel (*hakkōl gibbôrîm ʿōśê milḥāmāh*), including 7000 "men of valor" (*ʾanśê haḥayil*) and 1000 engineers (*heḥārāś wĕhammasgēr*). The surplus (2000) would simply represent parts of the population not reckoned as military personnel. Another possibility would be that, while 10,000 were designated for deportation, the number 8000 represents only those actually "brought captive (*wayĕbîʿēm gôlāh*) to Babylon" (v. 16).[133] This is less satisfying, since the verbs used in all cases refer directly to

---

[130] A. Malamat, "Maelstrom," 131. Unfortunately, the Babylonian tablet is broken at this point. The year 603 accords with the biblical statement that Jehoiakim submitted tribute three years (603—601). See the discussion following, Section E.

[131] See Chapter Three, Section I below. Compare 2 Kgs 24:6 (+ 2 Chron 36:8) and Jer 22:19 (+ 36:30). For a brief discussion, see Malamat, "Last Years," 210—11.

[132] For a discussion of these terms, which Malamat translates "armourer" (*masgēr*) and "sapper" (*ḥārāś*), indicating an occupation involved with fortifications, see "Maelstrom," 133; also, Gray, *I & II Kings,* 761.

[133] See the discussion above (Section D), concerning stages in the 701 Assyrian deportation of Judahite populations, and for a full treatment of these figures, Chapter Three, Section III/D.

deportation (vv. 14,15,16). In any case, it is highly unlikely that these reckonings represent two contradictory counts.

What is to be noted in our attempt to identify the "people of the land" is that the report focuses again on Jerusalemite populations. The text reads that Nebuchadnezzar carried away "all Jerusalem" (v. 14) and took them into captivity "from Jerusalem to Babylon" (v. 15). Military personnel, fortifications engineers, the king and the royal house all represent Jerusalem populations, especially during a state of siege (24:10). The "chief men of the land" (*'êlê hā'āreṣ*) were also carried off. These probably represented the leadership of the "people of the land" and they too seem to be a Jerusalem contingent. After these city populations were deported, only the poorest (*dallat*) of the "people of the land" were left. This sounds similar to the reference in the following chapter (25:12), but here there is no mention whatsoever of tilling or tending the land. In conclusion, it would again seem that the *'am hā'āreṣ* were among those numbered within Jerusalem.

Because the possibility has been raised that the "people of the land" may had only recently fled to the capital for safety, it is important to look briefly at reports in which they appear prior the period of Jerusalem's imminent destruction.

2 Kings 11:13—20; 21:19—26; 23:28—30

Although these are three distinct accounts from the reigns of Athaliah, Amon, and Josiah, respectively, all relate activities on the part of the "people of the land." Attention has already been paid to these accounts, since the role of the "people of the land" in maintaining the Davidic dynasty is so clearly demonstrated in them. One obvious thing to note in all three is that the "people of the land" are consistently active within the confines of Jerusalem. If they only represented the rural population, the text should supply narratives which depict them at work in Judah proper — the argument being that even if concern for the Davidic dynasty brings them into the capital, one would expect to see an account of them residing or active in the countryside. These do not exist. This is even more perplexing when the "people of the land" appear to be represented in their entirety (*kol 'am hā'āreṣ*), as in the overthrow of Athaliah (2 Kgs 11:14,18,20). Also, within this account there is a difference between the "people of the land" and just simply the "people" (vv. 13,17a,17b), as subtle as this may seem. Again, the "people of the land" are depicted alongside groups identifiable as Jerusalemite (priests of the temple; the servants, captains, and even trumpeters of the king).

Though it has been popular to see in 2 Kgs 11:20 a *contrast* between the city inhabitants and the rural "people of the land,"[134] this contradicts the sense of the larger passage, which makes nothing of such a contrast. Ishida's remarks are instructive here:

> Many scholars regarded Athaliah's overthrow as a "national revolution" because of the part taken by the "people of the land" in the revolt. Generally, they also find a contrast between the "people of the land" and the "city" in II Kings 11:20: "So all the people of the land rejoiced; and the city was quiet after Athaliah had been slain with the sword at the king's house" (cf. II Chron 23:21). However, the "people of the land" took neither the initiative nor the leadership in the revolt. The leader of it was Jehoiada the priest and the main power lay in the hands of the royal mercenaries. Evidently, both belonged to the "city". It seems, therefore, that the sentence *wehā'îr šāqātâ* implies only that "the city Jerusalem became peaceful" (*Royal Dynasties*, 164—65).

Though Ishida restricts unnecessarily the influence of the "people of the land" in the overthrow, he is right to note that "it appears that of the 'people of the land' who shared in Athaliah's overthrow actually only a small fraction came from the 'land'" (165). It "appears" this way precisely because the "people of the land" could in fact be considered a part of the Jerusalem population.

In conclusion, these accounts of activities of the "people of the land," prior to the military threat from the Babylonians, point to the strong unlikelihood "that in the *'am hā'āres* were incorporated all full-fledged citizens of Judah."[135] Rather, they act as though they were an integral part of the Jerusalemite population. The same is true of the reference at 2 Kgs 15:5, which indicates that the "people of the land" were governed by the co-regent Jotham. At this point suggestions must be made as to how a Jerusalemite population might come to be termed "people of the land."

It was noted above (Section D) that following both the Fall of Samaria (721 B. C.) and Sennacherib's invasion of Judah (701 B. C.), significant population shifts occurred in Judah. It has been argued that as a result of these two Assyrian incursions Jerusalem's population increased as much as 400 %, viz, from 6,000—8,000 to 24,000.[136] Excavations in the city of Jerusalem have uncovered a section of city-wall which was approximately 275 meters west of the Temple Mount, its general direction being

---

[134] Gordis' position is classic, ("Sectional Rivalry," 244), though he is not alone in his opinion (see Gray, *I & II Kings,* 580; de Vaux, *Institutions,* 71; Ishida, "Political Crises," 30).

[135] Talmon, "The Judaean *'am ha'ares,*" 75.

[136] Broshi, "Expansion of Jerusalem," 23; also, "Estimating the Population of Ancient Jerusalem," *BAR* 4 (1978) 10—15. L. Stager has questioned the extent of the growth ("The Archaeology of the East Slope of Jerusalem," *JNES* 41 [1982] 121) but not the essential fact of its having taken place.

northeast to southwest.[137] This wall is to be dated to around 700 B. C. and gives evidence of substantial growth in the capital to the west; this growth has been coordinated with Assyrian military action in the region, including both Northern and Southern Kingdoms. Refugee populations would have taken up residence in the environs of Jerusalem, some enclosed by this newly discovered wall, others simply in the near region of the wall.

The biblical evidence provides surprising verification of these findings. 2 Chron 32:5 mentions that Hezekiah not only repaired a broken wall, but also raised *another wall without (wĕlaḥûṣāh haḥômāh ʾaḥeret)*. 2 Chron 33:14 gives a rather detailed account of a wall constructed by Hezekiah's successor Manasseh, which others have likewise correlated with this same general population growth.[138] Moreover, such an outer wall helps clarify the long enigmatic location of the pool of Siloam, which Hezekiah built (2 Kgs 20:20) as a precautionary measure during the period of Assyrian threat; this pool is situated beyond the generally accepted line of the city wall, seemingly impossible to defend. But the newly discovered wall places the pool *inside* Jerusalem's defenses.[139] Furthermore, reference is made in texts from this period to a "Second Quarter" or "Second City" (*Mišneh*). It is reasonable to conclude that the section recently enclosed by new walls is being referred to here (2 Kgs 22:14; Zeph 1:10). Populations who are described as "dwelling on the wall" (*hayyōšĕbîm ʿal-haḥômāh* or *hāʿām ʾašer ʿal-haḥômāh, 2 Kgs 18:26,27*) are the same ones whom the delegation from Hezekiah fears will hear the Rabshekah's speech. They are probably refugee populations who have had firsthand experience with Assyrian occupation troops.

The biblical evidence confirms what has been uncovered through recent archeological research. Substantial population movements occurred not just after the events of 721 and 701 B. C., but throughout the seventh century. Jerusalem, even apart from theological claims for inviolability (Ps 46), was considered a place of greater refuge than the Judahite countryside. This would have been true even prior to the circumstances which led to the development of an even bolder statement of her special status (Isa 37:33—35). It can be assumed that throughout the 7th century Jerusalem experienced the influx of rural populations, even into the period of neo-Babylonian threat. Note, for example, the justification given by the cus-

---

[137] N. Avigad, "Excavations in the Jewish Quarter of the Old City of Jerusalem, 1970 (Second Preliminary Report)," *IEJ* 20 (1970) 129—140; Hillel Geva, "Excavations in the Citadel of Jerusalem," *IEJ* 33 (1983) 56; Y. Yadin, ed, *Jerusalem Revealed: Archaeology in the Holy City, 1908—1974* (New Haven & London: Yale University Press and the Israel Exploration Society, 1976) 44. For a complete summary of the earlier findings, see J. Simons, *Jerusalem in the Old Testament* (Leiden: Brill, 1952) 226—281.

[138] Dan Bahat, "The Wall of Manasseh in Jerusalem," *IEJ* 31 (1981) 235—6.

[139] Avigad, "Excavations," 133.

tommarily rural contingent of Rechabites ("you shall not build a house, but you shall live in tents all your days," Jer 35:7) when they are addressed by Jeremiah in Jerusalem proper:

> ... We have lived in tents and have obeyed and done all that Jonadab our father commanded us. But when Nebuchadnezzar king of Babylon came up against the land, we said, "Come, and let us go to Jerusalem for fear of the army of the Chaldeans and the army of the Syrians." So we are living in Jerusalem (Jer 35:10—11).

Here, then, is a remarkably clear, first-hand account of a rural population which was forced to take refuge inside the capital, due to military threat. Since this scene emerges from "the days of Jehoiakim" (35:1), we have confirmation of population movements into the capital toward the end of the 7th century and beginning of the 6th.

Having said something about the role and function the *AH* exercise in Kings, it is important to finally say something about their identity. These two factors have not always been well integrated.

First of all, there is a broad sense in which the term *AH* can be applied, indicating the whole population of a given region (including non-Israelite regions). The term *can* also be used in this sense as more specifically applied to Judah. As such it is akin to a designation such as *'am yĕhûdāh*. As such, it has given rise to theories about the relationship between Judahite dynastic kingship as initiated by David and his rural followers at Hebron (so Ishida, Talmon, Tadmor) and the "people of the land." This more general use of the term, indicating the wider population of a region, depends in part upon the perspective of the literature. In Ezekiel, when the term appears, it seems to be no more specific than the "people of the land of Judah," i.e., as they are to be contrasted with Judahites in the land of Babylonian exile.

When the term appears in the Books of Kings, the author has a more specific meaning in mind. This is due to the fact that the perspective of Kings is not predominantly Judahite (as, say, distinct from Ephraimite or all-Israelite), but Jerusalemite. From this perspective, the "people of the land" *can appear to be* the whole citizenry of Judah or Judah/Benjamin. The problem one confronts with such a reading involves squaring this broader sense of the term with the fact that the activities of the "people of the land" occur within the confines of Jerusalem. They could not have involved the whole citizenry of Judah. Rather than assume that the Dtr Historian was simply being general in his use of the term, another alternative is suggested: that the use of the term "people of the land" in the Books of Kings refers to those populations which did in fact come from the "land" but which had taken up residence in the capital. They were the refugee populations (or their descendents) who, in quite large numbers, had fled from the land to the city for safety, taking up residence both inside the major defensive walls of the capital and also in the immediate environs, both before and after the events of 701 and 721 B. C. In time, a new wall was built to enclose these populations in a "Second Quarter," mentioned in biblical texts of the period. It is a reasonable conjecture that, due to the large number of refugees from the land and the resultant population density within the city and the Second Quarter, populations dwelt not just near (within) the wall (Isa 36:12) but also outside of it. These populations would have resided in Jerusalem's immediate environs, so that refuge inside the city might be taken in time of particular threat.[140]

From the perspective of the Dtr Historian in Kings, these populations were considered the "people of the land." Given their recent movement to the urban Jerusalem, use of such a term was accurate. Though quite a sizeable number (upwards of 15,000), they could be distinguished geographically from the totality of Judahite populations and could at the same time function in close proximity to or actually within the capital city. This explains the description of their activities as recorded in the narratives of Kings. The actual term "people of the land" may have functioned in a broader sense in other biblical contexts (Ezekiel, Genesis). But given the specific historical and geographical perspective of the Kings' narratives, the narrower meaning does better justice to the details of the biblical text and what can be reconstructed about the pertinent historical events of the period.[141]

F. Summary and Transition

Because several distinct subjects have been treated in the preceding section (Shifting Political Allegiances; Queen Mother; People of the Land), a summary of conclusions reached is helpful at this juncture. Then analysis of the composition of Judahite society for the period of Jeremiah will be taken up.

The general historical overview of the period from Hezekiah through Amon has revealed a degree of internal conflict and disruption hitherto unfelt. The effect of Sennacherib's successful invasion on Judahite society

---

[140] The reference in Zeph 1:11 to the *maktēš* might have been to just such an outlying, but clearly "suburban" region. See Avigad, "Excavations," 134.

[141] The reference to the "people of the land" in 2 Kgs 11 could be problematic, since it is difficult to link up with population movements which can be demonstrated explicitly for a later period only. Either this is an anachronism or, more likely, a less specific use of the term, colored by later usage. Or, there may have been a similar population living in or near the capital at this period as well. The latter position is to be preferred, though the hard data is lacking. It seems plausible that, from the Jerusalemite-perspective of Kings, the "people of the land" were populations living in Jerusalem's more immediate environs — a fact which is easier to establish in the 7th century than the 8th or 9th.

in general and on affairs in the capital in particular was profound and irreversable.

Internal disruption is clearly evidenced during the reign of Manasseh. While for the most part he remained loyal to his Assyrian overlords, the rise in power of the Egyptians to the south complicated matters. Factions within the government doubtless emerged long before his death and the transference of power to Amon. This was conjectured as due to the fact of Amon's brief reign, the strong likelihood of other contenders to the throne, his unusual background (Jotbah, in Assyrian-held territory), his assassination by court servants, and the action (retaliatory or otherwise) by the "people of the land." There is no direct evidence linking the activity of the "people of the land" to one consistent political alignment or another (vis-à-vis Egypt or Assyria) in this period. It is a reasonable conjecture that factions existed within the realm, encouraged by Manasseh's advanced age, his protracted reign, and the strong likelihood that other (elder) brothers existed who were eventually by-passed at the selection of Amon. It was also noted that Amon might have been backed by a pro-Assyrian faction, due to his provincial background. In sum, the shifting external political circumstances did not promote internal stability, especially in a country which had already had a close brush with the Assyrians and which maintained any existence only through cautious vassalage. Assyria's own shifting fortunes, both in the region of Judah and beyond, also created a climate conducive to intrigue and political maneuvering in the capital.

A relatively clear picture has emerged of one significant group active during this period: the "people of the land." Certain lines of relationship between them and the queen-mother in Judah were noted, and between them both and the dynastic system peculiar to Judah. As they appear in the narratives of 2 Kings, the "people of the land" represent the rural population recently incorporated into the capital or its environs. As to the nature of their activity, the following can be concluded. As a result of problems related to the selection of a new king at the passing of the throne in Judah, they frequently intervene to exercise their own choice in the matter. Typically, they make their choice based upon the place of origin of the queen-mother, since her origin plays an obvious role in the king's own geographical, if not political, background. In all cases where they act, the king they choose and place on the throne has Judahite background. It is not at all surprising that they would back one who, like themselves, came from the territory of Judah into the environs of the capital. Furthermore, there is strong evidence that other candidates, with other geographical and political roots, existed at the time. This is clearly the case for both Josiah and Jehoahaz in the period presently under discussion.

It would overstep the evidence to claim that the "people of the land" had any special or historically significant allegiance to Davidic kingship *as such*. Rather, they accept the dynastic premise as it finds force in

Jerusalem and work within it in ways open to them, which, as has been noted, are not as restricted as commonly believed. Each passing of the throne, especially in this volatile period of Judahite history, presents its own options and particular challenges. This point is made in opposition to those who see the "people of the land" as a group with fixed historical and political background and inclinations, distinguished primarily by their loyalty to the Judahite dynastic enterprise.[142] If the conclusions reached here as to the background of the 'am hā'āreṣ are correct, among their number would be found refugees not only from the territory of Judah, but also from the nearby northern regions.[143] Neither must one assume the kind of fixed political or theological allegiance to the Davidic monarchy that is often assumed. If one wanted to find a succinct statement of their concept of kingship, it is best sought in the kind of sober declaration found at Deut 17:14—20.[144] They accepted kingship in at most a kind of *plene esse* sense, and this in contrast to certain other positions on the matter (2 Sam 7:14—17; Ps 2). In fact, the influence of specifically northern theological views of kingship probably shaped their own understanding. This explains why the "people of the land" are depicted as actively engaged in dynastic affairs in Judah in the period presently under discussion. In the Northern Kingdom there was a rich tradition of popular involvement in kingship and the affairs of state.

As to the political stance of the "people of the land" vis-à-vis external military powers, again it is best to assume no fixed agenda. Here one does well to examine the staunchly nationalistic, if not utopian, tone of much of Deuteronomy's core material for a clue as to the political attitude of the "people of the land." At this early period, when the option for either Egypt or Assyria was at best a kind of political nightmare, the "people of the land" probably chose to remain steadfastly independent, or at least held out for such a possibility against other views on the matter. Their choice of the boy-king Josiah at age eight, after the court assassination of Amon, reflects their desire to remain independent of political posturing toward any outside nation. They probably saw no necessary collision between the religio-nationalistic aspirations of Deuteronomy and the ag-

---

[142] Talmon, "'Am Ha 'areṣ," 74—75; Ishida, *Royal Dynasties,* 166 (by relating them in the early period of Judahite kingship to the "people of Judah," a tendency which he avoids for the later period).

[143] Ishida mentions this: "In addition, we can assume that the northern tribes, who *took refuge in Judah* from the catastrophe of Samaria in 722 B. C. (underscoring mine) and the subsequent disturbances, brought with them the strong tradition of the popular sovereignty and strengthened the people's voice in political affairs" ("Political Crises," 37). It is likely they were included among the "people of the land" during this period.

[144] J. A. Soggin, "Der jüdische 'Am-Hā'āreṣ und das Königtum in Judah," *VT* 13 (1963) 195; Kurt Galling, "Das Königsgesetz im Deuteronomium," *TLZ* 76 (1951) 134—8; L. Rost, "Sinaibund und Davidbund," *TLZ* 72 (1947) 129—34.

gressive military-political policies of their overlords in the larger ANE. Though von Rad has tried to account for the "decidedly martial" (45) tone of Deuteronomy by appeal to a theory of "holy-war" theology founded on real hopes for military resurgence in Judah, and though there is good support for such a theory in the military designs of Josiah years later, Deuteronomy can be read from a different perspective.[145] Nielsen has argued that much of Deuteronomy has "had to loosen the otherwise strong ties between religious and political activity" and has entered into the sphere of religio-theoretical paraenesis, soberly adjusted to the military-political realities of the day. These realities involved powerful ANE sovereigns who were capable of destroying and deporting whole nations.[146]

Nielsen's view is persuasive. The example of Samaria and the Judahite countryside would have been etched on the minds of the "people of the land." The "people of the land," holding to the tone of early dtr traditions, sought a king who would maintain the kind of rigorous independence permitted even vassal-states, rather than the kind of religious and political wavering evidenced for the reign of Manasseh. That real military and political advantage, based upon these same traditions of Deuteronomy, could be taken during periods in which the sovereign was less threatening is not to be denied. In fact, this is precisely what happens during the reign of Josiah. But from the perspective of Judah and the Book of Deuteronomy, this was more a fortunate turn of military/political events than the situation actually called for and plotted out in concrete terms within Deuteronomy. In other words, the sharp religious force of Deuteronomy could be translated into military/political action when and if the circumstances allowed, but this was not the primary stimulus for the authoring/transmitting of dtr traditions. Concrete hopes for the military resurgence of Judah may have emerged from these traditions. They did not give rise to them.

What emerges in the period following Josiah's short-lived experiment with aggressive political independence is a kind of prudent realism exercised by the "people of the land." At times the position of the *AH* appears "pro-Babylonian" — to the extent that it is a firm rejection of political intrigue or maneuvering with Egypt —[147] once the authority of the Neo-

---

[145] Gerhard von Rad, *Studies in Deuteronomy,* 45—73; E. Junge, *Der Wiederaufbau des Heerwesens des Reiches Juda unter Josia* (BWANT 23; Stuttgart: Kohlhammer, 1936).

[146] Eduard Nielsen, "Political Conditions," 106. See for example the highly conceptualized, wholly impracticable "Rules for Waging Holy War" in Deut 20:1—20.

[147] That Egypt plays a specifically negative role in Deuteronomy (17:16; 11:10; 16:1—12; 20:1; 24:18) is to be explained in large part by its literary setting in the Mosaic-Wilderness period. Is there evidence that such a negative role may have served a double purpose, viz, resulting from its specific relevance for the period in which the traditions actually came together (in a form approximating the final form of the text), the period presently under discussion when Egypt re-emerged as a new threat under a different guise? This may in turn reflect the animosity of the "people of the land" toward the Egyptians during this (7th century) period.

Babylonians is established in the region and once the prophetic voice of
Jeremiah counsels submission to the Babylonians as the "instrument of
Yahweh." Anticipating the analysis of Jeremiah traditions which follows
in Chapter Four, there is good reason to assume that important links exist
between the background and position of the "people of the land" and the
prophet Jeremiah — especially in terms of their respective attitudes toward
the proper place of Judahite monarchy and society within a changed and
more threatening political arena. These attitudes in turn have important
implications for reactions to the Exile which were forming in this period,
now found in the present Book of Jeremiah and other exilic material.
Along these lines, it is to be recalled that the "people of the land" represent
that portion of broader Judahite society most familiar with the events of
exile and deportation, having encountered in direct terms the Assyrian
onslaught and its aftermath not many years previously. Jeremiah's post-
597 counsel to "serve the king of Babylon and live" (27:17) may have its
ultimate roots within the political perspective of the "people of the land."
Uncompromising in the religious realm and in the demand for an Israel
set apart (see Deuteronomy), the "people of the land" were anxious to
avoid external political entanglements, even if the result was a loss of
political prestige and aggressive external military capability in the region.[148]

It should be obvious at this point that certain clear lines of relationship
exist between the early traditions and traditionists of Deuteronomy and
the "people of the land." Such a thesis has been explored before; it has
also been hotly debated.[149] It is impossible to enter into a complete

---

[148] The relationship between Jeremiah and certain key families with scribal roots (Shaphan
family) in Jerusalem will be explored in Chapter Four, in the context of an analysis of
an intermediate level of Jeremiah tradition termed the Scribal Chronicle. Scribal families
within the capital may also share the broader political perspective of the "people of the
land." A political statement such as outlined here can be found in this intermediate level
of Jeremiah tradition (primarily Jer 27—29* + 37—43*). See Chapter Four below.

[149] The critical debate is not so much over the linking of Deuteronomy in its early form to
the "people of the land," but to the Levites. For the latter theory, see especially, G. von
Rad, "The Provenance of Deuteronomy," *Studies*, 60—69, or Aage Bentzen, *Die Josian-
ischen Reformen und ihre Voraussetzungen* (Copenhagen: P. Haase & Sons, 1926); also J. A.
Soggin, "'am-ha'areṣ," 194 (with important refinements of von Rad esp. concerning
kingship). Rejected by, among others, Moshe Weinfeld, *Deuteronomy and the Deuteronomistic
School* (Oxford: University, 1972) 54—6. Weinfeld may be correct in his criticism of the
strictly levitical origin of Deuteronomy. He argues that it would be more reasonable to
see in the composers of Deuteronomy "a neutral circle which has access to different
types of literary material" (56). The "people of the land" would fit this description
admirably. He tries, however, to also tie the material to wisdom circles, in my view
leaving his own plea for neutrality behind. On the other hand, when he opts at a later
point for a specific circle of scribes or scribal families as involved with the "crystallization"
of dtr traditions, he is again on the right track, but again with unnecessary appeal to a
specific wisdom provenance. It would seem that one might reckon with the early dtr
traditions being nurtured and maintained by the "people of the land." Within this larger

discussion within the context of the present study. However, the following observations can be added. If this theory (in its narrower sense) of the origin of the "people of the land" is correct, then the supposed northern origin of much of the early D-material is also accounted for. The "people of the land" were comprised of those elements of both northern and southern territories who had escaped Assyrian deportation and had moved subsequently to the region of Jerusalem. With von Rad, many of the present statements concerning centralization of the cult are not primary to these traditions; rather the core material was concerned above all else with the establishment of a distinct "people of Yahweh," based upon ancient Mosaic traditions, holy and separate from the nations round about.[150]

These concerns, while voiced by various individuals at distinct periods, would be exceedingly apposite for such a group at a time when the influence of foreign culture and religion was at its zenith, and no distant phenomenon.[151] The geographical distinctions northern and southern only tell part of the story, and may be misleading.[152] In any event, with the Fall of the Northern Kingdom in 721 and the widespread disturbances in Judah in 701, these two groups, however distinct theologically or geographically, were brought together. Out of the crucible of these historical circumstances the traditions of Deuteronomy began to receive written form. It should be noted that the background of the prophet Jeremiah is remarkably similar to that of the "people of the land," in view of the fact that like them he was a refugee from the provinces (Anathoth) to Jerusalem. This has important implications for Jeremiah's own theological background and heritage, as well as for the subsequent prose development of his message. It is sufficient at this point to state that the form Jeremiah's post-597 statements take, concerning the remnant community in Judah

---

circle, and in the due course of time, scribal families emerged who gave not only the traditions of Deuteronomy specific literary shape, but also much of the present Book of Jeremiah, especially narratives concerned with an interpretation of the person of Jeremiah, active in the land, after the first (597) and second (587) deportations. More on this in Chapter Four.

[150] G. von Rad, *Studies,* 68 (following Adam Welch, *The Code of Deuteronomy* [New York: George H. Doran, 1924]). Literary formulation of concerns with centralization of the cult, as it finds expression in both the Dtr History and Deuteronomy, is a secondary development (especially in the latter) which emerged from a sober assessment of the whole history of pre-exilic Israel/Judah and an attempt to account for its tragic finale. This is not to say that there were no advocates of such a view of the cult in the pre-exilic period, only that in the earliest traditions of Deuteronomy this view did not find considerable attention; it emerges as a later compromise between what were perhaps even opposing views on the matter. (It may have formed an actual part of early [Jerusalemite] traditions which have now been taken up into the larger DtrH).

[151] Among others, see E. Nielsen, "Political Conditions," 106.

[152] See now Joseph Blenkinsopp, *A History of Israelite Prophecy* (Philadelphia: Fortress, 1984) esp. 16—17.

and the reality of deportation, have been influenced by his relationship, historical and theological, to the "people of the land."

There would be a certain benefit at this point in entering into a full discussion of the literary traditions of Jeremiah, given the direction of preceding remarks. However, an important historical period remains to be covered. In the interest of completeness, our socio/historical analysis continues at this point. It should also be stated that the period from the reign of Josiah until the Fall of Jerusalem in 587 B. C., covered in the next section, reveals a new factor of special significance for the development of Jeremiah traditions. This factor involves certain irregularities Judahite monarchy experiences, particularly after the death of Josiah. The evaluation of the respective kingships of Jehoiachin and Zedekiah, Judah's last two monarchs, sharply divides the traditions of Jeremiah and Ezekiel. The following section lays out the historical background and circumstances of this division. Chapter Three pursues this division more fully, within the context of developing Ezekiel traditions and the first report of the "Exile" provided at 2 Kings 24.

G. Shifting Political Allegiances, Judah, 640—597 B. C.

It is important to resume the survey of shifting political allegiances in Judah at this point. The survey thus far has only laid the groundwork for the historical situation relevant for the Book of Jeremiah. Time and space have been invested in this background material because it provides an excellent sense of the political climate in Judah and Jerusalem, a climate which remains relatively unchanged from the Fall of Samaria in 721 to the Fall of Judah in 587 B. C. This is due to the fact of Judah's reduced political and territorial status throughout this period. As has been noted, the period is also one throughout which the reality of exile and deportation is a familiar one, experienced in 721, 701, probably in the mid-600s, and of course in 597, 587, and again in the 580s.[153] Furthermore, certain key figures in the capital and countryside remain relatively consistent actors throughout this period, including the "people of the land," the queen mother, and various political factions at the royal court.

What emerges for especially the first 2 decades of Josiah's reign is a brief period of stability and real geographical expansion, occasioned by the decline in power of the Assyrians.[154] Most scholars now argue this

---

[153] Ezra 4:2 mentions deportations into the Northern Kingdom under Esarhaddon (670s?); 4:10 speaks of settlements in Samaria under Osnapper (= Assurbanipal), probably in the mid 600s. Jer 52:30 tells of a third deporation from Judah in the 23rd year of Nebuchadnezzar (582 B. C.), perhaps following the assassination of Gedaliah and as a reprisal for the slaying of Chaldean troops (41:3).

[154] Criticized for attempting too much chronological precision, yet an important essay, is Cross and Freedman's "Josiah's Revolt Against Assyria," *JNES* 12 (1953) 56—58.

decline was felt in Judah and Hatti-land as early as the 640s, that is, during the first years of Josiah's reign.[155]

These years come quickly to an end as new political forces seek to inherit the former Assyrian holdings, including Judah. It is probably significant that the death of Assurbanipal, the last important monarch in the Assyrian empire, coincides with the beginning of Jeremiah's prophetic activity in Jerusalem (627 B. C.). Jeremiah and Josiah are near contemporaries and probably experience something of the same hopes for religious and geographical restoration. But these concrete hopes are quickly dashed as the political situation worsens in Judah.

With the death of Josiah at Megiddo in 609, Judah gets a clear sense of the situation she must face in the years ahead. Four kings rule in a period just over two decades. Allegiances to Babylon and Egypt shift no less than six times. It is during this particularly tense political period that the prophet Jeremiah is active. The majority of his book contains material which situates itself in the post-609 years. In order to get some sense of the political situation during which he was active, as well as the impact political factors had on his prophetic activity and message, it is important to gain as full and accurate a description of events as possible. Fortunately, in this period a broad assortment of extra-biblical sources is available, making an almost year-to-year reckoning of events in Judah possible.

1. Josiah

Josiah was only eight when he became king of Judah. This means that though his reign was long (31 years) and eventful, he was still only 39 when tragically slain at Megiddo, nearly 30 years younger than his grandfather Manasseh at his death. There has already been cause to note that his mother, Jedidah, was originally from Bozkath, a Judahite town near Lachish. It was probably for this reason that he was selected and placed in power by the "people of the land" upon the assassination of his father Amon. It was further conjectured that the assassination was due to the presence of factions within the royal court, specifically an anti-Assyrian contingent which sought to remove Amon in favor of another candidate (probably a half-brother). What is unclear is whether the faction was anxious to throw off Assyrian vassalage in order to establish other external alliances (Egyptian) or simply to assert Judahite independence. Probably a combination of both factors was involved. It is possible to see in the developing policies of Josiah something of the kind of position most likely taken by the "people of the land," both because they placed him in power and also because they probably wielded significant influence over him in his early regnal years, as he grew to maturity.

---

[155] Cogan, *Imperialism,* 70—71; Spalinger, "Psammetichus: II," 52.

Though Chronicles and Kings date the reforms of Josiah to different periods (his 18th year, 621; or his 12th year, 627), it is significant that they are in agreement that no direct attempts at political independence were undertaken for over a decade, until Josiah was well in power. If anything, this suggests a cautious or conservative attitude on the part of the "people of the land" who no doubt remained his main support group. It also shows that while they may have had considerable influence over the king, they did not act independently of him. At any rate, though Assyrian influence had begun to decline in the region prior to the death of Assurbanipal (627 B. C.), no immediate change in Judahite policy vis-à-vis Assyria or Egypt is evidenced for this early period. The fact that no major upheavals occurred within Judah until a later period indicates the preference for stability under the vassalage agreement, such as it was in the 630s. Above all, it may simply have been the case that the "people of the land" saw Judah's best interests served not in political intrigue or re-alignment, but in conscientious adherence to the religious vision of the dtr traditions. If the political situation began to tolerate a more rigorous and independent religious stance on the part of Judah, this could be viewed as consistent with these same dtr traditions. But there is no evidence of this in Joshiah's early years. The point is that if one wanted to classify the "people of the land" in terms of political alignment for this period, some evidence of alignment in Josiah's *early years* would be expected, when their influence over him was the greatest. Instead the period is one of relative internal and external stability.

One other unusual if not significant fact to note about Josiah's early years is his fathering of two chidren, the first, Eliakim (Jehoiakim), when he was only 14, and Shallum (Jehoahaz) at age 16. Since Eliakim's mother, Zebidah, came from Rumah in Israelite (Galilean) territory, within the Assyrian province of *Magidu,* it is difficult to view the "people of the land," if they maintained the role in royal affairs it appears they did, as staunchly anti-Assyrian during this period (634 B. C.). However, his next two children were sons of the same mother, Hamutal from Libnah in Judah. Shallum (Jehoahaz) was born in 632 and Mattaniah (Zedekiah) in 619. A certain sense of internal stability must have obtained during this period, permitting Josiah's marriage to a non-Judahite wife (Zebidah). This stability was made possible because of the relatively quiet political situation.

When Josiah initiates his reforms, they are for the most part of a purely religious nature and are restricted to Judah proper (2 Kgs 23:4–14). Much of his reforming activity involves specific purification of the temple in Jerusalem, though mention is also made of purification in the cities of Judah (vv. 5,8). It is possible therefore to conceive of the primary reforms as taking place "from Geba to Beersheba" (2 Kgs 23:8). Without entering fully into a literary analysis of this complex chapter, it is clear that even

if one accepts the report of Samarian reforms (vv. 15—20) the Book of
Kings does not stress any religious reforms occurring beyond Bethel to
the north.[156] The very fact that the biblical account in Kings goes on to
tell of treachery at Megiddo (23:30) suggests that Josiah's control did not
extend here. The extent of Josiah's reform is a much debated topic.[157]
Chronicles offers a much broader geographical view of the reforms, and
recourse is often made to other biblical texts which would buttress the
view of an all-Israelite reform.[158]

Extra-biblical finds,[159] including inscriptional evidence at Mesad
Hashavyahu to the west, Arad inscriptions and fortress to the south, and
lmlk seal impressions within the Geba-Beersheba region and beyond are
difficult to evaluate. Some wish to see them as evidence of Josiah's wider
geographical reach, others of a kingdom consisting primarily of former
Judahite holdings in the south and west, and the Assyrian province of
Samerina to the north. This more conservative picture seems on the whole
the most reasonable hypothesis. It is to be noted as significant that even
this more restricted view of political and religious reform would certainly
be cause for celebration within the capital and countryside. At no period
since 721/701 did Judah experience this kind of sustained geographical
expansion; rather, she had to be content with defensive buttressing of the
city of David. The fact that the reduced kingdom of Samaria, that is, the
Assyrian province of *Samerina* established in 722, could be re-incorporated
by Judah at this period, when she was still theoretically an Assyrian vassal,
was no small accomplishment. It demonstrates the degree to which Assyrian hegemony over the region had declined. It also meant the influx of

---

[156] Compare 2 Chr 34:6,7,33. It should be remembered, however, that Chronicles has an
altogether different view of the Northern Kingdom than does Kings, and this view cuts
both ways: the Northern Kingdom never has any serious theological existence over
against Judah, and so its actual historical existence can at times be used for a variety of
purposes.

[157] Malamat, "Josiah's Bid," 271 ff.; A. Alt, "Judas Gaue unter Josia," *PJB* 21 (1925)
100—16; Z. Kallai, *The Northern Boundaries of Judah* (Jerusalem, 1960) 75 ff. [in Hebrew];
B. Mazar, *Bulletin of the Jewish Palestine Exploration Society* 8 (1940) 35—37; H. Reviv,
"Hezekiah to Josiah," 203—4; H. L. Ginsberg, "Judah and the Transjordan States,"
355—63; R. Nelson, *"Realpolitik* in Judah," *Scripture in Context: Essays on the Comparative
Method,* 183—9; J. Milgrom, *Beth Mikra* 44; Hayes & Miller, 463 ff.

[158] See, for example, H. L. Ginsberg, "Judah and the Transjordan States," 355—63.

[159] J. Naveh, "A Hebrew Letter from the Seventh Century B. C.," *IEJ* 10 (1960) 129—39;
12 (1962) 27—32; Y. Aharoni, "Arad: Its Inscriptions and Temple," *BA* 31 (1968) 2—32,
89—99; Y. Yadin, "The Historical Significance of Inscription 88 from Arad: A Suggestion," *IEJ* 26 (1976) 9—14; P. Welten, *Die Königs-Stemple: Ein Beitrag zur Militärpolitik
Judas unter Hiskia und Josia* (Wiesbaden: Abhandlungen des Deutschen Palästina-Vereins
4, 1969); A. D. Tushingham, "A Royal Israelite Seal (?) and the Royal Jar Handle Stamps,"
BASOR 200 (1970) 71—8; 201 (1971) 23—35; H. D. Lance, "The Royal Stamps and the
Kingdom of Josiah," *HTR* 64 (1971) 315—32; Hayes & Miller, 464 ff.

new populations from the north into Judah proper, along with greater communication between these two regions.

The presence of Jeremiah from Anathoth in the capital city during this period (probably as early as 627) explains the presence in the Book of Jeremiah of oracles clearly directed to the House of Israel as distinct from Judah (see for example, Jer 3:12—14). The term "Israel" is a reference to actual inhabitants of the Northern Kingdom or populations which, like the prophet Jeremiah, came from Israelite territory to settle in the capital. Among them may have been descendents of populations who had fled to Jerusalem from the Northern Kingdom years earlier after Samaria's fall. Here again the circumstances involve refugee populations within Jerusalem or her environs. The particular timing of Jeremiah's prophetic message during the reign of Josiah is also significant. It comes late enough in Josiah's reign that renewed hopes for the Northern Kingdom could emerge; it is also near enough to the rise of a new foe from the north, the Neo-Babylonians, that such hopes were intermingled with sober calls for repentence and renewal (Fall of Ninevah, 612 B. C.).

Prior to the accomplished ascendency of the Babylonians in the region (in the 580s), there was a scramble for the right of inheritance to the Assyrian empire that included the Egyptians under Psammetichus I (664—610), Necho II (610—594), Psammetichus II (594—588) and Apries (588—569). It is for this reason that Malamat, accurately charting the situation from the Judahite perspective, termed the period the "Egyptian-Babylonian Maelstrom." There is abundant evidence, biblical and extra-biblical, that such a power struggle did in fact take place, with far reaching implications for Judah. Though the Babylonians tend to maintain a higher profile in the biblical account, this is due to the decisive role they ultimately play vis-à-vis Judah and Jerusalem. But their hegemony over the region is not easily accomplished, and for over 2 decades Judah had to contend with several political alternatives open to them, including alignment with Egypt. During the main period of Jeremiah's prophetic activity, under the last four Davidic rulers, Judah was faced with the choice of allegiance to Egypt or Babylon. More than at any previous period, political alignment was a constant question within Judah, and concerns with just this issue permeate the Book of Jeremiah. Such a concern was all the more provocative given Jeremiah's early and consistent warning that submission to Babylon was the will of Yahweh.

It has recently been argued that the picture of conscious political posturing and alignment within Judah during much of this period is inaccurate, and that one would do better to speak only of a kind of *Realpolitik* when evaluating this period.[160] Consistent with such an approach is the downplaying of Judah's real military and political influence

---

[160] Richard Nelson, "*Realpolitik*".

vis-à-vis the larger powers (Egypt, Assyria, Babylon). To suggest, however, that political factors were not decisive within Jerusalem, either in terms of Judah's external alignment or with respect to internal disputes over such alignment, is a misreading of the biblical and extra-biblical evidence. There is good reason to suspect that, as Malamat has put it, "political orientation (was) an acute issue among the people of Judah."[161]

The biblical and extra-biblical evidence suggests that following the decline of Assyrian influence in Hatti-land, Judah had to contend first of all with the Egyptians under Psammetichus I, who were anxious to assert their own control over the region. It may have been the case that during Josiah's early years (630s), when the balance of power was still an open question, religious reform and political expansion occurred in a relative power vacuum; that is, apart from political alliance or agressive military stance. But quite quickly the broader international situation would change.

Nelson's objections to such a view of Judahite politics come to a head in his interpretation of Josiah's encounter with Necho II at Megiddo in 609 B. C. The boldest thesis he mounts is that, prior to this encounter, Josiah was no more or less hostile toward the Assyrians than was Manasseh; moreover, Judah was in fact a loyal ally of both Assyria and Egypt for this period (hence, the term *Realpolitik*). He speaks of "good relations" between Josiah and Psammetichus and develops the theory of an "Egypt-Judah-Assyria" alliance based upon texts from Jeremiah and Isaiah (185−86).[162] As for the actual account from Kings of Josiah at Megiddo (23:29), he argues that "Josiah went out from Megiddo to welcome his ally Neko," in order to "throw open the pass to the Egyptian advance" (188).[163] In order to further this interpretation he must assume, among other things, that the Chronicler has already misunderstood the report of Kings or intended "to lead us astray with his tale of a battle" (189), since 2 Chr 35:20 ff. clearly sees Josiah's mission as anti-Egyptian (and anti-Yahweh!). Nelson claims that the purpose of this narrative was to "provide a reason for Josiah's early and violent death" (188), but this could have been done without the Chronicler having to invent Josiah's opposition to Egyptian advances. Clearly the purpose of the Chronicler's expansions are more complex than Nelson proposes.

As has been stated, it is clear that Assyrian influence had already diminished by the time Josiah took the throne. Moreover, a virulently

---

[161] "Twilight of Judah," 129.

[162] Rather than, as is most often done, seeing Jer 2:18, 2:36 as evidence of political vacillation on the part of Judah, or more accurately, of certain factions within Jerusalem. See J. Milgrom, "The Date of Jeremiah, Chapter 2," *JNES* 14 (1955) 66−69, and J. Bright, *Jeremiah*, 14−18 (who wants to date the oracle after 609).

[163] On the basis of Josephus and the Babylonian Chronicle, in which Egypt is clearly seen as an ally, not an antagonist, of the Assyrians, read 2 Kgs 23:29 as Necho "went up to" rather than "against" the king of Assyria.

anti-Assyrian policy on the part of Josiah overstates the evidence. In this sense, Nelson is correct that the purpose of Josiah's activity at Megiddo was not to "prevent Egyptian aid from reaching Assyria in its final hour" (188); such a view places far too great an emphasis on possible or intended resuscitation of the Assyrians by the Egyptians. What then was Josiah up to?

Malamat has argued that while it is possible to speak of Egyptian-Assyrian rapprochement during part of this period, and especially after 616 when Egypt is depicted alongside Assyria as the common enemy of Nabopalassar in the Babylonian Chronicles, it is nevertheless a time when Egypt is interested in consolidating as much of Assyria's former holdings in Syria/Palestine as possible.[164] During the long reign of Psammetichus (664—610) the relationship between Egypt and Assyria is a complex one, moving through several distinct phases.[165] If one were to use the term *Realpolitik,* it might be a good description of the policy of the Egyptians under Psammetichus I, who saw benefit in alignment with Assyria only due to the fact of the emerging Neo-Babylonian threat. When Spalinger speaks of Egyptian-Assyrian cooperation against the Kushites in the earlier period of Esarhaddon and Assurbanipal,[166] it is nevertheless a fact that Egypt remained no equal partner but an Assyrian vassal; it is difficult, moreover, to extrapolate from this supposed cordiality in the early 7th century the tendency for similar friendly relations for the whole of the period under discussion.[167] The circumstances are quite different, with Egypt in a much more powerful role vis-à-vis Assyria. When Assyria's influence declined in Syria-Palestine, Egypt was in a good position to make a bid for control; this was not done, as Nelson proposes, in order to protect the region for the Assyrians as a partner in a Judah-Egypt-Assyria alliance. What he describes as the unexpected treachery of Necho II is better seen as the consistent policy of Egypt in the region, made more evident because of Josiah's conscious resistence to this new monarch.

---

[164] For the Babylonian material, see D. J. Wiseman, *Chronicles of Chaldean Kings (626—556 B. C.) in the British Museum"* (London: Trustees of the British Museum, 1961) [hereafter cited as *CCK*].

[165] Malamat, "Josiah's Bid," 272—3.

[166] A. Spalinger, "Assurbanipal and Egypt: A Source Study," *JAOS* 94 (1974) 316—28; "Esarhaddon and Egypt: An Analysis of the First Invasion of Egypt," *Or* 43 (1974) 295—326.

[167] Both he and Nelson are inclined toward this view ("Psammetichus, King of Egypt: II," *JARCE* 15 [1978] 49—57). Compare the studies of K. A. Kitchen (*The Third Intermediate Period in Egypt [1100—650]* [Warminster, 1972] 400—8), F. K. Kienitz (*Fischer Weltgeschichte 4, Die Altorientalischen Reiche III* [München: Fischer Bücherei, 1967] 190 ff.), Benedict Otzen (*Studien über Deuterosacharja* [Copenhagen: Prostant Apud Munksgaard, 1964] 87 ff.), and Alexander Scharff (*Ägypten und Vorderasien im Altertum* [München: F. Bruckmann, 1950] 180 ff.).

Evidence of Egyptian designs in Syria-Palestine is provided at numerous points. Herodotus (II, 157) speaks of the Egyptians under Psammetichus involved in a lengthy siege and conquest of Ashdod,[168] which has been confirmed by archaeological investigation.[169] An Egyptian stele from Psammetichus' 52nd year (612 B. C.) has been discovered in Phoenecia, and it claims sovereignty for Psammetichus over the Phoenecian coast.[170] Katzenstein makes note of a similar find at the coastal town of Arvad.[171] There is also evidence that the Egyptian army was bolstered throughout this period by the presence of Greek mercenaries, who were involved as well in maritime adventures under Necho II.[172] Similar mercenaries are mentioned in the Arad letters, and they seem to be a garrison dispatched by Necho II to the vassal kingdom of Judah.[173] The Aramaic letter commonly referred to as the Saqqara papyrus should also be mentioned at this point. Though probably from a slightly later period, it contains the urgent appeal of one Adon, a ruler in Philistia or Phoenecia, to the Pharaoh for assistance against the approaching Chaldean army. Here again, significant Egyptian control within the region must be assumed.[174]

Malamat has tried to demonstrate that Megiddo was in fact a logistics base for the Egyptians at the time when Josiah encountered Necho. The (short) cubit measure used at the fortress there indicates either Egyptian or Israelite control, as Malamat has argued; Nelson concedes this, but opts for Josianic rather than Egyptian control.[175] It seems, however, that the weight of the evidence confirms the theory of Malamat: the Egyptians were consciously involved in a scramble for inheritance of former Assyrian territory, and this both before and after the encounter between Necho and Josiah. In the years of gradual disintegration of Assyrian control over Judah, Josiah had been able to carve out a restored political state including

---

[168] For a discussion, see Malamat, "Last Wars," 218; H. Cazelles, "Sophonie, Jérémie, et les Scythes en Palestine," *RB* 74 (1967) = "Zephaniah, Jeremiah, and the Scythians in Palestine," in Leo G. Perdue, ed, *A Prophet to the Nations* (Winona Lake: Eisenbrauns, 1984) 129 ff. F. K. Kienitz dates the beginning of the siege to 655 B. C. (*Politische Geschichte,* 17).

[169] M. Dothan, "Ashdod II−III," *'Atiqot* 9−10 (1971) 21, 115.

[170] Freedy & Redford, "Dates in Ezekiel," 477.

[171] *The History of Tyre,* 299 n. 24; 313, n. 100.

[172] Katzenstein, *Tyre, 313.*

[173] Freedy and Redford, "Dates in Ezekiel," 478.

[174] For a full discussion, see articles by John Bright, "A New Letter in Aramaic, Written to a Pharaoh of Egypt," *BA* 12 (1949) 46−52; Joseph Fitzmyer, "The Aramaic Letter of King Adon to the Egyptian Pharaoh," *Bib* 46 (1965) 41−46; Siegfried Horn, "Where and When was the Aramaic Saqqara Papyrus Written?" *AUSS* 6 (1968). As the title of Horn's article indicates, there is some confusion as to the date and place of origin of the letter. The general consensus, however, since Albright's original proposal, is Ashkelon around 605. All agree that the letter emerges from a situation of Egyptian-Babylonian conflict over territory in Syria-Palestine.

[175] Malamat, "Josiah's Bid," 269−70; Nelson, "*Realpolitik,*" 187.

even *Samerina* to the north. In the late 620s and 610s, however, his control in the region was threatened by the presence of Egyptian forces, especially under the aggressive Necho II. It is for this reason that a confrontation occurred between Josiah and Necho at Megiddo, probably territory Josiah was in the process of bringing under Judahite control.

It should also be said that the clearest evidence for Egyptian influence in the region detrimental to Judah's interests is the role they continue to play long after the death of Josiah and the demise of the Assyrian empire. This moves our discussion firmly into the period of Jeremiah's prophetic activity. After Josiah's death at Megiddo, Necho took up military residence at Riblah (2 Kgs 23:33) in the province of Hamath and it was here that the newly installed king Jehoahaz was summoned after a reign of only three months. Jehoahaz is first incarcerated and then exiled to Egypt; his older brother, Eliakim, is placed in power and given a new name; the "people of the land" are taxed (2 Kgs 23:33—35). All of these actions were carried out by the same Necho who killed Josiah at Meggido. Though the Egyptians were signally defeated at Carchemish in 605 B. C., it is a testimony to their confidence in the region that they challenged the Neo-Babylonians at all in the distant territory of the Euphrates.[176] And despite their defeat, they are later successful enough in 601 to send the Babylonian army home for a full-year's refitting (*CCK*, 29—31,70—1). Following the brief and generally peaceful reign of Psammetichus II (594—588), Pharaoh Hophra (Apries) resumed an aggressive posture in the region. There is a record of a rebellion of Zedekiah against him.[177] In sum, Egyptian aggressive action is well-attested for the period immediately following the death of Josiah. It makes good sense to assume that similar political pressure was experienced in Judah especially in the latter years of Josiah's reign. With the decline of Assyrian influence in the region, it is understandable that Egypt sought a share of the inheritance.

Malamat has tried to argue that Josiah's action at Megiddo was carried out in part to place Judah in clear alignment with the emerging Neo-Babylonians, a move which would hopefully ensure Judah's continued political integrity.[178] This is difficult to determine. What can be inferred is that he saw no purpose in Egyptian hegemony over Judah, and the Egyptians were historically a more familiar quantity than the distant and lesser-known Chaldeans. Furthermore, from a certain perspective the Neo-Babylonians could be arguably conceived of as the liberators of Judah and the final destroyers of the Assyrian menace, which had held sway in the region for over a century (see Nahum). If Josiah was not pleased enough

---

[176] Kitchen, *Third Intermediate Period, 407.*

[177] See Freedy & Redford, "Dates in Ezekiel," 482; Cf. M. Greenberg ("Ezekiel 17 and the Policy of Psammetichus II," *JBL* 76 [1957] 304—9) for an earlier dating of the rebellion.

[178] "Last Years," 205—6; "Last Wars," 219.

at the prospect of the end of Assyrian rule to align himself with the Neo-Babylonians, at a minimum it is likely that he had hopes for a continued period of peace and stability in Judah, such as had been felt with the decline of Assyrian influence since the 640s. This hope saw better chance of fulfillment in the Babylonians than the Egyptians.

Several conclusions can be drawn. There is ample evidence that political factions existed within Judah during the reigns of Manasseh and Amon. After a decade of relative calm under young Josiah, Judah began to experience religious and political restoration, still within the limits of Assyrian vassalage. In the 620s, Egyptian influence is increasingly felt in the area and is perceived as a threat by Josiah. He is killed at Megiddo in a military encounter with Necho. With the rise of the Neo-Babylonians under Nebuchadnezzar, political alignment will again emerge as an important consideration within the capital, as Egypt and Babylon vie for control over the territory of Judah.

2. Jehoahaz (Shallum)

Just prior to the death of Josiah in 609 B. C. and the assumption of power by Jehoahaz in Jerusalem (2 Kgs 23:30), events on the international scene are relatively easy to reconstruct. The Babylonian Chronicle greatly assists in this. Together with the Medes, the Neo-Babylonians under Nabopolassar captured the city of Ashur in 614, Ninevah in 612, and Haran in 610 (*CCK*, 60 ff.). The Egyptians came to the aid of the failing Assyrians as early as 616, and they are mentioned as active alongside Assuruballit in 610 and 609 as well. The latter dates mark the attempt by the Assyrians, joined by Necho after the affair at Megiddo, to retake Haran. A "strong Egyptian army" crossed the Euphrates with Assuruballit but did not succeed in capturing the city, even after a long siege (*CCK*, 63). Although after this nothing further is said of the Assyrian monarch, Necho hurried south to take possession of Syria/Palestine.[179] It may even have been during the siege itself that Necho was able to return to his outpost at Riblah and summon Jehoahaz there.

The biblical text is fairly silent about the details of Jehoahaz' deposition. It appears that the actual sentencing and incarceration occurred in Riblah; it states that he was "put in bonds" (*wayya'asrēhû*) there precisely that "he might not reign in Jerusalem" (23:33). But Necho's other activities, including the installing of Jehoiakim and the taxing of the land, appear to have taken place in Judah itself, again testifying to the Pharaoh's power in the region. Both Jeremiah's dirge (22:11) and the Kings' report include the fact of Shallum's deportation to Egypt. Two other facts are worthy

---

[179] S. Herrmann, *A History of Israel in Old Testament Times* (London/Philadelphia: SCM/Fortress, 1975) 274.

of note. The "people of the land" were responsible for placing Shallum on the throne; their avoidance of his older brother Jehoiakim was probably due to his Galilean background. Whatever hopes the "people of the land" may have had for Shallum were quickly extinguished; note that they are mentioned specifically as being taxed by Jehoiakim in order to pay tribute to the Egyptians (2 Kgs 23:35). Secondly, while one can only assume that Necho made these important throne changes personally, the fact of Jehoiakim's pro-Egyptian loyalties must have been made known to him in such a way that his selection and installation where quickly carried out, because there is no mention of any time lapse or internal conflict following the removal of Jehoahaz. Apparently Jehoiakim was not alone in his pro-Egyptian stance, for he could not have assumed power so quickly and ruled as long as he did without significant support from a group within the capital. It is also reasonable to assume that they did not develop a pro-Egyptian attitude overnight. Such assumptions are borne about by further evidence from the Book of Jeremiah, but full treatment of this subject will be held off until a later point.

In the section above important factors have been described which played a role in the passing of the throne in Judah. Several conjectures were made about these factors, based upon the evidence provided for the succession of Amon and Josiah, as well as for previous successions. In the last 25 years of Judah's existence one moves out of the realm of conjecture onto firmer ground. The irregularities demonstrated in throne changes for Judah's last 4 kings mark this 25-year period as unique in the nearly 350-year history of the Davidic monarchy. At no point in the long history of the dynasty does kingship move horizontally, from brother to brother (or half-brother). This happens in the case of Jehoiakim succeeding Jehoahaz. An even odder instance is the succession of Zedekiah, another brother of Jehoahaz, after the reign of his own nephew Jehoiachin.

While it has been argued that the principle of primogeniture is fairly fundamental in Judah, exceptions to the principle do occur, though often these exceptions must be left in the realm of conjecture (e. g., Amon's succession). But for these last years clear evidence exists — precisely because more than one brother in a given generation assumes power — that the principle could be over-ruled. The clear reason for the irregularities involves the fact of forced throne changes due to external interference, though even here one might want to reckon with certain internal maneuvering (e. g., for Jehoiakim and Zedekiah). Josiah is killed by Necho; Jehoahaz is deported by the Egyptians; Jehoiakim is placed in power by Necho; his successor, Jehoiachin, is deported by the Babylonians; Zedekiah is in turn placed in power by Nebuchadnezzar. External interference is illustrated by the fact that each of these last four kings receives a new name upon taking power, signifying allegiance beyond Yahweh, to Pharaoh or the Babylonian King.[180] External interference leads to the appointment of a non-Davidic administrator following the deportation of Zedekiah, Gedaliah ben Ahikam ben Shaphan. After his assassination by a member of the royal family, power is held briefly by Johanon and Jeremiah. For both of these latter cases there is neither precedent nor analogy in either Judahite or Israelite versions of dynastic kingship.

The fact of external interference also explains one other unique circumstance in this period: the simultaneous kingships of Jehoiachin and Zedekiah, the former deported to Babylon, the latter king for 11 years in Judah.[181] Discussion of this unusual circumstance is postponed until Chapter Three.

It should also be stressed that external interference in this period affects more than monarchial and governmental circles. The whole of Judahite society undergoes irreversable changes. This is seen in the reality of Judah existing in part as "Israel," that is, as the people of Yahweh in a loose or completely severed relationship to the actual territory of Judah (or Israel). This new reality comes about due to deportations and exchanges of population heretofore experienced by the Northern Kingdom only. "Israel" now exists in dispersion, as well as in Judah proper. Internal instability during these last years results not only from external military threat but also from the changing self-definition of Israel/Judah. This unstable situation is first demonstrated in internal factional conflict, but it very soon turns into a conflict extending beyond Judah's borders, involving communities of Israelites in exile (see Jer 27–29).

The biblical notices indicate that Josiah had at least three sons, because they all eventually reign in Judah; Jehoiakim, the eldest, does not succeed to the throne at the death of his father.[182] It is unlikely that he had named a successor, given his early death at 39 at Megiddo. Immediately the

---

[180] See J. Gray, *I & II Kings*, 751; A. M. Honeymoon, "The Evidence for Regnal Names Among the Hebrews," *JBL* 67 (1948) 16 ff.

[181] Seen as significant in varying degrees by W. F. Albright ("The Seal of Eliakim and the Latest Preexilic History of Judah," *JBL* 51 [1932] 77–106; "King Joiachin in Exile," *BA* 5 [1942]), H. G. May ("Three Hebrew Seals and the Status of Exiled Jehoiakin," *AJSL* [1939] 146–8), A. Malamat ("Jeremiah and the Last Two Kings of Judah," *PEQ* 83 [1951] 81–87) and P. R. Ackroyd ("The History of Israel in the Exilic and Post-Exilic Periods," in *Tradition and Interpretation* [G. W. Anderson, ed; Oxford, 1979] 320 ff.). Malamat has made some modifications in his position based upon a more cautious evaluation of the extra-biblical evidence (seals), but the larger point remains the same ("Twilight," 138, n. 34).

[182] The biblical reports of Kings and Jeremiah provide the primary data for this treatment of Josiah's sons. Chronicles seems to understand Zedekiah as Jehoiachin's brother (2 Chr 36:10), probably because he ruled after Jehoiachin; 1 Chr 3:15–16 suggests that there are two Zedekiahs, both a (third) son of Josiah and a (second) son of Jehoiakim. It is not clear where the Chronicler got this information, since it clearly is in tension with the reports of Jeremiah and Kings, which consistently agree over the age and order of the last four kings.

"people of the land" intervene to place Jehoahaz, 2 years Jehoiakim's junior, on the throne; it is significant that at such times when no king was in power and the potential for internal unrest was high, it is the ʿam hāʾāreṣ who take action. Malamat also argues that the specific mention of the anointing of Jehoahaz by the "people of the land" (2 Kgs 23:30) is important, since anointing is only reported in the biblical record on occasions when dynasties are founded or successions contested.[183] Both Jehoahaz and Zedekiah had the same mother who, as noted, came from the Judahite countryside. The kind of political tolerance which allowed the marriage of Josiah to Zebidah from Rumah came to an end; it is likely that at this time Rumah was in Egyptian territory. Given Josiah's popularity and the tragedy of his death at Megiddo, Jehoiakim was viewed as a less than attractive candidate.[184]

All this would remain in the realm of conjecture were it not for the fact that after only three months on the throne, Jehoahaz is replaced by Necho and Jehoiakim made king in his place. Here one is on much firmer ground in assuming that Necho actually capitalized on Jehoiakim's pro-Egyptian background and leanings. Jehoiakim appears quite loyal to his Egyptian support; there is no mention of a revolt or reluctance to rule.[185] The tribute (ʿānaš) imposed by Necho (23:33) is only a third of that exacted by Sennacherib a century earlier; this too may indicate the desire on the part of Necho not to place Jehoiakim's already volatile kingship in jeopardy, vis-à-vis his subjects.[186] Jehoiakim in turn focuses the tax on the "people of the land," the main support group of his predecessor Jehoahaz and his father Josiah. The unavoidable conclusion is that the pro-Egyptian faction, quiet for much of Josiah's reign, emerged in full force as the Egyptians became a clear military and political force to reckon with in the region.

The earlier activity of the "people of the land" in placing Jehoahaz on the throne can also be construed as anti-Egyptian. It was noted above that the existence of political factions was not obvious for much of Josiah's 31-year tenure, due to the relative political stability in the area. The "people of the land" were more inclined toward cautious support for religious restoration and independence than for external political alignment. It can be assumed that as a result of more direct military and political pressure from two opposing directions, the "people of the land" are forced into a more virulent political stance. They hoped that in the person of Jehoahaz

---

[183] "Last Kings," 140, n. 7.

[184] This is the view of Malamat ("Last Years," 206) and Ihromi ("Die Königinmutter," 427).

[185] Even when it is recorded that Jehoiakim became servant of Nebuchadnezzar (2 Kgs 24:1), there is not a hint of Jehoiakim abandoning his Egyptian support. The deciding factor is that Egypt is forced to retreat (temporarily) from the region (24:7).

[186] J. Gray, I & II Kings, 750–1.

they would see a continuation of the independent policies of his father
Josiah. Unfortunately these hopes were crushed when he was summoned
to appear before Necho at his Syrian headquarters. Note again that
Jehoahaz' compliance demonstrates the power wielded by the Egyptians
in Syria/Palestine under Necho. It was not possible to challenge Necho's
authority, though he probably had hopes that Necho would allow Judah
to maintain a semblence of religious and political independence under his
leadership. But the time was not right for such tolerance on the part of
the Egyptian monarch; he was not through with his own political plans
in the wider region. Clearly Necho felt that a continuation of Josianic
policy in Judah was detrimental to his bid for control of the region. The
truth of this had been borne out at Megiddo. At the same time, he did
not have the same concerns about Jehoiakim, since he did not place his
own military leadership in control in the capital.

Apart from the brief notice in Kings (23:34), there are no further
details about the fate of Jehoahaz in the biblical record. In contrast to the
later treatment of Jehoiachin (2 Kgs 24:14—15) and Zedekiah (2 Kgs
25:6—12), the sentence of exile by the Egyptians falls on him alone, and
does not include any of the royal house or other citizenry from Jerusalem.
The only possible explanation for this is that Necho specifically sought to
separate him from the rest of the royal house (quite large at this point)
and single him out for punishment as an example to those remaining.
Ezekiel 19 includes a lamentation for the kings of Judah (called něśí'îm, in
characteristic Ezekiel fashion), and there is a brief reference to Jehoahaz
in vv. 2—4; he is specifically included, together with Zedekiah, because
both are carried off into exile (Egypt and Babylon).[187] Unfortunately, the
dirge reveals very little about Jehoahaz (or Zedekiah), because the language
of metaphor predominates (lion/whelp/young lion/prey/pit/hook/cage).

A more direct assessment is found in Jeremiah 22:10—12, though it
too is quite brief. This oracle concerning Jehoahaz falls in a larger section
of (judgment) oracles concerning his successors Jehoiakim and Jehoiachin,
and an even larger section on Judahite/Davidic kingship (Chs 21—24),
framed by judgment oracles against Zedekiah (21:1—10; 24:8—10).[188] The
tone of judgment over these kings is set in contrast to hope for the future,
in which Yahweh will raise up a "righteous branch" (ṣemaḥ ṣaddîq, 23:5).
Form-critically it is clear that each of the separate oracles against Jehoahaz,
Jehoiakim, and Jehoiachin once had a prior life as genuine oracles delivered
by the prophet Jeremiah. They have been brought together secondarily

---

[187] See the full discussion of this text in Chapter Three. Chapter 19 provides an extremely
important look at Ezekiel's perspective on kingship. It is important, among other reasons,
because it seems in tension with the Jeremiah perspective. If the analysis below is correct,
Jehoiakim and his son Jehoiachin do not even appear in Ezekiel's dirge.
[188] See the full discussion in Chapters Three and Four.

and fused with oracles concerning Zedekiah and his generation in order to form a complete and coherent statement on kingship.[189]

The form of the oracle concerning Jehoahaz is brief (vv. 10—12) in contrast to the oracle against Jehoiakim (vv. 13—23) and Jehoiachin (vv. 24—30), but it is also quite distinctive. The command to weep bitterly (*bĕkû bākô*) for Jehoahaz stands in clear contrast to the description of non-lamentation (v. 18) for his successor Jehoiakim; it is also meant to serve as a contrast to actual lamentation for Josiah, whose fate, while tragic, is compared with the worse fate of exile for Jehoahaz (10b,11). Although the oracle finds its place now in a context of judgment against the whole monarchial enterprise, it contains none of the severe force of censure found in the oracles against Jehoiakim and Jehoiachin (see vv. 19, 24—26). Rather, it is an oracle of lamentation for the tragic fate of Jehoahaz, glossed by a description of the actual circumstances of his exiling (vv. 11—12). It can be concluded that the exiling and death of Jehoahaz were viewed as a tragic end to hopes for restoration initiated by his father Josiah. It was for this reason, as well as for the very brief interval separating their deaths, that lamentations arose at the same time for them both.

3. Jehoiakim (Eliakim)

Upon entering the period of Jehoiakim's 11-year tenure as king of Judah, one turns a corner that is significant on historical and literary grounds for any analysis of the Book of Jeremiah. There is a sustained debate about the prophet Jeremiah's activity during Josiah's reign.[190] Jehoahaz is not even included with the other kings of Judah in the superscription to the Book of Jeremiah. As stated above, there is only one brief oracle (22:10—12) referring to Jehoahaz (in positive contrast to Jehoiakim) in the entire Book of Jeremiah.[191] But the reign of Jehoiakim had a clear impact on the person and message of the prophet Jeremiah,

---

[189] See the commentaries, or W. Thiel (*Redaktion 1—25,* 230—49). Further: R. P. Carroll, *From Chaos to Covenant,* 136—57.

[190] See now, most recently, the position of Norbert Lohfink, in the Colloquium Biblicum Lovaniense Volume, *Le Livre de Jérémie: Le Prophète et son milieu. Les Oracles et leur transmission* (P.-M. Bogaert, ed; Leuven: University Press, 1981). In the article "Der junge Jeremia als Propagandist und Poet: Zum Grundstock von Jer 30—31," (351—68) Lohfink joins Holladay ("A Coherent Chronology of Jeremiah's Early Career," 58—73) in arguing that Jeremiah makes no clear appearance in the book until the accession year of Jehoiakim. Unlike Holladay, however, he feels that attempts to say more than this (e. g., that the "thirteenth year" of Jer 1:2 is the prophet's birth-date) create more problems than they solve (351, n. 4).

[191] Moreover, he is not mentioned by name in Kings (23:34) as the actual predecessor of Jehoiakim — "Pharaoh Neco made Eliakim the son of Josiah king *in the place of his father Josiah.*" The Egyptians probably never considered him king — did Jehoiakim? See Malamat's discussion in "Last Years," 207.

for it was long, it was riddled with internal and external problems, and it fell directly on the central years of the prophet's activity.

Up to this point direct work with the Jeremiah tradition has not been undertaken, since much of the socio-historical data involved in our investigation pre-dates these texts.[192] The historicity of the material — that is, its reliability for historical reconstruction — is related to broader and often quite complex literary analyses; it is for this reason that a more directly literary evaluation of the Jeremiah tradition follows in Chapter Four. The present investigation deals primarily with details arising in the tradition (dates, personages, events) whose general veracity has not been questioned from a form- or redaction-critical perspective. When necessary, literary questions will be taken up which have a clear effect on historical reconstruction. The methodological commitment to treating socio-historical questions before literary analysis demands this line of approach.

Much of the arguably early material from Jeremiah, now located in chs. 1—20, 30—31, is undated and unrelated to any specific king (e. g., Josiah) or circumstance in the life of the prophet. Of those sections of the book explicitly related to Judahite kings, the majority tell of events during the reign of Zedekiah (chs. 21, 24, 27—29, 32—34, 51:59 ff., 52). But a number of chapters are also directly tied to the reign of Jehoiakim. These include: the Temple Sermon (Ch. 26) at the beginning of his reign; an oracle against Egypt/Jehoiakim (46:1—12) in his fourth year (605 B. C.); in the same year, perhaps at a later date, a speech counselling submission to Babylon, following Nebuchadnezzar's victory at Carchemish (25:1—29); in the same year, an account of the writing of Jeremiah's scroll (36:1—8); shortly thereafter, in November of his fifth year, the same scroll is read (vv. 11—19), destroyed (vv. 20—26) and rewritten (v. 32); a further oracle is delivered against Egypt, perhaps around 601, anticipating victory over the Egyptians (46:13—26); the account of the Rechabites' movement to Jerusalem (Ch. 35) is probably from Jehoiakim's final years, when the Babylonians sent raiding parties against Judah (2 Kgs 24:2; Jer 35:11).[193]

In these chapters, especially Chs. 26 and 36, a direct view is given of Jehoiakim's persecution of Jeremiah, and other prophets (26:23). An important glimpse is also provided of Jehoiakim's position vis-à-vis key families, scribes, ministers and officials in Jerusalem, many of whom are

---

[192] The majority view that the prophet began his prophetic activity in the "thirteenth year of Josiah" (627 B. C.) remains compelling. Though much of the poetic material in chs. 1—20, 30—31 is dateable to these years, texts from these chapters have not been cited because they are not explicitly dated (furthermore, they contain minimal historical data). More will be said about Jeremiah's early preaching in Chapter Four.

[193] Ch. 45:1—5 claims to be set in the fourth year of Jehoiakim, but its present placement in the book complicates this somewhat; Bright includes 19:1—2,10—11,14—15; 20:1—6 among material dated to the reign of Jehoiakim, but this too must be investigated at a later point.

named.[194] The clear impression the texts convey is of a king concerned with maintenance of the state and the survival of the capital at any cost. He regards the message and activity of the prophet Jeremiah, demanding Judah's submission to Babylon and calling for the destruction of the state unless the *tôrāh* of Yahweh is obeyed (26:1—6), as treasonous.

It should be stressed that all of these chapters, with the exception of Ch. 35, situate themselves at an historical period (609—604 B. C.) when submission to Babylon was by no means a necessity; it was not yet clear that Babylon would emerge as the superior power in the region. The Battle for Carchemish (*CCK*, 66) established Babylonian superiority over Egypt on the Euphrates and spelled the end of Assyria, but the question of control over Syria/Palestine was not closed in 605 B. C. In any event, a policy of submission to Babylon ran counter to the official policy of Jehoiakim, which undergirded his right to rule: viz, allegiance to Egypt. Especially during these years, Jeremiah's position as stated in 36:29 (from the mouth of Jehoiakim himself) stood squarely against the king's own position. As a result of Jehoiakim's recalcitrance, Jeremiah's own extreme sentence of judgment over him and his descendents is also included in the text, once in Jer 36:30—31 and again in Jer 22:13—23. Before examining these important texts for a clue to Jeremiah's evaluation of Jehoiakim and his house, it is necessary to construct a brief outline of significant internal and international events.

In 609, after the exiling of Jehoahaz, Jehoiakim undoubtably sought his right as eldest (2 Kgs 23:36) to the throne of Judah.[195] Unfortunately, the background of his selection by Necho is left unclear in 2 Kgs 23:34; there can only be conjecture about certain details based upon what is reported of his reign elsewhere in 2 Kings and in the Book of Jeremiah. There is a suggestion in 1 Esdras 1:36 that Jehoiakim had a hand in the overthrow of his half-brother, and based upon what is known of his subsequent career this is not difficult to believe.[196] It may even have been

---

[194] This particular material will be examined more closely in Chapter Four, in reference to the authorship of the Scribal Chronicle.

[195] This is the opinion of the majority of scholars, including Malamat ("Twilight," 126), Tadmor (*Encyclopedia Judaica*, "Jehoahaz," 1316), B. Oded (Hayes & Miller, eds, *History*, 469), Spalinger ("Egypt and Babylonia: A Survey [c. 620 B. C.—550 B. C.]," *Studien zur Altägyptischen Kultur* 5 [1977] 226), Ishida (*Royal Dynasties*, 151—54, 163—65). Cf. W. F. Albright ("The Seal of Eliakim," 92), who argues that Jehoahaz was in fact the eldest. He bases his opinion not on the information provided by the Chronicler (1 Chr 3:15) which is, as he rightly concludes, incorrect or confused, but on the fact that the information in 2 Kgs 23:36 is faulty since it implies that Josiah was only fourteen when he fathered Jehoiakim, "a most abnormal age even in Palestine" (92). This is an unusual fact, but the weight of the biblical evidence confirms it. 2 Kgs 23:31 and 23:36 are absolutely clear about the ages of Jehoahaz and Jehoiakim; see Ezek 19:1—4 and Jer 22:10—11 as well.

[196] See the remarks of Malamat ("Last Years," 207; "Twilight," 127) and Joseph Scharbert, *Die Prophetie Israels um 600 v. Chr.* (Köln: J. P. Bachem, 1967) 128—9.

the case that Jehoiakim ignored the reign of Jehoahaz in reckoning his own regnal years, though this involves the more complex question of chronology for this period. Even Kings ignores the reign of Jehoahaz at 23:34, as if the action by the "people of the land" was irregular or illegal. In any case the clear fact remains that Jehoahaz' reign was quite short (three months) as recorded by the Dtr Historian (23:31). When one considers that during this time Jehoahaz was occupied with a journey to Riblah, his actual tenure in Jerusalem is inconsequential, and so it likely seemed to Jehoiakim and his (pro-Egyptian) support group. It is not clear from 2 Kgs 23:34 whether Jehoiakim was installed by Necho in Jerusalem or by order from the Pharaoh from Riblah. The latter seems more probable, as a journey to Jerusalem is not specifically mentioned. If this was the case, then significant support for Jehoiakim was already in place; at any rate, no challenge to his kingship at his accession to the throne is known. However dormant the pro-Egyptian party may have been during the reign of Josiah, they now were the force to reckon with in the capital.

The irregularity of this entire affair must be emphasized: a younger prince is seized and anointed by the "people of the land"; he is almost immediately summoned to Riblah; his half-brother Eliakim is appointed king by Necho and given a new throne-name; the "people of the land" are taxed to pay tribute to Necho. At no point in the history of the dynasty do half-brothers succeed one another to the throne. The one exception took place in the Northern Kingdom: Jehoram of the Omri dynasty succeeded his brother Ahaziah. But this occurred only "because Ahaziah had no son" (2 Kgs 1:17).[197] The setting aside of the principle of primogeniture in order to place Jehoahaz on the throne was an event of major significance, which is why he was anointed.[198] What exists then for the first time in Judah is the potential for serious questions about the legitimacy of the reigning king. This is one of the key reasons for internal turmoil and instability in Judah and Jerusalem for this period, especially when one observes the continued irregularities in the dynastic system up to the Fall of Jerusalem and beyond. The question of the legitimacy of the reigning king will be taken up in the section that follows. It is sufficient at this point to make the observation that these irregularities had an impact on

---

[197] Ishida, *Royal Dynasties,* 152.

[198] Malamat ("Last Kings," 140) cites a Talmudic reference (Jer. *Horayot* 3,47) which states: "a king, the son of king, is only to be anointed in the case of a contested succession." Did the "people of the land" change Shallum's name to Jehoahaz ("Yahweh-has-seized") in order to stress Yahweh's special choice of him over Jehoiakim? Ishida (*Royal Dynasties,* 163, n. 42) notes that the use of the verb *lqḥ* at 2 Kgs 23:30 is striking (cf. 2 Sam 7:8). The use of this verb, and the change of name to Jehoahaz, suggests Yahweh's choice of Shallum just as David was "chosen" or "taken" from "tending the sheep" ('ănî lĕqaḥtîkā min-hannāweh mē'aḥar haṣṣō'n).

Judahite society and on Jeremiah's assessment of individual kings in this period.

Jehoiakim's 11-year reign can be partitioned into three periods: Egyptian Allegiance (609—604), Babylonian Vassalage (603—601), and Revolt Against Babylon (600—597). Although the question as to why some oracles in Jeremiah are explicitly dated while others are not is a complex one,[199] it is worth noting that the passages which give indication of date and setting fall chiefly in the first period. No passages can be dated with absolute confidence to the period of Babylonian vassalage, and very little is known of this time from either Jeremiah or Kings. Reports concerning the last period are found in Kings, especially with respect to the siege of the city and the broader circumstances of 597 (2 Kgs 24:1—7). Several oracles in the Book of Jeremiah concerning the Fall of Jerusalem, though undated, fit well in this final period. Included here are the units: Jer 12:7—13; Jer 13:15—27; Jer 14:2—9; Jer 14:17—22; Jer 15:5—9; there is general agreement that these oracles are not to be included among the secondary expansions of the deuteronomistic redaction.[200] The only question would be whether they were originally delivered on the later occasion of the Fall of Jerusalem in 587 B. C.[201] It is clear, however, that Jer 13:15 ff. comes from this period, since it contains a reference to Jehoiachin and Nehushta, the queen mother (13:18). The oracles against Jehoiakim (22:13—23) and Jehoiachin (22:24—30) should also be dated to this period, along with Jeremiah's word to the Rechabites (Ch. 35).

Throughout Jehoiakim's first five years Egyptian control was exercised over the region of Judah. Spalinger in particular has been helpful in defining the exact nature of this control.[202] In contrast to Nebuchadnezzar, Necho II never campaigned to bring about thorough military domination over Judah. This does not mean that the Egyptians failed to take the region seriously. Saite control over the Levant was real, and with respect to Syria and Phoenecia, could be strongly enforced. But it was more cautious, more commercially oriented, and more realistic than its Neo-Babylonian counterpart.[203] In designating Jehoiakim's first five years a period of Egyptian allegiance, it is to be stressed that Jehoiakim saw his

---

[199] See my remarks in Chapter Four, Section III/B.

[200] Thiel, *Redaktion* 1—25, 162 ff.

[201] See, for example, the analysis of Scharbert, *Prophetie*, 197—246.

[202] Anthony Spalinger, "Egypt and Babylonia: A Survey (c. 620 B. C.—550 B. C.)," *Studien zur Altägyptischen Kultur* 5 (1977) 221—44. Further: "The Concept of Monarchy in the Saite Epoch," *Or* 47 (1978) 12—36. The *SAK* article is an excellent supplement to the works of Malamat; other secondary sources for this period include H. J. Katzenstein's *Tyre* and Freedy & Redford's "Dates in Ezekiel." Henri Cazelles' contribution in the Colloquium Biblicum Lovaniense volume is also quite helpful ("La vie de Jérémie dans son contexte national et international," *Le Livre de Jérémie*, 21—39).

[203] Spalinger, "Egypt and Babylonia," 226 ff.

best interests served in loyalty to his Saite overlords. The only tribute exacted was in Jehoiakim's accession year, and this was only a nominal amount. What Jehoiakim probably expected in return was Egyptian military assistance. Unfortunately, when the years before the "first Fall" arrived, this assistance was lacking. Nevertheless, in the early period of his rule the Egyptians had a much greater potential for military strength, under the able leadership of Necho. Judah had seen an exhibition of this at Megiddo.

The Babylonian Chronicle assists greatly in reconstructing events on the international scene. At the period of Jehoiakim's accession, brought about by the Egyptians, Necho controlled the region "from the brook of Egypt to the river Euphrates" (2 Kgs 24:7).[204] During the years 608—606 the Neo-Babylonians, still under Nabopolassar, were involved in battles to the north, on the upper Euphrates and the Urartu border (CCK, 20). In 606/5 the Egyptians captured the Babylonian garrison at Kimuhu, a strategic site on the upper Euphrates, and Nabopolassar was forced to withdraw. In March 605 they took the initiative again and marched to capture Quramati; Nabopolassar had returned to Babylon in January of the same year, either because of poor health or age. In May/June of the same year the tide changed. The crown-prince Nebuchadnezzar led his forces to a decisive victory against the Egyptians ("to non-existence," CCK, 67) at Carchemish. The Chronicle states that at this time Nebuchadnezzar conquered the "whole area of the Hatti country," and in 604 "marched unopposed through Hatti-land." This is probably an exaggeration. Necho had not been in the field at Carchemish, and garrison troops were most likely the ones defeated.[205] Furthermore, it cannot be assumed that with this single victory the whole Levant came under Neo-Babylonian control; this would have required more active campaigning in the area. Egyptian control over the Philistine states and the *via maris* was not brought to an end by a Babylonian victory, however decisive, on the upper Euphrates.[206]

Several scholars argue that the Babylonian record is correct in depicting a thorough and immediate hegemony over Syria/Palestine by 604; they also conclude that Jehoiakim was among those kings who appeared before

---

[204] Malamat, "Twilight," 128, n. 10; also W. F. Albright, "Seal of Eliakim," 89—90, and S. Herrmann, *History,* 277.

[205] Wisemann, *CCK,* 24, 28; Katzenstein, *Tyre,* 306, n. 66.

[206] On the extent and nature of Egyptian hegemony over this area, see Spalinger, "Egypt and Babylonia," 227—231, and Katzenstein, *Tyre,* 304. Commentaries which urge the transposition of 2 Kgs 24:7 before 2 Kgs 24:1 in order to link directly Egypt's expulsion, Jehoiakim's vassalage, and Nebuchadnezzar's victory at Carchemish oversimplify the situation, even in the name of enlightened historical analysis (see even RSV notes). In one sense, the placement of 2 Kgs 24:7 is correct, since Egyptian influence remained in the area after 605 (and in fact, after 597 — see Jer 37:5).

Nebuchadnezzar, still in his accession year (604), to pay tribute.[207] The kings, however, are not named in the Chronicle and there is no evidence from the biblical record that Jehoiakim was among them.

What the account in 2 Kgs 24:1 reveals is that Jehoiakim was a Babylonian vassal for three years before he rebelled. With Malamat it is reasonable to settle on the events of 601 as those which would give the Judahite king cause to question his vassal-status.[208] The Babylonian Chronicle is quite candid that in this year Nebuchadnezzar's attempt to exercise control over the Egyptians failed (CCK, 29,71); in fact, the army was forced to return to Babylon for at least a year's refitting. From this set of events it is to be concluded that Jehoiakim paid tribute in 603, 602, and 601, and that when the Babylonians were forced to retreat from the region after the Egyptian non-victory in the winter of 601, he decided to rebel.

Fixing the date by determining the end of Babylonian vassalage, it is possible to determine the first year of tribute from Jehoiakim as 603 B. C. It is logical to assume that it took Nebuchadnezzar at least a full year to establish his control over Syria/Palestine and the territory of Judah, the confident tone of his own Chronicle notwithstanding.[209] Furthermore, there is no reason to assume that Jehoiakim quickly or easily shifted his allegiance from the Egyptians, who had after all placed him in power. What is more, the text relates that still in the fifth year of Jehoiakim (Jer 36:9), probably the winter of 604, the king had not yet given up his pro-Egyptian stance. But Nebuchadnezzar's victory over Ashkelon (CCK, 28,69) in November of that year convinced Jeremiah that submission to Babylon was long overdue. During a public fast a scroll containing his words was read before the people (Ch. 36). This is one of the prose sections of Jeremiah provided with a clear date during the reign of Jehoiakim.

Internal evidence from the Book of Jeremiah confirms what is now known about Egyptian influence in Judah during this period (609—604 B. C.). The oracle of judgment against Jehoiakim found in Jer 22:13—19 (20—23) is agreed by all to reflect Jeremiah's judgment over the king's unjust and ill-timed building project; furthermore, it is concluded by some

---

[207] Wisemann, CCK, 28. It might also be added at this juncture that the reports in Dan 1:1 ff. and possibly 2 Chr 36:6, which suggest a real or intended deportation of Jehoiakim (according to Dan 1:1, in his *third* year, together with a siege of Jerusalem and deportation) have in turn, influenced the accounts of Boressus and Josephus. With most scholars, they are to be taken as erroneous; their intention may be to make more accurate the "seventy-year" tally as a prediction of the length of exile (as found in Jeremiah). For a discussion of the issue, see Gerhard Larsson, "When did the Babylonian Captivity Begin?" *JTS* 18 (1967) 417—23. See also Chapter Three, Section I.

[208] "Twilight," 131—2. Also, Albright, "Seal of Eliakim," 89—90; S. Herrmann, *History,* 276—7.

[209] W. F. Albright, "Seal of Eliakim," 89—90.

that this project (see vv. 13—17) was carried out in conscious imitation of
Egyptian style.[210] In a series of articles, Yohanan Aharoni has steadfastly
maintained that a citadel/palace at Ramat Raḥel (probably biblical Beth-
haccherem, Jer 6:1) can be dated to this period.[211] The cite is about the
same distance from Jerusalem as Anathoth, lying to the southwest. Aharoni
has discovered certain details here (cedar ceiling beams; vermilion deco-
ration) that match the account of Jer 22:13—17. But the sheer size of the
building (90 × 50 m), its shape ("in a manner only used in royal palaces"),
and its proximity to Jerusalem are the most convincing indicators that this
was a royal building of some sort. Aharoni concludes that this palace/
citadel was the summer residence of Jehoiakim (note that his Jerusalem
residence is referred to as a winter house [bêt haḥōrep] in Jer 36:22) as well
as an important military outpost: "We may conjecture that it was an army
camp . . . which served as a huge military stronghold near Jerusalem, on
the main highway leading to the south."[212]

Originally its construction was dated by Aharoni to the latter years
of Jehoiakim. He reasoned it was built as a defensive outpost against the
Babylonians in the period following his revolt (c 600). R. De Vaux is,
however, correct in arguing for its construction during the first years of
his reign, when the question of Babylonian domination of the region was
not yet settled.[213] Whether or not it was built in Egyptian style is not
clear — Aharoni makes no reference to this in his analysis of the details
of the palace. However, if the dating of its construction in Jehoiakim's
first years is accurate, then it certainly would have required Egyptian
approval; at a minimum, it could not have been built if it was viewed by
Necho as an anti-Egyptian move. But most of all, there is no reason to
assume that the loyal Jehoiakim would have had such a plan in mind.[214]

---

[210] See, for example, the commentary of Rudolph ("nach ägyptischem Muster") (*Jeremia*,
121) and Malamat, "Last Years," 350, n 19. Compare also Bright (xlvii), Hyatt (*IDB*,
982), and Cazelles ("La vie de Jérémie," 32).

[211] "Excavations at Ramat Raḥel, 1954: Preliminary Report," *IEJ* 6 (1956) 102—11; 137—57;
"Excavations at Ramat Raḥel," *BA* 24 (1961) 98—118; *Excavations at Ramat Raḥel, Seasons
1959 and 1960* (Rome: Centro di Studi Semitici, 1962) esp. 60. The best summary can be
found in "Beth-Haccherem," *Archaeology and Old Testament Study* (D. Winton Thomas,
ed; Oxford: Clarendon, 1967) 178—83. For an excellent discussion and critical evaluation,
see R. De Vaux's review of Aharoni's 1962 work in *RB* 73 (1966) 270—1.

[212] "Beth-Haccherem," 178.

[213] *RB* 73, 271.

[214] Incidentally, it was at this same cite that the controversial seal with the inscription *l'lyqm
n'r Ywkn* was found. All have agreed that *Ywkn* (vocalized *Yawkin*) could be an abbreviated
form of *Yehôyākîn* or *Yôyākîn*. It is by no means clear that this Jehoiachin was the son
of Jehoiakim, the king (deported) of Judah, as Albright suggested ("Seal of Eliakim"),
or a private citizen (Nachman Avigad, "New Light on the Naʿar Seals," *Magnalia Dei:
The Mighty Acts of God* [FS G. E. Wright; F. M. Cross, Werner Lemke, Patrick Miller,
eds; Garden City: Doubleday, 1976] 294—300). See also A. Malamat, "Twilight," 138,
n. 34. The dual kingship issue will be discussed in Chapter Three following.

If these conclusions are correct, it is all the more clear why Jehoiakim and his palace construction were condemned by Jeremiah. Not only did such a project require forced labor (22:13b) and serve as a symbol of Jehoiakim's unjust (*bĕlōʾ mišpāṭ*) and illegitimate (*bĕlōʾ ṣedeq*) rule, it also promoted his pro-Egyptian policy, which, as already seen, stood at odds with Yahweh's will for Judah.

There is one other interesting detail which has been picked up in Jeremiah's oracles. It is quite likely that references to "Gilead" and "Lebanon" at Jer 22:6b,20,23 and 46:11 are allusions to this same palace of Jehoiakim, since the forests of these two regions provided the timber for the project (see 1 Kgs 7:2—5; Isa 22:8, "House of the Forest").[215] In this regard, de Jong has argued that in the oracle against Egypt (46:1—12), which almost all grant as authentic to the prophet Jeremiah, the rapprochement between Necho and Jehoiakim is hinted at and actively condemned by Jeremiah. The reference to Yahweh's vengeance in v. 10 is specifically related to revenge for the death of Josiah at Megiddo. De Jong even argues that, as in Ch 22, "Gilead" is an allusion to Jehoiakim's "House of Forest"; in other words, Egypt is called to seek assistance from his ally/ vassal Jehoiakim, but in so doing "both fall together" (v. 12). Whether this interpretation is accepted or not, it is clear that both segments of the oracle (vv. 1—12; vv. 13—24) are concerned with Egyptian aggression against the foe "in the north country" (v. 10).[216] The first is certainly to be dated to the period of Egyptian hegemony over Judah. Most likely, it was uttered by the prophet shortly before Carchemish (605 B. C.).[217]

One unusual reference to Egypt, also from this period, occurs at Jer 26:20—23. This brief notice, concerning the prophesying and political murder of one Uriah ben Shemaiah from Kiriath-jearim, is used to serve as an example of prophets who, like Jeremiah, preached judgment against Jerusalem (also Micah of Moresheth, vv. 18—19). It is interesting to note that when "King Jehoiakim, all his warriors and all the princes heard his words" and "sought to put him to death" (v. 21), Uriah chose to flee for refuge to Egypt. Possibly he believed he could find political asylum there,

---

[215] See especially C. de Jong, "Deux oracles contre les Nations, reflets de la politique etrangère de Joaquim," *Le Livre de Jérémie,* 369—79; also Bright, *Jeremiah,* 141; Rudolph, *Jeremia,* 119; Thiel, *Redaktion 1—25,* 239.

[216] The clearest allusions to the "palace of Jehoiakim" are found in Ch. 22 (v. 6b, 23) and Ch. 21 (v. 14b). In Ch. 46, the statement "Go up to Gilead and take balm, O virgin daughter of Egypt" is more difficult to see as a reference to this palace; as in 8:22, "Gilead" is also known for its healing balm. See M. Noth, "Beiträge zur Geschichte der Ostjordanlande: I. Das Land Gilead als Siedlungsgebiet israelitischer Sippen," *PJB* (1941) 98—9.

[217] Bright, *Jeremiah,* 308; John G. Snaith, "Literary Criticism and Historical Investigation in Jeremiah Chapter XLVI," *JSS* 46 (1972) 15—32.

but the reasons for his choice are not given.[218] With apparent ease he is extradicted to Jerusalem, again probably because of Jehoiakim's relationship with Necho and the Egyptians. Elnathon ben Achbor and "others with him" are responsible for bringing him back to the capital, but he is slain by Jehoiakim and cast in the burial ground of the common people (v. 23). It is significant that when Jeremiah issues his most severe oracle against Jehoiakim, preserved in two places (22:18−19; 36:30−31), a similar but worse fate is said to await him:

> With the burial of an ass he shall be buried, dragged and cast forth beyond the gates of Jerusalem (22:19)
> His dead body shall be cast out to the heat by day and the frost by night (36:30)

While it is unlikely that the Lachish Letters fit in this period, the same is not true of the Aramaic document referred to as the Saqqara Papyrus.[219] Only nine lines long, it records the urgent plea of an unknown ruler of an unknown territory, Adon, to the Egyptian Pharaoh, requesting military aid. Explicit mention is made to the threatening Babylonians; a vassal arrangement of some kind is presupposed between Adon and the Egyptians. Some have argued that Adon was the ruler of Ashkelon.[220] If this were true the letter could be dated fairly specifically, since the Babylonian Chronicle (*CCK*, 69) records that Ashkelon fell to the Babylonians in 604 B. C. However, with Horn it seems that speculations about the precise city from which Adon makes appeal are flawed simply from lack of details in the letter.[221]

What is certain is that conflict between Babylonia and Egypt forms the background of the letter. As such, it could fit at any time during the period between 609−580 B. C. Because it is fairly certain that Necho II and Jehoiakim had some kind of vassal arrangement or "mutual assistance pact" during 609−603, the letter could be seen as reflective of similar circumstances at a similar period. But there is no reason to exclude any time especially between 609−587 from consideration. The important point to note is that Egyptian activity in the region is presupposed (although

---

[218] It should be mentioned at this point that the unnamed prophet in the Lachish Letters was considered by Torczyner (*The Lachish Letters* [London: Oxford, 1938] 204−8) to be this same Uriah — almost all agree this is quite unlikely (see bibliography and discussion in Pardee, *Handbook*, 77). Furthermore, the letters better fit circumstances during Zedekiah's reign; accordingly, they will be discussed below.

[219] H. L. Ginsberg, "An Aramaic Contemporary of the Lachish Letters," *BASOR* 111 (1948) 24−27; J. Bright, "A New Letter in Aramaic, Written to a Pharaoh of Egypt," *BA* 12 (1949) 46−52; Joseph Fitzmyer, "The Aramaic Letter of King Adon to the Egyptian Pharaoh," *Bib* 46 (1965) 41−6; Siegfried Horn, "Where and When was the Aramaic Saqqara Papyrus Written?" *AUSS* 6 (1968) 30−45.

[220] Fitzmyer, Albright, Ginsberg, Bright.

[221] Horn, "Where and When?" 45. Ironically, the mention of Aphek (1 4) has been more problematic than helpful, since at least five "Apheks" are known.

lacking at the time the letter is written!). This argues for its placement at a period when Egyptian influence was at its potentially strongest point in Syria/Palestine. For the reasons rehearsed above, this period falls between Josiah's encounter at Megiddo (or a little earlier, see *CCK*, 62 ff.) and Jehoiakim's vassalage to Babylon (603—601 B. C.); if Jehoiakim expected Egyptian help after his revolt c. 600 B. C., then it could be dated to this period as well.[222]

2 Kings 24:1 says simply that "in his days" Nebuchadnezzar "came up" to Judah and Jehoiakim became his vassal for three years. The best evidence suggests that these three years were 603, 602, and 601. It is probably to these years that the Babylonian Chronicle makes reference when it speaks of Nebuchadnezzar's "marching unopposed" through Syria/Palestine (*CCK*, 70—1). Unfortunately the tablet is broken at significant points for the 2nd and 3rd years of Nebuchadnezzar (603 and 602 B. C.). But what is clear is that in 603 a "powerful army" was called up; the expression suggests an unusually concerted effort, directed in this instance toward Syria/Palestine (*CCK*, 28). Siegetowers and other heavy equipment are mentioned as well in the text. The entry for 602 does not help identify more specifically the objective of these campaigns, but what is clearly stated is that much tribute is collected from Hatti-land and taken to Akkad (*CCK*, 70, line 4). The entry for 601, Nebuchadnezzar's 4th year, mentions yet again his marching unopposed through Hatti-land; it is not until the winter of that year that the candid report of his losses against Necho appears. It can be confidently assumed that for these three years King Jehoiakim was among those paying tribute to Nebuchadnezzar. Only after the Babylonian loss and retreat at the end of 601 could Jehoiakim contemplate rebellion.

It is striking that there are no oracles in Jeremiah dated to this period of Babylonian vassalage. As mentioned above, the problem of dating is a complex one, especially since only certain selected passages (often in prose) are supplied with a date to begin with; this makes it difficult to state unequivocally that no material in the book emerged during these three years. What makes the period unusual is that Jehoiakim, through no choice of his own, actually obeys the word of Jerusalem to submit to the Babylonians as the servant of Yahweh. It would be tempting to try and piece together these three years as they relate to the person and activity of Jeremiah. The texts record, for instance, that he was prohibited from speaking in the temple by the fourth year (605) of Jehoiakim (Jer 36:5); it might be assumed that this command to silence extended to his entire public ministry, thereby explaining the lack of clearly dated material from this period. Some have tried to date many of his "confessions," as private

---

[222] All of the foregoing is dependent upon the assumption that Judah and Adon's region were in similar circumstances — an assumption impossible at this point to prove.

works, to this period.[223] But this raises the question as to tradition-history of this material, which is burdened by many complex issues.[224] Rather than add new theories to an already burgeoning number, it is enough to note that no prose sections, such as often focus on both the words and activity of the prophet, are dated to this period. Jehoiakim was probably a reluctant Babylonian vassal; these were not years when Jeremiah gloated over the success of his preaching.

This conclusion is confirmed when one notes (1) how quickly Jehoiakim seizes the opportunity to revolt in 600 B. C. and (2) how quickly Jeremiah resumes his harsh diatribe against the king (22:18—19), bitterly rejecting hopes for the avoidance of Babylonian vassalage or sanctuary in Jerusalem (9:10—11; 12:7—13; 15:5—9). The biblical texts say nothing explicit about Jehoiakim trusting in Egyptian assistance, but if the timing of the revolt was determined by Egyptian successes in 601, as seems likely, then Jehoiakim assumed he could count on Egyptian support in his bid for independence.[225] The Babylonians had been forced to retreat from the region following this battle. The Babylonian Chronicle reports that Nebuchadnezzar remained "in his own land" in 600/599 B. C. Only in the winter of 599 does he again muster this army and march to Hatti-land, though in this year he had to remain content with sending forth raiding parties against desert tribes. His objective in this year was both defensive: to guard the areas he still controlled (Riblah, Hamath) from Egyptian encroachment from the southwest; and offensive: to strengthen his own position in preparation for a thrust into Palestine and eventually Egypt.

It is significant that the Chronicle mentions the personal return of Nebuchadnezzar to Babylon in March 598 (*CCK*, 70—71); garrison troops were probably left behind in order to maintain Babylonian strength in the region to the west of Palestine. If it is supposed that such troops made retaliatory raids during the spring and summer of 598 B. C., an explanation is provided for the notice in 2 Kgs 24:2, which tells of harrassment from bands of Syrians, Ammonites, and Moabites, alongside certain "Chaldeans," probably garrison troops left behind in the region.[226] These various

---

[223] See, for example, Josef Scharbert (*Die Prophetie*, 188 ff.) who speaks of these as years when Jeremiah and Baruch fled for safety to the north and Jeremiah composed "die bitteren Klagen über die treulosen Mitbürger und Verwandten von Anatot (11:18—23)" and "über die scheinbare Sinnlosigkeit des eigenen Lebens in 15:10 ff. niedergeschrieben worden sein" (188).

[224] See, for example, the study of H. Graf Reventlow: *Liturgie und prophetisches Ich bei Jeremia* (Gütersloh: Gerd Mohn, 1963) 205—57; for a recent survey of options for interpretation, see Norbert Ittmann, *Die Konfessionen Jeremias: Ihre Bedeutung für die Verkündigung des Propheten* (WMANT 54; Neukirchen: Neukirchener, 1981) esp. 1—20.

[225] This is stated bluntly by Josephus (*Antiq. Jud.* X.6 (88—9) to be the actual situation; his historical reliability is however not beyond question.

[226] This is the view of Malamat, "Last Years," 209; Gray, *I & II Kings,* 758; Hayes & Miller, 470—1.

tribesmen "may have been induced to co-operate with Babylonian garrison troops in raids on those districts, including Judah, which were not loyal to Nebuchadnezzar."[227]

In the biblical account of the "first Fall of Jerusalem" (beginning at 2 Kgs 24:1—10) several significant features emerge when one takes the order of presentation seriously. Following the revolt of Jehoiakim, dateable to around 600, the emphasis falls first of all on this raiding activity (vv. 2—3) by area tribesmen; perhaps it had begun even prior to 598 B. C., the date suggested above. It is specifically this activity which is interpreted as occurring "according to the word of Yahweh" in order "to remove Judah out of his sight" (vv. 2—3). It is also in this particular context that the unusually cryptic notice of Jehoiakim's death (v. 6) is mentioned. The actual siege of the city by the servants of Nebuchadnezzar, as well as the appearance of the king himself, does not occur until after the death of Jehoiakim is reported. A reasonable assumption is that attacks on Judahite territory took place as early as 599 and continued right up to the time when Nebuchadnezzar appeared on the scene and formally captured the city (March 16, 597). Sometime prior to this date, at least three months according to the account of 2 Kgs 24:8, Jehoiakim died — the details of his death are not given.[228]

It has been stated that the "first Fall of Jerusalem" was an unusually swift and efficient affair, the siege itself lasting little more than a month or two.[229] This statement is misleading. Noth mounts the thesis that Nebuchadnezzar's decision to take Jerusalem was based upon the news of Jehoiakim's death, and the desire to place a ruler in power "after his own heart" (*CCK*, 71). Unfortunately, this makes it appear as though Nebuchadnezzar's decision was based solely on the fact of Jehoiakim's death, thereby collapsing the period of Babylonian pressure on the capital and the Judahite countryside. As noted, Nebuchadnezzar had for several years been strengthening his position in the region; moreover, the death of Jehoiakim probably came about precisely as a result of these raids or at least in the context of external military pressure on the capital. The report of 2 Kings (24:10) suggests that "servants" of Nebuchadnezzar were involved in the siege of Jerusalem prior to his appearance. In the context of earlier raiding activity directed at Judahite territory, the siege and military pressure on the capital is understandable, even before the "king of Akkad" put in an appearance.[230] The Babylonian Chronicle makes it

---

[227] Wiseman, *CCK*, 32.

[228] A full discussion of Jehoiakim's mysterious death follows in Chapter Three.

[229] M. Noth, "Die Einnahme von Jerusalem im Jahre 597 v. Chr.," *ZDPV* 74 (1958).

[230] Malamat ("Twilight," 133) states: "Jerusalem was already under full siege by 'his (Nebuchadnezzar's) servants', probably Babylonian occupation troops and possibly also auxiliary forces stationed in the West."

clear that the main objective of Nebuchadnezzar's campaign was the takeover of Jerusalem; but preparation for this campaign had been going on since 599. From the start, then, the campaign was directed against the rebellious Jehoiakim, who had throughout his reign made clear his pro-Egyptian loyalties.[231]

Additional proof of the extended nature of military pressure on Judah prior to the actual takeover of the capital in 597 B. C. is provided by several sources beyond the account of 2 Kgs 24:1—9. Several of the Arad ostraca (esp. § 24, § 40) tell of distinct military pressure from the Edomites in territory south of the capital (Ramath-Negeb); as such, they should probably be dated to this same period.[232] In other words, Edomites may have been among those raiding parties in league with the garrison troops of Nebuchadnezzar.[233] From the Book of Jeremiah, an extended prose passage (Ch. 35) dated only "in the days of Jehoiakim" also sheds light on circumstances in this period. Chapter 35 tells of the movement of the Rechabites to Jerusalem "for fear of the army of the Chaldeans and the army of the Syrians" (35:11). But far more relevant are the numerous oracles of Jeremiah which describe in extremely dark terms the approaching catastrophe of 597. Included here are the collection of statements from Jeremiah which anticipate the final destruction of the city and the wholesale deportation of its people (particularly within Chs. 9—15):

> "pastures of wilderness" (9:11) "a heap of ruins" (9:12) "lair of jackals" (9:12) "a desolation without inhabitant" (9:12) "ruined, utterly shamed" (9:20) "death in our windows" (9:22) "like dung upon the open field" (9:23) "a desolate wilderness" (12:10) "no flesh has peace" (12:12) "wholly taken into exile" (13:19) "a woman in travail" (13:21) "chaff driven by the wind from the desert" (13:24) "smitten with a great

---

[231] Noth acknowledges the presence of garrison troops in the region, but minimizes their role. The main reason for this is his desire to explain the odd timing of Nebuchadnezzar's campaign (in winter) by juxtaposing it with news of the death of Jehoiakim. Noth may be correct that Nebuchadnezzar had a stake in the issue of throne-changes in Judah. The point is that his designs on Judah were of a piece with much larger plans focused on Egypt. The time was right for mobilization toward the south and stabilization of the region. The death of Jehoiakim may have been a greater incentive in these plans. Incidentally, winter campaigns, as Noth himself is forced to admit, are not unknown in the Babylonian Chronicle.

[232] Pardee, *Handbook,* 29,61; Y. Aharoni, "Hebrew Ostraca from Tel Arad," *IEJ* 16 (1966) 1—7; "Three Hebrew Ostraca from Arad," *BASOR* 197 (1970) 18.

[233] Syriac of 2 Kgs 24:2 reads "Edomites" in place of "Aramaens." Though a distinct animosity toward Edom emerged in texts during the exilic period (Obadiah; Ps 137), it is not clear whether this was a result of specific events in 599—597 or on more scattered occasions throughout the immediate preexilic period. See Jer 27:2ff., which tells of a conference attended by Edom, Moab, Tyre, Ammon, and Sidon; also Jer 40:11ff. The situation was probably as volatile in these small Palestinian and Transjordanian states as it was in Judah proper. For a discussion, see Jacob M. Myers, "Edom and Judah in the Sixth-Fifth Centuries B. C.," *Near Eastern Studies in Honor of William Foxwell Albright* (Hans Goedicke, ed; Baltimore and London: Johns Hopkins, 1971) 377—92.

wound" (14:17) "slain by the sword, diseases of famine" (14:18) "I have destroyed my people" (15:7) "widows more than the sand of the sea" (15:8) "a destroyer at noonday" (15:8) "the rest I will give to the sword" (15:9)

The bleakness of impending circumstances is due in part to the hyperbole of prophetic invective. But this observation should not wrest the oracles from specific historical moorings. It has been be argued, for example, that Jeremiah simply foresaw a situation in terms more extreme than what actually occurred.[234] But the credibility of his vision would have been compromised if it bore no resemblence to events as they had begun to unfold, even as early as 599 B. C.

The poetic tradition at this juncture of the book accurately reflects the situation as it evolved in the events leading up to 597 B. C.[235] It is clear, for example, that the severity of pronouncements made by Jeremiah against both Jehoiakim (22:13–17) and Jehoiachin (22:24–30) was upheld in the reports of the treatment they both eventually received.[236] In this regard it is striking that one of the most extreme oracles announcing judgment on Judah (13:19) falls in the context of judgment over Jehoiachin and Nehushta, the Queen-mother (13:18). Here the announcement of total exile (v. 19) is tied to an event which the biblical text reports as having taken place: the capture of the king and queen mother in 597 B. C. (see 2 Kgs 24:12 ff.). Similarly, Martin Noth relates another prophetic saying in this same unit 13:18–19, "the cities of the Negeb shall be shut up, and none shall open to them" (v. 19a), to actual events of the period.[237] These

---

[234] Rudolph asks, concerning the finality of 13:18: "Daß Jer im Widerspruch zum tatsächlichen Geschehen von völliger Wegführung Judas redet, mag gesteigerter Ausdruck des Schmerzes sein (vgl. Thr 1:1,3,7), vielleicht wußte man aber auch zu dem Zeitpunkt, als Jer diese Worte sprach, noch nichts davon, daß Nebuchadnezzar milder vorging, als man befürchtet hatte" (*Jeremia*, 83).

[235] In his Jeremiah commentary, Bright states concerning 9:16–21: "These verses are a dirge over the ruin of Jerusalem, perhaps uttered on the very eve of the siege and deportation of 598/7" (73); concerning 10:17–25: "This section begins (vss. 17–18) with a brief oracle, no doubt uttered as the Babylonians closed in upon Jerusalem in 598/7 . . ." (73); concerning 12:7–13: ". . . a poem describing Yahweh's sorrowful rejection of his people, probably composed while Judah was being overrun by marauding bands just prior to the Babylonian attack in 598/7" (88); a similar opinion is registered for Ch. 13 (p. 95) and 15:5–9 (p. 111).

[236] This appears to be clearer for Jehoiachin than Jehoiakim (see Chapter Three, Section I). Bright states with regard to Jer 13: "Most of them (the poems in Ch. 13), were apparently composed not long before the first deportation, in 597; one of them, indeed (vss. 18–19), addressed to Jehoiachin and the Queen Mother (cf. II Kings xxiv 8, 12), clearly was uttered just prior to Jerusalem's surrender that year (*Jeremiah*, 95).

[237] He states (*History*, 283): ". . . the Negeb was lost to the kingdom of Judah at this time (598) and the southern frontier running north to the latitude of Hebron established, which is well known to us as the southern frontier of the latter province of Judah in the Persian period." He also conjectures that this territory was annexed to the Edomites, a view which now finds verification in the Arad correspondence. See note above.

various statements from Jeremiah are inexplicable in the context of a sudden and swift Babylonian campaign, as is proposed by Noth.

A more serious problem for interpretation of the exilic period arises when one considers the *finality* with which events in 597 are described by Jeremiah, especially when compared with the events of 587 B. C.[238] In the traditional view, the "first Fall" is regarded as a foreshadowing of a much more final Fall in 587 B. C. But this particular sequencing is by no means clear in the Babylonian Chronicle, where the emphasis falls on the capture of Jerusalem in 597 B. C.[239] Nor is it clear that greater severity of judgment falls upon the city, king, and inhabitants in 587 B. C. in the Book of Jeremiah (39:1−10).[240] In spite of the many divergences between them, the reports of deportations in Jer 52:28−30, 2 Kgs 24:14−17, and 2 Kgs 25:11−12 are in essential agreement that, in terms of numbers involved, the exile of 597 B. C. was more extensive than that of 587 B. C. The Book of Ezekiel assumes both deportations in the year 597 and the migration of Yahweh from the capital (Ezek 11:23). The implications of this for the possibility of continued life in the land, and for an interpretation of the significance of 597 events, will be explored in the next chapter.

It is the Book of Jeremiah that continues (beyond Chs. 9−15) to depict life in the land after 597 B. C. in unbroken fashion. Jeremiah is left as a prophet to chronicle events in the land up to the Fall of Jerusalem in 587 (and beyond), and his assessment of circumstances in Judah is far more difficult to interpret than what is reported in Ezekiel.[241] But it is above all in the final shape of the Deuteronomistic History (through Ch. 25) that one pictures the events of 597 B. C. as preliminary to the "final" assault and destruction of 587 B. C.

H. Conflict in History: Conclusions

In moving toward a discussion of the historical and theological relationship between the events of 597 and 587 B. C., a decisive factor in the growth and redactional shaping of the Jeremiah tradition is touched

---

[238] Scholars seeking to identify these oracles from Jeremiah (now distributed throughout chs. 9−15) with events of 587 rather than 597 may anticipate the problems which would arise in the traditional view of Judah's final years if they were (correctly) taken as descriptive of 597. See, for example, Josef Scharbert, *Die Propheten Israels,* 197−246.

[239] Unfortunately, there is no record of events for 587 B. C.

[240] See Chapter Four, Section IV.

[241] The complexity of the Jeremiah presentation has as much to do with redactional factors as with the prophet's own shifting attitudes and perspective. See the treatment in Chapter Four. Compare, for example, the word of Jeremiah at 21:6−10, 24:8−10, or 37:10, where the destruction of the city and death of all inhabitants and potential survivors is proclaimed, with the word at 27:11,17, 38:17, or 42:10, where the possibility of life in the land is not foreclosed.

upon. As such, it is appropriate at this point to bring the socio/historical survey of the pre-exilic period to a conclusion. The kinds of issues that must now be considered fall better within the context of a more specifically literary analysis of Jeremiah and other exilic traditions. But there is one further justification for breaking at this point in our analysis. Greater continuity within Israel (sociological, religious, tradition-historical) is generally perceived to have existed before and after 597 events than before and after their 587 counterpart. Because the reader is accustomed to viewing 597 events as preliminary to a more profoundly experienced, final end to life in the land in 587, the impact 597 events had on the community in Judah and especially on those deported to Babylon is not given its full force. Bringing the socio/historical survey to a close here is meant to emphasize the significance 597 events had for the broader Israel, both as a deported community in Babylon and as a remnant community in Judah.

Ironically, the Book of Jeremiah in its present form encourages and discourages an emphasis on 597 events. Just the existence of the prophet in Judah and the continuance of the prophetic voice beyond 597, among other things, indicates a measure of continuity in Judah for a remnant community and its new king. On the other hand, the impact of 597 is by no means ignored in the Jeremiah traditions.[242] Within the Book of Jeremiah, there is a broad slice of poetic material (Chs. 9—15) associating the judgment of Yahweh with 597 events. One also sees the impact 597 deportations had in terms of dividing Israel into remnant and exiled communities (see, for example, Chs. 27—29). In other words, the exiling of king and community in 597, together with increased Babylonian presence in the Judahite capital and countryside, had a profound impact on the development of Jeremiah traditions.

There is one other factor that needs to be considered when one looks at the full 52-chapter presentation of the Book of Jeremiah. Jeremiah traditions record the prophet active not just within the post-597 remnant community, but also in the post-587 years after the "Fall of Jerusalem" (Jer 39—43). This suggests that even when the report of 587 events is given its appropriate place within the Jeremiah presentation (Jer 39), this does not happen in such a way as to set them in absolute distinction to 597 circumstances. Both episodes — in 597 and then in 587 — had a profound effect. After both, a measure of continuity and discontinuity was experienced. In Chapter Three, alternative perspectives on the coordination of 597 and 587 events are explored, particularly as they involve a theological evaluation of the post-597 remnant community and king (Zedekiah), and a fuller statement of Yahweh's design for judgment and restoration.

---

[242] The impact of 597 has had a major effect on the Book of Ezekiel and the Deuteronomistic History (2 Kgs 24).

In this chapter the role conflict plays in Judahite society prior to the events of Exile has been closely observed. The role played by political factions within the capital was examined, especially as it affected the institution of the Davidic monarchy (Section II). On several important occasions, at the passing of the throne, the prominent place of the "people of the land" and other forces is to be noted within Judah, as these work to influence the designation of a Davidic king (II,E). Interventions in the monarchial enterprise occur with the intention of establishing for the Judahite Kingdom certain specific religious and political positions, vis-à-vis new and more powerful external military forces (II,F). In the period prior to the Exile, these interventions increase at both the internal and external level, to the point that Judah's broader religious and political stability becomes fractured (II,G). In 597 B. C., following a lengthy assault on capital and countryside, a sizeable portion of the Judahite community, together with the newly appointed king Jehoiachin, and prophet Ezekiel, is deported to Babylon.

Whatever internal conflict over Judahite monarchy, its legitimacy and place within the broader community, existed prior to the Exile did not come to an end in 597 B. C. The Book of Ezekiel and the final chapters of the Deuteronomistic History are vitally concerned to evaluate the significance of 597, within Yahweh's broader plan for Israel. At stake are questions concerning the finality of the judgment of 597, the validity of the remnant community, and Yahweh's plan for restoration. One of the best places to explore conflict over interpretation of the Exile is with respect to prophetic and so-called Dtr Historical evaluations of Judahite kingship, beyond the events of 597. An evaluation of Judahite kingship after 597 is directly related to questions concerning the legitimacy of the post-597 remnant community, and its place within Israel's future restoration.

These questions are explored in Chapter Three. The opening Section (I) analyzes the peculiar silence of the biblical record over circumstances surrounding the death of Jehoiakim. This subject is pursued not for its intrigue or general historical value. Rather, the silence of the record raises questions about the specific point of standing of the author of 2 Kgs 24. It is important to pinpoint this author's perspective because of the special quality of his narrative presentation of 597 events. This presentation now exists as an extensive yet penultimate word (2 Kgs 24) of the full Deuteronomistic History.

Chapter Three
The Dissolution of Judahite Kingship and Kingdom: The 597 Perspective of Ezekiel and the Deuteronomistic History

INTRODUCTION

Examination of conflict in Israel has brought us to a critical juncture in history. The Book of Jeremiah reaches a crescendo of judgment in the section of the book just reviewed (chs. 9—15), specifically around the events of 597 B. C. At this historical moment sizeable portions of the Judahite and Jerusalemite community were deported, including the king, royal house, religious, military, and governmental figures, as well as the general populace. Among their number, whatever its specific size, was the prophet Ezekiel. An entire literature and prophetic activity grows up in the context of the community in Exile, on the banks of the Chebar (distinct even from the later 2 Isaiah community and traditions).

From the perspective of Ezekiel, his literature, and his community, the events of 597 were as final as they appear to be in this one section of Jeremiah. There is an irony in the presentation, however, because the Jeremiah literature resumes (in uninterrupted fashion) prophetic discourse even after this "crescendo of judgment." In the present form of the book, this section remains a slice of prophetic vituperation, strangely located at the end of the first third of the book. A tone of finality seems unusual at this point in the presentation. A judgment is forcefully proclaimed and sharply described in the literature; then it actually comes about in the historical events of 599—597 B. C., culminating in the capture of Jerusalem on March 16, 597 B. C. But the continuation of life in Judah for the prophet Jeremiah, a new king, and a remnant community, beyond the dramatic vision of judgment, complicates any sequential presentation of events affecting all Israel. This fact sets the Book of Jeremiah off as a complex mixture of poetry and prose, judgment and hope, exile and restoration. The dramatic vision of judgment and the reality of a severed and deported community left its mark on the literature of Jeremiah and Ezekiel, as it did on the various other literatures of the period (2 Isaiah; the Dtr History; Obadiah; Lamentations; various Psalms). But it is the Book of Jeremiah alone which straddles the events of both 597 and 587, spanning the whole "exilic age." It is this fact which makes it a distinctive witness to the exilic period. In one sense, it is a pre-exilic, exilic, and post-exilic work, depending upon whether "exile" is construed as 597, 587, or for that matter 582 B. C. (see Jer 52:30).

It has been maintained that the *literary* complexity of the Book of Jeremiah has its roots in *historical* factors. Historical factors unique to this period called forth a theological conflict over normative interpretation of Judah's judgment, exile, and restoration. Although the 587 date often overshadows it in popular thought, the most decisive historical factor in this complex was the Exile and deportation of 597 B. C. 597 events permanently divided two communities of Judahites.

In this Chapter the impact of the 597 Exile on developing biblical traditions, specifically Ezekiel and the Deuteronomistic History, will be examined. In order to gain a point of entry into the discussion, an analysis of the perspective of the report of 597 events found in 2 Kings 24 is provided. This analysis probes one specific problem in the report: the failure to tell of circumstances surrounding the death of Jehoiakim. In attempting to solve this problem, other issues of importance for the investigation of theological conflict in the exilic period emerge. These involve Ezekiel's view of the Davidic monarchy and the broader post-597 Judahite community, and the concluding perspective of the Deuteronomistic History (2 Kings 24 + 25). This last topic extends into Chapter Four with an evaluation of conflict in the Jeremiah traditions. In what follows, a lengthy analysis of the missing burial notice for King Jehoiakim is undertaken in order to determine the narrative perspective of the author of 2 Kings 24.

It has been argued that surrounding the tragic death of Jehoiakim's father, Josiah, and the mysteriously brief report of his encounter with Necho in 2 Kings 23:29, there was a "conspiracy of silence."[1] This description seeks to account for the brevity of the Historian's report: a "conspiracy of silence" grew up around the events at Megiddo because Josiah's bid for Armageddon was such a dismal and embarrassing failure.[2] But for mystery and secondary confusion over details, the account of the death of Jehoiakim in 2 Kgs 24:6 is a more perplexing example of silence in the sources than what is recorded earlier about the death of his father — though for different reasons.

It is possible to discuss the theory of a "conspiracy of silence" with respect to the terse summary of 2 Kings 24:6b: "and Jehoiakim slept with his fathers." This terseness is significant enough to beg explanation, for at this point in Kings it is likely that the Dtr Historian was reporting almost contemporaneous events and in a good position to report far more than he has. His failure to mention the burial of Jehoiakim is striking. But alongside the unusually cryptic report of Kings, there are a number of statements regarding the death of Jehoiakim in other biblical and extra-biblical sources.

> (1) Jehoiakim was taken to Babylon (date unknown) by Nebuchadnezzar; since no mention is made of his death or burial, presumably he died in Babylon (2 Chr 36:6, MT);
>
> (2) Jehoiakim "slept with his fathers" and "was buried in the Garden of Uzza" (2 Chr 36:8, Lucian LXX);
>
> (3) Nebuchadnezzar besieged Jerusalem in Jehoiakim's third year (606), and took him and the vessels from the temple to Babylon; there is no mention of his return or death (Dan 1:1 ff.);
>
> (4) Jehoiakim, converted by Jeremiah's preaching, opened the gates of Jerusalem to Nebuchadnezzar, only to be slain and "thrown before the wall, without any burial" in fulfillment of the same Jeremiah's preaching (Josephus, *Antiq. Jud.* X.6.96 ff.).

---

[1] S. B. Frost, "The Death of Josiah: A Conspiracy of Silence," *JBL* 85 (1968) 369–82.

[2] To quote Frost: "We are left with a general conspiracy of silence on the subject of the death of Josiah because, given OT premises, no one could account for it theologically" (p 381). These events, while tersely reported, are nevertheless explicable, historically and theologically. Factors other than those suggested by Frost were involved, including decisions about what was truly significant in the literary flow of the Historian's narrative. In my view, Frost's is one of a burgeoning number of studies that places far too great an emphasis on the figure of Josiah, usually in order to defend a theory of a Josianic redaction of 1 & 2 Kings or a watershed "deuteronomic reform" in or around 620 B. C.

It would tempting to conclude that the mystery of the death of Jehoiakim was solved. However, the *embarrass de riches* with respect to available data in the biblical record only complicates matters. It looks as though explanations were drawn up in order to solve the riddle or harmonize existing traditions, the result being even greater confusion. But other possibilities cannot be ruled out. This is what makes the death of Jehoiakim a puzzle. Not only must silence about Jehoiakim's death be accounted for in strictly historical terms. Explanations must also be provided for how variant traditions about "just what happened" took shape.

The answer to the latter question conceivably lies within the narrative flow and specific literary context of each work, read apart from the others. But even this way of approaching the problem does not meet with clear success. It cannot be determined from the MT of 2 Chr 36:6 if Nebuchadnezzar actually deported Jehoiakim or only intended to do so. Commentators are divided on this question.[3] Moreover, the report that he reigned 11 years could mean either that he was deported and then allowed to return, in which case the non-mention of either his death or burial is odd; or that he was not deported until 597, that is, after he had reigned 11 years. Lucian at 2 Chr 36:8, by mentioning his burial in the "Garden of Uzza," obviously pictures his having returned to Jerusalem after an earlier deportation. Perhaps concerned that no burial was mentioned in 2 Kgs 24:6, he supplies this information. He may assume it squares with Jer 22:19 (". . . with the burial of an ass"), though his intention is difficult to determine. It is also not clear that a burial in the garden of Uzza was the kind of burial the prophet Jeremiah had in mind.[4] In any case, why is there no clear mention of his return to Jerusalem?

---

[3] See Edward L. Curtis (*The Books of Chronicles* [ICC; New York: Scribner's, 1910] 521) for a discussion; also, W. Rudolph (*Chronikbücher* [HAT; Tübingen: J. C. B. Mohr, 1955] 335 ff.).

[4] Jehoiakim literally gets off the hook. This issue has been argued both ways. Nelson (*Double Redaction,* 86), following several commentators (Wellhausen, Benzinger, Stade, Schwally, Eissfeldt) concludes that Lucian, precisely because he disagrees with the Jeremiah tradition, is *lectio difficilior* and therefore to be preferred over MT as providing the actual report of Jehoiakim's death (i.e., MT sought to ease the tension by striking out this reference). On the other hand, Gray (*I & II Kings,* 753), wondering if the garden of Uzza was at the confluence of the Kidron and Hinnom Valleys (a debated topic in its own right), suggests that "this would accord with Jeremiah's prediction that Jehoiakim would be 'buried with the burial of an ass' and 'cast forth beyond the gates of Jerusalem,'" (i.e., to the garden of Uzza). His view (and Gray admits there is much confusion here) is seconded by Malamat ("Last Years," 210): "Internment here, certainly lackluster because of the heavy siege, may be what Jeremiah meant when he prophesied the king's ignoble end." This seems like an unusual fulfillment (Josephus does not know of it), and the silence of Kings has not really been significantly improved upon. What is striking, however, is that Lucian can be considered *lectio difficilior* by one group of scholars and an accurate supplement by another. Clearly the question demands further study.

Daniel is not interested in the figure of Jehoiakim, but only in the provision of a setting for his tale in Ch. 1. Still, why could he not have chosen the more obvious figure of Jehoiachin, whom all the sources agree was deported to Babylon, or the better documented group of 597 B. C. deportees, for his story? Josephus seems to want to make composite sense not of these accounts, but of the Kings' report and the various Jeremiah traditions, especially 22:19 which tells of Jehoiakim's non-burial outside the walls.[5] His tale is relatively self-consistent, but in contrast to the terseness of Kings it suffers from a superfluity of detail (Jehoiachin's psychological state, etc.) thus calling into question its essential credibility. The overabundance of detail suggests that Josephus is not citing some private source, but simply weaving the best-possible report out of those known sources he deemed most accurate or authoritative. As such, Josephus' report is to be distinguished from the others at the outset. With the reports of Chronicles and Daniel one must entertain the possibility that the information they provide could have been drawn from independent sources or, in the case of Lucian, a different text-recension.

The obvious problem with the accounts of the Chronicler (MT) and Daniel is that nowhere in the nearly contemporaneous reporting of the Dtr Historian is there any mention of the deportation of Jehoiakim or others from Jerusalem. In this regard, Daniel 1:1, which actually supplies a date for such a deportation, is the most problematic since Jehoiakim's third year (606 B. C.) predates even the battle at Carchemish, when Nebuchadnezzar first established Babylonian ascendancy in the region (for that matter, Nabopolassar was still technically the Babylonian monarch in 606 B. C.). Moreover, and most telling, nothing is mentioned of this significant event in the Book of Jeremiah, which otherwise keeps the reader remarkably well informed at just this moment in history. Recall the importance placed at several points in Jeremiah upon Jehoiakim's 4th year. Jehoiakim spent this year in the Judahite, not the Babylonian capital.

Fortunately, it is possible to provide a motivation for the inclusion of these reports in Chronicles and Daniel. It is clear for example that a theme not found in the narrative structure of Kings can be spotted in 2 Chronicles, as well as in the continuation of the Chronicles narrative in Ezra: the theme of a seventy-year submission to Babylon as defining the length of God's punishment over Israel (2 Chr 36:21; Ezra 1:1).[6] The

---

[5] To use the expression of M. Noth ("Einnahme," 147), possible only in German, his *Unbegrabenbleiben*.

[6] Ezekiel does not seem to yet know of a fixed seventy-year period either. The closest thing is his term of exile in Ch. 4. Confusing as the scene in Ch. 4 is, a 70-year term is nowhere to be found there. The 70 years of Jer 29:10 ff. (also 25:12) is probably a secondary elaboration on the less specific (see 27:22) word of Jeremiah to the exiles, representing a more distant reflection on the exact term of exile/restoration. See Chapter Four, Section I.

presence of this theme in Chronicles explains why a report of Nebuchad-nezzar's deportation of Jehoiakim was included. In contrast to the complex account of 2 Kgs 23:31—24:17, which contains specifics about the role of the Egyptians and the Babylonians in overrunning Judah, Ch. 36 of 2 Chronicles is remarkably straightforward. Just as there is a deportation of Jehoahaz by Necho (36:4), of Jehoiachin (36:10) and Zedekiah (36:20) by Nebuchadnezzar, so too there is a deportation of Jehoiakim (36:6).[7]

In point of fact, a greater interest is displayed in the deportation of the temple vessels than in the kings themselves: part are taken with Jehoiakim (v. 7), part with Jehoiachin (v. 10), and the remainder with Zedekiah (v. 18). A merely "intended" deportation of Jehoiakim in v. 6 seems to be ruled out by the juxtaposition of this verse with what follows: "*Also* (i.e., in addition to Jehoiakim) Nebuchadnezzar carried part of the vessels of the house of the Lord to Babylon . . ." (36:7). To pursue for a moment the logic of the narrative, this is precisely why no burial or death notice follows. Jehoiakim did not return to Jerusalem but apparently died in exile. There is unclarity because more interest is shown in the fate of the temple vessels. Similarly, no burial or death notice is given for Jehoiachin or Zedekiah. As a matter of fact, a good deal of information is left out in the case of Zedekiah, arguably because the concern has shifted again to the temple vessels themselves. When Ezra picks up the story of restoration, interest is resumed in these same vessels (1:6 ff.), the true tokens of continuity over the 70-year duration.[8]

Other issues in Chronicles are simplified as well. Possible confusion about the precise relationship between Judah's last three kings is done away with by seeing Jehoiakim as the 36 (i.e., 25 + 11) year old father of 8-year old Jehoiachin, whose 21-year old *brother* (not uncle) Zedekiah then succeeded him on the throne.[9] The first time Nebuchadnezzar's name is mentioned, the period of submission presumably begins; there are no details about battles such as are found in Kings. The Chronicler does not provide a date for the events he records. He has taken the notice of an eleven-year reign of Jehoiakim over from Kings, even though it does not fit well with his report of a deportation, for reasons mentioned above. In this compressed narrative, the important thing for the Chronicler is a kind of prioritized simplicity: all of the last four kings were deported; with the taking of the vessels (and also the kings), the period of submission (not

---

[7] The Chronicler may have picked up the notion of a deported Jehoiakim from Ezek 19:1—9. See the remarks of Moshe Greenberg (*Ezekiel 1—20* [AB 22; Garden City: Doubleday, 1983] 356) and the discussion of this important text below.

[8] Peter R. Ackroyd, "The Temple Vessels — A Continuity Theme," *VTSup* 23 (1972) 166—81.

[9] See T. Willi, *Der Chronik als Auslegung. Untersuchungen zur literarischen Gestaltung der historischen Überlieferung Israels* (FRLANT 106; Göttingen: Vandenhoeck & Ruprecht, 1972) 106, n. 118.

rigidly dated) began. If confusion resulted from such a narrative, it was a confusion the Chronicler was willing to tolerate in order that other issues might receive due emphasis.

In a similar way, when the Book of Daniel actually attempts to date the deportation of Jehoiakim — the report of which was taken over from the Chronicler — this is done neither to falsify the record nor cleverly manipulate it in order that it might more accurately reflect a seventy-year tally.[10] With respect to Daniel's "the third year of Jehoiakim" (1:1), there is a good chance that the author simply grafted the number three from the report of Jehoiakim's three-year vassalage to Nebuchadnezzar from 2 Kgs 24:1.[11]

By demonstrating the clearly secondary nature of the reports of 2 Chr 36:6 ff. and Dan 1:1, several potential sources of confusion have been eliminated in the search for the circumstances surrounding the death of Jehoiakim. This has been done by providing a plausible explanation for why they evolved in the first place and how they function within the logic and limits of their own respective narrative frameworks. Yet the primary question remains: Why is the Dtr Historian silent about the death of King Jehoiakim?

That an actual problem exists with this silence ought first of all to be made clear. This can be done fairly readily by examining the wider assembly of death and burial notices for Judahite kings in 1 and 2 Kings. A full list of these appears on the first page of Chart 5. For the purpose of clarification, notices are divided between kings who died a natural death and those who did not. The first thing to be observed is that in almost all cases a notice of the burial of the king is provided. The exceptions can be easily explained for Jehoahaz, Jehoiachin, and Zedekiah, since all three were deported; neither is mention made of Athaliah's burial, but this presumably has to do with the (unusual) fact of her usurpation and resultant slaying.[12] This leaves only Hezekiah and Jehoiakim without burial notices.

Another thing to be observed from this list is that the expression "to sleep with one's fathers" is almost unfailingly completed with the expression "and was buried in X." It has been argued, therefore, that the first expression means nothing more than "X died," with further specifics about burial itself not discussed.[13] In other words, the two expressions are not interchangeable. Nor does one cover precisely the same territory as the

---

[10] Compare the gratuitous argument of G. Larsson, "When did the Babylonian Captivity Begin?" *JTS* 18 (1967) 417—18.

[11] See M. Noth, *History,* 282, n. 2; Norman Porteous, *Daniel* (OTL; Philadelphia: Westminster, 1979) 32.

[12] Compare the lack of burial notice for northern kings (CHART 5.3, nos. 32, 38, 39).

[13] N. J. Tromp, *Primitive Conceptions of Death and The Nether World in the Old Testament* (BO 21; Rome: Pontifical, 1969) 168—71.

other, regardless of how one views the effects of parallelism in biblical semantics. Tromp's position is borne out by a review of the expression's usage in 1 and 2 Kings. The older form of the expression "to be gathered to one's fathers" included within its semantic range the idea of burial. This is why, in contrast to our expression, it need not be completed with the (in this case) redundant "and was buried with . . .". With respect to the notice of 2 Kgs 24:6, then, the failure to mention the burial of Jehoiakim is noteworthy. That he "slept with his fathers" says nothing about his burial (or even non-burial).

It has been argued that use of the expression "to sleep with ones fathers" precluded the idea of a death from other than natural causes. If this were the case, then one would have to assume that Jehoiakim simply passed away, though this would be odd for a man as vigorous or as young (age 36) as Jehoiakim; it would also be fortuitous only a few months before the capture of the city by Nebuchadnezzar. But this notion is not upheld by the evidence in Chart 5. In sections 5.2 and 5.3 one finds reports of kings who were killed in conspiracy and battle: Amaziah of Judah and Ahab of Israel (marked ***). Yet the expression "sleep with ones fathers" is used of them both (I 22:40; II 14:22). In the case of Jehoiakim, use of the expression "he slept with his fathers" does not rule out the possibility that he, like Amaziah or Ahab, was killed in conspiracy, battle, or by some other unnatural cause. A burial notice, peaceful or otherwise, is missing.

Chart Five

Death and Burial Notices in 1 & 2 Kings

5.1 Natural Death and Burial for Judahite Kings

1)	I 2:10	David (a)
2)	I 11:43	Solomon (a)
3)	I 14:31	Rehoboam (b)
4)	I 15:8	Abijam (b)
5)	I 15:24	Asa (a)
6)	I 22:50	Jehoshaphat (b)
7)	II 8:24	Jehoram (b)
8)	II 15:7	Azariah/Uzziah (b)
9)	II 15:38	Jotham (b)
10)	II 16:20	Ahaz (b)

a = "slept with his fathers and was buried in the city of David"
b = "slept with his fathers and was buried with his fathers in the city of David"

5.2 Exceptional Circumstances, Judahite Kings

11)	II 9:28	Ahaziah (a)
12)	II 11:16	Athaliah (slain; no mention of burial)
13)	II 12:21	Jehoash (a)
14)	II 14:19	Amaziah (a) (b) (***)
15)	II 20:21	Hezekiah (b; no mention of burial)
16)	II 21:18	Manasseh (b; "buried in the garden . . . of Uzza")
17)	II 21:26	Amon (slain; buried in "his tomb in the garden of Uzza")
18)	II 23:29 – 30	Josiah (slain; buried "in his own tomb")
19)	II 23:34	Jehoahaz (deported; died in Egypt)
20)	II 24:6	Jehoiakim (b; no mention of burial)
21)	II 25:30	Jehoiachin (deported; not dead at time of report)
22)	II 25:7	Zedekiah (deported; no mention of burial)

a = slain; buried with his fathers in the city of David
b = formula: "slept with his fathers"

5.3 Unnatural Death for Israelite Kings

23)	I 15:27	Nadab (a)
24)	I 16:10	Elah (a)
25)	I 16:18	Zimri (a)
26)	I 22:37	Ahab (b) (c) (***)
27)	II 15:10	Zechariah (a)
28)	II 15:14	Shallum (a)
29)	II 15:25	Pekaiah (a)
30)	II 15:30	Pekah (a)
31)	II 17:4	Hoshea (d)

a = slain; no death ("slept with fathers") or burial formula
b = slain; burial notice included
c = formula: "slept with fathers" (I 22:40)
d = deported (?)

5.4 Natural Death for Israelite Kings

32)	I 14:20	Jeroboam (a; no burial notice)
33)	I 16:6	Baasha (a; buried at Tirvah)
34)	I 16:28	Omri (a; b)
35)	II 10:35	Jehu (a; b)
36)	II 13:9	Jehoahaz (a; b)
37)	II 13:13	Joash (a; b, with kings of Israel)

38)   II 14:29   Jeroboam (a, with the kings of Israel; no burial notice)
39)   II 15:22   Menahem (a; no burial notice)

a = formula: "slept with fathers"
b = formula: "and was buried in Samaria"

5.5 Significant Chronicles' Divergences

(5)   II 16:11—14   Asa (diseased; special tomb, funeral)
(7)   II 21:20   Jehoram (diseased; separate tomb in city of David)
(*)   II 24:16   Jehoiada the priest (buried with kings)
(13)   II 24:25   Jehoash (apostate; separate tomb in city of David)
(8)   II 26:23   Uzziah (leprous; royal burial field)
(10)   II 28:27   Ahaz (apostate; tomb in Jerusalem, but not royal tomb)
(15)   II 32:33   Hezekiah (buried on the ascent to the royal tomb)
(16)   II 33:20   Manasseh (buried in his house)
(17)   II 33:25   Amon (no mention of burial)
(19)   II 35:24   Josiah ("buried in the tombs of his fathers")
(20)   II 36:6 ff.   Jehoiakim, Jehoiachin, and Zedekiah [brother] (deported to Babylon w/temple vessels; died there)

It has been argued that in order to break the silence concerning the burial of Hezekiah one needs only turn to the report of the Chronicler at II 32:33.[14] The same pattern might then be followed with Jehoiakim. 2 Chron 32:33 records that Hezekiah was in fact buried "on the ascent of the tombs of the sons of David." Yeivin also turns to Chronicles (Ch 36) for information concerning the death and burial of Jehoiakim, though here he must go a step further to the LXX tradition (36:8). The MT of Chronicles is silent on the matter.[15] This silence, as argued above, is best explained as the result of the Chronicler's decision to include a report of Jehoiakim's deportation to Babylon. But is the Chronicler (MT or LXX) really of assistance in filling out lacunae in the Kings tradition, as Yeivin urges?

A brief survey of Section 5.5 makes this unlikely. Here one sees the remarkable latitude the Chronicler accorded himself in handling burial notices. Cases of extreme apostasy or disease appear to necessitate separate burial (nos. 5,7,13,8,10; cf. 5.1). The Chronicler is under the suspicion that the royal tomb was filled by the time of Hezekiah, since from Manasseh on (in 2 Kgs) kings are often buried in their own tomb rather than "in the city of David." This is part of the reason the Chronicler tells of Hezekiah being buried "on the ascent of the tombs of the sons of David."

---

[14] S. Yeivin, "The Sepulchers of the Kings of the House of David," *JNES* 7 (1948).
[15] "Sepulchers," 34, n. 47.

But the most likely explanation for the divergences in Chronicles has nothing to do with an independent source being put to use. Rather, the Chronicler is concerned with factors other than strict historical accuracy.[16] And in any event, he did not choose to invent a burial notice for Jehoiakim. Instead, as seen above, he had him deported.[17]

The lack of a burial notice for Jehoiakim would be in any other instance of no particular concern. As unusual as it is, it could be taken merely as a matter of inadvertance or the result of carelessness on the part of the Historian — something akin to explanations given for the silence about Hezekiah's burial. But in contrast to the silence regarding Hezekiah, as well as to what the Historian does have to say about all other kings' burials, the circumstances of Jehoiakim's death and burial receive special attention in a source outside of Kings/Chronicles: the Book of Jeremiah. For this reason the failure to include details about his death or burial in Kings is striking. Clearly Kings does not otherwise fail to supply information regarding Jehoiakim's 11-year tenure, so why is he silent at this point in the record?

Jeremiah's oracles against Jehoiakim, preserved at 22:18—19 and at 36:30, are forceful and specific. The first stresses that he will not be lamented in any normal fashion; the second indicates that "none that are his" (*lōʾ yihĕyeh lô*), e.g., none of his sons, will sit on the throne after him.[18] Both agree on the terms of his burial — it will not happen.

> With the burial of an ass he shall be buried, dragged and cast forth beyond the gates of Jerusalem (22:19)
> ... his dead body shall be cast out to the heat by day and the frost by night (36:30)

Morton Cogan has successfully demonstrated that while the hyperbolic threat of disinternment appears at several points in the Jeremiah tradition (see 7:33 ff.; 15:3, 16:4, 34:20), appearing as well as an infrequent motif in Assyrian literature, these two passages speak not of disinternment, but of non-burial.[19] He takes the two infinitive verbal forms in the first passage, *sāḥôb wĕhaṡlēk,* as a hendiadys, and translates: "dragged about — left unburied beyond the gates of Jerusalem."[20] The form *haṡlēk* he calls a technical term, "employed when speaking of the abandonment of an item with which one can or does not want to deal." Used in reference to

---

[16] See the remarks of P. R. Ackroyd in "History and Theology in the Writings of the Chronicler," *CTM* 38 (1967) 501—15.

[17] Perhaps following Ezek 19:5—9. See below, Section II/B.

[18] Jehoiachin reigned for only 3 months, so Jeremiah's word was for the most part upheld. For comparison, see also the oracle against Jehoiachin at 22:30.

[19] Morton Cogan, "A Note on Disinternment in Jeremiah," *Gratz College Anniversary Volume* (Philadelphia: Gratz College, 1971) 29—34.

[20] Literally: "dragged about as the result of being left unburied" ("Disinternment," 33).

the dead, it means "leave unburied."[21] He then enlists as evidence several neo-Assyrian citations which also speak of non-burial, both as an actual occurrence and as a curse/threat. For the purpose of comparison, the first of these will be reproduced.

niše mātišu sīḫu elīšu ušabšū
> the people of his land rebelled against him;

ina sūqi ālīšu šalamtasu iddūšu
> in the market-place of his city they left his body lying,

indaššarū pagaršu
> his carcass dragged to and fro.[22]

Two things should be noted here. First, this passage is not a threat, but involves an actual case of non-internment. Presumably, in the course of time the body would be buried — however, without the ceremony which customarily attended a royal burial. Second, as Cogan stresses, the passage speaks not of disinternment but of non-burial during the circumstances of civil war.

It can be concluded from Cogan's analysis that although the Book of Jeremiah contains numerous references to disinternment, which may simply originate in the context of a threat or curse yet to be realized,[23] these passages regarding the non-burial of Jehoiakim emerge from a far more concrete backdrop. During a state of siege the prophet Jeremiah would have utilised precisely such imagery of non-burial and, along with it, non-lamentation; no royal burial ceremony would have been possible (or following Jeremiah, permissable). These passages do not present implausible or merely hyperbolic language. Instead, they threaten King Jehoiakim with a death which would take place precisely during the circumstances of the 598/7 siege, a time when one would have to forego proper royal burial proceedings.[24]

At this point the original question resurfaces: Since Jehoiakim died some three months before the capture of the city (Dec 598),[25] why does

---

[21] Here he quotes himself ("Disinternment," 33) from "A Technical Term for Exposure," *JNES* 27 (1968) 133—5. Apparently the image of an ass's burial was employed to stress the ignoble nature of the funeral proceedings, not the manner of burial *per se*.

[22] Cited by Cogan ("Disinternment," 34) concerning the death of one Ahseri, king of Mannai, who died in a bloody civil war.

[23] See Jer 8:1—3; 7:33—34; 15:3—4; 16:1—4; 34:20 ff. These passages are found in secondary prose frameworks, often attributed to deuteronomists (in this context, see Deut 28:26). All have general referents ("this people"), as over against the two passages under discussion; all have to do with foreclosing the possibility of continued life in the land for "this people," viz, survivors of the 597 events.

[24] So Malamat, "Last Years," 210—11. It is impossible to agree with Malamat, anxious to harmonize the Jeremiah and Chronicles (LXX) traditions, that burial in the garden of Uzzah was what the prophet Jeremiah had in mind. Other reasons must be given for this divergent (LXX) tradition of the death of Jehoiakim.

[25] For a discussion of the dates involved, see Malamat, "Last Years," 210—11.

the Historian not provide more information about the circumstances of his death, especially in light of the Jeremiah material? The Babylonian Chronicle also mentions nothing about Jehoiakim or the circumstances of his death, though it must have occurred in the context of the capture of the city. Moreover, it was Jehoiakim, not his young son, against whom Nebuchadnezzar had set out to begin with. Yet all the annals report is: "In the seventh year, the month of Kislev, the king of Akkad (Nebuchadnezzar) mustered his troops, marched to Hattiland, and encamped against the city of Judah; on the second day of the month of Adar (March 16) he seized the city and captured the king. He appointed there a king of his own choice, and receiving heavy tribute, brought (it) to Babylon." [26] The general consensus is that the first king mentioned as captured (*ik-ta-šad*) by Nebuchadnezzar was the newly crowned Jehoiachin. The king favorably selected (*šarra ša libbi-šu*) to rule was another son of Josiah, Zedekiah. No mention is made of Jehoiakim. [27]

Jeremiah's threat of non-burial has been successfully grounded in the concrete events of the 598/7 siege of Jerusalem. It could be argued that Jeremiah's statement and the report of Kings are in not in fundamental

---

[26] A. K. Grayson, *Assyrian and Babylonian Chronicles. Texts from Cuneiform Sources* (New York, 1975) Vol. V. Grayson is paraphrased here. Other translations are often quite confusing about just what is brought (*ulterib*) to Babylon. For a sampling, see A. Malamat, "Last Years," 210; D. N. Freedman, "The Babylonian Chronicle," *BA* 19 (1956) 54; S. Herrmann, *History,* 278. In Ronald Clements' translation of Zimmerli's Ezekiel commentary (*Ezekiel 1;* [Hermeneia; Philadelphia: Fortress, 1979] 11) this annals' citation is rendered in English as "sent (him) to Babylon," presumably due to a confusion over the German object pronoun *ihn* (meaning here *Tribut,* not "him"). The implication of such a translation would be that Nebuchadnezzar appointed Jehoiachin king and then deported him, a notion which is not all that far-fetched, in light of what is known about Babylonian policy concerning dual kingship and regency elsewhere (see below). Moreover, this would in turn mean that the first king mentioned was Jehoiakim, thereby supplying the first important clue as to circumstances of his death (there are certain chronological problems with having Jehoiakim still king in Adar 597, beyond his 11th year). Wiseman is himself misleading in the translation "sent (them) to Babylon" (*CCK,* 73), which most scholars follow. His translation implies that some plural object was sent to Babylon by a Nebuchadnezzar who remained in Judah; presumably, Wiseman has a deportation in mind here, but the wrong verb appears in the annals. No object appears in the Akkadian with the verb *ulterib,* but the sentence structure implies that it was in fact the heavy tribute (*bi-lat-sa kabittu*) which he both received (*il-[qa-am-m]a*) and then brought to Babylon (cf. B. M. 21946, Rev 1 4). That he "brought it" rather than "sent it" (both translations are possible) is suggested by the fact that the citations for a given year normally end with the mention of the king's return to Babylon (with the verb *itur*[a] [ra]; compare B. M. 21946, Obv l. 20; Rev ll. 7,10,15,20,24). Since the verb is missing here, he apparently accompanied the tribute back to Babylon, perhaps departing before the deportations had begun. This fact may also be substantiated by the notice at II Chronicles 36:10, which states that at the turn of the year (Nisan 597) Nebuchadnezzar "sent" (*šalaḥ*) and had Jehoiachin brought (*wayěbi'ēhû*) to Babylon. More on this below.

[27] Here too the Babylonian Chronicle and Kings are in agreement.

disagreement.[28] Jeremiah really does not indicate the manner of Jehoiakim's death, only his burial. But it would seem that the prophet did not
have a natural death in mind, and while the Kings' note that he slept with
his fathers does not rule out the possibility of some sort of foul-play, it is
still unusually vague. It must also be said that, its concreteness aside,
Jeremiah's oracle need not have been fulfilled.[29] But is all this of much
help? In the final analysis, one is still left with a mysterious silence from
the Historian at a key point in his account.

There are those who have tried to fill in the missing details through
reasonable conjecture. Both Albright and Bright were unconvinced that
Jehoiakim died a natural death at age 36 and so argued that he was killed
in a *coup d'état*.[30] The party behind such an overthrow was, according to
Albright, a group of "nobles who were disaffected because of heavy
property losses sustained during the Chaldean punitive incursions" (91).
Bright felt Jehoiakim was assassinated because he was *persona non grata*
with the Babylonians; the hope was that Judah would "gain milder
treatment thereby" (327). From what has been uncovered concerning
internal instability in the capital and countryside from at least the time of
Amon forward, the likelihood of a palace *coup* cannot be ruled out. Bright's
theory, while not implausible, does not explain however why Jehoiakim's
son would have been selected over Zedekiah or some other candidate.
Would Jehoiachin not have been viewed by the Babylonians as merely a
continuation of his father's political untrustworthiness? The possibility
cannot be excluded of Jehoiakim's having been killed during the harsh
and no doubt tense days of the siege. Indeed, from what is known about
how Jehoiakim came to power, a coup of some sort remains a good
explanation of how he died. Given this fact, Kings' silence is all the more
perplexing.[31]

There is one possibility that would help explain the lack of a burial
notice in Kings and at the same time partially aid in clarifying Kings'
silence about Jehoiakim's death. This has to do with the specific perspective
from which the author of Kings is working at this point in the narrative.
The burial half of the problem will be examined first.

As pointed out above, Jeremiah's oracle against Jehoiakim is concerned more with the manner of his burial than with his death. Royal
burial in Judah involved a degree of appropriate ceremony. This was true

---

[28] Malamat, "Last Years," 211. Malamat still does not explain the circumstances of Jehoiakim's *death*.

[29] Even Albright noted, however, that usually unfulfilled predictions are glossed in some
way ("Seal of Eliakim," 90).

[30] W. F. Albright, "Seal of Eliakim," 90 ff.; John Bright, *History,* 326; *Jeremiah,* xlix.

[31] Incidentally, as creative as Albright and Bright were about the details of Jehoiakim's
death, they offered no explanation for Kings' silence on the matter.

even in cases when the king was slain in battle (2 Kgs 23:30).[32] Such
would not be possible during a state of siege, and particularly during a
siege as final as that envisioned by the prophet Jeremiah. It must be
stressed that whatever its essential accuracy, the oracle is written from
Jeremiah's own perspective. That he saw no possibility of Jehoiakim's
sons ruling after him (Jer 36:30) may mean more than that he was unhappy
with this particular Davidic branch (as over against Zedekiah, for example).[33] Rather, he saw the events of 597 as bringing to an end the Davidic
dynasty altogether (see esp. 13:18—19), as well as all existence in Judah
and Jerusalem. It is in this context that the oracle is delivered. Its burden
is that a royal burial for Jehoiakim is denied. Instead there will be the
kind of hurried burial normally reserved for animals. His dead body will
have to be hauled out beyond the city walls, with actual internment left
to others. It is a burial reserved for one caught up in a military disaster
he brought upon himself, due to his disobedience before Yahweh and
Nebuchadnezzar.

Having set this backdrop, what can be said about the Historian's
terse report in 2 Kgs 24:6? John Gray, following several older commentators, raised the possibility that Kings' silence on the details of Jehoiakim's
burial stemmed from the fact that these details were not known to him at
the time of his writing.[34] He attributed the "uncertainty" of secondary
traditions on the matter (LXX, Daniel, Josephus) to a confusion, or an
ignorance, that was there at the earliest moment. The question of the
Historian's perspective on matters he is chronicling is a crucial one since
it is tied to the way one envisions the redactional history of 1 and 2 Kings.
In other words, Gray used Kings's silence on the matter of Jehoiakim's
death as a way to determine where "the first Deuteronomistic compilation
ended and the exilic continuation began."[35] Relative silence, or lack of
details, about other matters (the revolt of Jehoiakim; exact beginning of
the siege) and especially about an interval he theorizes took place between
the death of Jehoiakim and the accession of Jehoiachin, also points to the
limited viewpoint of the exilic "redactor."

These additional factors are not as convincing as Gray's statements
concerning the death of Jehoiakim. The theory of a chronological interval
between the reigns of Jehoiakim and his son Jehoiachin is extremely

---

[32] Though only the bare minimum is provided in Kings, consistency in burial notices
regarding the royal tomb in the city of David indicates the concern shown for proper
burial for the Davidic line.

[33] But see Section II following.

[34] John Gray, *I & II Kings*, 753—4.

[35] *I & II Kings*, 753. In Gray's system, the terms "dtr compiler" and "dtr redactor" are to
be differentiated. The first draws upon annalistic source material and works in Judah,
the second imitates the style of the first and works after 597 in Babylon.

difficult to establish.[36] It is not clear that the Historian is any less inform-
ative at this point concerning details about the siege than he is at any
other place in the History. As Gray himself points out, the Historian's
normal style consists of "staccato statements of facts" in "annalistic sources
in the first compilation" (752), that is, throughout 2 Kings. And as Gray
and many others have recognized, there is much about Chapter 24 that is
more similar than dissimilar to what is found throughout the history, and
this in some contrast to the "continuous narrative style" (752) found in
Ch. 25. Recourse is often made to a theory of literary imitation, suggesting
that the "redactor" imitated the style of the "compiler," but this is a very
difficult theory to prove.[37] Moreover, almost all agree that the note in
24:7 looks like any other citation from annalistic sources in the "first
compilation."[38] The more pertinent question concerns the lack of stylistic
uniformity and the differing narrative technique and use of sources between
Chs. 24 and 25; complete discussion of this matter is taken up below.
More to the point: Does Gray's understanding of the redactional history
of Kings, which he shares with many proponents of a major Josianic
edition (Dtr 1), undercut his view on Kings' silence about Jehoiakim's
burial?

The question of Jehoiakim's burial can be separated from the other
issues raised by Gray with respect to the editing of Kings. On this single
question, Gray is essentially correct in his hunch about the Historian's
limited perspective, though for slightly different reasons. The deuteronomistic "compiler" worked up through the events of the 597 siege and
the accession of Jehoiachin. It is likely that he was among those deported
along with Jehoiachin in 597 B. C. The literary scope of his chronicling,
then, reached through all of Ch. 24, several secondary additions excepted.[39]
His concluding statement occurs in v. 20: "For because of the anger of
the LORD it came to the point in Jerusalem and Judah that he cast them
out from his presence."

There are two major reasons why this editor is silent about Jehoiakim's death and burial. With Gray and others, the editor simply did not
know all of the details concerning Jehoiakim's burial. There is also no
sure way, given the strong likelihood of a coup, to precisely date his death;
in other words one cannot be sure that the date of Jehoiachin's accession
is the same date as Jehoiakim's death. It no doubt fell sometime during
the latter days of the siege. Jehoiakim may have been captured or handed
over to the garrison troops in the area. If this occurred, then the precise

---

[36] Compare Malamat, "Last Years," 210 ff.
[37] Richard Nelson's work is heavily dependent upon just such a theory (*Double Redaction*,
36—40).
[38] Gray, *I & II Kings*, 758; even Nelson, *Double Redaction*, 83.
[39] See the exegetical discussion of 2 Kgs 24 below, Section III.

details of his death would have been unknown to the editor. But if he died a violent death at the hands of fellow Jerusalemites, as Bright and Albright conjecture, this fact would have been noted by the Historian. At any rate, if he was unsure about the circumstances of his death, then this would be even more true of his burial. From this limited perspective, he simply concluded his reign with the succinct entry: "and Jehoiakim slept with his fathers."

The second reason is related to the *literary form* of the Historian's narrative presentation. When one notes the positioning of the burial notices for Judahite kings, it is clear that the Historian never begins to fully record events of a successor's reign without first summarizing that of his predecessor. These summaries invariably include a death/burial notice. What was of paramount interests to the Historian was the Fall of Jerusalem. One is prepared to hear of this event already at 24:1; in fact, throughout the unit 24:1—7 there is a concern to make clear the ascendency of Nebuchadnezzar and the withdrawal of Egypt from the region (24:7). But the actual capture of the city did not take place until the reign of Jehoiachin, so the narrative hastens to this point. To move to this obviously crucial chapter in the history, the narrator simply concludes with the usual summary form (24:6), mentions the expulsion of the Egyptians, and then quickly picks up with the reign of Jehoiachin (24:8 ff.). This is a stylistic technique employed throughout Kings, and it argues for more than an imitative relationship between this chapter and what precedes. Given the significance of events he is recording, including the deportation of the King, royal family, temple vessels, some 10,000 others including himself — events which he understandably concluded were final — the circumstances of Jehoiakim's death paled in comparison. A notice of that death at 24:6 suffices. The circumstances of his burial were unknown, and at this particular historical moment capable of omission without clarification.

One final note: Was there a conspiracy of silence surrounding Jehoiakim's death that prevented the whole story being told? Such an interpretation is not required, given our analysis of Ch. 24. But it cannot be ruled out either, for several important reasons. In order to pursue this issue, however, a broader perspective is required on historical events in this period and on the precise status and nature of kingship in these last decades of Judah's existence. Such a perspective cannot be had without moving to the one other decisive witness for the period: the Book of Ezekiel. To anticipate a bit, consider two distinctive viewpoints on the Davidic dynasty and its scions. Jeremiah predicts in absolutely unequivocal terms the end of the Davidic line in the person of Jehoiakim (36:30). Then, in a time period that cannot have exceeded the three months of his royal tenure, he pronounces a similar judgment over Jehoiachin (22:30). In contrast to this, Ezekiel calls for the final destruction of the Davidic house of Zedekiah in equally forceful terms (21:25 ff.; 19:14; 12:12 ff.;

17:16 ff.), while at the same time singling out Jehoiachin as a topmost cedar-twig transplanted by Yahweh to Babylon (17:4) to be ultimately replanted by Yahweh on the mountains of Israel (17:22 ff.).[40] Out of this conflictual matrix a certain silence over the final days (death and burial) of Jehoiachin's father emerged. Or, at a minimum, this conflict saw to it that the silence was maintained, not to be disturbed by further commentary — at least within the narratives of the Deuteronomistic History.

---

[40] The finale of the Deuteronomistic History also comes to mind here (25:29), with its picture of the gracious treatment of Jehoiachin in exile. See Chapter Four, Section II.

II. THE 597 PERSPECTIVE OF EZEKIEL TRADITIONS

A. Judahite Kingship and Kingdom: An Introduction

There is a general consensus that the prophet Ezekiel was among those who were deported to Babylon with King Jehoiachin and the royal family (so Ezek 1:2). Like the prophet Jeremiah, Ezekiel has many specific things to say about individual Davidic kings, often termed by him "rulers" (from the nominal form *nāśî*').[41] Prior to the Fall of Jerusalem (33:21), direct references to Zedekiah, "rulers," Jehoiachin, or Jehoahaz (in descending order of frequency) can be found throughout the first part of the book (especially chs. 12, 17, 19, 21, 22). The Book of Ezekiel is remarkably well organized according to a system of dates, correlated with the exile of Jehoiachin (*lĕgālût hammelek yôyākîn*).[42] That this particular dating scheme has a significance all its own for understanding Ezekiel's stance toward King Jehoiachin, as well as the exiled community of 597, has been noted by interpreters.[43]

While he is not mentioned by name even a single time in the whole of the book, transparent references to King Zedekiah appear at 12:12; 17:5,13,20, etc; 19:12–13; 21:25.[44] There have been those who detected a certain ambivalence in Jeremiah's attitude toward the figure of Zedekiah.[45]

---

[41] It is difficult to provide an adequate translation for this term. Yet a precise definition of it is crucial for understanding Judahite kingship at this period.

[42] Ezek 1:2. For a discussion of Ezekiel's chronological system see: Walther Zimmerli, *Ezekiel 1*, 9–11; Moshe Greenberg, *Ezekiel 1–20*, 8–17; K. S. Freedy and D. B. Redford, "The Dates in Ezekiel in Relation to Biblical, Babylonian and Egyptian Sources," *JAOS* 90 (1970) 462–485; Jack Finegan, "The Chronology of Ezekiel," *JBL* 69 (1950) 61–66.

[43] W. F. Albright, "Seal of Eliakim," 93; "King Joiachin in Exile," *BA* 4 (1942) 54; Peter R. Ackroyd, "The History of Israel in the Exilic and Post Exilic Periods," *Tradition and Interpretation* (G. W. Anderson, ed; Oxford: University, 1979) 320; Freedy & Redford, "Dates in Ezekiel," 463; Herbert G. May, "Three Hebrew Seals and the Status of Exiled Jehoiakin," *AJSL* 56 (1939) 148; John W. Wevers, *Ezekiel* (NCB; Grand Rapids: Eerdmans, 1982) 43; Zimmerli, *Ezekiel 1*, 10–11. Cf., Martin Noth, "The Jerusalem Catastrophe of 587 B. C., and its Significance for Israel," *Laws of the Pentateuch and Other Studies* (D. R. Ap-Thomas, tr; Philadelphia: Fortress, 1967) 271.

[44] It will shown that the lion cub of 19:5–9 is also a reference to Zedekiah.

[45] These include, among others (see note above), Erich Zenger, "Die deuteronomistische Interpretation der Rehabilierung Jojachins," *BZ* 12 (1968) 16–30; Peter R. Ackroyd, "Aspects of the Jeremiah Tradition," *Indian Journal of Theology* 20 (1971) 1–12; "Historians and Prophets," *SEA* 33 (1968) 18–54; Martin Noth, "Jerusalem Catastrophe," 266 ff.; A. Malamat, "Jeremiah and the Last Two Kings of Judah," *PEQ* 83 (1951) 81–7; Klaus Baltzer, "Ende des Staates," 33–43; Christopher R. Seitz, "The Crisis of Interpretation over the Meaning and Purpose of the Exile," *VT* 35 (1985) 78–97.

The same is by no means true of the prophet Ezekiel. Without exception, when reference is made by Ezekiel to Zedekiah, the context is always one of sure and final judgment. Not once does Ezekiel use the term "king" (*melek*) when speaking of Zedekiah. He is the *nāśî* "unhallowed among the wicked" (21:30); the "strong stem" (*maṭṭēh ʿuzzāh*) "withered and consumed" (19:12); one of the "seed royal"[46] (*mizzeraʿ hammĕlûkāh*) not to be trusted (17:13); a fickle "seed of the land" (*mizzeraʿ hāʾāreṣ*) to be contrasted with Jerusalem's [her] exiled king (17:12, *malkāh*); a "topmost shoot" (*rōʾš yōnĕqôtāw*) from "the crown of a cedar" (*ṣammeret hāʾerez*) whom Yahweh will again plant on the mountains of Israel (17:23) to become a "noble cedar" (*ʾerez ʾaddîr*).[47] The fate in store for scion Zedekiah is more sobering. He must trade the symbols of his authority, scepter (19:14, *šēbeṭ limšôl*), turban and crown (21:31, *hammiṣnepet; hāʾăṭārāh*) for those of defeat, [my] net and snare (*rištî; mĕṣûdātî*, see 12:13; 17:20; 19:8).[48] Blinded (12:13), he shall be brought to Babylon for Yahweh's judgment (17:20, *wĕnišpaṭtî*) and will finally die there (12:13).[49]

It is fairly easy to differentiate between Ezekiel's evaluation of Zedekiah and Jehoiachin. At a minimum it can be concluded that for Ezekiel, Zedekiah's punishment was an absolute necessity. This was due to Zedekiah's political untrustworthiness (Ch. 17) as well as violations in the moral realm (Ch. 19), both of which were an affront to Yahweh's essential Holiness.[50] More than this can be said. The entire community under Zedekiah's rule in Judah is doomed (Chs. 5—9). Though their fate may be differently met (5:12; 6:11; 7:15; 14:21) in pestilence, sword, or famine, no segment of society is to be exempted (7:27; 13:1 ff.; 14:1 ff.).[51] Survivors, if there be any, must like Zedekiah appear in judgment before Yahweh (6:9—10; 14:22). The absolute thoroughness of the judgment is stressed above all else.

---

[46] Compare Jer 41:1 where the same term is used of the assassin Ishmael.

[47] For an English translation, see Greenberg, *Ezekiel 1—20*, 307—309.

[48] The reference at 19:8 is debated, falling as it does in a *qînāh* whose *dramatis personae* are not absolutely clear.

[49] The interpretation (and translation) of 21:32, where *mišpāṭ* is again spoken of in the context of Zedekiah's abasement, is one of the toughest challenges of the book. Is "judgment" (of Zedekiah, by Nebuchadnezzar) or "justice, right" (of Jehoiachin or a new ruler) spoken of here? When? In what (temporal) relationship to the destruction of Jerusalem (21:27,32)? What is the relationship of this verse (if any?) to Gen 49:10? See the discussion below.

[50] Sharp distinctions between these two arena are not warranted in the Ezekiel presentation (cf. Greenberg, *Ezekiel 1—20*, 359). In the present text of Ezekiel, in the section concerned with the figure of Zedekiah and the dynasty itself, there is a complex interweaving of these realms of human activity (Chs. 16 + 17; 18 + 19; 20 + 21). From Ezekiel's perspective, they are two sides of one coin.

[51] Yahweh's "four sore acts of judgment" (14:21) include *ḥereb wĕrāʿāb wĕḥayyāh rāʿāh* ("evil beasts") *wādeber*.

Given this particular perspective on affairs in Judah, it is not surprising that Ezekiel's evaluation of Zedekiah's political status is as unilaterally negative as it is. Even at the one moment when, hypothetically, Zedekiah's rule could have been perceived as established with a degree of legitimacy — that is, when Ezekiel acknowledges his selection by the great eagle Nebuchadnezzar (17:5) — the prophet is careful to avoid the employment of any term which might suggest that he was, in fact, *melek* of Judah. Instead, other terms are carefully chosen (17:5,13) which admit to only his royal lineage, and not his right to rule. There are only two "kings" mentioned in the passage, the *melek-bābel* and the *melek* of *yĕrûšālaim* (17:12), Nebuchadnezzar and Jehoiachin, the son of Jehoiakim and nephew of Zedekiah.[52]

Ezekiel's use of the term *nāśî'* has been the focus of much discussion.[53] Unfortunately, many who have attempted to clarify its usage have done so in the more narrow context of inquiry into Ezekiel's eschatology: even more specifically, the program of restoration in Chs. 40—48.[54] The term *nāśî'*, which appears 36 times in the entire book, has an undeniably central role to play in this concluding tradition-block (19 times in chs. 44, 45, 46, 48). Any discussion of the term, regardless of how one understands the proper relationship between chs. 40—48 and chs. 1—39, must be capable of illuminating its precise usage throughout the whole of the book. But it is possible to distinguish between Ezekiel's use of the term as applied to the phenomenon of kingship, as it exists in Judah and Babylon during this period, and the special use which is made of it in the future theocratic state of chs. 40—48.[55] This is all the more important given the fact that

---

[52] It should be noted that while Ezekiel cannot completely ignore the fact that Nebuchadnezzar did make Zedekiah king in Judah (17:16, *hammamlîk*), he himself will not give Zedekiah this title. The use of the hiphil of *mlk* here may have been occasioned by the reference to Nebuchadnezzar, *hammelek,* "the king," *hammamlîk,* "who made him king." At any rate, the clearest contrast is in vv. 12—13, between the king (Jehoiachin) and his officers (*śārîm*) and the "seed royal" (Zedekiah).

[53] Martin Noth, *Das System der Zwölf Stämme Israels* (BWANT IV/1; Stuttgart: Kohlhammer, 1930) 151—162; E. A. Speiser, "Background and Function of the Biblical *Nāśî'*," *CBQ* 25 (1963) 111—117; F. Hammershaimb, "Ezekiel's View of the Monarchy," *Pedersen Festschrift* (Copenhagen: Einar Munksgaard, 1953) 130—140; Zimmerli, *Ezekiel 1,* 209, 273, 364, and esp. 277—279; Wevers, *Ezekiel,* 65, 66, 113.

[54] Among others, see: Harmut Gese, *Der Verfassungsentwurf des Ezechiel (Kap. 40—48) traditionsgeschichtlich untersucht* (BHT 25; Tübingen: Mohr, 1957); Dieter Baltzer, *Ezekiel und Deuterojesaja: Berührungen in der Heilserwartung der beiden großen Exilspropheten* (BZAW 121; Berlin: de Gruyter, 1971) 136—141; Otto Procksch, "Fürst und Priester bei Hesekiel," *ZAW* 58 (1940/41) 99—133; Jon D. Levenson, "Who is the *Nāśî'* in Ezekiel's Theocracy," *Theology of the Program of Restoration of Ezekiel 40—48* (HSM 10; Missoula: Scholars, 1976) 57—69.

[55] If this conception stems from an Ezekiel school or later "traditionists" (the terminology varies), the reasons for such a distinction are all the more obvious. This is true even granting a certain measure of continuity and consistency of thought across redactional

Ezekiel's eschatological statements present a by no means uniform picture. This lack of uniformity is particularly apparent in the shifts in terminology for leadership across chs. 34, 37, and 40—48, where David will return as prince/shepherd (34:24) or king/shepherd (37:24), or where "the prince" plays a much more limited role in the future theocratic community (40—48).[56] Given the seemingly elastic nature of the terminology employed for Israel's future eschatological ruler, is it reasonable to expect a degree of consistency in the prophet's own use of language for rulers of Judah who play a specific role both in the early chapters of the Ezekiel corpus as well as in history itself? Such an expectation is entirely warranted in light of the perspective of the Book of Ezekiel and a wide assortment of biblical and extra-biblical sources for this period. In fact, it may be that in discussing the genesis of the term in Ezekiel a remarkably consistent and straightforward understanding of the *nāśî'* will emerge. Only in the course of time and as a result of its use in a more eschatological mode has the term undergone certain transformations.[57]

To point up the distinction between Ezekiel's own early and later use of the term *nāśî'*, not to mention later redactional alterations, let it be noted that while some scholars urge a sacral or "theological" dimension to the role in Ezekiel's view of the future *nāśî'*, almost no one would argue a similar position for Ezekiel's early use of the term.[58] Of the total occurrences (36) of the term *nāśî'* in the Book of Ezekiel, just under half (15) refer to contemporaneous "rulers" (see Chart 6). Of these, just under half (7) involve Israelite "rulers," including three specific references to Zedekiah. The general observation that the term *nāśî'* is not equivalent to *melek* but is a designation for a ruler with less political and territorial clout is upheld for two chief reasons: (1) the preponderance of references to "king" as applied to Nebuchadnezzar or Pharaoh (19×); and (2) related to this, the use of the term *nāśî'* for rulers of smaller territories (Judah,

---

boundaries (which many studies do not however stress). See Levenson's helpful summary (*Restoration*, 57—61); also, among others, Klaus Koch, "Die Eigenart der priesterschriftlichen Sinaigesetzgebung," *ZTK* 55 (1958) 40—41; Hammershaimb, "Ezekiel's View," 138; John Hartford-Battersby, *Studies in the Book of Ezekiel* (Cambridge: University, 1935) 63—4.

[56] Permutations in the role of "prince" can even be detected within chs. 40—48 themselves (see Zimmerli, *Ezekiel 2*, 538 ff.; Gese's *nāśî'* stratum, *Verfassungsentwurf*, 108 ff.).

[57] M. Noth (*System*, 152) states: ". . . die Verwendung von נשיא statt מלך im Buch Ezekiel (hat) nichts mit der geforderten besonderen Stellung des judäischen Königs im Zukunftsprogramm zu tun."

[58] Though see Zimmerli (*Ezekiel 1*, 364) who states, in reference to 17:11—21: "(The title) *mlk* expresses the plain political institution. *Nāśî'*, however, in being used for Davidic kings, contains a theological reflective character." Zimmerli's position simply cannot be upheld for the use of the term in chs. 7—21; nowhere is the "theological reflective" character clearly evidenced in these chapters.

Edom, Kedar).[59] This conclusion is not vitiated by the fact that reference is made to a *melek* of Edom (32:29), Tyre (28:12), or Judah (1:2; 17:12).[60] In the case of Edom and Tyre, these are countries significant enough to warrant reference to a "king," in Edom's case alongside a reference to "rulers" as well (32:29); so too Judah (7:27).[61] The reference to Jehoiachin as "king" may be more significant, but discussion of this will be postponed for a moment. The larger point to be made is that in Ezekiel's world-view, there are powerful kings (Nebuchadnezzar and Pharaoh) and numerous less powerful "rulers" (Edom, Kedar, "Sea" and "earth"). In Yahweh's economy, Nebuchadnezzar is in fact *melek mělākîm* "king of kings" (26:7). It is only a matter of time before this reality is fully established and acknowledged by the kings and rulers of the earth. Babylon is Yahweh's agent in establishing His universal dominion (21:31; 29:19; 30:24; 32:11).

Chart Six

Distribution of the Terms Nāśî' and Melek

Nāśî'

1. Total occurrences in the Old Testament: 119 ×
   a) Exodus/Numbers/Joshua (4/55/10): 69 ×
   b) Ezekiel: 36 ×
   c) All others (Gen, Lev, Kgs, Chr, Ezra): 14 ×
2. Occurrences in Ezekiel
   a) Contemporary *Nāśî'*: 15 ×
           Zedekiah: 3 × (12:10,12; 21:25)
           Israelite: 4 × (7:27; 19:1; 21:12; 22:6)
           Non-Israelite: 8 × ("Sea" 26:16; Kedar, 27:21; Egypt, 30:13; Edom, 32:29; Meshech/Tubal, 38:2,3; 39:1; "Earth" 39:18)
   b) Future *Nāśî'*: 21 × (34:24; 37:25; 44:3; 45:7,8,9,16,17,22; 46:2, 4,8,10,12,16,17,18; 48:21,21,22,23)

Melek

3. Occurrences in Ezekiel (33 ×)
   a) Contemporary: 28 ×
           Jehoiachin: 2 × (1:2; 17:12)

---

[59] E. A. Speiser, "*Nāśî'*, 111; Noth, *System,* 152.

[60] Nor is there any need to resort text-critically to LXX's lexical alterations in order to eliminate "problems" with the alternation between king/ruler; the MT is to be preferred (Greenberg, *Ezekiel 1—20,* 18—21; Levenson, *Restoration,* 64; Hammershaimb, "Ezekiel's View," 134; cf. Noth, *System,* 152).

[61] Where the terms "king" and "ruler" appear in so-called "synthetic" parallelism (7:27; 32:29), the conclusion is not to be reached that they are simply alternatives (Levenson, *Restoration,* 64).

General (Israelite): 1 × (7:27)
General (non-Israelite): 4 × (27:33,35; 28:17; 32:10)
Nebuchadnezzar: 13 × (17:12,16; 19:9; 21:19,21; 24:2; 26:7; 29:18,19; 30:10,24,25; 32:11)
Pharaoh: 6 × (29:2,3; 30:21,22; 31:2; 32:2)
Tyre: 1 × (28:12)
Edom: 1 × (32:29)

b) Other, Israelite: 3 × (43:7,7,9)
c) Future, "David": 2 × (37:22,24)

As mentioned above, it has been argued that there is little if any difference in Ezekiel's use of the terms *nāśî'* and *melek*. Levenson, for example, draws upon the single attestation outside of Ezekiel of the term "ruler" as applied to an Israelite king (1 Kgs 11:34) to argue that there is "no incongruity between a promise of eternal kingship to the Davidic house, with special reference to Solomon, and the designation of Solomon as *nāśî'* over Judah."[62] The pertinent section of the passage reads: "Nevertheless I will not take the whole kingdom out of his control, but will make him *nāśî'* all the days of his life" (1 Kgs 11:34). Levenson acknowledges that use of the term *nāśî'* at this point (the only occurrence of its kind in 1 & 2 Kings) was dictated by the announcement of reductions in Solomon's territorial and political hegemony: he was now ruler over the tribe of Judah only, the other ten having been promised by the Shilonite prophet Abijah to King Jeroboam. Yet he extrapolates from this that the question of political power, especially as it is related to the defining of the *nāśî'*, is of "lesser importance" than certain other presumably more theological issues.[63] Clearly, such a conclusion has been reached in the context of arguments concerning the identity of the future, messianic *nāśî'* in Ezekiel (chs. 40—48) and the desire to attribute to him certain Davidic characteristics. Levenson seeks to maximize continuity between the terms *nāśî'* and *melek* on the basis of this early text in Kings in order to argue for the same sense of continuity between the *nāśî'* of the restoration program and the *melek* of former days. But such an approach does not address the fundamental question as to why Ezekiel adopted the term *nāśî'* to begin with, much less why he tends to avoid a term like *melek* altogether when speaking of Israel's kings in chs. 1—21.

Almost all who have attempted to define the term *nāśî'* in Ezekiel have noted its strikingly infrequent appearance in the OT outside of

---

[62] *Restoration*, 64.

[63] *Restoration*, 64. He then goes on to conclude from their appearance side-by-side in Ezekiel 7:27 and 32:29 that the terms "ruler" and "king" are in "synthetic" or "impressionistic" parallelism, "the same unit of meaning expressed completely in each of the two clauses." This apparently means they are roughly or exactly identical. See also M. Greenberg, *Ezekiel 1—20*, 156—7.

Exodus/Numbers/Joshua (see Chart 6). Over 90 % of all occurrences are found in these books or in Ezekiel, Numbers itself claiming over half. There are a number of reasons given for this fact, which at first glance may seem unusual considering the time span (over a millennium) and literary difference (Hexateuch // Prophets) between these early books and the Ezekiel material. These problems disappear when it is noted that (1) the term *nāśî'* generally falls in those sections of the Hexateuch termed P; and (2) there is a clear relationship between the Ezekiel traditions and this same so-called Priestly Document (particularly in Ezekiel, chs. 40—48).

The biblical evidence indicates that the *něśî'ê hā'ēdāh* (Nu 4:34; 31:13; 32:2; Jos 9:15,18; 22:30) functioned in the pre-monarchic period as tribal leaders.[64] In the Book of Numbers, each of the twelve tribes has a representative *nāśî'*, who appears alongside other leaders of the congregation, including Moses and Aaron, priests, levites, and elders, when the Israelite community is assembled (e.g., Numbers 1—9). In the wilderness period, before the period of the *šōpěṭîm* or the later *mělākîm,* each tribe has its *nāśî'* who carries out fundamental administrative and leadership duties. Semantically, the term probably means one "called up," "nominated" or "lifted up" by the members of the tribes and various *bêt 'ābôt* whom they represent.[65] *Nāśî'* is the nominal (*qāṭîl*) form of the verb *nś'*, "to raise, lift," similar in form to other familiar terms, including *nābî'* "prophet," *nāgîd* "[king/leader] designate," *māšîaḥ* "anointed," *nādîb* "noble."[66]

Noth credits the use of the term *nāśî'* in Ezekiel to a basic misunderstanding (*Ermangelung*) of the original meaning intended by the Priestly writer, that is, the *nāśî'* as tribal spokesman. This is true of Ezekiel's application of the term to minor kings and rulers of the past and present, as well as to the future Israelite ruler of chs. 40—48. In this latter instance,

---

[64] Also *něśî'ê hammaṭṭôt* (Nu 7:2), *něśî'ê yiśrā'ēl* (Nu 1:44; 4:46; 7:2,84).

[65] Speiser notes the parallelism of Nu 1:16, which speaks of those "chosen of the assembly" (*qěrî'ê hā'ēdāh*), the "leaders of the their ancestral tribes" (*něśî'ê maṭṭôt 'ăbôtām*). On the relationship between the "father's house" and the tribe, see Speiser, "*Nāśî'*," 113. The three Levite clans each had a *nāśî'* (Nu 3:24).

[66] See Speiser, "*Nāśî'*," 114. There are passive and active *qāṭîl* forms (compare "anointed" and *qāṣîr* "harvester"), and some which appear to have both modalities — *nāśî'* and *nābî* are likely candidates. Noth considered the *nāśî'* one who "lifted up his voice," i.e., a spokesman (*System,* 151—62; *Exodus* [OTL; Philadelphia: Westminster, 1962] 187; *Numbers* [OTL; Philadelphia: Westminster, 1968] 19 ff.). For Noth, the office of *nāśî'* was quite old, dating back to the period of the Israelite federation (so-called "amphictyony") and even earlier, when the tribes had a separate existence. They were "permanent and perhaps lifelong tribal representatives" (*Numbers,* 19). Problems with the "amphictyony" concept itself do not undercut Noth's basic view of the *nāśî'*. However, the *nāśî'* was probably more of a secular than a religious figure (*System,* 159—161). Noth argued for the latter in part because of his understanding of the Israelite federation (see *System,* esp. 160).

according to Noth, the term was used primarily to avoid any suggestion that the new ruler would be the usual oriental *melek*. In other words, the priestly writer was the first to make widespread use of the term, which had roots stretching back to the pre-monarchic period and a sacral dimension due to the role of the *něśîʾîm* in the amphictyonic assembly. As a result of the coincidence of the priestly writer's proximity to the Book of Ezekiel, the term was picked up and (mis)applied there.

Apart from problems with Noth's conception of the sacral role of the *nāśîʾ* at the central shrine of the tribal federation, his understanding of the sequence of influence (early to P to Ezekiel) in adoption of the term is flawed. In the early period, the *nāśîʾ* was a leader of a smaller political and geographical unit, such as a tribe and/or a *bêt ʾāb*. In the period of the monarchy, the *melek* ruled over a fixed confederation of tribes. This was true for both the northern and southern monarchs, even though the Judahite king in particular ruled over a greatly reduced "kingdom" (so 1 Kgs 11:34). Once the term "king" was employed for David, however, it was maintained within the Judahite monarchy. Dynastic stability in Judah assured this.

After the death of Josiah, however, Judahite monarchy was threatened by major internal and external disruptions. These have already been discussed in some detail, and the important moments in Judah's earlier monarchial history have been outlined when the stability of the dynastic enterprise was threatened. It is reasonable to assume that part of the explanation for Ezekiel's employment of the term *nāśîʾ* is tied to the fact that the monarchy had to be quite differently conceived once Judah's king was deported to Babylon. There were other important considerations as well. With Josiah's tragic death at Megiddo only about decade earlier, the "people of the land" had intervened to place Jehoahaz on the throne, and in so doing had set aside the principle of primogeniture. Jehoahaz was deported to Egypt and never returned to Judah. His older brother ruled only as a result of Egyptian appointment, and for the greater part of his eleven-year rule there was instability in the capital. His death, as noted, remains a mystery about which there can only be reasonable conjecture. Zedekiah, in turn, rules only according to Babylonian privilege. He is the king "of Nebuchadnezzar's choice" (*šarru ša libbi-šu, CCK,* 73). Moreover, following the capture of the city in 597 the territory of Judah is greatly reduced in size and influence. As such, use of the term *nāśîʾ* by Ezekiel for the "Judahite ruler" of this period is understandable. The *nāśîʾ* of the wilderness period was a leader of a single tribal unit; the same was essentially true of the *nāśîʾ* Zedekiah.

In addition to these general historical observations, a number of other reasons can be given for Ezekiel's use of the term "ruler" rather than "king."

(1) Ezekiel conceives of this period, both in Judah and in Exile, as resembling Israel's years in the wilderness. A long sermon to this effect is provided in Ch. 20. The present judgment is likened to the judgment of the fathers in the "wilderness of the land of Egypt" (*bĕmidbar 'ereṣ miṣrāyim,* v. 36). While the respective allotments for Ezekiel's supine siege enactments (Ch. 4) are difficult to correlate with one another (390 + 40 days), the length of time that Ezekiel is to "bear the punishment of the house of Judah" on his right side is a 40-day period clearly related to the years of Israel's sojourn in the wilderness, "a day for each year" (4:6). And as the first wilderness period had its *nĕśî'îm,* so too does this wilderness period.[67]

(2) In Ezekiel's view, this is a period when there is a "king of kings" (26:7) and numerous other minor kings and princes. Such a view conforms well to the political situation in the period of the wilderness and occupation: Pharaoh is "king of kings" and Israel confronts many other smaller kings and princes in the wilderness and upon entry into the land (Amorite, Midian, Canaanite, Moabite; Jericho, Ai, Jerusalem, Heshbon, Hazor, Gilgal; See Numbers 21—23; 31—33; Deuteronomy 1—4; Joshua 2—12).

(3) It is a period when there is no kingdom of tribes in Judah, nor even an essentially strong Southern Kingdom. There is only the greatly reduced territory of the single tribe of Judah. Its "king" rules only through the favor of the Babylonian "king of kings." As in the wilderness period, the single tribe had not a *melek,* but a *nāśî'.*

(4) It is a period when, as in the wilderness and occupation years, there was no king in Israel (Ju 21:25). There were only kings of other countries (a situation that Israel was not to envy). The challenging question involves Ezekiel's view of the deported king Jehoiachin. It is certain that from his perspective in Babylon, "there was no king in Israel"; but was there a king in Exile?

(5) It is a period when, since the days of Josiah, there had been a plurality of leadership in the capital. Jehoiakim, Jehoahaz, and Zedekiah are three sons of Josiah who eventually rule in Jerusalem. Josiah may have had other wives, and certainly more sons. Jehoiakim's own son Jehoiachin ruled in Jerusalem, even while Zedekiah was still on the scene. From the so-called Weidner tablets, it is known that Jehoiachin had 5 sons himself![68] All of these royal "rulers" were

---

[67] Recall as well the way the wilderness years and the blessing/curse of Deuteronomy (Chs. 27—29) are linked to events far off in the future: the cursed loss of land and the Exile itself (28:28), to be followed by a blessed new Exodus (30:1—5).

[68] Some interpret the references as brothers, i.e., sons not of Jehoiachin but of Jehoiakim; the essential point remains the same. For texts and discussion, see Ernst Weidner, "Jojachin, König von Judah, in babylonischen Keilschrifttexten," *Mélanges Syriens offrets à Monsieur Réne Dussaud* (Paris: Paul Geuthner, 1939) 2.923—7.

approximate contemporaries in Jerusalem during this period. When the principle of primogeniture was set aside in the case of Jehoahaz' enthronement, and when right to rule in Judah is increasingly determined by external forces (Egypt; Babylon), what was to prevent any of the "seed royal" from seeking the throne? This is precisely the situation behind the assassination of Gedaliah by Ishmael, as well as the kidnapping of the kings' daughters in the period following the Fall of the city in 587 B. C. (Jer 41:1—18). The assumption of the throne by Zedekiah is also an unprecedented case of power passing within a generation (brother), even after it had already moved to the next generation (son).

(6) Add to this fact that in the period under discussion kings are increasingly able to trace their origin to the tribal districts outside of the capital (Jehoahaz: Judah; Jehoiakim: Zebulon; Zedekiah: Judah; even Josiah: Judah; see Chart 4 above) and Ezekiel's use of the term *nāśî'* is not only justifiable but accurate.

In the historical survey of the exilic period a growing tension was noted between capital and countryside. The discussion of the role of the "people of the land" demonstrated the degree to which Judahite influence had penetrated the capital and the monarchial system. In the last two decades of Judah's existence, only the mother of Jehoiachin comes from the capital. Josiah, Jehoahaz, Jehoiakim, and Zedekiah all trace their lineage to tribal regions beyond Jerusalem. From the perspective of the Books of Kings and Jeremiah, these last rulers are nevertheless "kings" in the traditional sense of the word. Despite the instability of the external political scene, with its impact on affairs in Jerusalem, Judah's last four rulers are not categorized as distinct in any way from their predecessors. But it is not clear that the same was true of Ezekiel's perspective on the Judahite monarchial enterprise. His use of the term *nāśî'* signals more than an idiosyncratic or nostalgic adoption of a title from the period of Israel's early years. It is one way that he points up certain distinctive features of the monarchy that obtain during this "wilderness period."

One question yet to be resolved concerns Ezekiel's evaluation of King Jehoiachin. Jehoiachin is the only Judahite ruler to merit the title *melek* in the Book of Ezekiel. This fact is significant in and of itself. But other observations can be made. He is the only king who comes to power in Judah during this period without Egyptian or Babylonian interference (cf. Jehoiakim; Zedekiah). The "people of the land" do not play a role in his accession. Nehushta, his mother, is from the capital. He is a king who is portrayed at 2 Kgs 24:12 as submitting without resistance to Nebuchadnezzar ("he gave himself up": *wayyēṣē' yĕhôyākîn melek-yĕhûdāh 'al-melek bābel*), together with his entire royal family. This is in complete conformity with Jeremiah's pronouncements concerning submission to Babylon, and

Ezekiel may understand his actions in this light. However, the picture of this same king as it appears in the Jeremiah traditions is not a positive one (22:24—30; 13:18—19). Conversely, Jehoiachin is the king who shares the same exilic fate as the prophet Ezekiel. The book orients itself in terms of the years of his exile. Though it moves beyond the historical period under discussion, it is clear that in the course of time hopes associated with the kingship of Jehoiachin never died out (2 Kgs 25:27—30; Hag 2:23; the scion Zerubbabel in Ezra), though transformations in the actual role of the monarchy are envisioned (Ez 40—48) and carried through.[69] The same cannot be said of King Zedekiah.

Apart from the general observations made above concerning the contrast between Jehoiachin and Zedekiah, there are two other key texts which may help pin down Ezekiel's view of Jehoiachin (19:1—14; 21:29—32 [Eng 24—27]). With this view in place, it should be possible to gain a clearer picture of the monarchy and its future within the restored Israel, as laid out in the early chapters of the Book of Ezekiel. What is of specific interest is the extent to which Ezekiel's view of the monarchy is the specific result of this prophet's interpretation of events leading up to and culminating in the deportations of 597 B. C. The degree to which he sees these events as final, definitive signs of Yahweh's judgment over Judah would exert considerable influence on his evaluation of the Judahite monarchy, both as an institution which contributed to the downfall of 597 B. C., and as it continues in Judah in the person of Zedekiah.

B. Dirge over Israel's Rulers (Ezek 19:1—14)

This particular text from Ezekiel has been notoriously successful in eliciting new and conflicting interpretations. Text critical problems abound, but they are hardly unfamiliar to the critical reader of Ezekiel. Here, perhaps due to its poetic form (somewhat striking in these early chapters; a poetic dirge would fit better in the middle of the book), the interpreter has the added burden of a certain pithiness in expression. It is not at all clear, for example, how one is to deal with the shifts from singular to plural in the third strophe (vv. 11—12), not to mention the shifts from masculine to feminine. As such, it is difficult to know whether the vine or strong bough(s) is/are being spoken of. If a plural reading is adopted for v. 11 (as the MT prefers), how does the the single "strong bough" appear in v. 12? There are several lexical difficulties (v. 9) and odd turns of expression (v. 10) that appear to have befuddled even our versional predecessors, who everywhere demonstrate an often oddly expressed desire to uncomplicate the MT. For this reason, the *lectio difficilior* of the MT

---

[69] Note the use of the term *nāśî'* as applied to Sheshbazzar in Ezra 1:8, and the new leadership patterns which emerge in the post-exilic community.

must be allowed to stand, if for no other reason than to take Ezekiel seriously as "more difficult prophet."

All interpreters seem to agree that the first strophe of the dirge (vv. 1—4) speaks of Jehoahaz. This is an odd fact in and of itself, since Jehoahaz' three-month and long-concluded reign would not warrant special commentary from Ezekiel. Scholars typically go one of two ways in dealing with the dirge's complex imparting of historical data. They either conclude that the dirge, taken as a whole, is primarily a metaphorical composition which rides high enough above the realm of history to require no coherent picture in the *bruta facta* it does on occasion record.[70] Others tend to be impressed by the glimpses of important detail the dirge relates when it is not being overly poetic, but cannot agree as to just who each of the various characters (lionness, cubs, vine, bough) represent on the dirge's subtle and confusing historical canvas.[71] In reality, both groups recognize the janus-like quality of the text before them, which presents enough of both the "typical" and the "special" that neither realm can be completely ignored. This is particularly evident when the figure of the lioness is taken by members of both groups as emblematic of Judah, thus allowing a key symbol to stand even as the cubs take on quite concrete historical characteristics.

Text I

Ezekiel 19:1—14

(1) Now you, lift up a qinah to Israel's rulers, and say:

(2) What a lioness was your mother
    among lions
Couching amoung young lions
    rearing her cubs

(3) She raised one of her cubs
    he became a young lion
He learned to tear prey
    he devoured men

(4) Nations heard of him
    in their snare he was caught

---

[70] M. Greenberg, *Ezekiel 1—20,* 356—9; to a certain extent, Zimmerli (*Ezekiel 1,* 388—98) fits better in this group than the other.

[71] J. Wevers, *Ezekiel,* 112—14; Noth, "Jerusalem Catastrophe," 271—276; Eichrodt, *Ezekiel,* 249—58; W. L. Brownlee, "Two Elegies on the Fall of Judah," *Studies in the History of Religions* 21.1 [Leiden: Brill, 1972] 93—103; Georg Froher, *Ezechiel* [HAT 13; Tübingen: J. C. B. Mohr, 1955] 104—7.

They brought him in shackles
   to the land of Egypt

(5) When she saw how she waited
   her hope died out
She took another of her cubs
   set him as a young lion

(6) He roved among lions
   he became a young lion
He learned to tear prey
   he devoured men

(7) He knew his widows
   he made desolate their cities
The land, all of it, was appalled
   at the sound of his roar

(8) Nations set upon him
   from surrounding provinces
They spread their net upon him
   in their snare he was caught

(9) They put him, shackled, in neckstocks
   they brought him to the king of Babylon
     [brought him in custody]
That his voice might no longer be heard
   on the mountains of Israel

(10) Your mother was like a vine in your blood
   planted by waters
She became fruitful and ramified
   from much water

(11) She had strong boughs
   (fit) for rulers' scepters
Its height reached to the clouds
   it was seen in its height
   with its mass of branches

(12) But she was uprooted in fury
   hurled to the earth
East wind dried up her fruit
   they broke off and withered
As for the strong bough —
   fire consumed it

(13) Now she is planted in the wilderness
   in a land dry and thirsty

(14) Fire went forth from the bough
    devoured its shoots and fruit
Now there is no strong bough in it
    (fit) for a ruler's scepter
This is a qinah, and it has become a qinah.

Notes and Commentary (vv. 1—14)

(1) *nĕśî'ê* "rulers" (pl). Though this word can appear in Ezekiel (MT) in the singular (7:27; cf. Ch. 22), G's singular is not to be preferred (cf. Greenberg's discussion, *Ezekiel 1—20,* 349). Not only does the dirge speak of several "rulers" (clear even in vv. 1—9); it never did otherwise. This is made evident by several factors. The dirge draws upon several sources (Zeph 3:3; Na 2:12—14) for its lion imagery, but its chief inspiration (outside of other Ezekiel material!) is Gen 49:9—12. Use of language from this old poem is witnessed across all three strophes of the dirge, including the odd shift to the vine and scepter motif in vv. 10 ff. (Gen 49:10,11). This particular juxta-position suggests an unusually constructed but essentially unified composition (*contra* Eichrodt, *Ezekiel,* 256, who would see this as "a too systematic utilization of remote literary models"). When one considers the use made of this same Gen passage in Ezek 21:36, the unavoidable explanation for the juxtaposition of images found here is that the prophet has the entirety of the Genesis poem in mind (so W. Moran, "Gen 49:10 and its Use in Ezek 21:32," *Bib* 39 [1958] 405—25; *contra* Levenson, *Restoration,* 77).

(2) The 3:2 or medium/short line, perhaps in view of the dirge genre, is consistently maintained through v. 9; only 9a seems overloaded. For "lion" (*'aryēh*), "couching" (*rābaṣ*), "cub" (*gûr*), see Gen 49:9—12, where the subject is not Judah's mother but Judah; hence the masculine forms there, and the feminine here (*rābāṣāh; ribbĕtāh*). Even the appearance there of *lābî'* is not the evocation of a female lion image (Gen 49:9); it is merely an alternative word in parallelism for *'aryēh* (Skinner, *Genesis* [ICC; New York: Scribners, 1917] 519; C. Westermann, *Genesis* [BK I/3; Neukirchen/Vluyn: Neukirchener, 1982]). This is further shown by the feminine vocalization provided at Ezek 19:2, which suggests the Massoretes considered *lābî'* masculine (Skinner, *Genesis;* Greenberg, *Ezekiel 1—20,* 350; Zimmerli, *Ezekiel 1,* 388). It also suggests that Ezekiel's dirge will shift attention from the whelp alone (Gen 49) to the mother (vv. 2, 3, 5, 10—12) and whelp(s) together (vv. 3, 4, 6—9, 11—14).

(3) In Gen 49:9, it is the cub himself who "grows up" (*'ālîtā*) "on prey" (*miṭṭerep*). Here the focus is on the mother's role in rearing and raising (*watta'al*), and the cub's learning to "tear prey" (*liṭrāp-ṭerep*) (so Greenberg, *Ezekiel 1—20,* 350). Note how these images are precisely re-employed for the second cub (v. 6). For "devouring" see Ezek 34:2,10, where the shepherds are condemned for this, and esp. 22:25.

(4) For a discussion of "net" and "shackles," see Greenberg, *Ezekiel 1—20,* 351; cf. Zimmerli, *Ezekiel 1,* 389. Whether one reads "pit" or "hooks" as alternatives may not seem significant exegetically; but it could assist in determining just how metaphorically or historically to take the references (i.e., are they images from lion hunting or human capture?) Note that the images of being taken in a net (*bĕšaḥtām nitpāś*) and shackles (*baḥaḥîm*) appear again in reference to the second cub (vv. 8, 9). This repetition suggests a more literary than historical allusion. The same is not true of the other details in the fuller second strophe.

(5) Reading the obscure *nôḥălāh* (an unprecedented *niphal* of *yḥl?*) with the help of Syriac *'wḥl* (Greenberg, *Ezekiel 1—20*, 351). The reference is to waiting in vain for Jehoahaz to return from Egypt.

(6) Employment of same imagery from v. 3. However, this cub needs no motherly rearing (cf. v. 3); he is simply set up as a *kěpîr*, and is confirmed as such by grazing with other lions (v. 6). This minor detail, since it is a departure from the set theme of rearing in the first strophe, may be significant. Where there are plusses over and above typical elements in the poem, one is entitled to search for a more historical allusion (see v. 9).

(7) Ezek 22:25 says of "the evil princes" that they have "made many widows" *'almĕnôtêhā ḥirbû*. Since this passage includes the constellation of offenses also mentioned in the dirge (". . . roaring lion tearing prey; they have devoured human lives . . ."), it is reasonable to assume that the unusual expression *wayyēda' 'almĕnôtâw* is related to the expression of 22:25. "Knowing", then, is unrelated to sexual knowledge and has the nuance "count," "take note," "acknowledge" (Greenberg, *Ezekiel 1—20, 351*).

(8) Again, typical motifs are repeated from v. 4.

(9) Apart from lexical difficulties (esp. *bassûgar; bammĕṣōdôt; see* the full discussion of Zimmerli, *Ezekiel 1,* 390; M. Noth, "Jerusalem Catastrophe," 273) which require the use of Akkadian cognates for elucidation, the chief problem of v. 9 is that the neat 3:2 pattern is suddenly dispensed with. Noth and Zimmerli agree there are additions but disagree on just what they are, Noth opting for "and they brought him to the king of Babylon" as the "explanatory gloss" ("Jerusalem Catastrophe," 273), Zimmerli for both "shackled" (he reads "with hooks") and "where they brought him into custody," *yĕbi'uhû bammĕṣōdôt* (*Ezekiel 1,* 390). Greenberg mentions no difficulty. Noth wishes to dispense with the first because of his interpretation of the cub as Jehoiakim (a view held by virtually no one), on the theory that Jehoiakim was only captured/imprisoned, but not deported, and died in Jerusalem. [Our inquiry into the death of Jehoiakim in the section above would be greatly aided by this additional bit of information; however, Noth's interpretation creates more problems than it solves — see discussion below.] Apart from the fact that, technically speaking, the phrase as it stands need not be interpreted as referring to a deportation (since Jehoiakim could have been handed over to the king of Babylon while he was in Judah), the more likely candidate for an addition would be a final rather than an internal gloss. Such an addition would have been included when it was known by Ezekiel or later traditionists that Zedekiah had in fact been taken into Babylonian custody. But such a view cannot be upheld until it is firmly established that the subject of the second strophe (and the third) is King Zedekiah.

(10) In the third strophe, while the figure of the mother is continued, she is now a vine; the cubs are now branches. Note that Gen 49:9—12, beyond the image of the lion, also offers a vine (v. 11), a staff (v. 10), and blood (v. 12); the unusual juxtaposition of images across the strophes of the dirge (lion/vine) are also found, together with others, in Gen 49:9—12. This cannot be mere coincidence, but suggests an intricate re-use by Ezekiel of this oracle concerning Judah. Many read "Vine in your vineyard" (*krmk*); others delete altogether (there are MSS with both; see Zimmerli's discussion, *Ezekiel 1,* 390). However, Syriac, Vulgate, and LXX (Symmachus; Theodotion) seem to read MT's *bĕdāmĕkā*, and this unusual expression is to be preferred. The reference is to the blood shed by the vine's branches ("your blood"), Jehoahaz and Zedekiah (see Greenberg's discussion, *Ezekiel 1—20,* 353); Ezekiel elsewhere refers to this as

the crime of the rulers (22:6). Images from chs. 17 (and 15) are re-employed here: the vine is planted by much water (v. 10), it gives forth many branches and fruit (vv. 10—11), it is uprooted and withered by the east wind (v. 12), and it is consumed with fire (v. 12; cf. 15:7).

(11) The plural forms of the MT (*maṭṭôt; šiḇṭê mōšĕlîm*) are to be preferred; as Greenberg accurately notes, they refer to royal scions of Judah (*Ezekiel 1—20*, 353), and more specifically, to the scions of Hamutal referred to in the first two stanzas (and possibly others?). The movement to the singular bough and staff occurs in vv. 12, 13.

(12) Compare 17:9—10 for the images of uprooting and withering. The line is oddly divided and the subject of *hitpārĕqû wĕyāḇēšû* is not clear; "boughs," though plural, are too far away (v. 11); the fruit (though singular? perhaps collective?) fits the image of breaking off and withering better than the following "strong bough," which is now singular (cf. v. 11). The sequence is as follows: first the fruit falls off and withers; then fire consumes the single strong bough, which must represent the second cub Zedekiah.

(13/14) After all this, the vine is then planted in the wilderness and fire spreads from the single bough to destroy all possible growth. On the basis of what seems like a strained logic or an over-accumulation of punishment, this additional verse (14) is often deleted as "a late interpretive remark to v. 12b" (Zimmerli, *Ezekiel,* 391,8; also M. Noth "Jerusalem Catastrophe," 274—6, who sees it and the reference to the strong rod(s) in v. 12 as a secondary attempt to relate the oracle to Zedekiah). But as Greenberg points out, multiple punishment is a familiar motif in Ezekiel (Ch. 17; 16:40). Furthermore, the combination of burning and re-planting occurs precisely because both are mentioned in Ezekiel (15:5; 17:9 ff.). The historical allusion may be to the further elimination of any possible rulers from this vine; 2 Kgs 25:7 reports that the sons of Zedekiah were slain after he was taken to Riblah.

Upon leaving the first strophe, problems in interpretation are encountered. Those who interpret the second cub as Jehoiakim appeal to a chronological logic (Jehoahaz— Jehoiakim) and above all to the particular applicability of details in this strophe to his situation.[72] Moreover, it is quite likely that the Chronicler and Daniel were early proponents of this interpretation, erroneously assuming a chronological sequencing in the dirge.[73] Those who opt for Jehoiachin have the common deportee-fate of its subject (vv. 4,9) on their side.[74] They are not bothered by seeming lack

---

[72] M. Noth is a modern representative of this view ("Jerusalem Catastrophe," 273). Zedekiah is ruled out for him since "the description in the second stanza of the young lion spreading terror all around hardly fits the weak and fearful Zedekiah." In Noth's view, the third stanza concerns Jehoiachin. So far as can be determined, Noth stands alone in this Jehoahaz/Jehoiakim/Jehoiachin theory, which requires a good deal of textual surgery both here and elsewhere in Ezekiel (although see G. A. Cooke, *Ezekiel* [ICC; Edingburgh: Clark, 1936]). Noth misses the mark badly when he goes on to conclude that Zedekiah finds no place in the whole dirge because he is not considered one of the *nĕśî'ê yiśrā'ēl* by Ezekiel (p. 277); also Wevers, *Ezekiel,* 113. Is it not Zedekiah alone who can be unequivocally identified as a *nāśî'* in Ezekiel (see Chart 6)?!

[73] See Greenberg, *Ezekiel 1—20,* 356; Andre LaCocque, *Daniel* (Atlanta: John Knox, 1979) 25.

[74] Zimmerli (*Ezekiel 1,* 394) speaks of "the parallelism of deportation to West and East" which Ezekiel picked up from Hosea (9:3); Greenberg, *Ezekiel 1—20,* 356; Wevers, *Ezekiel,* 113.

of historical applicability, since in their view the dirge is here simply relating typical details.[75] The non-mention of Jehoiakim is, in Zimmerli's view, "thematically conditioned" (395). By this he seems to mean three separate things: (1) the dirge refers only to kings "who were in no way important politically," or (2) who "gain prominence from their common fate of deportation," or (3) the dirge draws upon the laments against kings in Jeremiah (Ch. 22), in which, according to Zimmerli, only Jehoahaz and Jehoiachin are technically lamented.[76]

None of these explanations is particularly illuminating. Since reference is ultimately made to Zedekiah in the third strophe of the dirge, his political importance or non-importance is no decisive factor in his inclusion or non-inclusion in the second strophe.[77] With reference to the second issue, Zedekiah is of course deported, and in a manner not unlike that which is described in vv. 8—9. The most telling point here is that when reference is made in Ezekiel to a forceful capture and deportation of an Israelite *nāśî*, it is this language which is used and the *nāśî* spoken of is not Jehoiachin but Zedekiah. Zedekiah meets snare and net and removal to Babylon in 12:13 and again in 17:20 — in this latter passage, his "common fate of deportation" stands in absolute contrast to King Jehoiachin's removal by Yahweh to Babylon (17:4,22—24). Our controlling assumption is that there is an important literary relationship between the dirge and other sections of Ezekiel. This is rejected by Zimmerli and others; it will have to be further demonstrated below.[78] In any event, the "common fate of deportation" shared by Zedekiah is a much more prominent theme in Ezekiel than that of King Jehoiachin. Finally, Zimmerli's distinction between the laments for Jehoahaz and Jehoiachin in Jer

---

[75] In answer to the question, "How could Jehoiachin be depicted as a ferocious man-eater (v. 7)?" the response is simply that similar hyperbole was used with Jehoahaz in the first strophe, whose career was equally ephemeral. But the imagery of terror is actually increased in the second strophe. And what of the other seemingly specific allusions that go beyond the typicality of the Jehoahaz strophe? Jehoiachin's reign does not begin after a period of waiting (v. 5); the details of v. 9 suggest the capture of a resistent king, which by no means squares with the report of Jehoiachin's capture in 2 Kgs 24:12 ff.

[76] Zimmerli, *Ezekiel 1*, 394.

[77] Zimmerli tries to eliminate this as a consideration by taking the references to Zedekiah in the third strophe as secondary additions (*Ezekiel 1*, 397), thus destroying a unity of theme the dirge originally maintained.

[78] M. Noth's remarks on this subject are somewhat typical. He says, rejecting the possibility that reference to the vine as Zedekiah in Ch. 17 could be carried over to the third strophe of the dirge in Ch. 19: "Ezek. XVII and XIX are completely independent units; the prophet was free to use whatever images he wished, and the interpretation of each unit must be sought quite independently" ("Jerusalem Catastrophe," 275). As if to demonstrate his own idiosyncratic use of this rule, Noth proceeds then to interpret Ezek 17:22—24 armed with a specific interpretation of the vine of Ch. 19 as pointing to Jehoiachin (p. 277). Zimmerli's appeal to the fact of secondary additions helps destroy the possibility of interpreting the dirge clearly on the basis of other Ezekiel passages.

22:10 — 12 and 24 — 30 and that of Jehoiakim (vv. 13 — 23) is groundless and has no bearing on the interpretation of the dirge, in any formal sense. If it did, one might look for the sequence Jeremiah adopts, that is, the chronological one: Jehoahaz, Jehoiakim, Jehoiachin.[79] If anything, it is the omission of Jehoiachin from Ezekiel's dirge that is striking in view of Jeremiah's own potent pronouncements against him.

A third group favors Zedekiah for the cub of the second strophe. As has been noted, they too appeal to the fact of his deportation to Babylon, referred to in 19:9, but prefer beyond this to identify the lioness of 19:2 with an actual mother, Hamutal, who was in fact mother of the two brother cubs Jehoahaz and Zedekiah (2 Kgs 23:31; 24:18).[80] This interpretative move is a controversial one, usually dismissed as a *tour de force* which demolishes the dirge's ability to convey its metaphorical message. Greenberg is typically efficient in his rejection of the Hamutal-hypothesis, terming it "a gratuitous enhancement of a wholly obscure person" which "reduces the pathetic grandeur" of the allegory, in which "fidelty to history is subordinated to the elegeic theme of onetime glory turned into disgrace and ruin."[81]

Such a strong judgment cannot be lightly dismissed. But as already noted, it is clear that the dirge participates in the realms of both allegory and history. Moreover, there is a way to adjudicate the value of historical allusions without completely rejecting one side of the history/allegory combination of the dirge.

It is first of all to be noted that the dirge is not an original composition in the strict sense of the word. Its language and motifs are drawn from sources both within Ezekiel, that is, consistent with the prophet's own literary and theological perspective, and from other sections of the OT, notably Gen 49:9 — 12, but also Na 2:10 — 12 and Zeph 3:3 — 5.[82] This fact should at the outset guard against overblown notions of the dirge's independence, either as a poetic masterpiece disinterested in the mundane realms, or as a political puzzle conceived apart from other clear patterns in Ezekiel. Since the prophet shows himself interested in specific details related to the Judahite monarchy and her individual monarchs elsewhere

---

[79] Pronouncements against Zedekiah introduce (Ch. 21) and conclude (Ch. 24) this larger unit, as if to allow the strongest denunciation to fall on Zedekiah and the post-597 community (21:7 — 10; 24:8 — 10) in Judah. See Pohlmann (*Studien,* 41 ff.), Ackroyd ("Historians," 52, n. 25), Nicholson (*Preaching,* 42), Seitz ("Crisis," 86 — 92), and Carroll (*Chaos,* 136 — 57).

[80] Apparently suggested early on by Richard Kraetzschmar, *Das Buch Ezechiel* (HKAT; Göttingen: Vandenhoeck & Ruprecht, 1900). See now, W. Eichrodt, *Ezekiel,* 254 — 5; G. Fohrer, *Ezechiel,* 105 — 6; Peter Craigie, *Ezekiel* (Philadelphia: Westminster, 1983) 139 — 41; Brownlee entertains this possibility ("Elegies," 102), but ends up with Zedekiah here even as he takes the lioness to be Judah.

[81] *Ezekiel 1 — 20,* 357.

[82] Greenberg, *Ezekiel 1 — 20,* 357.

(chs. 12, 17, 21), there is good reason to expect as much here. In fact, the dirge is a virtual summary of Ezekiel's evaluation of the monarchy, as it finds expression at random moments throughout the book.

Dirges and various forms of pronouncements against kings and rulers are found in the central part of the Book of Ezekiel (Chs. 27—32). These envision the final carrying out of judgment against an assembly of disparate foreign powers, at the hand (or sword) of the commissioned Nebuchadnezzar. The early positioning of Ezekiel's dirge against Israel's own rulers (Ch. 19) is therefore significant. It signals, in proleptic fashion, the full end of the Judahite monarchy. This is implied in the final line: the poem is a dirge, and it has become a dirge. That Zedekiah, Judah's last ruler, would have been exempted from a lamentation covering the final period of a nation's potential strength is most unlikely. Zedekiah is clearly one of the subjects of the dirge's third strophe. As the majority of scholars have noted, he is the strong bough mentioned in vv. 12—13, which fire not only consumes, but from which fire spreads to the whole vine, leaving it in the end with no ruler's staff (v. 14) where once it had many (v. 11).

The image of the vine (*gepen*) is known elsewhere in Ezekiel, and the prophet clearly means to establish no new use of it here in the dirge. In Ch. 15, the wood (*ʿēṣ*) of the vine is evaluated by Yahweh and the prophet, in the specific context of other types of wood (*mikkol-ʿēṣ*) from trees of the forest (*baʿăṣê hayyāʿar*). When burned, there is nothing of use left of the vinewood; in fact, there is not much use for it before it is burned (v. 5). It is the wood (*ʿēṣ*) of this vine that is identified with the inhabitants of Jerusalem (vv. 6—8), who like the vine (*gepen*) of 19:9 meet their fate through fire. In Ch. 17, not the wood but the vine itself appears as a main character, along with eagles and a special kind of tree from the forest, a cedar.

The vine is everywhere contrasted with the cedar. The cedar's topmost growth is taken to Babylon; the vine stays in the land. In fact, the vine begins its growth as a "seed of the land." As in Ch. 19, the vine has many branches (17:7); it is re-planted by abundant waters (17:8); it is to be pulled up, withered and smitten by the east wind (17:10). It appears from the interpretation of 17:13 ff. that the "seed of the land" (17:5) from which the vine grew was "one of the seed royal"; since in what follows this "royal seed" is clearly Zedekiah, it appears that the *gepen* is in fact Zedekiah. The "inhabitants of Jerusalem" from Ch. 15 are then the "wood" of this vine, which is deemed worthless and burned, just as is the vine itself in Ch. 19. But the identification of the vine with Zedekiah is not absolutely clear. It is not the cedar which is identified with Jehoiachin in vv. 22—24, but the "lofty crown" (*miṣṣammeret*) and "topmost shoot" (*mērōʾš yōnĕqôtāw*) of the cedar. It would seem that the cedar and the vine represent two contrasting royal plants with their respective forms of growth: shoot (Jehoiachin) and branch (Zedekiah). This is precisely the way the image is developed in Ch. 19. There are many branches on the vine (19:10) which merit a ruler's scepter (v. 11). One emerges which is stronger than the others. It is from this same branch, however, that a fire is started which consumes the whole vine and brings to an end the possibility of further rule: "there remains in it no strong staff, no scepter for a ruler" (v. 14).

The same image of growth and generation is picked up in the intervening chapter (18), which concerns itself exclusively with the problem of the effect of the sins of one generation on the next. This is developed by speaking of the relationship between the behavior of the father and the sons begotten by him. The chapter concludes with the question, "Why will you die, O House of Israel?" rather than turn and live (18:32). In this context, the impact of the opening verse of chapter 19 is all the more sharply felt: "Lift up a dirge for the rulers of Israel."

The dirge continues the motif of generation ("rearing," "raising" in vv. 2, 3, 5), but now speaks of the relationship between mother and son under the image of lioness and whelp, followed by the now-familiar vine and branch. It is by no means likely, given the specificity of imagery in chs. 15 and 17, that the lioness is merely emblematic of Judah (whose inhabitants, incidentally, appeared as the "wood of the vine" in ch. 15). One must look to the more focused image of Judahite dynasty, especially since the image of vine/branch is maintained in vv. 10—14. But here the question arises: Why does the prophet move to a distinctly new image of royal power, the lioness? Up to this point, the imagery of plant-world growth sufficed.

As all who have worked closely with this passage have noted, the lion image is taken up by Ezekiel from Gen 49:9—12, by way of its more recent transformations in the prophetic discourse of Nahum and Zephaniah. If the image of the lion in Gen 49:9—12 was employed to stress a kind of power typical of the royal office as promised Judah, in Nahum and Zephaniah it has become a symbol of wanton ferocity, first for the figure of the Assyrian destroyer (Na 2:10—12) and then for various representatives of Judah's own leadership. These include officials, judges, prophets, priests (Zeph 3:2—5). In Ezekiel, the lion becomes the symbol most appropriate for Israel's "rulers" (Ezek 22:25—27).

The key question never satisfactorily answered by those who take the lioness as a symbol for Judah, or even for the royal house in general, is just why the female image of lioness/mother (19:2) is picked up and developed at all. It is not enough to speak of the reference to Judah as a lion in Gen 49:9—12 as justification for the lioness image.[83] The dirge

---

[83] Wevers, *Ezekiel*, 113; Zimmerli, *Ezekiel 1*, 394. Greenberg (*Ezekiel 1—20*, 356) mentions Ezek 16; 23:2; Hos 2:4; or Isa 50:1 as possible sources for the mother-lion image, "emblem" of the dynasty. In Ezekiel, the city Jerusalem is an unfaithful wife (Ch. 16; 23); in Hosea, she is the unfaithful wife Israel; in Isaiah (post-dates the Ezekiel dirge?),

cannot be adequately understood without close attention to the way in which language from Gen 49:9—12 has been picked up by Ezekiel. On the basis of this text's very clear utilization in the dirge, one would have expected the focus to remain with the lion itself, Judah, or Judah's ruler(s). But the appearance of the lion's *mother* in the dirge is by no means necessitated (or even suggested) by anything in the oracle concerning Judah. There is an opening reference to Judah as a cub (v. 9a), but it is a status Judah quickly outgrows (v. 9b). Moreover, based upon the literary context of Ezekiel itself, and the dirge's juxtaposition with Ch. 18, one might have expected a father lion in 19:2 to continue the father/son theme of Ch. 18. Instead, the mother of the lion is spoken of in the opening verses. And, as many have noted, the mother/lioness plays no merely incidental role in the dirge; in many ways, she is its central character, for she alone appears in all three strophes.[84] This centrality can also be detected in the way in which Ezek 19:1—19 has consciously transformed the language of Gen 49:9—12: the *lābîʾ* becomes the *lĕbîyyāʾ;* where once the lion was commanded to grow on prey (*ʿalîtā*), now the mother raises (*wataʿal*) the cub; it is she who "couches" (*rābāṣāh*), not he (*rābaṣ*) as in Gen 49:9b; it is her role in rearing that is stressed in the first two stanzas (vv. 2, 3, 5).

For these many reasons, the interpretation of the lioness as Hamutal is not as far-fetched as many have suggested.[85] Identification of the lioness/mother (*māh ʾimmekā lĕbîyyāʾ*) with an actual mother is the one positive way to explain Ezekiel's adoption of the female image here, an image which is not developed in Gen 49:9—12. Given the dirge's movement into the realm of history at other points, it is by no means a misreading to suggest the same here. This need not be done in such a way as to unnecessarily focus on an otherwise "wholly obscure person." As was shown in the preceding chapter, the mother of the king could be important for reasons other than her personality or (theoretical) office.[86] Rather, the importance of the image of the mother/lion lies in its representing a particular royal house, whose scions Jehoahaz and Zedekiah both become king in Judah.[87]

---

she is the cast-off Jerusalem. It is not clear how these sources would move Ezekiel to the adoption of the mother-lion image. There seems to be a contrast between Ezekiel's use of female imagery in chs. 16, 23 and ch. 19; the decisive difference is that in Ch. 19, he is drawing in a direct way upon one text: Gen 49:9—12.

[84] Greenberg aptly states: "This dominance of the mother in the figures must be accorded its due in determining her identity" (*Ezekiel 1—20,* 355).

[85] Alternatively, Eichrodt terms the theory that the lioness is the personification of Judah "far-fetched" (*Ezekiel,* 254).

[86] *Contra* Kraetzschmar and Eichrodt (*Ezekiel,* 254).

[87] Emphasis by some on the lion as the personification of the Judahite royal house was not incorrect, but merely lacked sufficient precision.

There are other reasons, largely negative, for identifying the lioness of the dirge as the mother of kings Jehoahaz/Zedekiah. It has been noted that the mention of Jehoahaz — an otherwise unknown person in Ezekiel's presentation and an obscure figure in 2 Kings as well — in the first strophe of the dirge seems odd. Ironically, it is Jehoahaz alone who can be so quickly identified, because of the reference to his Egyptian deportation (19:4). His appearance is explained by those who see the second cub as Jehoiachin as due to the motif of East/West deportation, picked up from Hosea (11:11), and dependent upon the western deportee being Jehoiachin. But this is hardly convincing. First of all, the same motif, if it was in fact utilized by Ezekiel, really says nothing about the figure chosen to represent the deportation west. Zedekiah, who was deported to Babylon after 587 B. C., could fit the bill as easily as Jehoiachin. Secondly, no amount of appeal to "political unimportance" as a theme which governs the dirge can blunt the fact of transparent references to real activity in the second strophe. Are allusions to "knowing widows," "desolating cities," "surrounding provinces" or "neckstocks" all that typical, especially when they go well beyond elements one could rightfully call "typical" in the first strophe? Stated another way, one may hunt a lion with a snare or nets (v. 4a and v. 8b), but one does not put a lion in neckstocks (v. 9a). At this point the dirge moves beyond the realm of metaphor. Such a description better fits the report of Zedekiah's actual capture and deportation.[88]

If the interpretation of the lioness as the mother and royal progenitor of kings Jehoahaz and Zedekiah is correct, this leads to another important conclusion: nowhere in the dirge does King Jehoiachin appear.[89] If one adds to this fact that not once in the Book of Ezekiel is Jehoiachin directly referred to with the term *nāśî'*, but instead with *melek*, it is to be concluded that his non-mention in the dirge is conditioned by his unique status in the Book of Ezekiel. Since in Ezekiel's estimation Jehoiachin is not *nāśî'* but *melek*, one should have been tipped off by 19:1 ("lift up a dirge to Israel's rulers") not to expect to find a reference to him in the dirge. In answer to Zimmerli's question, "Would Ezekiel . . . have left out of reckoning the king with whom he shared this fate (deportation) and according to whose years he, as an exile, dated his prophetic messages?" the response is: "Yes" and for precisely the reasons he states.[90] Wevers' remarks are also to be noted. He indicates a preference for Jehoiachin over Zedekiah as the second cub, since "Ezekiel recognized Jehoiachin as

---

[88] See 2 Kgs 25:7. Moreover, Jehoiachin is not put in neckstocks.

[89] Nor for that matter, does his father Jehoiakim appear. This is related to the "conspiracy of silence" question mentioned in Section I above.

[90] *Ezekiel 1*, 394.

king (cf. on 1.2), but Zedekiah only as regent."[91] Again, it is for precisely this reason that Jehoiachin is omitted from the dirge. Is there any further evidence in the Book of Ezekiel for this conclusion?

In the allegory of the cedar (Ch. 17), the top-twig is agreed by all to represent Jehoiachin. The very reason for the differentiated images of cedar and vine in Ch. 17 (+ 15) is to underscore the distinction Ezekiel makes between the line of Jehoiachin and the "branch" of Zedekiah, the latter traceable to Hamutal of Libnah. More than this can be said. The cedar symbolizes legitimate monarchial rule, issuing from Davidic roots. As such, in this context one of the infrequent uses of the term *melek* (for a Judahite king) is employed by the prophet (17:12; 1:2). To avoid confusion about such a distinction, when Ezekiel makes reference to Zedekiah he generally uses a term which has no pejorative connotations (*nāśî'*), but which stresses the more general concept of rule or leadership (as in the wilderness period).[92] A "ruler" can become a "king" (Saul; David), depending upon the extent of his rule and the legitimacy of his selection. But a ruler need not have these attributes. A king must have them.[93] Zedekiah is a ruler or scion ("branch" or "seed royal", 17:13); Jehoiachin is king.

What is decisive in this historical period is that both Jehoahaz and Zedekiah trace their Davidic lineage in a manner distinct from Jehoiakim and Jehoiachin. This distinctiveness lies precisely in their not having the same mother as Jehoiakim, the father of Judah's deported king Jehoiachin. Moreover, Jehoahaz and Zedekiah share a rural Judahite background. The former was placed in power by the "people of the land" in fundamental disregard for the elder Jehoiakim; the latter ruled only by Babylonian privilege. Many of these factors have already been discussed in sections above (Chapter 2) and final conclusions will be drawn below (Section C & E). At this point it is enough to note that a clear distinction has been made by Ezekiel between the cedar of Jehoiachin and the vine of Jehoahaz/

---

[91] *Ezekiel,* 113.

[92] In Ch. 17, he uses the neutral expressions "seed royal" and "seed of the land."

[93] It is unfortunately beyond the scope of the present inquiry to explore why, ultimately, the term *nāśî'* is employed more frequently than *melek* in chs. 40—48. Such a discussion would have to explain the precise relationship between these chapters and Ezekiel's own thought, or (if they are taken as the prophet's own statements) between Ezekiel's evaluation of contemporary events and his larger view of the future. It should be noted that both terms appear together in chs. 34 and 37, just as they do in 7:27. [It has been argued on the basis of this latter passage that king/ruler are interchangeable terms, since they appear in "impressionistic parallelism" (Levenson, *Restoration,* 64; see also Greenberg, *Ezekiel 1—20,* 156); but three levels are envisioned: king/ruler/people of the land, comparable to (and parallel to?!) the triad prophet/priest/elder in 7:26 (cf. *king/śārîm* "officials"/people of the land in Jer 44:21 or officials/judges/prophets/priests in Zeph 3:3 ff.). Is one to believe that prophet/priest or priest/elder in 7:26 are interchangeable?]

Zedekiah, based upon unique circumstances in the monarchy at this important historical period.

In composing his dirge over Israel's rulers, Ezekiel continued certain fundamental images already developed in chs. 15 and 17. These find their place in the third strophe of the dirge, where the branches of a vine become royal scepters but then are destroyed, bringing an end to the vine itself and its fruit. But Ezekiel was also aware of a key oracle concerning the special status given the tribe of Judah, which is now found at Gen 49:9−12. In this oracle, Judah is described as a fierce lion who is accorded respect by his brothers and enemies alike (vv. 8−9). His rule is symbolized by his scepter and staff (49:10), such as the ruler of the pre-monarchic period might possess.[94] Though the oracle makes reference to the transference of power, this event lies in the future (v. 10).[95] Either he or the future ruler live in an almost paradisial splendor, in which one can actually tie up their foal at a vine (without it being consumed) and wash garments in the "blood" of grapes.[96]

In this oracle there appears the precise constellation of images which also find their place in Ezekiel's dirge. It is possible that Ezekiel's use of this old oracle involved a type of *literary* midrash of a text which now exists at Gen 49:9−12. More likely, the oracle was known to Ezekiel in oral form, and its juxtaposition of images, though unusual in the dirge, had a kind of coherence in the original oracle. But in the dirge the controlling theme is one of termination, not endurance. In the dirge the vine is consumed (cf. 49:11a); the lion(s) are captured in snares (cf. 49:9b); the scepter departs (cf. 49:10a).

The element introduced to the old oracle by Ezekiel involved the figure of the progenitor (mother-lion), which he had developed previously under the symbols of vine and branches[97] and discussed more directly in terms of cross-generational sin in Ch. 18. But because certain distinctions already existed in Ezekiel's assessment of the royal monarchy (and its specifically political dimension), this introduction of the mother-lion went well beyond the general topic of royal rule gone afoul. By bringing in the

---

[94] See, for example, Exodus 4,7; Numbers 17,20; and later, Isa 9:4; 10:5,24; 14:5.

[95] An extremely difficult crux which, because it lies behind another key Ezekiel passage (27:31), must be discussed below.

[96] It is not clear who is being referred to here, Judah or the coming one. For a brief discussion, see G. von Rad, *Genesis* (Philadelphia: Westminster, 1970) 424−5. This passage attracted commentary from more than Ezekiel; see Nu 24:12; Mi 5:1; Zech 9:9.

[97] The symbol of the branch is a familiar and appropriate way to talk about royal scions; see, most notably, Isa 11:1; Jer 23:5. What is distinctive is Ezekiel's talk of a *vine* branch; the vine is not usually the symbol of royal growth, but of Israel (see Isa 5:3; Jer 6:9; Hos 10:1). The cedar, on the other hand, is a symbol of royal majesty (1 Kgs 6; 2 Kgs 14:9; Jer 22:7,14,15,23); and for the contrast of images (fig tree, vine, bramble, cedar), such as is found in Ezekiel, see Ju 9:7−15, esp. 9:15. Ezekiel may adopt the vine image since he sees Zedekiah as a "seed of the land", rather than a royal cedar (17:5).

specific figure of the mother of the king, a more focused judgment on the monarchy is made by the prophet. And indeed, in the final analysis she becomes the chief character of the whole dirge, unifying all three stanzas.

In focusing on her young lion-whelp Zedekiah (as was the case in the vine/strong branch motif from Ch. 17), it was natural enough to begin with a reference to her first cub Jehoahaz, though he otherwise plays no direct role in the Book of Ezekiel. In so doing, Ezekiel retards the action by describing the fate of the first young cub netted and carried off, and a mother who tires waiting for his return. Then the dirge moves to the character next in importance to the mother-lion: her second cub Zedekiah. He also plays a main role next to her in the last strophe. A certain symmetry is maintained in the third strophe, however, by talking about "boughs" (pl) rather than just the one "strong bough"; in this way, the initial reference to Jehoahaz is not completely forgotten.[98] The third strophe simply focuses on the final destruction of the whole vine, all its branches and fruit. In that context, the significant role of the one "strong bough" which became a ruler's scepter (Zedekiah) is given its just attention. But in the end, "there remains in it no strong bough (fit) for a ruler's scepter" (v. 14). The lamentation over Hamutal and her cubs is to be taken up: it has become a dirge.

C. Summary and Transition

This analysis of Ch. 19 has provided important insight into Ezekiel's perspective on the Judahite monarchy. Several significant factors have been determined. (1) It is clear that Ezekiel differentiates between the royal line of Jehoiachin and that of Zedekiah. (2) As this relates to Zedekiah, the prophet calls for an absolute end to his rule or the assumption of rule by any in his line. (3) The prophet draws upon stock language in the dirge that can be responsibly identified elsewhere in Ezekiel; that is to say, one can expect a degree of consistency in the thought of the prophet across chapter divisions. (4) An especially noteworthy text outside Ezekiel is Gen 49:9—12; the prophet clearly draws upon this text, in ironic fashion, in order to depict the end of the monarchy as it is represented in Zedekiah.

Points one and four, in particular, may be linked for reasons beyond their more specific relationship to the dirge. Gen 49:8—12, a text with difficulties in its own right, focuses on the special characteristics of the tribe of Judah. It not only describes the royal and political rule to be exercised by Judah (vv. 8—10a); it also tells of the coming of a new era,

---

[98] Moreover, the possibility that there were other scions "from the land" cannot be ruled out. Greenberg (*Ezekiel 1*, 356) says of the interpretation of the second cub as Zedekiah that "the vine allegory must go over the same ground" again. This is only partially correct, and misses certain important features that unify the whole dirge.

in which the "obedience of the peoples" will belong to either Judah (as foreshadowing David) or to "the one to whom belongs the ruler's staff," suggesting a future transference of power to some unknown ruler.[99] The problems of interpretation center on the difficult v. 10b. These have been discussed fully by scores of commentators, with no apparent consensus forthcoming.[100]

It is important to establish the best possible working translation of this key verse. But integrally related to this task is the question as to the oracle's relevance for Ezekiel. If it can be established that Ezekiel did more than utilize in his dirge the somewhat unusual configuration of images appearing in this old oracle, and that he took the oracle's message as specifically related to his evaluation of the future of the monarchy in his own day, then some incidental clue might be gained as to the proper translation of v. 10b, as the more important topic of this chapter comes into prominence: Ezekiel's view of the Judahite monarchy. Stated more conservatively, the "original" reading of Gen 49:10b may or may not be recoverable.[101] But what can potentially be determined is (1) how Ezekiel

---

[99] Our preference is: "Until the one comes to whom it belongs," reading the subject of the admittedly difficult *'ad kî-yābō'* as a person, the referent of *šellô* (MT, *šîlōh*) as the same person, the possessor of "it", the staff of v. 10a.

[100] W. L. Moran terms Gen 49:10 "perhaps the most famous *crux interpretum* in the entire Old Testament" ("Gen 49,10/Ez 21,32", 405). For a full list of early readings, see John Skinner, *Genesis* (ICC; New York: Scribners, 1917) 519—24; for more recent bibliography, see Claus Westermann, *Genesis* (BK I/3; Neukirchen/Vluyn: Neukirchener, 1982) 243—6. A modern critical miscellany would include: (1) for the historical place-name reading (Shiloh), J. Lindblom, "The Political Background of the Shilo Oracle," *VTSup* 1 (1953) 78—87; O. Eissfeldt, "Silo und Jerusalem," *VTSup* 4 (1957) 138—47; J. A. Emerton, "Some Difficult Words in Genesis 49," *Words and Meanings: Essays Presented to David Winton Thomas* (P. R. Ackroyd, Barnabas Lindars, eds; Cambridge: University, 1968) 81—88; (Shelah), E. M. Good, "The 'Blessing' on Judah, Gen 49:8—12," *JBL* 82 (1963); (2) for *šilu/šelu* the (more obscure!) Akkadian cognate "prince", among others see F. Nötscher, "Gen 49,10: שׁילה = akkad. *šēlu*," *ZAW* 47 (1929) 323—5; G. R. Driver, *JTS* 23 (1921,2) 70; S. Mowinckel, *He that Cometh* (G. W. Anderson, trans; Nashville: Abingdon, 1956) 244; [for a careful demolition of this theory, see Moran, "Gen 49,10/Ez 21,32," 406—9]; (3) for *šay lô* "until tribute is brought to him" (apparently an early proposal by S. R. Driver), see especially W. L. Moran, "Gen 49,10/Ez 21,32," 412 ff.; F. M. Cross, D. N. Freedman, "Studies in Ancient Yahwistic Poetry" (Baltimore, 1950); tentatively, E. A. Speiser, *Genesis* (AB; Garden City: Doubleday, 1964) 366; (4) for *mōšĕlōh* "ruler" (BH), see BHS apparatus; G. von Rad, *Genesis*, 424—5; C. Westermann, *Genesis*, 262—3; (5) for *šellô* "whose it is", see BHS apparatus; J. Skinner, *Genesis*, 523. Though it makes for admittedly difficult syntax as Moran points out (p. 409 and quoting Dillmann [*KHAT Genesis*, 1886, 458]: "kein Satz und gar nicht zu verstehen"), this last reading has in its favor that, though lacking a desirable smoothness in style, it is taken this way by almost all the versions, not to mention the prophet Ezekiel himself (21:32)! Moran grants the latter even while arguing for an originally different reading at Gen 49:10b, which the prophet apparently misinterpreted.

[101] Ezekiel probably correctly understood the oracle at v. 10b as meaning *šellô;* he reproduces a rough equivalent of this in his *'ăšer-lô* (which also suggests he is not "reading a text"

understood the meaning of the verse, and (2) what impact that meaning had on his evaluation of the monarchy.

The issue can be pursued one step further. Since in more than one option for translation the oracle concerning Judah speaks of a transference of power (from "Judah" to the "one who will come"; from Judah to the "ruler" or "prince") rather than an absolute end to power, it might also be assumed that Ezekiel had more in mind than just the announcement of the end of the line of Zedekiah. Skinner points out an important feature in the oracle concerning Judah, which in some sense transcends transla-tional difficulties:

> The logical relation of the two halves of the v. (10) is clear: the state of things described by 10a shall endure *until* — something happens which shall inaugarate a still more glorious future. Whether this event shall be the advent of a person — an ideal Ruler — who shall take the scepter out of Judah's hands, or a crisis in the fortunes of Judah which shall raise that tribe to the height of its destiny, is a question on which no final opinion can be expressed (*Genesis*, 520—1).

The notion of "terms to Judah's history" (as Moran calls it) is inherent in the oracle no matter what option for translation is selected, since the basic sense of *'ad kî-yābō'* is not debated. Since Ezekiel at several points (17:20; 19:14; 21:31—33) announces the end of one term (viz, the monarchy as represented in Zedekiah), what might this imply about the beginning of another term? More specifically, just how is this notion of "terms in history" related to the status of exiled King Jehoiachin and the possibility of his future rule? These would be important questions in their own right within the context of the Book of Ezekiel alone. But the fact that in Ezek 21:32 there is a direct allusion — if not quote — from Gen 49:10 (in the context of an oracle of judgment over the "wicked prince" Zedekiah) indicates that the relationship between Ezekiel and the oracle concerning Judah is more than coincidental. This is all the more true given the established relationship between Ezekiel and Gen 49:8—12 elsewhere, in the dirge of Ch. 19.[102] One key question remains: Did the prophet Ezekiel

---

but citing from memory an oracle concerning Judah he, as well as his hearers, knew well). At any event, Ezekiel remains the earliest "pre-versional" clue as to the sense of the phrase. The only other possibility is that Gen 49:10 was secondarily adjusted in light of Ezekiel's (coincidentally) close parallel at 21:32. Again, in view of Ezekiel's use of Gen 49 in the dirge, this is unlikely.

[102] This point is made quite forcefully by Moran, "Gen 49,10/Ez 21,32," 417. Levenson (*Restoration,* 77) is willing to accept Moran's emendation *šay lô* at Gen 49:10 but not his conclusion that, even though Ezekiel may misinterpret Gen 49, there is an undeniable relationship between this text and Ezek 21:32. It is difficult to adjudicate this disagree-ment. Moran does not adequately account for Ezekiel's alleged misinterpretation. Leven-son ignores the obvious relationship between Gen 49 and Ezek 21 by not giving due attention to the oracle's use in the dirge at Ch. 19. But he seems to be on the right track in raising the objection to Moran: "If Ezek 21:32 is under the influence of Gn 49:10, then surely some such reading must underlie the *'ăšer-lô* of the former passage" (77). It is for this reason that *šellô* is not only taken by Ezekiel as the reading (hearing) at Gen 49:10 (so, Moran, 417, n. 1), it was the original sense of the line.

see the message of this old oracle as addressing the circumstances of the monarchy in his own day? If so, in what sense did it inform his evaluation of Zedekiah, Jehoiachin, and the future of the Judahite monarchy?

D. The Near Future of the Monarchy: Ezek 21:29—32 [Eng 21:24—27]

Discussion of Ezekiel's understanding of the future of the monarchy is related to the prophet's larger vision of the restored community. As noted, statements on this subject are found primarily in chs. 34, 37 and 40—48. But other brief notices appear in the early chapters (e.g., 11:17—21; 16:59—63; 20:33—44). It has been argued that mention of restoration at this point in the book may be evidence of secondary levels of tradition, somewhat on the pattern of early pre-exilic collections of prophecy where oracles of restoration supplement a flat picture of judgment. But such a view is not convincing for two reasons. First of all, these statements lack the kind of enthusiastic intensity and breadth of application characteristic of secondary additions to the pre-exilic books (see Mi 7:8—20; Amos 9:11—15; Hos 14:4—7). Note for example, the sober reserve of 16:59—63; or the way in which hopes for the future in 11:17—21 emerge in the context of a clear, pre-587 B. C. episode: the challenge thrown to the exiles by the inhabitants of Jerusalem that the land is theirs. The second reason involves the peculiar editorial history of the Book of Ezekiel. In comparison with pre-exilic prophetic collections, in which primary and supplementary levels of tradition may be separated by centuries, the overwhelming critical consensus would see in Ezekiel a much more compressed period of supplementation and secondary enrichment.[103] So even granting the secondary nature of certain sections of Ezekiel, it is not required that theological discontinuity or distortion be major factors in the development of the tradition.

There is one good example of an oracle of restoration that very few would deny to the prophet Ezekiel.[104] This is the oracle concerning the

---

[103] This enables one to conceive of the prophet as active in the formation of his own "tradition" in a way for which there is largely no analogy in the pre-exilic period. See Eichrodt (*Ezekiel*, 229) or Zimmerli (*Ezekiel 1*, 368) on 17:22—24, a passage to be discussed shortly. The broader critical judgments of Zimmerli could be taken as indicative of the present period of interpretation (*Ezekiel 1*, esp. 68—64). Though Greenberg can take issue with what he sees as abuses in modern canons of authenticity (*Ezekiel 1—20*, 20 ff.), the critical distance between himself and, for example, Zimmerli is minimal when contrasted with Weippert and Thiel in Jeremiah studies. [Critical analysis of Ezek 40—48 is a separate problem altogether.]

[104] Note for example that Zimmerli (*Ezekiel 1*, 368) and Eichrodt (*Ezekiel*, 229) attribute the oracle (17:22—24) to Ezekiel (similar in content to chs. 34, 37), while still seeing it as a further development of the original allegory of Ch. 17. Levenson argues vigorously for the unit's (17:22—24) essential continuity with what precedes (*Restoration*, 79 ff.). It is much clearer that v. 24 is secondary than vv. 22—23.

restoration of the Davidic dynasty now found at the conclusion of the
extended allegory/interpretation of Ch. 17. This oracle (vv. 22—24) is
concerned with the specific issue of future monarchial rule:

> I myself will take from the lofty crown of the cedar (*miṣṣameret hā'erez hārāmāh*) and
> set it (out); from the topmost shoots (*mērō'š yōnĕqôtāw*) I will pluck a tender one; and
> I myself will plant (it) upon a high and lofty mountain (17:22).[105]

The oracle goes on to talk of how "the tender one" becomes a great cedar,
putting forth boughs and even fruit! This takes place that all the trees
might know how "I Yahweh bring low the high tree, and make high the
low tree, dry up the green tree, and make the dry tree flourish" (v. 24).

Long before modern commentators, Rashi interpreted the final verse
(24) as applying in more particular terms to "the nations" (high tree made
low), Zedekiah and his offspring (green tree dried up), Jehoiachin and,
eventually, Zerubbabel his grandson (dry tree made green).[106] In this
narrower instance, with Greenberg, Rashi's interpretation does seem like
a "particularization which goes beyond the text"; rather, this concluding
verse offers a general assessment tied to Yahweh's declaration of complete
sovereignty (cf. 21:31). Utilizing the tree imagery already in place, its
larger point concerns reversals made possible only by the Almighty, not
further interpretations of the main allegory. This is shown by the fact that
the attributes "high" and "low" are not kept absolutely distinct in the
allegory itself. Thus, the "tender one" is plucked from the top of a high
cedar, while the vine remains a low plant, even at its most arrogant
moments (v. 8). As such, the image of raising the low and lowering the
high does not correlate easily with the specific images of vine and cedar.[107]

But an interpretation related to Jehoiachin is certainly attempted in
vv. 22—23. All the imagery from vv. 3—4 is carried over intact, including
the key terms *ṣammeret hā'ārez* and *rō'š yĕnîqôtāw* (17:3,4/22), thereby picking
up and concluding the story of the cedar-crown that was spared destruction
by transplantation to Babylon (v. 4). Though it is not often mentioned by
commentators, the theme of King Jehoiachin's planting and re-planting

---

[105] For translation, see Greenberg, *Ezekiel 1—20,* 309 ff.

[106] Cited in Greenberg, together with apt criticism (*Ezekiel 1—20,* 317).

[107] Neither does the dry/green contrast fit well for cedar/vine. "Dry" and "green" may seem,
respectively, to fit the political realities of Jehoiachin and Zedekiah, about to be reversed
by Yahweh. Unfortunately, the main allegory did not pursue this tack, and this final
verse is too cryptic to depend upon for additional information. Compare also Levenson's
remarks, *Restoration,* 79 ff. He seems to interpret the high tree brought low and the dried-
up green tree as Zedekiah, without reference to the specific figure of Jehoiachin. It is
clear that beyond what it might say about Yahweh's sovereignty, the specific context in
which this assertion is made is a chapter concerning the monarchy. But vv. 22—23 seem
more essential to the original unity of Ch. 17 than this final verse, which has probably
been supplied on the basis of a *nachinterpretation* of 21:31 (where the identical imagery,
high/low, is pursued).

— so central in Ch. 17 — is certainly one key reason that a dirge over him as "ruler" in Ch. 19 is unlikely. It is clear that in this oracle of restoration, not Jehoiachin himself but a new tender shoot "from the lofty crown" is replanted, that is, one from his line. All this hardly suggests the appropriateness of a funeral dirge for Jehoiachin. Rather, while in the dirge the vine grew large (19:10—11) and then was destroyed along with its strongest growth, this original shoot of the tall tree (v. 4) becomes a great cedar (v. 23) with much growth, capable of sustaining life and providing shade for all. So while strictly speaking the final image (17:24) does not demand an interpretation related to Jehoiachin and Zedekiah, the same is not true of the oracle concerning the ultimate fate of the cedar crown (vv. 22—23), especially in light of the dirge over the vine and branch in 19:10—14 (cf. 17:5—21). It must also be said that the oracle does not stress the re-enthronement of Jehoiachin himself, however much the prophet considers his kingship as legitimate. Rather, it is from his line that a new cedar is to sprout, when, yet in the future and presumably along with this replanting, the replanting of the wider community takes place (37:26).

Full discussion of Israel's restoration would move beyond the more pressing task: determining Ezekiel's perspective on the monarchy during the exilic period. It is important to note in Ch. 17's oracle of restoration that Jehoiachin's special status as king is not rescinded by the prophet (see also 37:24). Anticipating a bit (regarding 21:32), an outright transfer of power from Zedekiah to Jehoiachin, as re-instated monarch, is not envisioned. More accurately, since Zedekiah is never considered legitimate *melek* by Ezekiel, he is never in a position to hand over rule to Jehoiachin. Rather, he is the *nāśî'* for whom a dirge is to be taken up.

1. Ezek 21:29—32: A Vision of Restoration?

Even as Ch. 19 describes the end of the monarchy in the land, and even as it participates in bringing the end about (v. 14), the actual judgment of Yahweh over the monarchy as well as the whole land must wait. Much in these early chapters merely anticipates the fall of the city and the judgment of Yahweh over Israel and the nations, through a series of intricate sign-acts, in which the prophet is to enact that fall and judgment (4:1—17; 5:1—4; 12:1—7; 12:17—20; 21:1—5; 24:3—14). On other occasions, allegories or riddles, together with their interpretations by the prophet, explain the nature of events that will take place (Chs. 15—17; 23). The "vision" enables the prophet to gain an adequate view of events in the land, as well as a clear picture of what is to transpire (Chs. 8—11). On other occasions, the prophet merely "prophesies" against the land (*wě'attāh ben-'ādām hinnābē'*), and in so doing a fairly precise description is usually given of events as they are to take place (Ch. 6; 13; 21); often such prophesying comes in the familiar context of the prophetic reception of "the word of Yahweh" (*wayĕhî dĕbar-YHWH ʾēlay lēʾmōr,* Chs. 21—24). In all of this, a compelling picture of Yahweh's judgment over Israel and the nations (Chs. 25—32) emerges.

There is one particular oracle of judgment given in the context of general punishment for Jerusalem concerning the "profane, wicked *nāśîʾ*" (21:32—43); in view of Ezekiel's evaluation of the monarchy, this oracle demands greater attention. This is true because it is one of the key texts in which Zedekiah transparently appears under the more general guise of *nāśîʾ* (see also 12:10,12). But there is another factor which links this text with discussion of the monarchy, especially as it has centered on Ezek 19:1—14. This is the relationship it like the dirge shares with Gen 49:8—12. It was argued above that correct interpretation of the dirge could only follow from a proper acknowledgement of the dirge's debt to the oracle of Gen 49:9—12. Though correct translation of the famous crux at v. 10 of that oracle is problematic, the same cannot be said for the remainder of the oracle. Moreover, it is largely apart from the difficult v. 10b that language parallels are to be detected between Ezek 19:1—14 and Gen 49:9—12. In that instance, then, we were not reduced to interpreting the dirge *obscurum per obscurius.*

In the oracle against Zedekiah at 21:32 an obscure phrase does occur. An attempt to read the MT as literally as possible results in the following translation: "Distortion, distortion, distortion I will make it (*ʾăśîmennāh*); even this (*zōʾt*) has not been until (before) the coming of one to whom belongs judgment (*ʿad-bōʾ ʾăšer-lô hammišpāṭ*), and I will give it (*ûnĕtattîw*)."[108] There are at least three pronominal elements whose referents (it; this; it) are unclear; recourse to the larger context is of limited help. The feminine forms (it; this) most likely express feminine neutrality.[109] In v. 31, the most immediate context, the phrase *zōʾt lōʾ-zōʾt* appears, with the most likely sense of "this is not this" (lit.) or "this will not stay as it is," referring to the present state of affairs including the monarchy under the wicked prince. Hence the command to "remove the turban" and "take off the crown."

Adopting the translation of "distortion" suggested by Moran, however, makes it unlikely that the "it" of this verse refers in such a specific way to the monarchy.[110] In fact, even in verse 31 the general sense of "it" as "present state of affairs" is to be preferred in order to capture the larger

---

[108] See the fine discussion of W. Moran, to whom much here is indebted: "Gen 49,10/Ez 21,32," 416 ff.

[109] Moran, "Gen 49,10/Ez 21,32," 419; Zimmerli, "neuter generality," *Ezekiel 1,* 439.

[110] As Moran points out, a translation "ruin" for *ʿawwāh* is not without problems. Even in Is 24:1, the sense from the verb ("to bend, twist") is still implied. As he puts it *"zōʾt* means everything, the extremes high and low, and it is everything that is distorted" (420).

picture of Yahweh's bringing in chaos-like destruction on the whole city, monarchy and citizenry alike. The "this," then, simply pursues the image into v. 32. A better translation, in light of this connection with v. 31, might read: "Distortion, distortion, distortion I will make it, even such as has not been." For the specific sense of *gam-zō't lō' hāyāh,* compare Ezek 5:9, which in a similar context of judgment indicates Yahweh will do "what he has never yet done" (*wĕ'āśîtî bāk 'ēt 'ăšer lō'-'āśîtî*). The problem appears to be the past tense implied in *hāyāh* and accordingly Moran emends to *thyh,* which has support in LXX *estai.* But this problem only emerges when the phrase is juxtaposed with the following *'ad-bō' 'ăšer-lô;* the translation seems temporally illogical: "even such has not been, until the coming of the one to whom belongs . . .".

The force of the problem is blunted when it is recalled that here the prophet Ezekiel is making use of a familiar phrase from an oracle he cited earlier in Ch. 19. As noted above, there is strong reason for assuming that the oracle concerning Judah read at this point *'ad-kî yābō' šellô,* "until the one comes to whom it belongs." If Ezekiel wanted not only to make his citation of the oracle clear, but also stress the notion implicit therein of a term reaching an end (and a new term beginning), then this would have required employing the phrase almost verbatim, even if the result was a certain roughness in syntax.

This argument can be further substantiated when the final section of the phrase is translated: "Distortion, distortion, distortion, I will make it; even such has not been 'until he comes to whom belongs' — *mišpāṭ,* and I will have it executed." In the original oracle, the new term to be inaugurated was one in which "the obedience of the peoples" (v. 10b) would be given to the one who had received the "ruler's staff." In Ezekiel's use of the oracle, the hearers are jarred by the coming one's display of power: *mišpāṭ.* But this is not, as if frequently suggested, because the image of *mišpāṭ* "judgment" is to be rigidly contrasted with "right" (perhaps one might expect *ṣedeq*).[111] It is because *mišpāṭ* in the context of Ezekiel's discourse is the chief attribute of Yahweh, and his appointed executer of that judgment, Nebuchadnezzar. Accordingly, his is now "the obedience of the peoples" (Gen 49:10b), including Israel.

It is primarily by appeal to the larger context of Ezekiel that one is able to understand the impact of this oracle. Many have argued quite forcefully that what Ezekiel is speaking of here is the coming of one to whom belongs *the right to rule,* namely, Jehoiachin, or a future Judahite

---

[111] Certainly in Gen 49:10, the ruler's staff and scepter symbolize both the power to judge and the legitimacy to rule. This is a familiar motif in the OT. For example, the pairing of *mišpāṭ* and *ṣedeq* occurs in Jer 22:13 (non-attributes of Jehoiakim!) and Isa 11:1–5.

ruler.[112] But as Moran points out, all the imagery of vv. 29—31, not to mention the broader context of Ch. 21, is of judgment — specifically, judgment over the city and its monarch. The notion of a transfer of power to a new and legitimate ruler suggests the transfer to a new age, such as is suggested in Gen 49:8—12, for example. But such imagery is never developed in the context of this chapter. The context remains one of judgment.[113] The prophet depends upon the old oracle to provide a fitting word to the situation of the monarchy in Judah. But he radically dislodges its view of a new day of promised power to Judah's proud ruler (Gen 49:8—10). To the one who comes will be *mišpāṭ*, and Yahweh has this judgment carried out (*ûnětattîw*). In this sense, the "coming one" from Gen 49 is as much Yahweh as it is his agent of judgment, Nebuchadnezzar.[114]

One other point can be made concerning Ezekiel's use of the oracle concerning Judah. The old oracle clearly spoke about a *future* event: the coming of one to whom belonged the ruler's scepter. This is seen in the use of the imperfect *yābō'*. Ezekiel has not completely placed this future event at the present moment of his speaking. Though he uses the participial *bō'*, it is still an event which, though on the horizon, must wait until its divinely appointed moment (see also 21:35). What was in the old oracle a moment in the distant future (see also Nu 24:17) has become in Ezekiel a moment in the very near future. He can speak of the wicked prince "whose day has come//the time of final sin" (*'ăšer-bā' yômô* [note the perfect of this same verb]//*bĕ'ēt 'awôn qēṣ*, v. 30), but at the same time imply that the wider judgment of Yahweh, as described in vv. 31—32, still awaits. This is consistent with the logic of Ch. 17, in which much of the same imagery appears. The judgment of Zedekiah claims a particular focus there (17:13—20) apart from the broader issue of Yahweh's sovereign rule (17:24) and his judgment over Israel as a whole.

The precise temporal sequence of events as described in this brief oracle is admittedly complex.[115] On the other hand, it appears as though

---

[112] For a full list of options in translation and interpretation, see Zimmerli (*Ezekiel 1*, 447) who otherwise rejects this reading. Fohrer opts for Jehoiachin; he states, concerning Ezekiel's adaptation of Gen 49: "Er hat jene dunklen Worte in seiner Weise interpretiert und auf Jojachin gedeutet" (*Ezechiel*, 126). Eichrodt (*Ezekiel*, 303—4) speaks of "the new world that will come into being after the judgment has been carried out by the one commissioned by God for the purpose."

[113] To cite Moran: ". . . it seems most improbable that in a context in which everything speaks of ruin and destruction, both before and after, in one short phrase of two words we should have a promise of restoration: such a *volte face* is without parallel in Ezekiel" (419).

[114] As has been noted, the only time the phrase *ntn mšpṭ* occurs in Ezekiel, it speaks of Yahweh's "giving judgment" over to the northern hoards (23:24). But even in this case it cannot be forgotten that the main executor of the judgment remains Yahweh, not Nebuchadnezzar.

[115] For a good discussion, see Eichrodt, *Ezekiel*, 303.

a scene of judgment over Zedekiah is in present effect. This is seen in the language: "whose day has come" (cf. 7:5—9). Yet there is at the same time, if the reading argued for is correct, a postponement of a more final judgment (v. 32). Close attention to Ezekiel's broader design for judgment as it appears in Chs. 1—32 shows this sequencing to be quite in order.

2. Design for Judgment in Ezekiel

The theme of judgment is most prominently introduced in Ezek 5:1—17. Utilizing the image of the sword (*ḥereb*), which also appears as the central image in Ch. 21, the prophet is commanded to shave head and beard (symbolizing surrender of power), and then divide the hair into thirds with a balance. These thirds relate to three phases of judgment execution, as it is called in 5:8: *wĕ ̔āśîtî bĕtôkēk mišpāṭîm*. One phase concerns death by fire in the city (*bĕtôk hā ̔îr*); a later one, death by sword "round about it (the city)" (*sĕbîbôtêhā*); the final one, death by sword where this last third is scattered, that is, in diaspora. Of this last third, a small portion survives; but even of these, some will perish from the fire started in phase one, presumably an indication that punishment can pursue even survivors in dispersion (compare 14:22—23).[116] Note the similarity between the image of "fire going forth" utilized here (5:4, *tēṣē ̓- ̓ēš*) and in the final strophe of the dirge (19:14, *wattēṣē ̓ ̓ēš*).

The concept of phases to punishment occurs in a variant form at 5:12. There a third die in the city by pestilence (*baddeber*) and famine (*bārā ̔āb*); a third by sword round about; a third is pursued by sword wherever scattered. Again, the final third does not die outright, as seems to be the case in the first two phases. Rather, they become a reproach (*ḥerpāh*), taunt (*gĕdûpāh*), warning (*mûsār*), and horror (*mĕšammāh*) to the nations where they find themselves, a testimony to the thoroughness of Yahweh's judgment (*ba ̔ăśôtî bāk šĕpāṭîm*).[117]

Chapter 6 simply illustrates in narrative form what is implied in Chapter 5. The same general design for judgment is activated: sword in city and environs (vv. 1—7; 11—14); pursuing judgment on scattered survivors (vv. 8—10). Chapter 7 focuses more particularly on the judgment over "the inhabitant of the land" (v. 7). Now-familiar images reappear, including *ḥereb, deber, rā ̔āb*. Insofar as it concentrates on the fate of the land and its inhabitants apart from the concept of dispersion, the desolation will be complete; the existence of survivors is only a pitiful indication of

---

[116] Greenberg, *Ezekiel 1—20*, 110.

[117] The similarity between Ezekiel's design for judgment and that of the Exilic Redaction of Jeremiah will be discussed in Chapter Four, below. Jer 43:8—44:30 is especially noteworthy in this regard. In their descent to Egypt, the "remnant of Judah" becomes the final third of Ezekiel's design for judgment.

the extent of punishment (vv. 16 ff.). All levels of society are affected (v. 27). Each according to his own way will be judged: *middarkām 'e'ĕśeh 'ôtām; ûbĕmišpĕṭêhem 'ešpĕṭēm.*

There are several important patterns to be observed in these opening chapters. First, the more general language of judgment is fairly uniform. Typically, Yahweh "executes judgments," expressed with some combination of the verb *'śh* and object *mišpāṭ*. (5:8,10,15; 11:9) or with both verbal and object elements from *špṭ*, as in *'ešpōṭ 'etkem* (11:10; 18:30), *ûšĕpaṭṭîk* (7:3), or *bĕmišpĕṭêhem 'ešpĕṭem* (7:27). The verb *ntn* is also notable in contexts of judgment. It appears in parallelism with *špṭ* at 7:3,8; 11:9. One of its clear uses is suggested at 11:9, viz, the notion that Yahweh gives Israel into the hands of foreigners, this constituting one form of Yahweh's judgment: "And I will bring you forth out of the midst of (the city), and give you into the hands of foreigners, and execute judgments on you" (11:9). This is more directly expressed at 23:24, where Yahweh "commits" his *mišpāṭ* to others, in this instance the northern hoards: *wĕnātattî lipnêhem mišpāṭ ûšĕpāṭûk bĕmišpĕṭêhem.* This is also a central motif of the oracles against nations in Ezekiel (chs 25—32), where alongside Yahweh's judgments (25:11; 28:22,26; 30:14,19) the sword is given over to Nebuchadnezzar, chief executor of Yahweh's punishment (30:24—26; 32:11).

The second point to be made concerns the "plurality of judgment" expressed in the concept of phases to judgment and in the simple use of the plural *mišpāṭîm* for Yahweh's action against Israel (5:8,10,15; 7:27; 11:9). Both senses are captured in the phrase: Yahweh's "four sore acts of judgment" (*'arba'at šĕpāṭay,* 14:21). This suggests that judgment is not static, but goes through certain phases. It should also be noted that Ezekiel does not conceive of his own 597-community in this design for judgment, presumably since *mišpāṭ* has already been received by them. The phases of judgment are future events, about to take place (12:27—28) and awaiting their allotted moment.

In the chapters immediately surrounding Ch. 21, the theme of judgment plays a prominent role. Both Chs. 20 and 22 begin with the rhetorical question put to Ezekiel "Will you judge?" (*hătišpōṭ 'ōtām hătišpôṭ,* 20:4; 22:1), with the sense: "Will you (not) judge? — Judge!"[118] The same theme is resumed at 23:36, following the indictment against the wicked sisters Jerusalem and Samaria: "Son of man, will you judge Oholah and Oholibah? Then declare to them their abominable deeds." Moreover, the term "judgments" in the more specific sense of "ordinances" (///ḥuqqôtay, v. 10 ff.) permeates Ch. 20. Because Israel has rejected Yahweh's earlier "judgments" by not "executing them" (*mišpāṭay lō'-'ăśû*), there will be a new wilderness, a *midbar hā'ammîm,* in which Yahweh will enter into

---

[118] See commentaries.

judgment with Israel face to face (*wĕnišpaṭṭî 'ittĕkem šām pānîm 'el-pānîm*, 20:35).

Ch. 21 is organized around the theme of Yahweh's sword (21:8,13,16,19,24,33,30); it is divided into three basic units, each introduced by the phrase: *wayĕhî dĕbar-YHWH 'ēlay lē'mōr* (21:1—12; 13—22; 23—37).[119] The first unit is composed of allegory/bridge (v. 5)/interpretation, linking fire and sword (as in "phase one," see above). The second tells of the sword being "given into the hand of the slayer" (*lātēt 'ōtāh bĕyad-hôrēg*), a not unfamiliar motif. The third describes the approach of the slayer, Nebuchadnezzar, at a point of decision: whether to move on Jerusalem or Rabbat bene-Ammon. When the lot falls for Jerusalem, its inhabitants are depicted as incredulous (v. 28), because of oaths they have sworn with Nebuchadnezzar (17:16). But "he gives evidence of their breach, to ensnare them" (21:28).[120] Note the use of the verb *tpś* "ensnare," familiar from the dirge (19:4,8) and 17:20, other contexts concerned with the punishment and capture of Zedekiah. Here, however, a plural subject is involved, presumably "all Jerusalem."

The plural subject is continued on into the unit of particular interest for us, Ezek 21:29—32. The *lākēn kōh-'āmar 'ădōnāy YHWH* and *ya'an* which introduce the unit indicate the nature of its content: a judgment oracle. The plural subject is then picked up: "Because you (pl) have shown evidence of your breach, by uncovering your transgressions, by revealing your sins in all your actions, because you have been convicted, with a strong hand you will be taken." The *'āwōn* of all the people (see v. 28) is shown to be more extensive than (political) breach of covenant with Nebuchadnezzar. Note that the same verb (*tpś*) appears, applied here to the taking of this plural subject. Note too that the judgment itself, within the temporal logic of the oracle, lies still in the future. By contrast, in v. 30 there is a shift in tempus and subject. The *wĕ'attāh* indicates the abruptness of this change, as now the *ḥālāl rāšā' nĕśî' yiśrā'ēl* is singled out and addressed. His day has come, "at the time of his final breach": *bā' yômô bĕ'ēt 'āwōn qēṣ*.[121] In Ezekiel's design for judgment, the notion of a "day" arriving which spells judgment is laid out in Ch. 7. There one hears of "the end coming" (vv. 1, 3, 6: *qēṣ bā'* or *haqqēṣ 'ālāyik*) and the time and day arriving (v. 7: *bā' hā'ēt qārôb hayyôm*). In some sense, then, this final end is conceived of as coming upon Zedekiah even at the moment of the

---

[119] The addressing phrase *ben-'ādām* also further subdivides these units (see 21:2,7,14,19,24,33).

[120] Interpreting *wĕhû'-mazkîr* (lit: he brings their *'āwōn* to remembrance) in a more juridical sense (see Zimmerli for discussion, *Ezekiel 1*, 445). *'āwōn* refers to the breach of covenant (see 17:16 ff.).

[121] We maintain the sense of "breach" for *'āwōn* (as clarified in v. 28), rather than "punishment" for that breach (cf. RSV and commentators).

oracle's delivery. This is a familiar concept from the dirge, but here the reader is much closer to the end, if not right upon it.

What occurs here is a rhetorical device whose intent is to single out the fate of Zedekiah. His judgment is forcefully and individually proclaimed. In that context, his judgment is distinct from the fate of wider Israel not just in intensity, but also temporally. For in vv. 31b—32 there is movement back to a more general punishment, yet in the future (*ăśîmennāh; ûnĕtattîw*), underscored by citation of the old oracle from Gen 49:10b: ". . . until he comes to whom belongs *mišpāṭ*" (21:32). So even as the oracle is delivered, and even as it appears to find present fulfillment in Zedekiah, in the broader temporal logic of the Book of Ezekiel the final judgment over all Israel (as well as the nations) is yet to come. In the immediate context of Ch. 21 (vv. 33—37), this is demonstrated by the theme of delay in judgment for the Ammonites (v. 35). But the clearest perspective on the temporal design for judgment is provided by the larger book itself. Jerusalem continues to meet indictment for her sins in Chs. 22—23. In terms of strict chronology, Ch. 24 is situated roughly a year before the Fall occurred (588: 9th year, 10th month, 10th day). 24:2 even relates that the siege is just beginning; there is no report of the fall until 33:21 (586: 11th year, 10th month, 5th day). [122] Chs. 25—32 are concerned with laying out the judgment program for the nations. In point of fact, there are no further references to Zedekiah as an individual. [123] In this sense, the statement of judgment against him at 21:32 can be taken as distinct temporally, if the rhetorical force of the passage is not forgotten. But as for Israel, she stands on the very edge of a judgment that still awaits its final fulfillment. Given Ezekiel's early statements on Yahweh's design for judgment (Chs. 5—7), judgment is not co-terminus with just the fall of the city (33:21). Yahweh executes judgments, only a third of which involve the fall of the city.

Based upon an evaluation of Ezekiel's broader design for judgment, it is possible to accurately interpret the narrower judgment oracle at Ezek 21:29—32. Utilizing the old oracle from Gen 49:10 in an almost verbatim citation, Ezekiel draws upon the notion of terms to Judah's monarchial history found there. But instead of highlighting the theme of an internal transfer of power and authority, from Judah to the one who comes, Ezekiel reverses the force of the oracle and tells of a transfer of power from Judah's royal "ruler" to one who comes from outside her own royal house: Nebuchadnezzar. Insofar as Nebuchadnezzar receives this transfer

---

[122] MT: *bištê ʿeśrēh* ("twelfth").

[123] If the MT *nĕbîʾêhā* "(her) prophets" is read at 22:25, rather than "princes" (LXX), there are also no further general references to the *nĕśîʾê yiśrāʾēl*. Note Ezekiel's somewhat uncommon use of *śārîm* at 22:27. In Ezek 11:1, 17:12, and 22:27, the term refers to "officials" rather than royal "princes".

at Yahweh's behest, Yahweh himself comes to execute judgment over his own ruler and people. All this correlates quite well with the picture Ezekiel draws upon Yahweh's design for judgment. A new age of messianic power is not ushered in here, as some have maintained, though this theme is not without expression at other points in the Ezekiel tradition. The final act of judgment is described. In a proleptic sense typical for Ezekiel, it begins to have effect. Only after this great execution of judgment are descriptions of the new age, with a new people and ruler (Chs. 33–37), apposite.

E. Conclusions: Ezekiel's View of the Davidic Monarchy

With proper emphasis on Ch. 19, together with the collection of statements from surrounding chapters (esp. 15–21), a full and coherent picture of Ezekiel's perspective on the Judahite Monarchy emerges. Jehoiachin is exempted from Ezekiel's negative appraisal of the Judahite monarchy, in sharp contrast to Zedekiah. The extreme sentence of judgment over Zedekiah occurs for two reasons. The chief factor is Zedekiah's failure to acknowledge that his right to rule comes only as a result of Yahweh's choice of Nebuchadnezzar, and by extension, Nebuchadnezzar's covenant with him as vassal — not because he is king by dynastic right, as his predecessors could assert. Zedekiah demonstrates his guilt (ʿāwôn, 21:30; 17:18) in this respect through his political untrustworthiness, in relying on Egypt in hopes of avoiding submission to Babylon. In Ezekiel's view, such an action was above all treason against Yahweh. By following this course, Zedekiah deludes himself about the legitimacy of his rule and the kingly independence of his activity. The second factor emerges from Ezekiel's understanding of monarchial legitimacy as it is specifically related to his vision of future leadership in the restored state. The oracle of restoration at Ezek 17:22–23 suggests strongly that Ezekiel never foreclosed on the prospect of future leadership emerging from the line of Jehoiachin, however much he may have envisioned it as a new and transformed leadership.[124] The most serious threat to such a view was the co-existence of a royal line equally in a position to assert the legitimacy of its claim to (present and future) rule. Faced with such a threat, the prophet denounced not just Zedekiah but the entire line of "rulers" emerging from Hamutal as dead (Ezek 19).

This distinctive view of Zedekiah's monarchial status involves a number of factors specifically related to Ezekiel's status as 597-deportee/ prophet. From his perspective, all life in the land stands under the judgment of Yahweh (chs. 5–6). If this perspective is not the direct consequence of the counterassertion of legitimacy on the part of those in the land (ch.

---

[124] In essential agreement with Levenson (*Restoration,* 77 ff.).

11), it is certainly emboldened by it. On two occasions (11:15; 33:24) it is made absolutely clear that those in the land could assert not only the right to exist; they could claim as well that the sentence of judgment had fallen, not on them, but on those taken in the 597 Exile. Ezekiel rejects this with all possible vehemence. The city as well as its rulers are under a death sentence.

While up to this point monarchial legitimacy had turned on the question of Davidic lineage, grounded in Nathan's charter to David (2 Samuel 7), from Ezekiel's perspective the last king to merit the title in this customary sense was Jehoiachin. He was deported, and with that deportation a return to the wilderness period had begun. In his place not a legitimate king, but a ruler, admittedly of royal stock (a collateral "vine branch") was placed in charge.[125] From the prophet's perspective, Judah's monarchial history had entered a new phase. Now the "king of kings" (26:7) was Nebuchadnezzar, under authority of the divine king, Yahweh himself. The final sentence of judgment over Judah had been passed even as the events of 597 took place. The day of execution of that judgment would not be long in coming (7:5—13; 12:28). There is nowhere in the Book of Ezekiel the suggestion that the judgment over the land has come and gone, or that it has come for the deportees only. The events of 597 signalled the true end of Judah, despite the "fictional" existence of a people and king ("ruler") in the land. It would only remain a question of time before Yahweh's "four sore acts of judgment" reached their allotted end, overtaking those who had been spared judgment in 597 as well as those who would appear to do so in 587.[126]

It should be stated that on this issue there is absolutely no equivocation in the Book of Ezekiel. A full end must be made before a full beginning can commence. Restoration begins with those who have met the judgment of Yahweh. In a very real sense, the fate of deportation and exile remains the only sure sign that the sentence of judgment has been passed and that, accordingly, restoration can begin. Stated another way, there is no hint in the Book of Ezekiel of a restoration apart from the fate of exile:

> "I will gather you from the peoples, and assemble you out of the countries where you have been scattered, and I will give you the land of Israel." And when they come

---

[125] From Nebuchadnezzar's perspective, this was probably a good move. Compare the situation in Jer 39 ff., after the 587 events.

[126] See 5:3 ff.; 6:8 ff.; 15:7; and especially 14:22, where those in exile will be "consoled" by the very fact that "survivors" nevertheless met the full force of Yahweh's judgment. In this sense their "survival" is only a testimony to their sins and the appropriateness of Yahweh's dispensation of evil: ". . . when you see their ways and their deeds you will be consoled for the evil I brought upon Jerusalem . . ." (for text and commentary, see Greenberg, *Ezekiel 1—20,* 257—62; Zimmerli, *Ezekiel 1,* 315—6).

there, they will remove from it all its detestable things and all its abominations (11:17—18);

"As I live, says the LORD God, surely with a mighty hand and an outstretched arm, and with wrath poured out, I will be king over you. I will bring you out from the peoples and gather you out of the countries where you are scattered . . . (20:33 ff.);

"I myself will search out for my sheep . . . and I will bring them out from the peoples and gather them from the countries . . ." (34:12—14);

"I will take you from the nations, and gather you from the countries, and bring you into your own land . . ." (36:24 ff.).

This is as true for the king as for the people (17:22—23; 37:22 ff.).

The situation is not as unambiguous in the Book of Jeremiah. The prophet Jeremiah is, of course, not deported in 597; for that matter, he is a survivor of the 587 deportations. For over eleven years he functions as a prophet in Judah, contemporaneous with Ezekiel's prophetic career in Exile. Statements concerning the status of Judah's last four kings have been preserved in the Jeremiah traditions, and they stand in considerable tension with Ezekiel's evaluation of the monarchy (see, among others, Jer 22:28—30; 36:31). The same can be said of his perspective on Yahweh's design for judgment and the place of the remnant Judahite community. At some points the Jeremiah tradition appears to be almost identical to accounts in Ezekiel (see Jer 7:30—33; 9:11—15; 11:16; 11:22; 14:15—16; 21:3—6; 24:8—10). On other occasions, Ezekiel and Jeremiah tradition appears in irreduceable tension (see for example, Jeremiah's pre-587 statements and actions at 27:17, 32:6—15, 38:17 ff.; or post-587, 40:6, 42:7 ff.).

There are several reasons for this similarity and dissimilarity. In view of the temporal proximity of these two prophetic traditions and the strong likelihood that the Book of Jeremiah received secondary enrichment in Babylonian Exile, it is probable that an Exilic Redaction, sharing much in common with the theological stance of the Ezekiel traditions, has influenced the Jeremiah traditions on the subject of Yahweh's fuller design for judgment. The design for judgment of the Exilic Redaction has the same basic style, vocabulary, and theological emphases as the Ezekiel material. Like Ezekiel, it stresses the irreversability and absolute thoroughness of the punishment. Its view of restoration as centered on a deported people alone is also unmistakeable (see especially 16:14—15; 24:4—7; 32:15,36—44 [redaction of 32:1—14]).[127]

An early, pre-597 level of tradition was noted in Jeremiah concerned with the absolute finality of judgment, the thoroughness of punishment, and the fate of deportation from the land (Chs. 9—15). It was the existence of this authentic level of tradition that justified the development of a similar, but far more comprehensive picture of judgment by the Exilic

---

[127] For a discussion of these passages, see Chapter Four.

Redaction.[128] From the perspective of the Ezekiel traditions upon which this redactional level in Jeremiah is based, the events of 597 were indeed pivotal. But however much these traditions from Jeremiah stimulated the development of the Golah Redaction, they are by no means the final word of the Book of Jeremiah; they are quickly overshadowed by reports which reach well beyond the events of the first deportation. Unlike the Ezekiel community, Jeremiah and a substantial portion of the Judahite population survived the 597-exile to remain in the land. As noted above, the fact of survival and continued existence in the land "complicates" the prophetic activity and developing traditions of Jeremiah in a way for which there is no analogy in the Ezekiel traditions. This is particularly true of those Jeremiah traditions which developed after 597, which address the contrasting realities of exile and continued life in the land. Stated simply, the Exilic Redaction has sought to "uncomplicate" Jeremiah's perspective on such matters in favor of a single, comprehensive statement of judgment, exile, and restoration, such as can be seen in the Book of Ezekiel. Jeremiah's language concerning the coming disaster of 597 (Chs. 9—15) has been pressed into service by the Exilic Redaction to anticipate the complete punishment of the land — even as Jeremiah himself remained in Judah and took the possibility of continued life there seriously.[129]

The layer of tradition supplied by the Exilic Redaction now forms an inextricable part of the Jeremiah traditions as a whole.[130] This redactional level can be detected as early as Ch. 1 and as late as Ch. 52, but it is especially noteworthy in chs. 21—45, that section of Jeremiah which focuses on life in the land in the post-597 period. Detailed analysis of the Book of Jeremiah, with an eye to uncovering this redactional layer, will follow in Chapter Four.

On the basis of our analysis of the Ezekiel traditions, it is clear that legitimate existence for a people or ruler in the land is foreclosed from the moment of Jehoiachin's capture and the first deportations. Admittedly, there is a brief delay before the prophet's career commences (Ezek 1:2, 5th year of Jehoiachin's exile), but this is not a significant factor. From the beginning of Ezekiel's prophetic activity the verdict over the land is absolute and final. Whatever else the extensive throne-chariot vision of Ch. 1 might portend, the reader comes away with a clear impression of

---

[128] See the remarks in Chapter Four, Section III.

[129] In Jeremiah's view, continued life in the land after 597 required submission to Babylon: "Serve the king of Babylon and live. Why should this city become a desolation?" (Jer 27:17).

[130] Compare the contrasting language even within a single chapter (Ch. 21). Within 21:1—7, v. 7 eliminates the possibility of survival after 587 B. C., even as 21:8—10 counsels surrender that "you might live and have your life as a prize of war" (v. 8). Or note the shift from 27:16—18 (vessels to remain in Jerusalem) to 27:19—22 (vessels to go to Babylon).

Yahweh's transcendent mobility, a characteristic which anticipates the ultimate removal of God's *kābôd* from the Jerusalem temple and his appearance to Ezekiel among the exiles (10:20). The implication of this is clear: God has taken his glory from Judah and revealed himself to the *Gôlāh*. And when the prophet is himself stricken over the severity and finality of Yahweh's sentence over the land (11:13), he is immediately put in mind of the verdict passed over the Golah by those who were spared deportation to remain in the land:

> They have gone far from the LORD; to us this land is given for a possession (Ezek 11:15).[131]

It is clear that more than property rights are at stake. A theological assessment is being made by those in Judah: God has "removed" those deported (v. 16). Yahweh's word in response is both a rejection of this verdict and a promise to those removed. They will be gathered, they will receive the land, they will receive "new hearts," and Yahweh will be their God (vv. 16−20). But in the meantime, he will be a "small sanctuary for them in the lands in which they come" (v. 16: *wā'ĕhî lāhem lĕmiqdāš mĕ'aṭ bā'ărāsôt 'ăšer-bā'û šām*). For he "removes" himself from the inhabitants of Jerusalem and their sanctuary:

> And the glory of Yahweh went up from the midst of the city, and stood upon the mountain which is on the east side of the city. And the spirit lifted me up and brought me in the vision by the spirit of God into Chaldea, to the exiles (Ezek 11:23−24).

Even as this perspective from the Book of Ezekiel is put in place, the fact remains that Jeremiah's prophetic activity continued beyond the events of 597, as did the existence of a community and king in Judah. His theological perspective on events is of necessity distinct from Ezekiel's, given the different historical fate he endured. The extent and nature of that distinctiveness is yet to be determined. At this point it is enough to make some general suggestions, in light of this assessment of Ezekiel's perspective on the monarchy, life in the land, the status of the exiles, and God's design for judgment and restoration.[132]

---

[131] Reading perfect *rāḥaqû* rather than the imperative *raḥaqû* (MT) on the basis of v. 16, but the major point remains the same in either case. Note how the first half of the verse, in clarifying the "they" of exile, states somewhat repetitively, "Son of man, your brethren, even your own brethren, your next of kin (MT), and the whole house of Israel [are those] of whom the inhabitants of Jerusalem say: They have gone . . .". "Next of kin" (lit, "redemption-men") is relevant in this context because the inhabitants of Jerusalem are claiming certain property rights, among other things. The emphasis also seems to fall on the extent of exile, possibly including even earlier (northern) deportations. For a full discussion, see Greenberg, *Ezekiel 1−20*, 189.

[132] One feature of the Ezekiel 597 perspective to keep in mind when reviewing post-597 Jeremiah traditions below is the former's negative assessment of Zedekiah. In a similar fashion, the Exilic Redaction works to blunt any positive stance taken toward him by the prophet Jeremiah, especially in that portion of the tradition to be termed the Scribal Chronicle (Jer 37−43*).

Before moving to the Jeremiah traditions, there is one other perspective on life in the land and exile after 597 B. C. that must be examined. This is the perspective of 2 Kings 24—25, the finale of the DtrH, which like Jeremiah and Ezekiel gives an accounting of this wider historical period. There is good reason to assume that the final chapters of Kings will shed some additional light on the question of contrasting evaluations of the exile, since they record events related to the "capture" of 597 and the "fall" of 587 B. C. But more importantly, the whole of the DtrH draws to a close around precisely these events of exile and deportation. It is reasonable to assume that as the unknown author/redactor completed this comprehensive theological survey of Israel's long history, the final chapters would play a particularly important role. These chapters will now be examined.

III. THE SEQUENTIAL PRESENTATION OF "CAPTURE" AND "FALL"

A. Historical Narratives in Jeremiah and 2 Kings: An Introduction

Further information about the events of 597 and 587 is found in the last two chapters of the Book of Kings. There are several points of contact between these historical reports and a similar form of narrative within Jeremiah, noteworthy among them 2 Kings 25 || Jeremiah 39 & 52. Moreover, brief mention is made in Jeremiah to the events of 597 in a manner similar to 2 Kings 24 (Jer 27:20; 29:2; 37:1). With respect to the reporting of 597/587 events, the points of contact between the Jeremiah and Kings traditions are such that literary dependence, common editorial background, or some other explanation must be given to account for the nearly word-for-word correlation between them.[133] An examination of the subtle differences between the accounts is also a fruitful enterprise, suggesting distinctive emphases within a given literary context.

When confronted in the biblical record with parallel reports, it is important to try and determine which is to have historical precedence. Only then can certain questions of a more historical or factual nature be pursued ("what really happened" at the Fall of Jerusalem). But it is an equally important task to assess how each report functions in its own literary context, attempting to account for why reports provide different information in different literary presentations. Obviously this task cannot be carried through successfully without first reaching a decision about the tradition history of the material, prior to its inclusion in specific literary structures.[134]

Determination of prior tradition is especially important in the case of 2 Kings 24/25 and the parallel Jeremiah material. It was pointed out above that while the Book of Jeremiah includes a section of poetic material related to the siege and capture of 597 B. C., this section is not the final word of the Jeremiah traditions, in original or final form. The reader is moved quickly beyond this material to the core of the book (Chs. 21—45),

---

[133] Traditional commentary has long recognized the resemblances between the Jeremiah and Kings material, even to the extent of attributing authorship of Kings to the prophet Jeremiah (*B Bat* 14b—15a). This view no doubt arose for a variety of reasons. On the literary level, it may have stemmed from the presence of closely related historical narratives, viz, Jeremiah 52 and 2 Kings 25. A modern form of this view sees the commonality in terms of secondary levels of tradition, viz, material in Kings and Jeremiah under deuteronomistic influence.

[134] For a discussion of the importance of assessing "pluriformity" in biblical narrative, see Peter R. Ackroyd, "Historians and Prophets," *SEA* 33 (1968) 18 ff.

which deals with post-597 events. It should be noted that the detailed superscription to the Jeremiah corpus does not mention the deportations of 597 or the figure of Jehoiachin, moving instead from Josiah to Jehoiakim to Zedekiah to the captivity of 587 B. C. Another important observation can be made in light of the perceived parallels with Kings. There is relatively little literary correspondence between 2 Kings 24, the chapter dealing with 597 events, and the Jeremiah material. Where parallel material is found (Jer 27:20; 29:1−2 || 2 Kgs 24:10−17) it is scanty. The fuller, more organically connected account appears to be from Kings. This account is utilized in a cursory way to provide editorial settings in Jeremiah (see esp. 29:1−3). Most feel that here Jeremiah has been secondarily expanded on the basis of reports of 597 deportations from 2 Kings 24.[135]

By contrast, there is a great deal of correspondence between 2 Kings 25 and the Jeremiah material. This is most obviously true in the case of Jeremiah 52, which is virtually identical to 2 Kings 25. Minor divergences, in view of the otherwise overwhelming correspondences, are intriguing; there is also a major divergence, concerning the summary of deportations (Jer 52:28−30). These divergences will be discussed below. More notable in this regard is the fact of their identical placement, as the final chapters in their respective works.

The question of literary dependence vis-à-vis the Jeremiah material is much more complicated in the case of 2 Kings 25 than 2 Kings 24. It appears as though Jeremiah 52 is a better candidate for dependence on 2 Kings 25 than the reverse, but the same cannot be as easily said about the relationship between 2 Kings 25 and Jer 39:1−10, narratives which both describe the Fall of Jerusalem. Opinions are divided within critical circles on the direction of literary dependence, though 2 Kings 25 is perceived by the majority of scholars as prior to Jeremiah 39. This holds true despite the obvious narrative location Jer 39:1−10 shares with surrounding chapters (Jeremiah 37−43).[136] These chapters appear to have a great deal of firsthand information related to the person of the prophet and the circumstances of the Fall of Jerusalem, not to mention post-587 events − so much so that they are considered by some the core of a document traceable to Jeremiah's own disciples, if not the ephemeral Baruch. By contrast, Jeremiah is not even mentioned in 2 Kings 25, nor is the material concerned with chronicling life after the fall (Jer 40−43) included. Numerous other details are lacking in this compressed account of Kings.[137] If the literary unity of the Jeremiah material is both original and early, that is, contem-

---

[135] There is critical agreement on this. See Bright, *Jeremiah*, 208; Rudolph, *Jeremiah*, 148,152; Thompson, *Jeremiah*, 544.

[136] See the full discussion of Jer 39:1−10 below.

[137] Walter Dietrich, *Prophetie und Geschichte* (FRLANT 108; Göttingen: Vandenhoeck & Ruprecht, 1972) 140, n. 119.

poraneous with events recorded, then the conclusion would appear to be that 2 Kings 25 was drawn from the fuller account of Jeremiah 37—43.[138] Another possibility would be to entertain a theory of a "common source" for them both.[139] But in either case, following this line of argument, what 2 Kings 25 lacks over against Jer 37—43 or a hypothetical "common source" would have to be considered an "omission," however one accounts for this fact.[140]

The specific question of the literary relationship between Jeremiah and Kings traditions presents a problem in its own right. But at the outset, an observation related to the editorial history of Kings can be made in light of the relationship between 2 Kings 24 and 25 and the Jeremiah material. It is to be noted that, the question of literary dependence aside, there is far greater correspondence between Ch. 25 of Kings and the Jeremiah material than Ch. 24. The events of 597 are not even mentioned in the book's superscription. This suggests that as the Jeremiah material was shaped and given final form, 587 events had already emerged as more crucial to the 52-chapter presentation than their earlier 597 counterpart. But a sensitive reading of the Jeremiah material, especially Chs. 21—45, indicates that the situation was not so clear prior to 587 B. C.

This thesis can be illustrated at a point outside the Jeremiah traditions themselves, specifically, within the presentation of the Deuteronomistic History. It should be noted that there is far more similarity in editorial style and general presentation between 2 Kings 24 (the "penultimate chapter") and the preceding chapters of the Dtr History, than between 2 Kings 25 ("final chapter") and the same material. Stated differently, 2 Kings 25 appears to have been developed subsequent to 2 Kings 24, and under different conditions.[141] This would be established beyond reasonable

---

[138] Martin Noth, *The Deuteronomistic History* (JSOTSS 15; Sheffield: JSOT Press, 1981), 74. He states, "These sections are so deeply imbedded in Jer 39—41, that they must be original there" (137, n. 69). Noth has taken a minority stand on this issue; most follow Duhm's 1901 analysis of Jer 39 (*Jeremia,* 309) and argue that Jer 39:1—14 is derived from 2 Kgs 25:1—20 (excepting the plusses at 39:3,13).

[139] Sigmund Mowinckel, *Komposition,* 29 ff.

[140] See, for example, Karl-Friedrich Pohlmann, "Erwägungen zum Schlußkapitel des deuteronomistischen Geschichtswerkes," *Textgemäß: Aufsätze und Beiträge zur Hermeutik des Alten Testaments* (FS E. Würthwein, 1979). The sub-title drives the important point home, "Oder: Warum wird der Prophet Jeremia in 2 Kön 22—25 nicht erwähnt?" Pohlmann's remarks are concerned primarily with 2 Kgs 25:22 ff. — 2 Kgs 25:1—21 he considers prior to Jeremiah 39. The scholary literature on the broader subject of the literary relationship between 2 Kings 25 and Jeremiah 39 & 52 is enormous, and will be cited at the appropriate point below.

[141] See our remarks above. Incidentally, this is a telling complication in the Dtr 1/Dtr 2 theory as laid out by Cross and Nelson. Dtr 2 theoretically includes a uniform level of redaction, represented in 2 Kings 24 and 25 (the material following the death of Josiah). But a comparison of chs. 24 and 25 suggests a different use of sources, distinct narrative style, and peculiar tradition history for each.

doubt if it were shown that 2 Kings 25, in distinction to 2 Kings 24, was dependent upon the Jeremiah traditions regarding the Fall of Jerusalem in 587 B. C., now found at Jeremiah 37—43. The question resurfaces of the impact of 597 events on the redactional development of the Jeremiah tradition. If 2 Kings 24 is shown to have a tradition history distinct from 2 Kings 25, also affected would be the conception of their respective evaluations of the "fall" and "capture" episodes of Judah's final days, as well as the coordination of these as distinct "phases." This section is concerned to explore just such a question, before moving to an analysis of the Jeremiah traditions themselves.

An important point to make in conclusion is that the question of the relationship between 2 Kings 24 and 25 is a problem in its own right, apart from the way the relationship between Jeremiah 39/52 and this latter chapter from Kings is conceived. Therefore, the report of capture and fall in 2 Kings 24, and its growth to final form, will first be examined. Then its editorial history and provenance will be compared with that of 2 Kings 25, as well as Jeremiah 39 and 52 and other exilic witnesses.

B. 2 Kings 24: Final Chapter?

Reading the essentially coherent final form of the narrative, 2 Kings 24 presents a sober account of the events surrounding the 597 siege, capture, and deportation of Judah and Jerusalem (24:20). It should be stated at the outset that though the narrative touches on the reigns of three separate Judahite kings, the unifying theme of the whole chapter concerns this one central subject: events leading up to the deportations of 597 B. C. As noted above, the chapter hastens to its main burden, anticipated even in vv. 2—4: the report of the approach of Nebuchadnezzar (v. 11) during the siege, the surrender of King Jehoiachin and his royal entourage (v. 12), and their capture and deportation to Babylon (vv. 13—16). Apart from the king and his family, a substantial portion of the population is also placed into custody and "carried away" (*wĕhiglāh*, v. 14), the figure given initially at 10,000 *gôlāh*. This includes governmental (*śārîm*) military (*gibbôrê haḥayil*) and general Jerusalemite citizenry. Over and above this figure are included artisans and smiths (*wĕkol-heḥārāš wĕ-hammasgēr*), apparently members of guilds within the city.[142]

It is often assumed that some sort of difficulty in the narrative flow is encountered at this juncture (v. 15 ff.), since much of the information already given is repeated, with what appears to be an unfortunate degree of variation. Specifically, vv. 15—16 tell of the exiling of Jehoiachin, his mother, his wives, his courtisans (*sārîsâw*) and certain leading men of the

---

[142] J. Gray, *I & II Kings,* 761. Malamat ("Last Years," 211) speaks of "armorers and sappers, the auxiliary technical personnel." See also "Twilight of Judah," 133, n. 24.

land (*'êlê hā'āreṣ hôlîḵ*). Additional figures are given in v. 16, including 7000 soldiers (*ḵol 'anšê haḥayil*) and 1000 of the same artisan/smith group mentioned in the preceding verses. Actually, the problem is not all that severe in v. 15. It does seem, however, that new numbers are given at v. 16 (7000 + 1000) which do not square with v. 14 (10,000).[143]

A further problem related to the two sets of different numbers given is also reported to exist in the narrative. Stated simply, with its fourfold repetition of "all" (i. e., "all" Jerusalem, princes, soldiers, and craftsmen) and its blunt summary that "none remained," v. 14 sounds too final and would appear to be contradicted by, among other things, the presence of Ch. 25.[144] Moreover, v. 14 seems to be of a piece with v. 13, which likewise tells of "all" the royal and religious treasures (*'ôṣĕrôt*) being carried off by the king of Babylon. Gray argues, for example, that this statement is "flatly contradicted" by Jer 27:19 ff. (which mentions vessels left in the temple).[145] As a result of the seemingly exaggerated tone shared by vv. 13 and 14, as well as the problems in narrative flow encountered in trying to coordinate vv. 13—14 with vv. 15—16, the former unit is often considered an intrusive addition, meant to anticipate the full fall of the city in 587 B. C.[146] By contrast vv. 15—16 are generally taken as some sort of accurate historical record, though the numbers here (7000 + 1000) and in vv. 13—14 (10,000) are taken in both cases as rather approximate reckonings when seen over against the entry at Jer 52:28 (3023 Judahites), regarded as authentic because it supplies an "un-round" number.[147] The problem with the reckoning of deportees may not, however, be that crucial within the context of Ch. 24 itself. After all, the numbers given are admittedly general and are, in any event, attached to different groups[148];

---

[143] For a discussion of the problem, see Malamat, "Twilight," 133 ff.

[144] See Gray, *I & II Kings*, 760—1; Ernst Würthwein, *Die Bücher der Könige: 1. Kön 17—2. Kön 25* (ATD; Göttingen: Vandenhoeck & Ruprecht, 1984) 473; G. H. Jones, *1 and 2 Kings* (NCB; Grand Rapids: Eerdmans, 1984) 2.637; further: W. Dietrich, *Prophetie und Geschichte*, 140.

[145] Gray, *I & II Kings*, 760; Jones, *1 and 2 Kings*, 637. Würthwein (*Könige*, 473) sees the statement as contradicted by Ch. 25 (vv. 13—14).

[146] So Gray, Würthwein, Jones (see note above); for further discussion and bibliographic reference, see R. Nelson, *Double Redaction*, 88.

[147] Note the difference in the year (7th) and the group (Judahites) in the Jeremiah 52 notice. Both factors must be taken into consideration. Malamat ("Twilight," 133) says of the number from Jer 52:28, that it is "based undoubtably on some official source." Malamat seeks to eliminate differences in the separate reckonings by appeal to a two-stage deportation: a "limited" 7th year one of 3023 Judahites (Jer 52:28) and a second principal phase, "comprised of the cream of Jerusalem and thousands of her defenders" (134), viz, the 7000 of 2 Kgs 24:16. This proposal was suggested earlier in rabbinic commentary, viz, 7000 + 3000 = 10,000 (see Malamat, "Twilight," 134, n. 27, for the citation). See the discussion below.

[148] Gray (*I & II Kings*, 761) terms them "approximations on the part of a later redactor." In the first case, 10,000 would appear to refer to "all Jerusalem and all the princes and

their coordination with the report at Jer 52:28 would appear a more difficult undertaking. The more telling objections to reading vv. 13—14 within the narrative flow are connected with the charge of redundancy and finality. This in turn begs the larger question as to the overall structure and tradition history of the chapter.

Gray's analysis of the constituent parts of Ch. 24 is fairly typical; it is reproduced here for the purpose of illustration:

(1) Annals' Citation: v. 1
(2) Dtr Redaction (w/historical nucleus): vv. 2—3
(3) Dtr Compilation (or Redactional imitation of the same): vv. 5—6
(4) Annals' Citation: v. 7
(5) Dtr Redaction (in style of Compiler): vv. 8—9
(6) Dtr Redaction (historical narrative): vv. 10—12
(7) Anachronistic Supplement: vv. 13—14
(8) Dtr Redaction (historical narrative): vv. 15—17
(9) Dtr Redaction (in style of Compiler): vv. 18—20a

The obvious thing to note is that 9 individual units, representing at least 4 levels of tradition, are detected within the space of just 20 verses.[149] These levels point to familiar characters within Gray's larger analysis of the Dtr History: (1) "annals" represents source material (pre-dtr) utilized by the (2) "dtr compiler" who works prior to the exile, his chronicle in turn edited by a (3) "dtr redactor" who, in this period, imitates the compiler's style (vv. 8—9; 18—20a) and, as shown in vv. 10—12, 15—17, can have access to sound historical material, unlike (4) a still later supplementary level. The Redactor's presence is often noted by his "homiletical" tone. In Gray's judgment, this gives him away at vv. 3, 4 and 18 ff.[150] But Gray must acknowledge his lack of homiletical style at points in Ch. 24 and conclude that there is, on occasion, historical veracity to his sermonizing (as in vv. 2—4 and 10—12, 15—17).

The redactional theory of Gray, quite convincing at other points in the DtrH, appears to break down at Ch. 24. Gray adapts a theory otherwise credibly used to explain the interaction between source and redaction in the DtrH in order to analyze literary traditions at a completely unique point in Israel's history: the capture and deportation of Judah/Jerusalem. This is a moment with no real analogy in Israel's history (short of the

---

all the mighty men"; in the second instance, 7000 refers to, specifically, the soldiers, and 1000 to the artisans/craftsmen. This issue will be addressed shortly, in light of the additional report from Jer 52:27 ff.

[149] Würthwein's analysis is similar (*Könige,* 467 ff.). He identifies a healthier pre-dtr level (24:1—2a; 10—12, 15—17), a similar post-dtr level at vv. 13—14, and a general dtr (Dtr-G) level at vv. 2b—4, 5—6, and 8—9.

[150] Similarly, Würthwein (*Könige,* 467 ff.), though in his schema these statements are distributed between Dtr-N (vv. 3—4, 20a) and Dtr-P (v. 2b), secondary redactional levels to the basis document, Dtr-G.

later events of 587 B. C.), when source, compilation, and redaction (to use his terms) are relatively interrelated phases. At this point in time, three originally distinct moments in the growth to final form of the DtrH begin to collapse. When Gray tries to extend his usual analysis into this chapter, the result seems too mechanical. Moreover, the surest sign of a theory's failure is the need for constant qualification. In Ch. 24 one sees Redaction "imitative" of Compilation (24:5,8 ff.,18 ff.), Historical Narration imbedded within Redaction (24:2 ff.,10 ff.), and Annals' citations too brief or too isolated to merit the classification (24:1,7). As if to signal his own discomfort with the theory's applicability here, Gray uses the terms "possibly" or "probably" over a dozen times in this brief section, a tendency he is usually successful in avoiding.

In sum, the presence of at least three literary levels is not to be doubted at specific points within the broader Dtr History. Nor is it unlikely that reflexes of such levels can be detected in Ch. 24. However, given the strong likelihood that the final shapers of Ch. 24 were among those exiled in 597 B. C., the period separating "source" and "redaction" on purely historical grounds is too compressed for the minute literary divisions attempted by Gray (or Würthwein). For this reason, fidelity to an otherwise coherent theory must at this juncture be set aside, given the historical factors involved. The only way to appreciate the unique status of Ch. 24 is to have clearly in mind the way redaction, compilation and original source were brought together earlier in the History. It then becomes apparent that something of the same process is at work in Ch. 24, only here redactor, compiler and source are much more intimately related. In fact, they are probably represented in a single phase of literary production. This makes perfect sense if the "redactors" are at this point "compiling" on the basis of their own "sources."

Gray has a slightly different proposal. He makes the important observation that "there is no clear indication of the point at which the first Deuteronomistic compilation ended and the exilic continuation began" (753). One explanation would be that the presence of such a literary seam is not to be expected, since the division he makes between compilation/ redaction is artificial — but this follows from a different understanding of the way the chapter is composed. Gray does attempt to uncover the circumstances which would lead to such a literary division. He argues that the failure to mention the details of Jehoiakim's revolt and death indicates a "definite break in the records" (753). In other words:

> ... the first Deuteronomistic compilation ended between the outbreak of the revolt and death of Jehoiakim, and after a certain hiatus the history was continued after the Exile, possibly by the redactor (753).

Alongside this, he offers a more complicated bit of evidence for a split between Judahite compilation and Exilic redaction, viz, that in 24:12 (the

8th year of Nebuchadnezzar) one confronts the "first dating in Kings by a foreign chronology" (753).[151]

The first argument is avowedly an *e silentio* one. The subject of Jehoiakim's death has been treated above, and there is no compelling reason to use the fact of silence in this one instance to defend a hiatus between source and redaction. Moreover, it is not clear that an exilic redactor would be in any better or worse position to know the details than a Judahite compiler. The period that would separate their activity could not be much more than a decade. This is far too short a time to warrant a distinction between availability to sources for the compiler and redactor. In any event, details of Jehoiakim's death are not likely to have been restricted to "sources." In sum, the failure to mention the circumstances of Jehoiakim's death is as much a mystery for a Judahite redactor as an Exilic compiler.

The second argument advanced by Gray makes no particular sense in the more limited framework of Kings itself. One can entertain the notion of "foreign chronology" for the "8th year of Nebuchadnezzar" at 24:12 only when this entry is placed alongside that of Jer 52:28: "This is the number of the people whom Nebuchadnezzar carried away captive: in the seventh year, 3023 Judahites."[152] Though at other points Gray follows the critical consensus in seeing Jeremiah 52 as later than 2 Kings 24—25, he takes this one unit (vv. 28—30) as an exception. He views it as an early deportation list, based upon "reliable Palestinian authority" (760). Such a theory puts Gray in the unfortunate position of having to clarify the redactor's failure to utilize the list, which, as Gray admits, "[he] could have consulted had he wished" (754).[153]

Even granting the complexity surrounding chronological systems for this period, Gray's explanations are convoluted and unnecessary. Ironically, in assessing the relationship between Jeremiah 52 and 2 Kings 24, the opposite position is more commonly defended, viz, that the Jer 52:28—30 dates (7th year; 18th year; 23rd year) reflect a foreign chronology (the

---

[151] By this he means more than dating by reference to the Babylonian king. At a later place he states more directly, "The dating in the eighth year of Nebuchadnezzar is surely from a Jew in Mesopotamia" (759 ff.), that is, one who had adopted the calendric and chronological systems of Babylon as opposed to Palestine.

[152] The term "Judahite" (*yĕhûdîm*) appears to be distinctive, since in the context of this unit (Jer 52:28—30), other phrases are employed: In the 18th year of Nebuchadnezzar, he carried away captive from Jerusalem (*mîrûšālaim*) 832 persons (*nepeš*); in the twenty-third year ... Judahites (*yĕhûdîm*) 745 persons (*nepeš*).

[153] At another place Gray states, "The figures of Jeremiah probably represent the authority of a mature contemporary as distinct from that of an exilic redactor, who may still, of course, have been one of the deportees sufficiently mature to take accurate note" (761—2). This is precisely the problem with Gray's analysis — the time-period envisioned is far too compressed. One is speaking of sources and redactors who are separated neither by age nor provenance!

post-dating system effective in Babylon) while 2 Kgs 24:12 is based on a Palestinian reckoning.[154] Generally, the whole of Jeremiah 52, including the deportation list, is taken as later than and based upon 2 Kings 25.[155] Others emend Jer 52:28 from 7th to 17th year, an equally unnecessary move.[156]

Unfortunately, the issue of chronology is so burdened by factors beyond critical control that it is difficult to use shifts in reckoning as proof of new provenance.[157] The one thing that does seem certain is that Jer 52:28−30 is a summarizing entry, later than 2 Kings 24 and based upon an official list.[158] Since the capture of the city took place near the turn of the year (March 16), the captivity of Jehoiachin could be plausibly dated to the 8th year of Nebuchadnezzar's reign (2 Kgs 24:12). The events of capture and deportation certainly carried over well into the following year. More to the point, this date could have been supplied by either an exilic redactor or a Judahite compiler. As such, it is impossible to use it as evidence of a hiatus separating the work of the compiler and redactor.

Having reviewed Gray's analysis, as well as the text of 2 Kings 24, an alternative proposal suggests itself: the author of 2 Kings 24 was among those deported in 597 B. C. In the case of 2 Kings 24, he functioned as both redactor and compiler.[159] As such, he had access to material which can logically be termed "sources" or "annals" only at other points in the tradition history of Kings. But he also functioned as compiler and redactor,

---

[154] W. F. Albright, *BASOR* 143 (1956) 28−33; D. N. Freedman, "The Babylonian Chronicle," *BA* 19 (1956) 50−60; Freedy & Redford, "Dates in Ezekiel," 466; Nelson, *Double Redaction*, 26.

[155] Jones, *1 and 2 Kings*, 2.641; Rudolph, *Jeremia*, 277,80 (calls vv. 28−30 a "besondere Quelle" but not an earlier source); Noth, *Deuteronomistic History*, 138, n. 69; Dietrich, *Prophetie*, 140, n. 119.

[156] Rudolph, *Jeremia*, 280.

[157] Do the dates refer consistently to captivity or deportation? In the instance of the 597 events, it is clear that circumstances took place around the "turn of the year" (2 Chron 36:11), thus making it even more difficult to know whose year, or what precise date was ultimately adopted. How explicitly were events dated by scribes? What kind of latitude did a scribe have with respect to the adoption of his or the conqueror's system? What kind of tolerance for discrepency was operative? For example, how can a scribe give different dates at one point when tradition provided others? All scholars have ways in which they provide answers to these questions, either indirectly or directly, and these in turn inform their conclusions. But in many respects, the answers to these and other questions cannot be determined with complete assurance. Even W. F. Albright remained skeptical about the possibility of attaining thorough and consistent precision in chronological reckoning (see Hayes & Miller, "Appendix: Chronology of the Israelite and Judaean Kings," *History*, 678 ff.). From his respected position, this was more a counsel of caution than despair.

[158] See discussion below.

[159] This is the important distinction to be made with respect to Gray's analysis. For even Gray can talk of the exilic redactor "who may still, of course, have been one of the deportees . . ." (762).

when, in this instance, he gave an accounting of events which brought about the downfall of the nation. These were events of which he had firsthand experience.

Such a view has important implications for this analysis of the theological perspective from Babylon, emerging from the 597 exilic community, and suggests the possibility of kinship with the Ezekiel traditions. Before turning to this issue, several specific questions related to the literary integrity of Ch. 24 must be addressed. The first involves the so-called homiletic tone detected at points in the chapter. The second has to do with the reputed secondary nature of the unit 24:13—14.

Beyond its compressed historical narration, one also notices terse theological assessments in Ch. 24, which Gray has argued give evidence of secondary redactional development. Yet what is obvious in Gray's analysis is the difficulty he has in isolating these notices on purely literary grounds. Rather, they are separated because of a prior commitment to, among other things, the notion that theological comment is a redactional and not a "compilational" activity.[160] However, at least in the case of vv. 2—3*, 13 and 20a, theological comment is far too well integrated into the narrative.[161] Moreover, if an exilic author is responsible for the major compiling and editorial work in the chapter, it would have been extremely odd — if not out-and-out implausible — for him to have avoided making a theological judgment at this point in the narrative. After all, from his perspective life in Judah had come to an end. Given this fact it is all the more likely that he provided the terse theological conclusions he did. These frame the chapter, anticipating the Fall in vv. 2—3, and commenting on it in summary fashion in v. 20: "For because of the anger of the LORD it came to the point in Jerusalem and Judah that he cast them out from his presence."

One of the ironies of critical analysis is that once a section has been determined as secondary, one can also conjecture as to why it is "missing." Proponents of a double redaction theory for Kings, with a Josianic Edition supplemented by Dtr 2 (= 2 Kings 24—25), frequently point out that there is no lengthy peroration on the Fall of Jerusalem equivalent to what

---

[160] On 24:20a, Gray states: "Composed after the pattern of the Deuteronomistic compiler, but with a homiletic note on the main event, the revolt against Babylon, which reveals the Deuteronomistic redactor" (762). See also, Dietrich, *Prophetie,* 139 ff.; Würthwein, *Könige,* 474.

[161] The grounding of the Fall in the sins of Manasseh (v. 4) does not appear as literarily integrated. Moreover, while vv. 2,3 (read *'ap* for MT *pî*) and 20a appear to present a common theme (Yahweh's wrath at Judah/Jerusalem's sins), v. 4 focuses on the specific sins of Manasseh. The so-called summary (for Jehoiachin: 24:8—9) and introduction (for Zedekiah: 24:18—19) formulae, which also typically contain evaluations, are another subject altogether. See the comments below. The evaluation of Zedekiah (24:18—19; 20b) may well have been added when Ch. 25 was brought into coordination with Ch. 24.

is found at 2 Kings 17 on the Fall of Samaria.[162] There are many explanations that help account for the breadth of the report at 2 Kings 17,
notable among them that 2 Kings 17 has itself received healthy secondary
enrichment. It has, after all, had a longer time in which to receive such
enrichment. Whatever its original scope, the narrative undoubtably continued to function in the Southern Kingdom beyond 721 as an apt
theological lesson, drawing upon the example of Samaria's fall (a little
over a century for reflection). This observation, however, gives only
relative assistance in pursuing the question as to why no commentary of
comparable force appears on the occasion of Jerusalem's final collapse.

It is mistaken to look to Ch. 25 for such commentary, even though
as the final word of the history it appears to be the logical place for such
a report to be found. The odd thing to note is that Ch. 24 really has more
to say by way of theological comment than Ch. 25. This raises certain
fundamental questions as to the present coordination of these two chapters,
which will be addressed shortly. But setting these considerations aside for
a moment, it cannot be concluded that an assessment analogous to what
exists for the events of 721 B. C. is altogether lacking. Rather, the intriguing
thing to note is that it surfaces in relationship to the events of 597 rather
than 587. By contrast, the narrative of Ch. 25, as has been pointed out, is
rather flat, content to provide a kind of detailed factual account which
does seem oddly devoid of theological comment. Even 25:21, which is
often called upon to fill this role, hardly does an adequate job: "So Judah
was taken out of exile into its land." If there is a fuller theological comment
in the chapter, it is associated with Jehoiachin's release; this report occupies
four verses and the significant final position of the entire work (25:27−30).
But this unit speaks more to the subject of restoration than judgment. For
theological reflection on the Fall of Jerusalem, the reader is driven back
to the narrative of Ch. 24.

C. Theological Commentary in Ch. 24

There is a general scholarly consensus that Ch. 24 has received a layer
of theological commentary it did not originally have (so, Würthwein,
Dietrich, Gray, Cross and Nelson). It is important to note that such a
view depends in large measure on the kind of split between source and
redaction, or compilation and redaction suggested by Gray and reviewed

---

[162] The evaluation of F. M. Cross (*Canaanite Myth,* 288) is curiously patronizing: "The
omission of a final, edifying discourse on the fall of chosen Zion and the Davidic crown
is better explained by attributing these final terse paragraphs of the history to a less
articulate Exilic editor." It is unlikely that the terseness has anything to do with an
editor's tendency toward "inarticulate" reporting. R. Nelson eliminates all verses with
theological comment from Ch. 24, including vv. 2−4, 13−14, and 20 (*Double Redaction,*
88−89).

on the preceding pages. Cross and Nelson file the layer of commentary in Dtr 2; Dietrich and Würthwein speak of more minute divisions, including "prophetic" and "nomistic" dtr levels of redaction. There is a measure of truth in the observation that the theological commentary in Ch. 24 is not necessarily of one piece. Three distinct forms of theological comment can be identified in Ch. 24, apart from evaluations which appear in the usual summary/introduction formulae (vv. 8—9; vv. 18—19).

The first is also the best integrated. It argues that Judah and Jerusalem fell because of the anger of Yahweh. This form of comment is found in vv. 1—3* and 20a, i.e., verses which frame the entire chapter. Though most commentators seek to eliminate YHWH as subject of v. 2, substituting instead Nebuchadnezzar (from v. 1), there is no particularly sound versional support for this.[163] The idea of Nebuchadnezzar sending out auxiliary troops is not to be ruled out on logical grounds. In fact, it makes good military sense, as was argued in Chapter Two. But the notion of YHWH as subject of the hostile activity against Judah and Jehoiakim (v. 2, *wayĕšallaḥ YHWH bô*) squares well with the overall sense of the verse, clarified in 2b: *wayĕšallĕḥēm bîhûdāh lĕhaʾăbîdô kidĕbar YHWH ʾăšer dibber bĕyad ʿabādâw hannĕbîʾîm,* "and he sent them [bands] into Judah to destroy it, according to the word of YHWH which he spoke by his servants the prophets" (it is to be noted that the Chaldeans are also sent by YHWH, presumably including Nebuchadnezzar). In this reading, vv. 1—2 form a sensible unit: YHWH sends troops out against the rebellious Jehoiakim and Judah itself. Verse three continues specifically with the broader object of the hostility, Judah, and now grounds the judgment more fully: *ʾak ʿal-pî YHWH hāyĕtāh bîhûdāh lĕhāsîr mēʿal pānâw,* "Yes, it was at the command of YHWH that this happened in Judah, to remove [Judah] from his presence." There is some versional support for reading *ʾap* instead of *pî:* "Yes, it was due to the anger of YHWH that . . ."; this reading may be preferable.[164] For when one looks at the concluding verse of Ch. 24, a remarkably similar statement occurs, which appears to be a resumptive note of conclusion: *kî ʿal-ʾap YHWH hāyĕtāh bîrûšālaim ûbîhûdāh ʿad-hišlikô ʾōtām mēʿal pānâw,* "for it was due to the wrath of YHWH that this happened in Jerusalem and Judah, until he cast them out from his presence." The similarity with v. 3a is striking. Note that in

---

[163] See *BHS* apparatus; Gray (with caution), *I & II Kings,* 757; Würthwein, *Könige,* 468; Hayes & Miller, *History,* 470. Jones, following Dietrich, who sees 2b as a secondary gloss from Dtr-P, is typical in his text-critical judgment: "the subject of the sentence, the LORD sent, is an addition that is omitted from the GK." (*1 and 2 Kings,* 634). There is another possibility, viz, no subject in LXX/B due to its having fallen out; YHWH may simply have been assumed as subject.

[164] It is not, however, required for the broader interpretation defended here. The basic point to make concerns resemblances between vv. 1—3a and 20a. Würthwein adopts this reading, viz, "Nur wegen des Zornes Jahwes geschah dies an Judah . . ." (*Könige,* 468).

both v. 3a and v. 4a, the same basic language and syntax is employed, as well as the same object: Judah, or Jerusalem/Judah. The fate of the king, in other words, is not considered apart from that of Judah and Jerusalem. If the evaluation notices are part of the original narrative, it was their specific task to comment on the more particular judgment regarding the king, which they do: Jehoiachin did evil, as did his father (v. 9); Zedekiah did evil, as did Jehoiakim (v. 19).[165] But the focus of these framing theological comments (vv. 1—3a; 20a) is on YHWH's activity against Judah in general.

It has been argued that the phrase "by his servants the prophets" (v. 2b) indicates secondary reflection because it is too general.[166] But the same argument cuts both ways. Perhaps a general statement is called for in order that the true subject of the judgment, YHWH, might have central attention. Cross is "struck by the weakness of the phrase" in another context, 2 Kgs 21:2—15, a passage predicting the fall of Jerusalem ("wiped like a plate") because of the sins of Manasseh.[167] It may be an indication of the secondary nature of that passage in its context, but the same cannot be said of the phrase as it appears in 24:2b. Without it, the theological justification for the Fall appears based upon the wrath of Yahweh alone — a wrath which could be viewed as arbitrary unless related to the actual activity of the people. Mention of the prophets, and in fact, all "his servants the prophets," brings clearly to mind the whole wider history and phenomenon of prophets who, up to this point in time, had warned Israel by calling her to account for her activity. As such, it is effective precisely because it invokes the entire legacy of Israelite and Judahite prophets. Moreover, its "generality" may be consistent with the style of the chapter as a whole (see the round numbers of deportees), a feature which is explicable if the author regarded Ch. 24 as a final evaluation. But this needs to be explored more fully below.

This leads to the second form of theological comment in Ch. 24, that which focuses on the sins of the monarchy. As v. 3 continues in the MT, an additional comment, or justification for the fall, emerges in relationship to the "sins of Manasseh." Arguments for rough syntax in v. 4 (viz, "also for the innocent blood ... for he filled Jerusalem") are convincing. Moreover, the switch to the sins of Manasseh in the context of an otherwise coherent v. 3 seems abrupt. In other words, v. 3b and v. 4 may well be of a one piece. This unit provides a supplementary reason why "YHWH

---

[165] Incidentally, here is an intriguing bit of variation in formulae whose reputed "stereotyp-icality" in Chs. 24—25 leads Nelson to a theory of uniform redaction in "Dtr 2". What is to be noted is that Zedekiah does not do evil according to his nephew/predecessor (Jehoiachin) or his father (Josiah), but "according to all that (his brother) Jehoiakim did."

[166] For discussion, see Nelson, *Double Redaction*, 88 ff.

[167] F. M. Cross, *Canaanite Myth*, 285—6.

removed Judah out of his presence," in this case drawing upon the rather specific, earlier historical activity of the monarch Manasseh. With Cross and Nelson, this addition (vv. 3b—4), narrowly focused on the particular sins of Manasseh, seems secondary and related to the motif developed in Ch. 21:2—15, thus anticipating 24:3b—4.[168] As such it provides an additional explanation for the fall of Jerusalem related to monarchial responsibility. As noted, within the broader context of Ch. 24 the king's activity and fate appears to be linked with that of Judah and Jerusalem. The individual king may receive the usual summary evaluation related to his deeds. But in the end, the same judgment falls for them both. This is made clear in the deportation lists of 24:10 ff.

The third form of theological comment appears in the unit 24:13—14. Here the removal of temple treasures and the cutting up of vessels is specifically linked to an earlier prediction of Yahweh. Most commentators acknowledge the rather odd appearance of such a specific prophecy/fulfillment motif at this point. 24:13 seems to make reference to 2 Kgs 20:12—19, a narrative in which Isaiah delivers an oracle to Hezekiah predicting the carrying off of temple vessels not by the Assyrians in his day but by the later Babylonians. To Nelson's credit, he has recognized the importance of this prophecy/fulfillment link for his theory of a dual redaction and has, accordingly, treated 24:13 in a special appendix.[169] For if it can be shown that this link is integral to the "first edition" of the DtrH and not merely tacked on by a secondary dtr 2 redactor, then the force of arguments which defend Chs. 24—25 as a unified (dtr 2) redaction would be seriously undercut.[170]

Directly related to an investigation of whether the prophecy/fulfillment motif of 24:13 is integral to the main edition of the DtrH is a further consideration. There is an oft-stated conviction that the unit 24:13—14, which contains a theological assessment related to the temple vessels, is a secondary and intrusive (pre-trusive) addition whose presence makes vv. 15 ff. appear redundant. These verses must be looked at for the obvious reason that they — like vv. 1—3a and v. 20a — offer a theological assessment of the Fall: in this case, associating the removal of certain treasures from the House of Yahweh and the spoilation of other vessels "which Solomon king of Israel had made" with Yahweh's earlier foretelling.

---

[168] Nelson, *Double Redaction,* 88—89; Cross, *Canaanite Myth,* 158.

[169] *Double Redaction,* 129 ff.

[170] It should be apparent at this point that we view Ch. 24 as more integrally related to the broader history than most, including all modern proponents of the classic "double redaction" hypothesis. Typically, Chs. 24 and 25 are together seen as the supplementary appendix to the main edition, Josianic or otherwise. Another position is possible. Ch. 24 may well form the conclusion to a main history, composed by a 597 deportee. This edition has been brought up to date by the supplementary Ch. 25.

But the unit is important for another reason. Verse 14 seems to operate from the perspective that these 597 events resulted in the wholesale carrying off of Judah/Jerusalem. The verse is frequently attributed to a theological *tendenz* operative for a later supplementer who sought to depict a wholly vacated Judah.[171] But apart from the picture widespread deportations might give of a theologically "empty" Judah, the finality of verse 14 ("none remained") also suggests that whoever was responsible for its inclusion saw the 597 deportations of king and nation as signaling a major event in Judah's history, if not the probable end of her existence. There may be an implicit theological judgment involved in the numbers given in 24:13—14. But the larger point to make is that for the author of Ch. 24, these 597 events had an integrity all their own. They are not depicted as a "phase" which anticipates a later, dramatic finale. So while the question to be answered is whether such a view was secondarily supplied at 24:13—14, it must be acknowledged that this unit is not the only place where such a theme surfaces in the chapter. Its literary integrity is defended at 1—3a and 20a. It is also to be noted at this juncture that none of the critics surveyed question the authenticity of 24:10—12,15—17; this is the "original" unit, intruded upon by 24:13—14. But close attention to vv. 15—17 shows that it too, like 24:13—14, can make use of the adjective "all" when referring to deportees ("all soldiers", "all able men"). It makes fuller reference to actual groups deported ("courtisans," "chief men," "soldiers," "able men," "warriors"). Moreover, its numbers (7000 + 1000) are similar to those supplied in the unit whose integrity is in question, both in actual count and in terms of its approximate quality.[172]

If the unit 24:13—14 can be shown to be integral to the chapter, one more piece of evidence will be provided for the notion that it is Ch. 24, not Ch. 25 (or Ch. 23), which actually forms the conclusion to the first main edition of the Books of Kings. It may well be the presence of Ch. 25 which potentially confuses the otherwise coherent description of Ch. 24. This description sees the events of 597 as coming about due to Yahweh's will (v. 2), in fulfillment of the word spoken by Him through the prophets (v. 2), at a point when His anger could no longer be abated (v. 20).

D. 24:13—14: An Anachronistic Supplement?

The charges against the unit 24:13—14 being included in Ch. 24 are fourfold. They include (1) redundancy, (2) lack of harmony (numbers of deportees), (3) contradiction (re: vessels, empty land), as well as (4) more

---

[171] See Würthwein, *Könige*, 473; Gray, *I & II Kings*, 760.

[172] Würthwein notes this fact and brackets v. 16, a sign that complications in the larger editorial theory exist. For him the number 8000 is, following Janssen (*Exilszeit*, 32), both a large approximation and a potentially secondary gloss, in conflict with the fact of Zedekiah's necessary troop support later (*Könige*, 472).

general questions about the prophecy/fulfillment link to 2 Kgs 20:12—19. Though his order is different, Nelson summarizes the objections as follows:

> . . . almost all commentators agree that v. 13 and perhaps 14 are really a post-redactional insertion into 2 Kings 24. First, vv. 12 and 15 fit together as a narrative about the royal imprisonment and exile. Second, *miššam* in 13 has a remote antecedent; the city has not been mentioned since 11. Third, these verses are redundant, for 15—16 deal with the same subject. Fourth, the figures given in 14 are hard to harmonize with those given in 16. Finally, the concept that all the treasure was plundered and all the important men of Jerusalem exiled would be unlikely for an editor whose horizon of thought included the plundering and deportation of 587 (*Double Redaction,* 88).

Nelson's first objection has been discussed above; it is not clear that v. 15 says anything contradicted by vv. 13—14 — the more serious charge here would be redundancy. His second objection is not clear; in relationship to v. 13, is v. 11 to be considered remote? But these problems are inconsequential when compared to the others, which do warrant discussion. Most notable among them is the concluding objection.

Looking ahead, another issue needs to be raised in connection with the observation made by Gray and others that vv. 13—14 anticipate the Fall of 587 and were added for this reason.[173] Is this a logical motivation for the inclusion of a supplement at this point in the narrative? Why would a supplement be added which blatantly contradicts the present narrative arrangement of Chs. 24 and 25?[174] The possibility that vv. 13—14 were inserted to "anticipate" the events of 587 seems to be ruled out precisely because of the strain it puts on the presentation of Ch. 25, and especially its own statements regarding temple vessels (25:13—17).[175] Nelson sees it as unlikely that an editor "whose horizon of thought included the plundering and deportation of 587" would be responsible for this unit. Here he puts his finger on the problem. It would be exactly the later supplementer, more than any other candidate, who would have had the events of 587 and the literary witness of Ch. 25 on the "horizon" of his thought. If the "addition" is attributed to him, one would need to account for his seeming ignorance or his disregard for the present narrative logic which spans chs. 24 & 25. There is another possibility. The only candidate who could have conceived of the events of 597 apart from those of 587 would be an author whose own horizon of thought was focused on and limited to the final circumstances of 597 B. C. — in other words, an author whose

---

[173] Jones, *1 and 2 Kings,* 637; Gray, *I & II Kings,* 760—1; Würthwein, *Könige,* 473.

[174] Put another way, why would one intentionally create an anachronism? Jones, following Gray, states: "It is obvious that this later addition incorrectly connects looting predicted in connection with the final fall of the city in 587 B. C. with the earlier surrender of 598 B. C." (*1 and 2 Kings,* 637). Such an obvious error is unlikely.

[175] It seems far more likely that the author of Ch. 25 was forced to coordinate his later presentation, as best he could, with the presentation that tradition had already supplied in Ch. 24. See the discussion below.

historical and theological perspective did not originally extend beyond Ch. 24. As a 597 deportee, it would have appeared to him that all Judah/ Jerusalem had been "cast from Yahweh's presence" (24:20a). In order to defend this view, the specific literary objections must be examined more closely.

1. Redundancy

There appears to be repetition of certain details across vv. 10—12 and vv. 13—14. But this repetition is not so extreme as many claim. The circumstances leading up to the ultimate deportation to Babylon (first explicitly mentioned in v. 15) seem to proceed in stages. This is completely consistent with what is known about both Assyrian and Babylonian deportations.[176] First the city is besieged by auxiliary forces (v. 10); then Nebuchadnezzar arrives on the scene (v. 11); then Jehoiachin and his immediate royal entourage surrender; a note tells in what year this occurred (v. 12). Then (v. 13), treasures (*ʾôṣĕrôt*) from the temple and the king's house are reported to have been "brought out" (*wayyôṣēʾ*); moreover, certain gold vessels (*kĕlê hazzāhāb*) "which Solomon made" were hacked up (*wayĕqaṣṣēṣ*). Up to this point the proceedings are not unusual, beyond the fact that the author interprets the removal of vessels as occurring "as YHWH had foretold." Nebuchadnezzar's own chronicle, terse though the entry is, reports that the Babylonian monarch left with more than deported Judahites; what the usual "heavy tribute" (*bi-lat-sa kabittu, CCK,* 72) included is not spelled out. But it is not likely that the temple and royal treasuries would have been left alone by the Babylonians when "receiving tribute."

A major problem is often identified in vv. 14 following. First the carrying off (*wĕhiglāh*) of (1) all Jerusalem (apparently general population), (2) all officials (*śārîm*), (3) and all the military (*gibbôrê haḥayil*) is reported. These three groups number 10,000. Then, in the context of the same sentence, reference is made to "all the craftsmen and smiths." As if in conclusion, the report then indicates that "none remained" except the "poorest of the people of the land" (*dallat ʿam-hāʾāreṣ*). In Chapter Two it was argued that this latter group refers to a delineable social group, composed primarily of rural citizenry living within the geographical limits and protection of Jerusalem. Poorer elements of the group were not marked for deportation; presumably, their deportation was more trouble than it was worth. Those who identify a problem argue that the same

---

[176] See Bustenay Oded, *Mass Deportations and Deportees in the Neo-Assyrian Empire* (Wiesbaden: Reichart, 1979); Stephan Stohlmann, "The Judaean Exile" (full citation in n. 8, p. 16 above). See the discussion of the deportations from Judah in 721 B. C. above. It was to be noted that the capture, counting of prisoners, resettlement, and final deportation could be separate stages.

basic information is repeated in vv. 15—16. However, v. 15 is concerned with the specific deportation of the royal family and court (king, mother, wives, courtisans, leading men), groups not mentioned in vv. 13—14, but rather (partially) in vv. 11 ff. Earlier, only the surrender and placement in custody of Jehoiachin (v. 12) was reported. Moreover, this is the first time that Babylon is explicitly mentioned as the point both of destination and arrival for the deportees: *mîrûšālaim bābelāh*. It should be remembered that other possibilities for a re-settlement were available.[177]

In other words, vv. 15,16 make explicit what is not required in the interpretation of v. 14; furthermore, the specific reference to Babylon, repeated twice in the brief space of these two verses, may suggest the actual point of standing of the author (viz, in Exile). Verse 16 then supplies additional figures: 7000 soldiers and 1000 craftsmen and smiths. These numbers will be examined in more detail below, especially in light of the lower figures given at Jer 52:28. It is to be noted here that these figures do not necessarily contradict, or more importantly, repeat information given in v. 14. If anything, they are simply more specific about the numbers for these two groups, which were not given above. In fact, the focus of the verse seems to be on the final clause: "all of them strong and fit for war" — this is what sets these 8000 apart. It is what makes them different for example from the "poorest of the people of the land" who were left behind, because they could not make the journey or because they were not seen as a threat. If anything, the thrust of this final note is on the willful or resigned obedience of that portion of the population most in a position to resist. In conclusion, there is nothing in vv. 13—14 that necessitates a charge of redundancy. In fact, certain details mentioned there cannot be omitted without explanation.[178]

2. Contradiction and Lack of Harmony in Numbers of Deportees

Actually, as critics note, the greater problem with the deportee listings involves the special witness of Jer 52:28 ff., which tells of 3023 having been deported in the 7th (not 8th; cf. 2 Kgs 24:8) year of Nebuchadnezzar. Within this unit, it is argued that the number 10,000 (v. 14) has been artificially derived by reference to the original figures of v. 16.[179] There are a number of problems with this theory. First, Gray and Würthwein are not sure that even the numbers of v. 16 are without problems, particularly in light of Jer 52 but also in and of themselves. Within the logic of their respective systems, such scepticism is necessitated. For the figures of

---

[177] For Neo-Assyrian practices, see Oded's analysis (citation above).

[178] Was Nebuchadnezzar really content with taking prisoners and leaving the temple and royal treasures alone?

[179] Gray, *I & II Kings,* 761; Würthwein, *Könige,* 472—3.

v. 16 are not radically different from those given in v. 14, and in both cases they suggest fairly widespread deportations. This is precisely the tone of v. 14 as a whole, and this is for them the most troublesome verse in the chapter with its suggestion that "all Jerusalem" was carried off.

There is another general difficulty with their "anachronistic supplement" theory. If the supplementer is late, as they argue, he is also arguably in a position to know the figures of Jer 52:28, and one might have expected a lengthier attempt at coordination. This does not happen. Rather, the figure at v. 14 only works in strict relationship to v. 16. As argued above, the logic appears to be one moving toward greater specificity: of the 10,000 mentioned in v. 14, 7000 are specified as military troops; in v. 14 the tally of artisans/craftsmen is not given — it is supplied in v. 16 (1000). Strictly speaking, this suggests a total of 11,000, in logical groups: 3000, general population and civil officials; 7000 military personnel; 1000 artisans. The reason for the greater specificity in v. 16 appears to be connected with the fact of this 8000 being "fit for war."

There are several observations which can be made about these numbers. First, they are all general figures (10,000; 7000; 1000). This suggests that they are not supplied on the basis of some official tally but rather are *ad hoc* approximations, perhaps made by one who was himself deported. Though the figures above are presented systematically, the system is a quite general one which conceives of three levels of society: royal/civil (king, royal entourage, officials); military ("men of war," "mighty men," technical support); general population ("all" Jerusalem; "people of the land"). Second, the figures that are supplied function in complete independence from the list of Jer 52:28. It has been argued by some that these two lists are to be integrated in order to produce a first-stage deportation in year 7 of 3023 "Judeans" (Jer 52:28), a second-stage in year 8 of 7000 from Jerusalem (2 Kgs 24:16?), the total equaling 10,000 (2 Kgs 24:14).[180] Such a theory is more a testimony to ingenuity than a credible reading of the texts themselves, for (1) 2 Kgs 24 knows nothing at all about two stages in a deportation, much less any 7th year phase; alternatively, (2) Jer 52 knows nothing about an 8th year stage, or the 7000 "missing" deportees, largely military or otherwise "fit for war," and (3) 2 Kgs 24 never supplies a figure of 3023/3000, nor demonstrates any interest in the number; neither is a "Judahite" group mentioned at any point in the narrative. The only way such a theory can work is by first adding the two lists together and

---

[180] This theory appears in modern form in the work of A. Malamat, "Twilight," 134 ff.; "Last Years," 211. Malamat does make important mention of texts from Jeremiah (13:18—19) which, as noted, speak to Jeremiah's perspective on the anticipated severity of the 597 events. "Judah" is of course mentioned as deported in 2 Kgs 24:20 as well. But never in the lists given in vv. 13—17 are "Judahites" as such singled out as a deported entity, as happens in Jer 52:28 (and 30).

then deriving those figures required for a given context. But this will not account for why certain selections were made in one context and not others. More plausibly, the lists are independent of one another.

As most contend, Jer 52 is a later list drawn from an official source. Not only does it conceive of a different chronology (7th/18th/23rd), based on the post-dating system familiar to a later Babylonian exile; it also knows of a later deportation in Nebuchadnezzar's 23rd year.[181] No mention is made of this deportation in either 2 Kgs 24 or 25, and the notice seems to function in coordination with the narrative only found in Jeremiah (Chs. 40 ff.), which chronicles life in Judah after 587 B.C. In the list the more accurate "Nebuchadrezzar" (*Nabu-kudurri-usur*) appears instead of the "Nebuchadnezzar" of 2 Kings 24/25, again suggesting an accuracy resulting from a later exilic perspective. Moreover, each number is given in direct, almost mechanical relationship to "the X year of Nebuchadrezzar." The figures, in contrast to 2 Kgs 24:14 ff., are quite specific (3023/832/745). All this suggests that the author of Jer 52:28−30 has drawn his list from an independent, Babylonian source. Why the figures given are lower is a matter of pure conjecture. Montgomery suggested that they referred only to adult males, but use of the term *nepeš,* at least at 52:28, seems to rule this out.[182] The lower figures may be connected with the particular scope and nature of the document from which they were drawn, but this is pure conjecture. Perhaps they refer to a more particular group of Exiles, in a single locale, from the perspective of Exile itself. This is impossible to determine.

Upon returning to the more general deportation list in 2 Kings 24, several further observations can be made. Though the numbers are higher, they do not represent the entire population. Estimates of Jerusalem's population alone for this period, even granting depletions due to the state of siege, are far greater than the maximum figure given at 2 Kgs 24:14 (11,000).[183] In light of this, what is to be made of the tone of finality which appears in 24:14: "all Jerusalem" and "none remained"? Here the third and main objection to taking vv. 13−14 as integral to Ch. 24 is confronted, viz, the apparent contradiction with events recorded in Ch. 25. Without minimizing the difficulty, it is suggested that use of the term "all" here is meant neither as (1) a precise judgment with an eye toward numerical accuracy, nor (2) a tendentious theological judgment supplied secondarily. It is simply another general assessment from the perspective

---

181 See, among others, John Bright, *Jeremiah,* 369.
182 *Kings* (ICC; Edingburgh: Clark, 1951) 556.
183 Broshi estimated the population following the deportations in 701 B.C. to be around 24,000 ("Expansion of Jerusalem," *IEJ* 24 [1974] 24). Even if this figure is high, as some have suggested, a deportation of 11,000 is a long way from clearing out the population altogether — which is not what the author intends to suggest.

of the exilic author of Ch. 24. So far as he was concerned, Yahweh had
cast Judah/Jerusalem from His presence (24:20a); this involved the king
and royal family, as well as large numbers of Jerusalemites.

The question as to whether such an assessment involves a negative
theological judgment is more difficult to answer. The question of ongoing
life in the land, its legitimacy and/or threat to the exilic community, would
more likely occasion a pejorative supplement in Ch. 25 than 24. However,
one does see in the Ezekiel's traditions, developed shortly after the 597
deportations, a sharp judgment over those in Judah. The answer to the
question of possible *tendenz* in 24:14 depends in large measure on when
the whole chapter was drawn up. If the description in Ch. 24 of 597 events
followed shortly upon those events themselves, then the concern was
probably directed more toward the chronicling of significant details than
the wrestling with theological questions related to the legitimacy of
ongoing life in the land.[184] What terse theological summary does appear
in the chapter seems to see such a question as a moot one, or at least one
which warrants no full-blown discussion such as is found in Ezekiel. As
such, statements like "none remained" arose more from reflection on the
tragic circumstances of capture and deportation for those exiled than from
the desire to consciously condemn those remaining, a move which is
curiously muted in this otherwise straightforward narrative. In any event,
this discussion has already moved toward an analysis of the author's, not
a supplementer's, perspective. This is consistent with the argument defended here that vv. 13—14 form an integral part of the wider Ch. 24 narrative.

3. The Taking of Treasures

> . . . and he brought forth from there all the treasures of the house of YHWH, and the
> treasures of the house of the king, and he cut up all the vessels of gold which Solomon,
> King of Israel, had made in the temple of YHWH, just as YHWH said (24:13).

This passage must be looked at for two reasons. First, Gray maintains
that the "spoilation" of v. 13b "is flatly contradicted by Jer 27:19 ff.," a
passage which indicates the presence of temple vessels in Jerusalem after
the events of 597 B. C.[185] In fact, Gray argues that 24:13 was inserted as
a reflection on the Jer 27:22 "at a time later than the main Deuteronomistic
redaction of Kings, when the edition of Jeremiah was familiar, about the
end of Exile or even later" (760). Jones is of a similiar mind. He attributes
the mention of the spoilation at this point to a later redactor who
"incorrectly connects looting predicted in connection with the fall of the

---

[184] Even mention of the death and burial of King Jehoiakim is missing. See the discussion
above, Section I.

[185] Gray, *I & II Kings,* 760.

city in 587 B. C. with the earlier surrender of 598 B. C."[186] In this sense, if the logic is correctly followed, 24:13 would appear to contradict 25:13 ff. as well as Jer 27:19 ff. There is a second objection raised against the authenticity of the passage in its present context. Jones, following Dietrich's analysis, sees the phrase "as YHWH said" as part of a "fulfillment of prophecy theme" (637), and on this basis dismisses the passage as secondary. Recognizing the unusual nature of the fulfillment, and the possibility that here one sees "a solid structural connection between sections which the present study has assigned to different authors," Nelson proceeds with more caution.[187]

The specific fulfillment mentioned in this unit is related to Isaiah's prediction in 2 Kgs 20:12−19 that the Babylonians would carry off "all that is in your (Hezekiah's) house, and that which your fathers have stored up ('āṣĕrû) till this day" (20:17). Isaiah also envisions the carrying off to Babylon of Hezekiah's successors, where they will be sārîsîm in the palace of the king of Babylon" (20:18). All this is to occur because Hezekiah unwisely showed his treasures to the delegation of Merodach-Baladan (*Marduk-apal-idinna*).

As Nelson rightly points out, if the prophetic narrative of 2 Kgs 18:13−20:19 (Isa 36−39) is early (not secondarily retouched or composed as a bald *vaticinium ex eventu*), then the reference made to it at 2 Kgs 24:13 could be an integral link within the scope of a first edition of Kings. This would in turn call into question the Josianic date and provenance for Dtr 1. Of course another possibility is available, and this is the one Nelson adopts. Granting an early date for the prophetic narrative of 2 Kgs 18:13−20:19, and no significant retouching at esp. 20:12−19, he still attributes the link at 24:13 to an exilic editor or a later glossator (132). As he notes, this is "the simplest solution to his dilemma" (131). Nothing in the early narrative required a later fulfillment (reference is not made to it in Jer 27−28); however, a later hand which "understood the structural technique of prophecy-fulfillment" (132) went ahead and established the literary link at 24:13.

Nelson's findings are reproduced in some detail because he was initially correct about the threat of the prophecy-fulfillment link at 24:13 to his conception of the scope of the first edition of Kings. Moreover, certain issues raised by him make clear how ill-formed are the objections of those who see 24:13 bluntly contradicting Jeremiah's statements in Ch. 27/28 or the later narrative of 2 Kgs 25. In order to gain better perspective on both issues raised thus far, it is fair to ask again just what is being depicted in the scene at 2 Kgs 24:13.

---

[186] Jones, *1 and 2 Kings,* 637.
[187] Nelson, *Double Redaction,* 129 ff.

In a broader literary context where verbs which clearly imply deportation and removal to Babylon are used (*wĕhiglāh; wayyegel*), v. 13 speaks more specifically of Nebuchadnezzar bringing forth (*wayyōṣē'*) items from royal house and temple house, as well as hacking up gold vessels. The sense of *miššām* ("from there") implies that he brought the treasures out from either the temple/royal precints or Jerusalem itself, prior to their full transfer into the Babylonian camp as such. This sounds like a public display of Babylonian superiority and the privilege of the conqueror. Presumably, then, certain treasures were taken away by the Babylonians when deportation proceedings actually got underway (*bi-lat-sa kabittu il-[qa-am-m]a ana babili[KI] ulterib, CCK,* 72). The items mentioned are specifically termed "treasures" and gold vessels, that is, objects of more than strictly religious value. By contrast, see the listing of 25:13—17, which mentions pillars with elaborate networks, dishes, pots, snuffers, firepans, sea and stands, and more.

In the passage under discussion it is never specifically said that any of the gold vessels are carried off; rather, they are cut up.[188] On the basis of Jer 27/28, however, one is able to infer — and this in precise contradistinction to Gray and others — that temple vessels (*kēlīm*) were among other items (and population) carried off to Babylon (27:16,18; 28:3). The crucial question in Jer 27/28 concerns whether vessels already carried off, just like the community already carried off, are there for just a few years or for good (see 27:16; 28:3).[189] Gray points to 27:19 as contradicting 24:13, presumably because it mentions vessels still in Jerusalem (e. g., "the rest of the vessels which are left in the city"). But this is patently not the case. His conclusion stems from the gratuitous isolation of one verse in a chapter whose message clearly implies that a portion of the temple vessels were deported in 597 B. C. Furthermore, there is good evidence that secondary supplementation has confused not 2 Kgs 24, but this Jeremiah text. After all, 2 Kgs 24:13 does not stress the carrying off of *vessels,* but the bringing forth and probable carrying off of *treasures* (see Jer 20:10 for reference to treasures) and the desecration of vessels. In other words, the hypothetical supplementer at 2 Kgs 24:13 has done a fairly poor job summarizing the burden of Jer 27:19 ff. and glossing Ch. 24 on the basis of it.

A more likely explanation is that Jer 27:19—22 forms a redactional supplement to an otherwise coherent prophetic narrative. The burden of

---

[188] Again, this desecration of objects of religious value sounds like, among other things, a display of Babylonian authority.

[189] In this context, recall the sentiments expressed in Ezek 11:15 ff. The establishment of a proper timetable (Hananiah: 2 years? Ezekiel: 40 years? Jeremiah: 70 years?) would assist in coming to grips with the question of exile and deportation — of obvious concern to those deported, and apparently no less so for those in Judah.

Jer 27:16—18 is remarkably straightforward: (1) vessels carried off to Babylon will not return; (2) "serve the King of Babylon and live" (see Jer 27:1—15), (3) that the vessels which he did not take might remain. These three statements are integrally linked and quite logical in their sequence and in the larger context of the chapter (vv. 1—15). In the following unit (vv. 19—22) there is a shift to a foregone judgment: (1) vessels left in the city will be carried off; (2) they will remain for an unknown interval; (3) then they will be returned. This theme has nothing in common with vv. 16—18. In fact, the literary evidence of v. 19 (". . . concerning the pillars, the sea, the stands, and the rest of the vessels which are left in the city . . .") suggests that the unit is based upon 2 Kgs 25:13 ff. or the general logic of its presentation: namely, that the bulk of religious furnishings from the temple were taken in 587 B. C., not 597 B. C. This logic already presupposes the existence of 24:13; the reverse (viz, that 24:13 was developed on the basis of Jer 27:19 ff.) is far more difficult to envision. Furthermore, evidence of the redactional nature of Jer 27:19 ff. is provided by the extensive repetition in verses 19—21:

> For thus says YHWH concerning the pillars, etc. . . . which Nebuchadnezzar king of Babylon did not take away, when he took into exile from Jerusalem to Babylon Jeconiah the son of Jehoiakim, king of Judah, and all the nobels of Jerusalem — thus says YHWH, concerning the vessels . . .[190]

The better candidate for redactional supplementation is Jer 27:19—22, not 2 Kgs 24:13—14, on both logical and literary grounds. It has been supplied on the basis of the present narrative sequence in Chs. 24 and 25 of 2 Kings, in which the hauling off of primarily royal and temple treasure occurs in 597 B. C., followed by more extensive and more specific stripping of the temple in 587 B. C. Within the Book of Jeremiah, the unit blunts the force of statements in 27:1—18, which consistently maintain that life in Judah (and Edom, Moab, Ammon, Tyre, Sidon) is possible if nation and king submit to Babylonian authority (27:5—7,11,13,17), granted by Yahweh Himself (27:5—7). By contrast, this supplement clearly implies that such a possibility is ruled out, and shifts the focus to the inevitable removal of all vessels to Babylon. This is an editorial technique consistently displayed in that layer of tradition capable of isolation in Jeremiah and classification as emerging from an Exilic Redaction. More will be said on the larger contours of this redactional effort below.

On the basis of this analysis of the relationship between 2 Kgs 24:13—14, Jer 27, and 2 Kgs 25:13 ff., several concluding remarks can now be made about the so-called "prophecy-fulfillment" motif signaled at

---

[190] V. 20 appears to be a distillation of 2 Kgs 24:12—16, another indication of the proper direction of dependence. For a better example of this, see 28:2, which is most assuredly drawn from 2 Kgs 24:12—16 (Bright, *Jeremiah*, 208).

24:13. It is important to note that the prophetic narrative in 2 Kgs 20:12 ff. says nothing whatsoever about Hezekiah giving the Babylonians a tour of the temple, beyond the general statement that "there was nothing which he did not show them . . . in all his kingdom" (20:13). Rather, the emissaries were treated to an examination of his store-house (*kol-bêt někōtōh*), armory (*bêt kēlâw*), and more generally, "all that was found among his treasures" (*kol-'ăšer nimṣā' bě'ôṣěrōtâw*). When the oracle is delivered to Hezekiah by Isaiah (vv. 16—18) the focus remains more on royal wealth ("what your fathers have stored up") than temple furnishings, and is concerned more narrowly with the fate of Hezekiah and his successors ("some of your sons who are born to you") than the broader population.

Returning to the notice of looting at 2 Kgs 24:13, what can be said about the statement "as YHWH said"? It appears to function in reference to the broader report that both royal house and YHWH's house had treasures removed, and that vessels of gold made by Solomon were cut up. In other words, the prediction that treasures would be hauled off, as reported at 2 Kgs 20:17, is picked up at 24:13. The focus of both remains with the royal treasures, not temple furnishings (compare 25:13 ff.). But the fact that YHWH's house was also raided is noted because such an event did in fact take place, together with spoilation of vessels by Babylonian troops. The point is that what is here encompassed by the quite general statement "as YHWH said" ("formula" is too strong) is by no means a full-blown, mechanical construction of a fulfillment from prophecy link. Rather, it is an *ad hoc* statement from the author of 2 Kgs 24 who was familiar with if not the literary witness of 2 Kgs 20, then certainly the tradition of an oracle delivered by the prophet Isaiah a century earlier.

There is one further point to be made that may shed light on the statement of 24:14 that "none remained," a statement which appears exaggerated or seemingly contradicted by the presence of Ch. 25. In Isaiah's oracle to Hezekiah, as it is preserved at 2 Kgs 20:17 ff., following the prediction that the royal treasures will be taken to Babylon, the concluding statement is made: ". . . nothing shall be left, says YHWH" (*lō'-yiwwātēr dābār 'āmar YHWH*). Not only does the Isaianic oracle indicate the origin of the reference in 24:13, "as YHWH said" (*ka'ăšer dibber YHWH*), it also includes the phrase whose reflex appears now in 24:14, in reference not to treasures but populace, in the form: "none remained (*lō' niš'ar*) except the poorest of the people of the land." Unfortunately, the phrases are too general to say anything further. But if this suggestion is correct, it would go a long way toward explaining the problem explored above (viz, the depiction of a land emptied of inhabitants in 597 B. C.). If this depiction in fact draws upon the prophetic prediction of Isaiah, this provides a possible explanation for its apparent overstatement.

What is to be concluded from this analysis is that a close relationship exists between 2 Kgs 24:13 ff. and 2 Kgs 20:12 ff. Nothing stands in the way of seeing the report in 2 Kgs 24 of 597 B. C. deportations as having been composed by someone sensitive to the oracle of the prophet Isaiah, now found at 2 Kgs 20:12—19. Whoever composed this final chapter saw Isaiah's predictions of royal treasures and royal house deported to Babylon fulfilled in the events of 597 B. C., which witnessed these two chief events and more. Isaiah was just one of the many prophets sent by Yahweh to announce this specific judgment upon Judah (24:2 ff.).

Considerations of time and space prevent the kind of full-scale literary analysis required to establish the precise tradition history of the Isaiah prophetic legend now found in both 2 Kgs 18—20 and Isa 36—39, much less the important role the narrative plays in formulating the redactional development of the Deuteronomistic History. Nelson's concise treatment (Appendix, 129—132) is a helpful introduction to the nature of the problem. Nothing stands in the way of treating the Isaiah legend as dependent upon authentic pre-exilic traditions, oral and literary. This is the conclusion reached by Nelson himself. But in contrast to his analysis, it makes far greater sense to assign the terse fulfillment notice of 2 Kgs 24:13, linking 597 looting with the word of Yahweh spoken through Isaiah, to the same author at work throughout Ch. 24.[191] It was this same author who began work on the first primary edition of the Books of Kings, which had its conclusion in Ch. 24 and the historical events of 597. This author is to be located in Babylon along with those who, like himself, experienced the capture of the city and the deportations of 597 B. C.

E. The Literary Scope of Ch. 24

On the basis of this analysis of Ch. 24, it can be concluded that the original form of the narrative chronicling the important events of 597 B. C. was roughly the same as exists in the canonical MT. Verses which critics considered controversial due to content or style, especially those which present some brief form of theological comment (vv. 2—3a; 13—14; 20), cannot be easily isolated as a separate level of tradition. Moreover, one unit in particular (vv. 13—14), increasingly viewed as a post-redactional supplement, not only functions logically in its literary context; it also provides specific information essential to the movement of the narrative presentation. It was also questioned how a chapter which gave report of the crucial events of 597, including the deportation of king, royal family, officials, and a sizeable portion of the general populace, could operate without some level of theological commentary. It was concluded that while

---

[191] Note the preference for anonymity regarding specific prophets in 2 Kgs 24:2 and 24:13 (i. e., Isaiah is not mentioned by name). As mentioned above, YHWH gets direct credit for His word, not the individual prophet (24:2).

the theme of "the sins of Manasseh" (v. 3b—4) seemed roughly integrated on a literary level, and dependent upon a more specific reflection on the relationship between monarchial sin and the fall of the city, the other notices concerned with providing commentary on the fall are far more compact and remarkably straightforward.[192] These include the linking of the catastrophe with the prior word of YHWH spoken through the prophets (v. 2), and in one case, a specific word delivered by YHWH to Hezekiah (v. 13). The concern to link a specific event with YHWH's prior word, in the particularly theocentric manner seen here, is evidenced in another work of a slightly later period, Second Isaiah (see Isa 41:21 ff.; 42:23 ff.; 44:26; 45:18 ff.). The final theological comment of the chapter is also consistent with the other notices: "For because of the anger of YHWH it came to the point in Judah and Jerusalem that he cast them out from his presence."

In light of this literary analysis, the remarkable thing to note is just how consistently 2 Kings 24 depicts the events of 597 B. C. as final events. This is particularly true of the level of tradition whose authenticity is here defended, but it can also be detected in verses not generally viewed as secondary. After all, the unit encompassing vv. 10—12; 15—17 knows of sizeable deportations and, at a minimum, testifies to the efficiency of Babylonian military might and the thoroughness with which she established control over affairs in Judah. This is consistent with the report of the Babylonian Chronicle, which tells of capture, tribute and deportation, as well as the appointment of a new king. In a more subtle way, it is also consistent with the portrayal of 2 Kings 25, which should be viewed as a kind of post-script to Ch. 24. It is unfortunate that no record has survived in the Babylonian Chronicle related to 587 events, the discussion of which now forms the final chapter of Judah's history. In any event, one important thing to note is that in the records that have survived, including all biblical accounts, the deportations in 597 B. C. are consistently listed as more comprehensive than those in 587 B. C. Again, this strengthens the view that the author of Ch. 24 initially composed this chapter as an assessment of Judah's history in its final stages. From the standpoint of the historical sources, it appears he was entirely justified in this assessment.

In the midst of the unusual catalog of acts of supremacy (siege; capture; tribute; deportation), the Babylonian Chronicle relates that after Nebuchadnezzar captured the king, he appointed another king, "after his

---

[192] The theme of "the sins of Manasseh" finds full expression in Ch. 21, including the notion that Manasseh's sins "contaminated" the people: "he seduced them" (v. 9), "he made Judah also to sin" (v. 11). The bridge unit to Ch. 24 appears in 23:26—27. This is most likely a secondary development, in which the sins of the people, which evoke the wrath of Yahweh, are "traced back" to the chief monarchial culprit, evoking a still greater wrath (23:26, Judah → Manasseh). The sins of Manasseh are such that they can even override Hezekiah's (21:3) and Josiah's (22:1; 23:25) exemplary behavior.

own heart" (*šarra ša libbi-šu*). On the basis of this entry, most assume that the king captured (*šarra ik-ta-šad*) was Jehoiachin, while the new king appointed was his uncle Zedekiah. There is no reason to question this, and it appears that confirmation exists in the biblical record at 2 Kgs 24:17: "And the king of Babylon made Mattaniah, Jehoiachin's uncle, king in his stead, and changed his name to Zedekiah." Beyond this strict notice, similar in form to 2 Kgs 23:34 (Jehoiakim), no further details related to the appointment are given. Perhaps this is not too odd. After all, the compressed narrative of Kings likewise fails to mention details surrounding the death and burial of Jehoiakim. On this subject, the biblical and Babylonian records are equally silent. It is difficult to know how to assess the selectivity of details presented in the 2 Kings 24 narrative, and arguments regarding "silence" in sources can be tricky, especially when the pattern for succinct reporting is firmly in place.

A more complete Ch. 24 has been argued for than most would allow. But the final question to be pursued at this point follows from some of the broader historical observations made on the basis of this literary analysis. Specifically, are references to Zedekiah in Ch. 24 (vv. 17—20) an integral part of the original narrative? The question must be pursued for obvious reasons. If the author of Ch. 24 saw the events of 597 as more final than one is accustomed to think, then to what extent did he view the appointment of Zedekiah as important to his narrative?

On the basis of Ezekiel traditions, which are placed at a slightly later period but from the same 597 perspective, Zedekiah was clearly viewed in some quarters as *nāśî'*, in distinction to *melek*. Beyond what this implied in more general terms about Ezekiel's notion of a "wilderness period" inaugurated by the 597 deportations (with its respective forms of leadership), it underscored a more specific concern over the legitimacy of "king" and community in post-597 Judah. Moreover, these Ezekiel traditions demonstrated support for the legitimacy of Jehoiachin, and restoration of the monarchy through his line. This position was directly threatened by the appointment and continuing rule of Zedekiah in Judah. In the balance were larger questions related to the role of the exilic community in YHWH's plan of restoration, over against the community in Judah. Many have argued that the Babylonians themselves played upon tensions inherent in Judah by appointing a "regent" king who at the same time had a collateral counterpart in Babylon.[193] There may be a measure of truth in

---

[193] The extra-biblical evidence which initially suggested that Jehoiachin was still considered king *de jure* by groups in the land has, after further scrutiny, received less than enthusiastic support. For the full discussion, see the following: W. F. Albright, "The Seal of Eliakim"; "King Jehoiachin in Exile"; H. G. May, "Three Hebrew Seals"; A. Malamat, "Jeremiah and the Last Two Kings of Judah"; "Twilight of Judah" [modified]; N. Avigad, "*Na'ar* Seals". Most recently, David Ussishkin ("Royal Judaean Storage Jars and Private Seal

this, though it is difficult to know whether such an appointment was a conscious attempt at destabilization, which could cause unnecessary unrest and, from the Babylonian perspective, time-consuming intervention, or merely the reasoned selection of an obvious candidate. Furthermore, it would have been impossible to predict just how the appointment would be viewed internally. As the analysis has thus far shown, the effect it did have in Judah and in Babylon was far from neutral.

The literary movement from v. 16 to v. 20 in 2 Kings 24, and continuing on into Ch. 25 is rough. This is due in part to the interruption by the summary formula for Zedekiah (24:18 — 19). There is no particular problem with the siege in Zedekiah's 9th year and running up to his capture in the 11th year (v. 7). But one unusual fact is that nothing whatsoever is reported of the period between the 597 deportations until the 9th year of Zedekiah — almost a decade of silence. There are those who have carefully noted other inexplicable silences in Ch. 25, notably, the lack of reference to Jeremiah or the post-587 events involving the community around Gedaliah.[194] In view of the healthy traditions available regarding such matters (Jeremiah 39 ff.), the silence does seem odd. It is however rarely noted that the silence regarding 9 full years of Zedekiah's reign, beyond the passing comment that he rebelled (24:20b), is really more puzzling. Again, healthy traditions exist in Jeremiah. Even allowing for lack of direct proximity to events, (1) it is clear that contact and correspondence existed between exilic and Judahite communities in this period (Jeremiah 27 — 29; the Book of Ezekiel), and (2) certainly affairs from the reign of Zedekiah were not completely unknown to an author of 2 Kings 25, who one might reasonably conclude was at work in Babylon.[195] All this considered, use of the term "silence" is not a wholly improper way to talk

---

Impressions," *BASOR* 223 [1976]) concludes: "the Elyakim handles antedate Jehoiachin's reign" (p. 11). The more general observations, based upon the biblical evidence itself, still however uphold the notion that a conflict existed in this period, within the Judahite and Babylonian communities, and between them, over the question of monarchial legitimacy, for the present and future. See: Peter Ackroyd, "Aspects of the Jeremiah Tradition" (1971); "The History of Israel in the Exilic and Post-Exilic Periods" (1979); K. Baltzer, "Das Ende des Staates Judah und die Messias-Frage" (1961); M. Noth, "Jerusalem Catastrophe" (1967); W. Zimmerli, *Ezekiel 1,* 13 ff.

[194] Noth's verdict is oft-cited and controversial: "It may seem strange that Dtr. does not so much as mention Jeremiah here, after borrowing the whole narrative of the end of the history of Judah from Baruch's account of Jeremiah which is essentially about the personal fate of Jeremiah. But in this context Dtr. was concerned only with public officials" (*Dtr History,* 138, n. 71). Compare especially, K.-F. Pohlmann, "Erwägungen zum Schlußkapitel"; W. Dietrich, *Prophetie,* 140; Mowinckel, *Komposition,* 29 ff.

[195] *Contra* Mowinckel (*Komposition,* 29 ff.) who assumed rather mechanically that 2 Kings 25 reported nothing about Jeremiah or post-587 events because the common source below Jeremiah 39 ff., which he utilized, did not have this information. This is far too literary an understanding of the way information becomes available or unavailable. For a discussion of the precise literary relationship between Jeremiah 39 and 2 Kings 25, see below, 377 ff.

about the selectivity of the narrative at 2 Kings 25. What can be inferred about precise authorial intention is far more difficult to establish.

Reference is made to this fact because of the way Chs. 24 and 25 of 2 Kings are presently linked. It was argued above that 24:20a functions in the original narrative in coordination with 24:1—3a and 13; in other words, v. 20a is related primarily to the events described in Ch. 24, not Ch. 25. These three well-placed statements present a coherent theological precis related to the 597 Fall of Jerusalem. With this observation in place, vv. 17—19, concerned as they are with information related to the subsequent reign of Zedekiah, seem out of place. For verse 20 begins with a causal *kî* that relates only with difficulty to v. 19. The *'ōtām* of 20a clearly points to the focus of the sentence remaining more generally with Judah and Jerusalem — not with king Zedekiah, or even further, with Jehoiachin. As such, the sentence forms a general and yet focused summary of the whole chapter, a fitting conclusion to the reports of siege/capture/deportation such as exist in vv. 10—16. Verse 17 is a special problem and must be considered in a moment.

For the purpose of comparison, note how this precise literary unit (24:18—20) has been put to use in Jeremiah 52. This is the final chapter of the Jeremiah traditions and one which is not from Jeremiah himself (see the notice at Jer 51:64). In this literary framework, the unit 52:1—3 (= 2 Kgs 24:18—20) functions as the thematic introduction to the events of 587 B. C. In other words, its primary point of reference is not the literary equivalent of 2 Kings 24, for which it served as conclusion, but the literary equivalent of 2 Kings 25, for which it now serves as introduction.

One further point can be made. Because Jer 52:4 ff. is practically a duplicate of 2 Kings 25, and because the latter has no (597) deportation list such as exists at 2 Kgs 24:10 ff., Jeremiah 52 now includes its own, three-stage deportation notice at 52:28—30. This is the only significant plus it has over and above 2 Kings 25. Whatever problems may result from the special chronology it adopts, the presence of this list in Jeremiah 52 can be explained as resulting from the decision to sever Ch. 25 from Ch. 24, in order to provide this particular conclusion to the Book of Jeremiah. However, when it is observed that Jeremiah 52 is not simply a carbon-copy of 2 Kings 25, but a copy prefaced by 2 Kgs 24:18—20 and adjusted by the inclusion of Jer 52:28—30, another important point suggests itself. It is only because the unit 24:18—20 originally functioned as a conclusion to the events of 597, and not the introduction to Ch. 25 and the events of 587, that an adjustment such as is found in Jer 52:28—30 was necessitated. For now the statement, "Because of the anger of YHWH things came to such a pass in Jerusalem and Judah that he cast them out from his presence," is made to serve as the comprehensive introductory rubric under which not just the "final fall" of 587 (52:29), or even the preliminary "capture" of 597 (52:28), but also the later deportation of 582/

3 is classified. Incidentally, this provides further evidence of the precise literary development from 2 Kings 24 to 25 to Jeremiah 52. More specifically, it supports the contention that the summary statement of the earlier 2 Kings 24 (v. 20a) originally functioned in reference to Ch. 24 alone, and the particular events of 597 B. C.

Returning to 2 Kings 24, a precise description of the literary scope of the chapter's conclusion is still needed. First of all, it is to be noted that 24:18—19 is the typical summary formula provided for kings throughout the DtrH, in this case regarding Zedekiah. By mentioning the total years of Zedekiah's reign (11), it clearly has a perspective presupposing Zedekiah's capture, if not all of Ch. 25 as a literary product. The other information it gives (mother; her father's place of origin) is not remarkable, and in this sense it resembles other formulae. One of the main pillars of the "Josianic Edition + Dtr 2" theory has been the conclusion that marked stereotypicality in formulae is evidenced from the death of Josiah to the fall of 587 B. C., thereby suggesting a uniform if not unimaginative Dtr 2 Editor.[196] At first glance, there seems to be some merit in this observation. But closer attention demonstrates its inadequacy. The fact that at 24:19 the evil deeds of Zedekiah are traced not to father, nor predecessor, but brother, does not square with a concept of Dtr 2 as unimaginative or "woodenly imitative." The most obvious thing to note is that this completely unprecedented ascription of sin to a collateral king (half-brother) is the result of the highly unusual succession pattern from the death of Josiah onward. But this only strenghtens the arguments against a second editor's consistent stereotypicality; rather, he was forced, as elsewhere in Kings, to take into account the exigencies and special circumstances of each ruler. A second point follows from this. Nothing stood in the way of a "wooden" editor attributing the evil of Zedekiah to his predecessor Jehoiachin, the latter's 3-month tenure notwithstanding. For if the editor was as inflexible as is claimed, such an attribution would be no more difficult than his original decision to attribute evils deeds to the constantly besieged and only vaguely "evil" Jehoiachin to begin with. Moreover, close attention to the tracing of sin from the reign of Hezekiah onward, inclusive of the period claimed for Dtr-2, shows a remarkable flexibility and a consistent internal logic, right up to the fall of the city. This tracing of sin is diagrammed in Chart 7 (next page).

Neither Hezekiah nor Josiah follow the ways of evil fathers, and therefore circumstances potentially begin anew after their tenure. Since Manasseh had a "fresh tenure" preceding his own, the editor had a slight problem. But he initially attributes Manasseh's evil to the effect of the surrounding nations, and expressly states that he did not do as his father

---

[196] Nelson, *Double Redaction*, 36 ff. For the characterizations of Dtr 2 by Cross and Nelson, see discussion above, pp. 20—21.

Hezekiah (II 21:3). A similar problem existed for the successors of the incomparably righteous Josiah (II 23:25), who were definitely "not like him" (v. 25b). This problem was dealt with in two ways. The first, which is an independent and secondary move, attributes the inevitability of the Fall of the city to the sins of Manasseh (23:26—27). It is concerned to tie the evil of Judah to monarchial evil (see Ch. 21) in order to account for the Fall of Judah. The second motif, and the one pertinent to the summary formulae, is more specifically concerned to trace evil in the monarchy as such. While the editor could trace the evil of Amon to Manasseh, or that of Jehoiachin to his immediate father, Jehoiakim, the same option was not available to him for the sons of Josiah, three of whom eventually rule. As a result, the concept of general evil of "all his fathers" is utilized. This general theme is by no means a display of the lack of imagination in a secondary dtr-2 editor. First of all, it is one variation among others in the History; secondly, it emerges in the formulae for Jehoahaz and Jehoiakim precisely because their father Josiah did not do evil.

Chart Seven

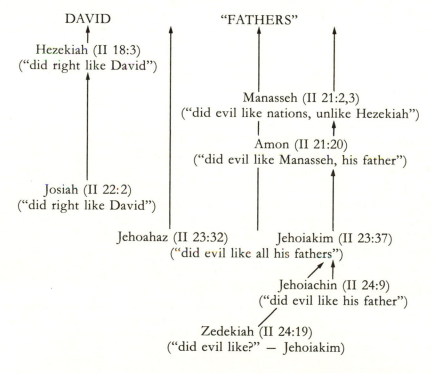

With this complete picture in place, it is possible to return to the summary formula for Zedekiah at 2 Kgs 24:18—19. The question begs itself: Why when a pattern for handling the evil of half-brothers Jehoahaz and Zedekiah was firmly in place did an editor not trace the evil of Zedekiah to "all his fathers," but to the specific figure of Jehoiakim, his half-brother? One might have anticipated such a move in the case of Jehoiakim (viz, the tracing of his sin to Jehoahaz) when instead the theme of "all his fathers" adopted for Jehoahaz was maintained. The answer is twofold. Unlike Jehoahaz and Jehoiakim, Zedekiah ruled after the interval of his nephew's reign, and only by Babylonian appointment. Both factors may have called into question the legitimacy of his rule. But the first factor implied that evil already attributed to Jehoiachin (II 24:9) and traced back to his father Jehoiakim, could in fact be evil capable of effect on his successor Zedekiah. So the question turned not so much on the adoption of the formula "like all his fathers" for Zedekiah, but rather on the adoption of the formula, "like Jehoiachin." What is to be made of the decision to trace the evil of Zedekiah to Jehoiakim rather than to "all his fathers" or to Jehoiachin? The answer to this question is related to the final notice of the DtrH at 2 Kgs 25:27—30.

Turning to the final form of the DtrH, including the whole of 2 Kings 25, one encounters as the crucial final word of the history those verses (27—30) which tell of the pardon, release, and special treatment of Jehoiachin by the Babylonian monarch Evil-Merodach. This unit has been the subject of much discussion.[197] The discussion centers on how to assess the relative significance of a concluding unit which offers a picture of hope, undeniably clear and centered on the monarchy, but which is either too brief to deserve special attention or far too overshadowed by the otherwise consistently negative thrust of the history as a whole. Others imply a tacked-on literary status for the unit, which admittedly reverses the tone and changes the subject of 2 Kings 25.[198] Larger questions regarding the theological importance of the unit for the whole History aside, the final notice of 2 Kgs 25:27—30 (Jer 52:31—34) jumps beyond the narrative framework of Ch. 25, into the 37th year of Jehoiachin (560 B. C.). Because it continues the chronological movement of the deportation unit discussed above (Jer 52:28—30), picking up with the 37th captivity year of Jehoiachin (cf. Ezekiel's system) and the accession year of Evil-Merodach, it seems less intrusive following Jer 52:28—30 than 2 Kgs

---

[197] See especially G. von Rad, *Deuteronomium Studien* (Göttingen: Vandenhoeck & Ruprecht, 1947) 63—4; *Old Testament Theology* (New York: Harper & Row, 1962) 334—7; M. Noth, *Dtr History*, 98; J. Gray, *I & II Kings*, 42; F. M. Cross, *Canaanite Myth*, 277; H. W. Wolff, "Das Kerygma des deuteronomistischen Geschichtswerkes," *ZAW* 73 (1961) 171—86; E. Zenger, "Rehabilitierung Jojachins," 16 ff.; Klaus Baltzer, "Messias-Frage," 38 ff.; Pohlmann, "Schlußkapitel," 107 ff.

[198] Gray, *I & II Kings,* 773 ff.; Dietrich (*Prophetie,* 142), "Der Bericht in 2. Kön 25,27—30 dagegen atmet einen ganz anderen Geist."

25:26.[199] Actually, there is only the appearance of greater integration in Jeremiah 52, because of the chronological movement of 52:28—30. The unit has its own tradition history, separate from other material in 2 Kings 25 (and Jeremiah 52).

Some conclusions about the present juxtapositioning of 2 Kings 24 and 2 Kings 25 can now be drawn, based upon observations made up to this point. The departure in the summary formula for Zedekiah (2 Kgs 24:18—19) from the scheme adopted for tracing the evil of Jehoahaz and Jehoiakim indicates the presence of a different hand at work in this unit. In isolation, this would be an extremely difficult theory to prove. But when one attempts to penetrate the logic of the unique summary formula at the seam between 2 Kings 24 and 25, the thesis argued here receives surprising confirmation. For the refusal to bring the evil of Zedekiah into relationship with that already mentioned for Jehoiachin (2 Kgs 24:8) anticipates the final word of the Deuteronomistic History (25:27—30). This notice clearly underscores if not the possibility of the continuance of Davidic rule though the line of Jehoiachin, then certainly the fact of his pardon and favorable treatment — and this in clear contrast to Zedekiah.[200] 2 Kings 25 very quickly moves to a description of the tragic fate of Judah's last monarch, including his blinding by Babylonian officials. This action foreclosed the possibility of his future rule, and the mention of the death of his sons likewise drove the same point home.

On a literary level, the uniting of Chs. 24 and 25 was accomplished as follows. The same editor who was responsible for bringing 2 Kings 25:27—30 into play as the final word of the DtrH was also responsible for merging Chs. 24 and 25 of Kings. This was done by placing the summary formula for Zedekiah, which traced his evil activity to Jehoiakim, between the reports of 597 deportations (vv. 10—16) and the concluding theological summary of the events of 597 (v. 20a). As mentioned above, v. 20a functioned originally as the concluding word to these deportations. At a later time, Jer 52:1—27 was drafted from 2 Kgs 24:18—25:26 and brought into play as the final word of the Jeremiah traditions, together with its own special tradition at 52:28—34.[201] The status of vv. 17 and 20b is more difficult to determine. They are either transition statements meant to aid in the placement of the summary formula at this point, or they were part of the original Ch. 24. It is unlikely that the exilic editor responsible for Ch. 24 would fail to mention Zedekiah's appointment

---

[199] See Gray, *I & II Kings,* 773.

[200] See Zenger ("Rehabilitierung," 28 ff.) who speaks of Zedekiah as "Gegenspieler zu Jehoiachin"; Dietrich (*Prophetie,* 143) mindful of Kings' omission of the Gedaliah governorship concludes: "Vermutlich wollte er [DtrN] damit klarstellen, daß es im Lande Juda keinerlei Alternative zu Jojachin mehr gab." Also, Baltzer, "Messias-Frage," 37 ff.

[201] It knows of the death of Zedekiah and perhaps even Jehoiachin (compare 2 Kgs 25:30 and Jer 52:34).

(v. 17). On the other hand, the notice at 20b carries the entire burden of reporting on 9 full years of Zedekiah's reign, in the space of just 4 words: *wayyimrōd ṣiděqiyyāhû běmelek bābel.* As such, it is a transitional editorial addition, meant to bring Ch. 25 into perspective with Ch. 24 in as brief a fashion as possible. As will be shown below on the basis of an investigation of the parallel Jeremiah material, the actual core of 2 Kgs 25 (1−12; 18−21; 22−26) was drawn up on the basis of a special level of Jeremiah tradition which now exists at Jeremiah 37−43* and which was made available to an exilic editor after the 587/582 deportations indicated at Jer 52:29−30. Its juxtaposition with the final chapter relating 597 events (Ch. 24) was accomplished in the manner just described.

F. Final Remarks

In his analysis of the Deuteronomistic History, Nelson correctly noted that one of the persistent problems in dual redaction theories of the composition of Kings has been "the determination of where the work of the first author ended."[202] F. M. Cross felt he had solved the problem of the lack of peroration in Chs. 24/25, the present conclusion of Kings, by placing the "climactic section" earlier, at 2 Kgs 22:1−23:25.[203] In so doing, he felt he had discovered the "end" of a primary edition of Kings, which for him was a Josiah-era document extolling this monarch's faithfulness to the Davidic covenant (one primary-edition "theme"). The other primary-edition theme, concerned with the sins of Jeroboam, received its healthy conclusion at 2 Kings 17:1−23. According to this approach, peroration signaled climactic conclusion.

An obvious problem with Cross' procedure was pointed out above. There is no particular reason to assume that lengthy peroration ought to indicate the conclusion of a work. As in 2 Kings 17, the chapter which comments on the Fall of Samaria and which gave Cross the hunch that something comparable was "missing" for Judah, peroration can just as easily be attributed to the secondary accumulation of related commentary as to the long-windedness of a first editor. This also explains the lengthy, and rather disjointed, collection of literary units in 2 Kings 22−23, Cross' first-edition finale.[204] This first edition, he claimed, was brought up to date by the laconic if not inarticulate supplementation of 2 Kings 24/25.

---

[202] Nelson, *Double Redaction,* 16.

[203] F. M. Cross, Canaanite Myth, 278 ff.

[204] Most contemporary studies point out the obvious secondary nature of much material in 2 Kings 22−23 − to an even greater degree than for Ch. 24! Among others, see A. D. H. Mayes, *Deuteronomy* (NCB; London: Oliphants, 1979) 85 ff.; Norbert Lohfink, "Die Bundesurkunde des Königs Josias," *Bib* 44 (1963); Martin Rose, "Bemerkungen zum historischen Fundament des Josia-Bildes in II Reg 22 f.," *ZAW* 89 (1977) 50−63; Helmut Hollenstein, "Literarkritische Erwägungen zum Bericht über die Reformmaßnahmen Josias 2 Kön. XXIII 4 ff.," *VT* 27 (1977) 321−36; W. Dietrich, "Josia und das Gesetzbuch," *VT* 27 (1977) 13−35.

In the section just completed, this increasingly popular theory of Kings' redactional development has been challenged. One of the persistent problems, if not the central problem, of such a theory has been addressed. Search for a conclusion to a first edition leads beyond 2 Kings 22 to 2 Kings 24. Lengthy peroration, not necessarily a sign of an original conclusion, may be lacking here, but not theological comment. Moreover, this chapter gives clear evidence on many levels of kinship with the preceding chapters of Kings. Common authorship is far more likely than a theory of literary imitation, which is in any event difficult to prove. Furthermore, if it can be shown that 2 Kings 25 was originally drawn from a specific level of tradition available from Jeremiah (Chs. 37—43*), then a separate tradition history for 2 Kings 25 distinct from 2 Kings 24 will be established. This would provide solid evidence for positing an original division between these two "concluding chapters," above and beyond what has already been established about the summary nature of 2 Kings 24 itself.

Full attention to the whole of 2 Kings 25 cannot be paid until the parallel Jeremiah material is examined. However, at this point it is possible to say something about the distinct tradition history of Ch. 25, over against that of Ch. 24. Even among those who question whether Ch. 25 has in its entirety been drawn up on the basis of pre-existing Jeremiah material (esp. Jeremiah 39), there is general agreement that the unit vv. 22—26 is dependent on this source (Jeremiah 40/41).[205] In passing it should be mentioned that this ought to provide support for the conclusion that the majority of Ch. 25 finds it way to final form due to healthy supplementation from Jeremiah traditions (so Noth). In addition, the temple inventory of vv. 13—17 looks as though it was drawn from an independent list, available to one in Babylon familiar with what was taken. For the special report concerning the death of remaining leaders at Riblah (vv. 18—21), one might likewise turn to a 587 deportee who was privy to this information. The final unit of Ch. 25, concerning the freeing of Jehoiachin (vv. 27—30), is obviously not dependent upon sources in Judah. The larger point is this: whatever one determines about the sources behind 25:1—21, it is obvious that several units of the chapter have a particular tradition history distinct from the material presented in Ch. 24. Moreover, it is likely that the hand responsible for bringing these units (13—17; 18—21; 22—26;

---

[205] Pohlmann, "Erwägungen," 95 ff.; Baltzer, "Messias-Frage," 37; Zenger, "Rehabilitierung," 17; Dietrich, *Prophetie,* 140; Würthwein, *Könige,* 479 ff.; Gray, *I & II Kings,* 770. Noth argues that the whole chapter is excerpted from Jeremiah, with the exception of the final notice (vv. 27—30), for which Dtr drew "on his own knowledge" (*Dtr History,* 74; 138, n. 71). Wanke (*Baruchschrift,* 115) follows Mowinckel in positing a common source below both 2 Kings 25 and the Jeremiah text. His argument for the better tradition at 2 Kgs 25:22—26 (cf. Jeremiah 40—43) is extremely subtle and, on the whole, unconvincing.

27 — 30) into their present position in Ch. 25 is also responsible for the present juxtaposition of the entire chapter with Ch. 24. Consequently, the editorial activity evidenced by the final redactor is quite distinct from that noted in Ch. 24, and even presupposes the existence of Ch. 24 in its original form.

This leads to the conclusion that at least two distinct stages of editorial work are represented by these two chapters: Ch. 24 formed the original conclusion of the primary edition of Kings, from the exilic perspective of 597 B. C. Ch. 25 is an editorial supplement whose intention is to coordinate Ch. 24 — and the entire History — with subsequent 587 events and direct the reader to a future beyond these events (vv. 27 — 30). The notion of a uniform Dtr-2 redaction, spanning chapters 24/25 and offering a flat update to a Josianic edition, does not do justice to the complex literary and tradition-historical nature of the material. Moreover, such a theory tends to obscure the logic behind the compositional process in Kings at this crucial moment in Israel's history. The evidence indicates that the separate circumstances of 597 and 587 gave rise to separate accountings of the "fall" of Judah. In their present form, Ch. 24 has been coordinated with Ch. 25 in such a way that its "fall" represents a preliminary "capture" episode before the final "fall" and destruction of the city in Ch. 25. This way of envisioning Judah's final years is historically accurate. But it is an accuracy which could only be achieved once both "phases" had been completed. Only at this point could a coordinated literary presentation of events emerge.

IV. THE 597 PERSPECTIVE OF EZEKIEL
AND THE DEUTERONOMISTIC HISTORY

Conclusions

On the basis of this investigation of the biblical witness to the Exile of 597 found in Ezekiel and the Deuteronomistic History, the following conclusions can be drawn. The Ezekiel traditions, theologically more developed than 2 Kings 24 and working from a later historical perspective, give the fuller evaluation of the respective communities in Babylon and Judah, following the events of 597. These traditions seek to establish a portrayal of past judgment and future restoration focused on the Golah community deported from Judah in 597. Within the traditions of Ezekiel, the deported king Jehoiachin functions as representative of the broader deported community. He is the topmost cedar twig, ultimately to be replanted. Judgment was executed on him and the Babylonian community in the fate of 597 deportation itself.

A concomitant of this portrayal of Jehoiachin and the exilic community is the theological evaluation of Zedekiah and the Judahite remnant. While the prophet Jeremiah is never mentioned in the Ezekiel traditions (see also the DtrH), the post-597 community, its leadership and especially its "ruler" are topics of considerable discussion. In general terms, the Judahite community is condemned for ongoing idolatry, an idolatry stretching back through the pre-exilic period to the days of the wilderness. In more specific terms, the severity of this general indictment can be accounted for by observing the stance taken by the Judahite remnant toward those deported in 597. The charge is made that deportation is a sign of God's displeasure and a casting-off of the exilic community by Yahweh. Ezekiel counters this charge with a thorough vision of judgment, yet to be realized but already set in motion with the events of 597, which awaits the community in Judah and their "ruler." The conclusion to be reached is that the ultimate sequence adopted in the historical and prophetic material (viz, 597 events inaugurating a season of judgment over Judah which reaches to 587 B. C. and beyond) has its earliest roots in the Ezekiel traditions. The Ezekiel traditions develop this sequential portrayal in order to address the question of ongoing life in Judah, over against God's ultimate plan for Israel's restoration out of Exile.

The analysis of 2 Kings 24 undertaken above suggests that the Ezekiel programme for judgment was developed subsequent to its own perspective on 597 events. Based upon a thorough literary analysis, it has been argued that the composition of 2 Kings 24 took place shortly after the events of 597 themselves. In sharp distinction to prevailing views, 2 Kings 24 is to be viewed as the original conclusion to a developing Dtr History. 2 Kings 24 sees 597 events as decisively accomplishing Yahweh's judgment over Judah, just as the prophets had warned. There is no discussion of ongoing life in Judah, nor are questions related to the general future, much less the monarchy and restoration, raised. In distinction to the Ezekiel traditions, there is also no discussion of judgments yet to be accomplished, in 587 or at some later point. It is the secondary juxtapositioning of 2 Kings 24 and 2 Kings 25 that brings the final word of the Deuteronomistic History into rough co-ordination with the normative Ezekiel perspective.

All this has important implications for Jeremiah analysis to be taken up in the next chapter. Like 2 Kings 24, the Jeremiah traditions stress the severity and finality of 597 events from the Judahite perspective. Like the final form of the Dtr History, the Jeremiah traditions are eventually brought into co-ordination with the Ezekiel perspective, with respect to the vision of judgment and restoration in 597 and 587 events. But the process is a gradual one and involves considerable redactional intervention.

One of the places where the greatest tension exists between developing Ezekiel and Jeremiah traditions is in the evaluation of the Judahite monarchy, represented in Jehoiachin and Zedekiah. While Jeremiah does not blindly endorse Judah's last Davidic king, his attitude toward Zedekiah and the post-597 remnant is far more nuanced than what is found in Ezekiel. Conversely, lacking a focus on the restoration of the 597 exiles so central in Ezekiel, Jeremiah's attitude toward Jehoiachin (and his father Jehoiakim) stands in direct contradiction to the view of Ezekiel. In the final form of Jeremiah, tensions between the 597 perspective of Ezekiel and Jeremiah have been considerably blunted by the redactional supplementation termed here the Exilic Redaction. In co-ordination with Ezekiel traditions, this redactional layer seeks to provide in the final presentation of the book a more uniform, consistent message of judgment over life in Judah, beginning but by no means ending in 597 events. As will be seen shortly, the situation was far more complex within the developing Jeremiah traditions themselves.

Chapter Four
The Impact of Exile on Developing Jeremiah Traditions

INTRODUCTION

Specific observations can now be made about the relationship between the "dual-conclusion" of Kings, the Book of Ezekiel, and Jeremiah material examined to this point. Furthermore, anticipating the analysis of the fuller post-597 traditions of Jeremiah which appears in this chapter, specific proposals can be made about the ways in which contrasting evaluations of the events of 597 B. C. have played a major role in the redactional history of the Book of Jeremiah. With some general understanding of the emphasis the Ezekiel traditions place upon these events, assisted by the narrower perspective of 2 Kings 24, it is now possible to look more critically at the complex Jeremiah material. The essential thesis of this study is that the literary complexity of the book results from secondary redactional enrichment, brought about by a conflict over normative inter-pretation of the Exile. The conflict is most focused at this particular historical moment, when as a result of the extensive deportations of 597 "Israel" is comprised of an exiled community in Babylon and a remnant community in Judah. In what follows, our analysis is focused by comparing attitudes toward the monarchy and the broader post-597 community, in Exile and especially in Judah, as these emerge in Jeremiah, 2 Kings 24, Ezekiel, and 2 Kings 25. This inquiry leads to the heart of the redactional complexity which involves all major tradition blocks of the present text of Jeremiah.

Chapter Four is organized as follows. Sections I, II, and III will sketch out the differing interpretations of the impact of the 597 Exile as found in the Deuteronomistic History (esp. 2 Kings 24 + 25) and the Book of Jeremiah. The perspective of Ezekiel and 2 Kings 24, as treated above, forms the background for this discussion. In addition, section III will examine the peculiar chronological organization of the present Jere-miah traditions as a means of introducing the redaction-critical approach adopted here. The bulk of the chapter (section IV) will focus on the isolation of a particular level of tradition within the present Book of Jeremiah, to be termed the Scribal Chronicle, now located primarily at Jer 37—45. This level of tradition represents an intermediate position between the pre-597 oracles of Jeremiah and later redactional supplementation.

Theologically, it holds out for the existence of the remnant community and its leadership, in Judah, in the post-597 and post-587 periods. In the final form of the Book of Jeremiah, the Scribal Chronicle has been modified by extensive editorial reworking from the Exilic Redaction. Theologically, the Exilic Redaction is most closely aligned with the developing Ezekiel traditions, particularly as it evaluates the legitimacy of the post-597 Judahite community, its king (Zedekiah) and other leaders (Gedaliah; Johanan), and the place of that community within the ultimate restoration of Israel.

Tradition-historically, 2 Kings 24 appears to have been composed earlier than the Ezekiel material. Not only does its historical coverage pre-date Ezekiel by a short period, it is not as theologically reflective as the developing Ezekiel traditions. The chronicling of history is still the major thrust of 2 Kings 24, even as it supplies terse theological comment. This chapter is concerned to say that Judah and Jerusalem were cast out because of the anger of Yahweh, after extensive prophetic warning. In fact, this is a theological position readily seen in the message of Jeremiah, one specific prophet notable for warning Judah at this period (see Jer 1—20). It can be assumed that within the portion of society deported from Judah, among whom was the author of 2 Kings 24, there were those familiar with "the word of YHWH which he spoke" through this particular prophetic servant (2 Kgs 24:1—3a). 2 Kings 24 must have come together relatively soon after the deportations to Babylon. For no evidence as yet exists of extensive theological conflict — over monarchial legitimacy, life in the land, the exilic fate, and the future restoration — which surfaces in bold form in Ezekiel and Jeremiah 21—45, and to more subtle extent, in 2 Kings 25 and Jeremiah 52.

2 Kings 24 does provide a brief glimpse at the figure of Jehoiachin, and several things can be inferred on the basis of his presentation in this chapter. On the one hand, there is no attempt to present Jehoiachin as unique within the monarchy, either because he ruled for such a short time (and therefore was exempt from evaluation) or because he was tragically deported. The narrative is straightforward at this point. Despite his brief rule, "he did evil like all his fathers." He is deported with the broader community, and accorded no special status. In this sense, the narrative appears to present events as they occurred. On the other hand, the presentation makes clear that consistent with the developing (post-597) message of Jeremiah, Jehoiachin is not rebellious before Nebuchadnezzar. At one level, the king's decision may simply have been a judicious acknowledgement of inevitable Babylonian supremacy. Yet, in distinct contrast to his successor Zedekiah (see 2 Kgs 25:1—7), Jehoiachin "gives himself up to the king of Babylon." This fact is specifically noted in the Kings narrative (24:12). At best, a sober respect for Jehoiachin can be detected within the tradition at this point, which also notes that those who were deported were "fit for war": that is, capable of rebellion, yet willing to submit.

It is interesting to observe the relationship between the portrayal of 597 events in 2 Kings 24, especially the depiction of king and populace as submitting to Babylonian authority, and one specific theme which emerges in Jeremiah 21—45. In the post-597 years in Judah, the prophet Jeremiah consistently counsels those who remain in the land to go out and submit to Nebuchadnezzar, and thereby claim their lives as "a prize of war" (27:12 ff.; 21:9 ff.; 38:17; further, 39:18 and 45:5).[1] One obvious suggestion for the point of origin of such counsel is the set of circumstances which Jeremiah and the whole Judahite populace experienced in the 597 siege, capture and deportations. On the basis of this experience, the prophet had firsthand evidence of lives which were spared, because king and populace had "gone out and submitted" to Nebuchadnezzar. Drawing upon this firsthand experience, the prophet had every reason to insist in his post-597 counsel to king and people that following submission, the city would not be burned with fire — this was precisely the sequence of events as Jeremiah had experienced them in 597, and as they are now presented in 2 Kings 24. King and people submitted; lives and the city were spared. Another clear possibility, and one which Jeremiah develops shortly after the 597 deportations, is that one could submit, have one's life spared, and continue to live in the land (". . . I will leave on [his] own land, to till and dwell there, says YHWH," 27:11).[2] The obvious thing to note in this regard is that in the 597 takeover and deportations a portion of the population had been permitted to remain in Judah, including Jeremiah, prophets, priests, scribes, monarch, and general populace. Submission, willful or otherwise, involved in their case not just having their lives spared, but also the opportunity to continue living in Judah proper.

---

[1] It does not sound as though such action necessitates deportation (though see the development at 39:17 and 45:5); at a minimum, it may prevent further hostility (esp. 38:17 and 27:17, "Why should this city become a desolation?").

[2] Unfortunately, the precise date of 27:1 is a matter of ongoing debate. MT ("beginning of the reign of Jehoiakim") is obviously in error (due to 26:1?) since Zedekiah is the king who appears in the chapter (27:3, etc.). LXX lacks a date citation. Some commentators prefer to read "accession year of Zedekiah" (Syriac) which would allow us to locate this counsel of Jeremiah immediately after 597 events. But if 28:1 ff. and 27:1 ff. form a unit, the year 594 (5th month of Zedekiah's 4th year) suggests itself (Bright, *Jeremiah*, 201; Wanke, *Baruchschrift*, 19 ff.; Rudolph, *Jeremia*, 146). Moreover, if the council of nations, often referred to as an "anti-Babylonian conference," came together as a result of troubles in Nebuchadnezzar's army, or the accession of Psammetichus II, the date 594/3 works better. For details and bibliographic summary of dating attempts, see Malamat, "Twilight," 135 ff.; also Greenberg, "Ezekiel 17 and the Policy of Psammetichus II," *JBL* 76 (1957) 305; Freedy & Redford, "Dates in Ezekiel," 470. It should be mentioned that Chs. 27 and 28 could refer to events in 597 and 594, respectively (following Syr: "beginning of the reign of Zedekiah" at 27:1), without seriously affecting the present unity of the chapters or the logic of the presentation. It appears from 28:1 as though the two chapters may have been secondarily coordinated. See H. Seebass, *ZAW* 82 (1970) 449—52. After all is said, Jeremiah's counsel is only relatively better grounded by positing a 597, rather than a 594, date for Ch. 27. The basic issue remains the same.

It is important to note that this particular "submit and live" counsel plays no significant role in Jeremiah's message in the years prior to 597 B. C. (see Jeremiah 1—20). Up to this point in time, the powerful imagery of military destruction and deportation had dominated the prophet's description of impending judgment. In 597 B. C., this language took on concrete form. It is only after the fulfillment of the prophetic word that a unique shift occurred in the prophet's perspective on the present and future. The concrete circumstances of 597 gave the prophet Jeremiah and his message a startling and forceful validation; at the same time, these circumstances gave rise to a distinct transformation of that message for the post-597 community in Judah who had experienced and survived the catastrophe. This transformation included a new focus directed toward the necessity of Judah's submission to Babylon, away from the often hyperbolic vision of military punishment as a judgment upon Judah's sins (Jer 9:10,18,21; 12:11; 14:8 ff.).[3] Such a specific shift can only be due to the fact that in the concrete events of 597 B. C. the word of the prophet had received some measure of confirmation. The "foe from the north" had descended (Jer 13:20). Judah had been "taken into Exile" (Jer 13:19). Only the depletions in population were perhaps not as expected, in view of the often extreme (pre-597) language of Jeremiah (9:10,18). But the extent of deportations, including the king and royal family, testified to the sureness of fulfillment.

Because Jeremiah was not deported, his message to the post-597 community had to address the altered circumstances of this "remnant" community (the šĕʾērît yĕrûšālaim, Jer 24:8). One of the unique features of the historical moment involved the new way in which "Israel" had to conceive of her independent political status. With a significant part of the population in Babylonian Exile, it would no longer be possible to talk about rebellion and independence in the same terms once entertained. In this sense, Israel faced a set of circumstances which demanded a radical change in political and theological self-definition. Similarly, with the events of 597 intimately experienced by the Judahite community, it would be possible for the prophet to talk about submission to Babylon in a way that had tangible resonance for these "survivors in the land." After all, their 597 submission had meant the opportunity to continue to live in Judah. When Jeremiah in the post-597 years exclaims, "Why should this city become a desolation?" (Jer 27:17), more than a rhetorical use of language is implied. No portion of the post-597 community could hear such language without being forced to reflect on the fortune which it had been their fate to enjoy, in distinction to the exiled community in Babylon.

---

[3] Such punishment continues to play a direct role in the prophet's vision of the future, if Judah refuses to submit.

The difference between pre- and post-597 language in the Book of Jeremiah can be illustrated on the basis of the prophet's evaluation of the monarchy. After 597, certain fundamental distinctions emerge between Jeremiah's perspective on the monarchy, due to his status as a survivor in Judah, and that of Ezekiel or the author of 2 Kings 25. In the pre-597 years, Jeremiah held out no hope for the continuance of the Davidic monarchy in the persons and line of Jehoiakim and Jehoiachin. These two monarchs, father and son, are the focus of some of the strongest denunciation of the whole book. Of Jehoiakim it is said: he will receive the "burial of an ass" (22:19), cast forth from Jerusalem during the anticipated siege. Jehoiachin will survive the siege but be cast off: "I will hurl you and the mother who bore you, into another country, where you were not born, and there you will die" (22:26). And as this oracle continues, it announces that Jehoiachin will be "childless," because his children shall never return to Judah nor rule again (see also 36:30−31). In one sense, this sharp denunciation of the monarchy prior to 597 is perfectly consistent with Jeremiah's vision of judgment for the wider community.

When this language is placed in the context of Jeremiah's post-597 statements to the monarchy and wider community, counselling submission and the possibility of continued life in the land, the only explanation for the shift in tone is the actual experience of 597 events. At this historical moment the perspective dramatically changes. When Jeremiah's words to the monarchial line of Jehoiachin are set alongside similar language from Ezekiel, the tension between the two is irreduceable. What emerges as a sharp denunciation in Jeremiah, a neutral or perhaps respectful depiction in 2 Kings 24, takes a decidedly supportive turn in the Ezekiel traditions. The "cast-off signet ring" without returning descendent (Jeremiah 22) becomes the "topmost twig of a cedar" who will be replanted and restored to a majesty unprecedented (Ezekiel 17). By contrast, the Judahite successor Zedekiah, as well as his whole house and line, is the recipient of strong and bitter denunciation (Ezekiel 19/21).[4]

Within the Jeremiah traditions, no attempt is made to reverse the harsh line adopted toward the monarchy as represented in Jehoiakim and Jehoiachin.[5] Zedekiah takes the throne, and insofar as he follows the prophetic counsel of Jeremiah to submit before Babylon he is depicted as a worthy king (37:21; 38:14−20,24−28). Questions with respect to his legitimacy, in view of Jehoiachin's presence among the exiles, are not a matter of ongoing interest in the Book of Jeremiah. Put another way,

---

[4] The original signet-ring image of Jeremiah is picked up and more directly reversed in Haggai 2:23, on behalf of Zerubbabel, the grandson of Jehoiachin.
[5] The pronouncements remain in all their severity. They are only relatively blunted by redactional emphasis on the disobedience of Judah's last monarch, Zedekiah. See the full discussion below.

Jeremiah does not appear to reckon with the possibility of Jehoiachin's continued rule or, even further, the continuance of that rule by his sons (see 23:6). If such a position finds expression, it is associated with the prophet Hananiah, who takes his stand on the issue as follows:

> Thus says YHWH of hosts: I have broken the yoke of the king of Babylon. Within two years I will bring back to this place all the vessels of YHWH's house, which Nebuchadnezzar king of Babylon took away . . . I will also bring back to this place Jeconiah son of Jehoiakim, king of Judah who went to Babylon . . . (28:2—4).

Note how for Hananiah, Jehoiachin's returning rule is linked to the promise of Babylonian defeat and the return of the wider Golah community. Jeremiah's negative response to this false prophet conforms with earlier statements he delivered regarding Jehoiachin. His response is also consistent with the message presented after 597 to both those in the land and those in Exile: "all shall serve Nebuchadnezzar" (Jer 27:7; 28:14). Submission is required for Jehoiachin in Babylon as much as for Zedekiah in Judah. If anything, it is Hananiah's message which is justly viewed as an attempt to subvert Jeremiah's post-597 counsel, even as it promises the return of the Golah community. Zedekiah's legitimacy, as such, is never called into question by Jeremiah, anymore than Gedaliah's post-587 rule is a matter of specific debate — both are capable of proper rule. Neither does concern with the future restoration of Jehoiachin fall within the horizon of Jeremiah's thought. This is perfectly consistent with his stress on submission to Babylon.

The conclusion that emerges from a careful reading of Jeremiah 27—29 is that concern for the specific restoration of Jehoiachin or the broader deported community began very quickly to merge with hopes for Babylonian overthrow. This is evidenced both in Judah (Hananiah) and in Babylon (false prophets and dreamers, 29:8 ff.). As such, this concern collides with Jeremiah's own response to the crisis of 597, both for those in Exile and those in Judah. Instead, Jeremiah simply directs those in Babylon to "seek the welfare of the city where I have sent you into exile" and not to follow the counsel of prophets there or in Judah who dream deceitful dreams (29:7—9), no doubt regarding swift return to Judah. If Jeremiah's conception of a 70-year term of Exile is original (29:10), then it is almost double the figure suggested in the Book of Ezekiel (for "forty years" see 4:6).[6] Both are quite familiar periods of time in the OT. Statements at Jer 27:7 and 29:6, which appear in the core of their respective chapters, are in essential agreement on a three-generation (father, son, grandson) stay in Babylon, and it may be that this is the original conception

---

[6] In this context, note the opening words of Second Isaiah, ". . . her time of service is ended . . . she has received from YHWH's hand, double for all her sins" (40:2).

of Jeremiah.[7] An obvious extrapolation would be a specific 70-year term (Jer 25:12).[8] Only in this sense, is a "70-year term" original to the prophet's thinking. In the context of Hananiah's earlier statements, as well as the unknown advice of prophets in Babylon, Jeremiah's message to the exiles was doubtless unpopular:

> Build houses and live in them; plant gardens and eat their produce. Take wives and have sons and daughters; take wives for your sons, and give your daughters in marriage, that they may bear sons and daughters; multiply there, and do not decrease (29:5—6).

Note that the imperatives "build" (*běnû*) and "plant" (*niṭĕʿû*) pick up the opening commission to the prophet "to build and to plant" (1:10), without adjustment for the exilic fate. Jeremiah apparently saw it as quite consistent with his prophetic commission to address these words to a deported community, and their descendents for two generations, without specific regard for a restoration focused on return to Judah.

In their present form, chs. 27—29 have received extensive editorial overlay, whose purpose is to focus more specifically on the fate of the exiles, as well as to condemn the post-597 community in Judah. This overlay often disrupts the narrative logic (see 27:19—22; 29:16—19). In

---

[7] See Rudolph (*Jeremia,* 157) for a discussion. Secondarily, the originally loose sense of the three-generation motif was lost in favor of more fixed, strictly numerical interpretations (esp. "the desolation of Jerusalem," Dan 9:2; but also, 2 Chron 36:21). Is the enigmatic 30th year of Ezekiel (1:1) an attempt — secondary and admittedly illogical — to bring the 40-year term into coordination with Jeremiah's three generation period (30 + 40 = 70)?

[8] The status of 29:10—14, in which the 70-year term appears, is unclear. Does the shift to the specific topic of return from Babylon, after 70 years, go beyond the narrower concern of the preceding section, viz, the encouragement of the Golah community in Babylon proper? It appears as though exilic welfare (*šālôm*) of Jer 29:7 has been re-interpreted to mean a welfare which is "not evil", "a future and a hope" (Jer 29:11). This welfare focuses specifically on return "to the place from which I sent you into exile" (29:14). For a different interpretation, see Wanke, *Baruchschrift,* 40 ff. (following Rudolph). Jer 29:10—14 appears to have entered the text together with the clearly supplemental 29:16—19 (see the discussion following). Vv. 11—14 are remarkably similar to the language and overall thrust of Deut 30:1—10 and 1 Kgs 8:33—34, passages which clearly presuppose the exile and point to the likelihood of an exilic author, working from the same perspective as the exilic redaction of Jeremiah (see esp. 3:24—25; 5:18—19; 12:14—17; 16:14—15; 23:7—8; 24:4—7; 30:1—3,8—9; 31:27—29; 32:16—44; 33). The fixed expression *šûb šĕbût*, which appears in 1st person form at v. 14, may develop a metaphorical sense "restore the fortunes" at a later period (see, for example, the Psalter), but at this historical juncture when exile is more real than metaphorical, the phrase would be better rendered "reverse the exile" or "return from exile." Furthermore, v. 15 seems to be directly related to vv. 8—9 of the preceding unit. See Thiel's perceptive analysis and concluding remark: "Vielmehr werden 16—19[20] der gleichen Hand zuzuweisen sein, die auch 10—14 und K. 24 formulierte, also D" (*Redaktion 26—45,* 17—18). Instead of "D" one might better talk about an exilic redactor closely aligned with the Ezekiel traditions.

the section above the first supplement was examined, in which the hauling off of remaining temple vessels is demanded in a context which otherwise depicts continued life in the land for vessels and post-597 community as a serious possibility. Even Bright considers the latter passage (29:16—20) intrusive.[9] The unit 29:15,20—32 contains a sharp rebuke of prophets (Ahab ben Kolaiah; Zedekiah ben Maaseiah) who have spoken "lying words" in Babylon, and who have sent letters (Shemaiah of Nehelam) to Judah demanding that Jeremiah be punished precisely because of his words to the deported community (// 29:4 ff.), "Your exile will be long" (29:28). As in 22:24 (Jehoiachin) and 28:16 (Hananiah), Jeremiah's forceful response calls for harsh punishment on Shemaiah and his descendents:

> He shall not have any living one among this people, and he shall not see the good that I will do to my people, says YHWH, for he has spoken rebellion against YHWH (29:32).

In the broader literary context of Ch. 29, the "good" which Yahweh promises to do for his people arguably includes the "good" he does for those in Judah as much as the "good" he has in store for the exiles. In the latter case, this good is related to welfare YHWH grants within the welfare of Babylon itself (29:7).

In the context of strong rebuke to prophets within the exilic community, Jeremiah's opening address to "all you exiles whom I sent away from Babylon" (29:20) sounds equally sharp. On the basis of this perceived rebuke of the broader deported community, the unit 29:16—19 now finds its place, at least in the MT (cf., LXX), as a preface to the address to "all you exiles" (29:20). It presupposes the failure of the post-597 community in Judah to hear the words not of Babylonian but of Judahite prophets "which I persistently sent" (29:19). The bitterness of the attack on king and "all the people who dwell in this city, your kinsmen who did not go out with you into exile" is as compressed and virulent as anything in the wider Book of Jeremiah; it looks particularly out of place in this three-chapter block.[10] Not only does it interrupt the original narrative flow (v. 15 to v. 21); it awkwardly, and boldly, severs the connection between the rebuke (20 ff.) and the exiles' claim to prophetic presence (v. 15). Now it appears that the word spoken by Yahweh in condemnation of the post-597 community (vv. 16—19) is somehow related to prophetic activity in Babylon.

It is likely that this insertion was made by the exilic community under the prophetic authority of Ezekiel. Its language closely mirrors the condemnatory litanies found in the Book of Ezekiel (sword, famine, pestilence;

---

[9] *Jeremiah,* 209 ff. Verse 20, however, maintains the narrative flow from v. 15 and ought to be retained.

[10] See the discussion of Thiel, *Redaktion 26—45,* 11—18.

horror, curse, terror, hissing, reproach). The same language does appear in Jeremiah (14:11—16; 15:1—4; 21:6 ff.; 25:9 ff.; 32:24; 38:2). But do these fixed constellations of language originate with Jeremiah in his attack on the post-597 community, or do they emerge in an editorial layer of Jeremiah under the influence of the Ezekiel traditions?[11] The best clue for answering this difficult question is provided in the unit presently under discussion. Not only is a perspective from exile clearly presupposed by the use of the 2nd-person forms in v. 16, "your kinsmen who did not go out with you" (*'ăḥêkem; 'ittĕkem*), resulting in a contrast between "you" (exile) and "them" (Judah), the conflictual matrix out of which the unit speaks seems strikingly similar to what was uncovered at Ezek 11:14 ff. and 33:24 ff.[12] When these various factors are taken as a whole, the rationale for the unit's inclusion is clear. It attempts to blunt the force of 29:15,21—32 by prefacing Jeremiah's strong words to the exilic community and its prophets with yet stronger words to the post-597 community in Judah — *they* are the ones who have persistently refused the word of Yahweh spoken by his servants the prophets.

This particular form of editorial supplementation can be noted else-where in the Book of Jeremiah (see Chs. 21 and 24; 37:1—2; 38:23; 42:15—22). Such supplementation generally operates by prefacing authen-tic Jeremiah material (even when such juxtapositioning strains the narrative flow) in order to either (1) blunt the force of subsequent material, or (2) foreclose on possibilities or alternatives later explored.[13] One further observation on the actual style of supplementation can also be made. There is only one way to account for the existence of seams in the present Jeremiah narrative (e. g., 29:15/16). It must have been the case that the prior material could not be altered once the authority of the prophet and the tradition associated with him was accepted.[14] All that could be done

---

[11] It is to be recalled that we do not doubt Jeremiah utilized similar language in the pre-597 years (see Chs. 9—15 and our listing above, p. 239). But the listing we provided showed far greater flexibility and variety in imagery than the fixed triad "plague, pestilence, famine" or the catalogue "terror, reproach, byword, horror, hissing," in whatever order it appears. If Ezekiel developed genuine Jeremiah language, its source could well be Jer 14:17—18, where several of the key terms (sword; diseases of famine) together with others (wound; blow) appear in the context of a pre-597 lament. Yet there is no fixed grouping here (cf. 15:1—4). For these fixed constellations, Ezekiel shows a far greater preference. For a brief discussion, see W. Thiel, *Redaktion 1—25*, 186 ff.

[12] Note too that Jeremiah (29:20) speaks of those whom Yahweh "sent away from Jerusalem to Babylon" (*šillaḥtî mîrûšālaim bābelāh*), not unlike the charge from those "inhabitants of Jerusalem" in Ezekiel 11:15, concerning those who have "gone far from YHWH." The *piel* of *šlḥ* is not used at 29:16 to describe those who did not "go forth" (*lō'-yāṣĕ'û*) with the exiles.

[13] Concluding supplements are also made, as in 27:19—22, 32:16—44, or Ch. 44.

[14] This is the literary concomitant of the "vitality of the prophetic word" (P. R. Ackroyd, "The Vitality of the Word of God in the Old Testament," *ASTI* 1 [1962] 7—23). The prophetic word was only relatively maleable (rearrangement/addition — not subtraction).

by way of editorial comment had to proceed through supplementation, anticipatory remark, or the rearrangement of material. All three moves are evidenced in the Jeremiah text, to a degree unequalled in the entire prophetic corpus.

The only explanation for the thoroughness and comprehensiveness with which secondary work on the Jeremiah traditions has been carried out is the presence of a contemporaneous, equally authoritative, prophetic collection: the traditions of Ezekiel. More detailed treatment will follow on the wider activity witnessed in the editorial transformations of the Book of Jeremiah, attributed to an Exilic Redaction. But it is important at this juncture to note the clear correspondences between this redactional level in Jeremiah and the traditions of Ezekiel. In view of the fact that any editorial work on Jeremiah would take place at the same time when Ezekiel material was taking shape, and considering the strong likelihood that such editorial work took place in Babylonian exile, Ezekielan influence on Jeremiah is not difficult to imagine. In fact, in view of all that has been established concerning tensions between the Golah community and the community in Judah, the reverse is far more difficult to conceive: that the Ezekiel material is dependent upon the final form of Jeremiah.[15] First, all the evidence in the post-exilic literature suggests that it was from the Golah community that normative statements of Israel's past, including the prophetic vision, and future emerged. Second, the editorial movement of the Jeremiah traditions suggests transformations in the direction of the Ezekiel material, and not the reverse. Third, the Book of Jeremiah received "final form" only after the traditions were loosed from their original prophetic figure, in this case a Jeremiah whose descent into Egypt necessarily distanced him from the community from which the restoration, in Judah, would emerge. It was also this community that shaped the "final form" of the present (MT) Jeremiah text.[16]

---

[15] A study which looks at this question in isolation is J. W. Miller, *Das Verhältnis Jeremias und Hesekiels* (1955). Yet it suffers from far too flat a literary and theological conception of the Jeremiah traditions, as though a single static tradition, in the form that exists in the present text of Jeremiah, was available *in toto* to Ezekiel. Moreover, it only treats a select portion of the broader Jeremiah material and thus fails to account for its full and complex nature. One far more restricted variation of this theory will be examined below: that the Jeremiah traditions available to Ezekiel were, logically, those which a 597-deportee could draw upon, that is, pre-597 statements (Jeremiah 1—20*). These probably remained normative, since their burden was that Judah was to be "taken into Exile out of her land" (Jer 13:19). The kind of post-597 developments in Jeremiah posited above either "fell on deaf ears," or, from the perspective of the Golah community, were capable of gross misinterpretation. This is precisely the pattern that can be detected in the Book of Jeremiah, which in Chs. 27—29 points to this rapidly developing conflict.

[16] The assumption of a Babylonian provenance for the MT of Jeremiah is also borne out by recent text-critical work. A detailed discussion of the conclusions established by close text-critical work (esp. E. Tov) lies beyond the scope of this study. It appears that

These three points are best illustrated by the development in Ezekiel of a comprehensive vision of restoration, which ultimately embraces themes not originally highlighted in Jeremiah: restoration of the house of Jehoiachin and a focus on the return of the Golah. In the text of Jeremiah (24:8 ff.; 29:17), the reflex of this latter theme is seen in the contrast between the "good figs" (those exiled in 597) and the "vile figs" (the post-597 community in Judah), as well as in a sweeping vision of restoration found throughout the present book, specifically related to the theme: gathering and return from exile.[17] While the figure of Jehoiachin (and his royal line) is impossible to reinstate, due to the strong denunciation associated with him in the Jeremiah tradition (22:30), it was possible in the Exilic Redaction to insure that his condemnation was balanced by equally negative statements directed toward his successor Zedekiah (e. g., the two frame-units, Chs. 21 & 24). These statements are of a piece with the view of the Exilic Redaction and the Ezekiel traditions that the wider post-597 community was an experiment in disobedience. Though the verdict is not registered in original Jeremiah traditions until the final descent into Egypt — and even at this point the depiction moves beyond flat condemnation — the present text of Jeremiah indicates that even as existence begins for the post-597 community, it stands under the judgment of Yahweh (24:1−10). The specific figure of Zedekiah is singled out in both Chs. 21 (v. 7 ff.) and 24 (v. 8 ff.) as monarch and chief representative of the abortive 597-community. His proleptic condemnation in these chapters, before the narrative appears which actually relates his capture and sentencing (Chs. 37−39), presents a counterbalance to the judgment over Jehoiachin in 22:24−30, thereby anticipating and quashing any potential hopes associated with his rule or that of his sons. The final retrieval of Jehoiachin's royal line took place outside of the Jeremiah traditions themselves (Ezekiel). Before turning to questions regarding the unusual redactional arrangement of Jeremiah 21−36/37−45, it is important to look at the specific way the focus returns to Jehoiachin and hopes associated with his royal line in the final presentation of 2 Kings 25. It is to be recalled that this same material eventually appears as the final word of the Book of Jeremiah, at Jer 52.

---

especially in the case of Jeremiah, where a decidedly shorter and differently arranged text exists in the LXX, text analysis begins to merge with redactional analysis. Differences in hypothetical Egyptian or Palestinian "recensions" of Jeremiah may have as much to do with editorial as with strictly textual issues. See E. Tov, "Some Aspects of the Textual and Literary History of the Book of Jeremiah," *Le Livre de Jérémie*, 145−67; S. Talmon, "The Old Testament Text," *Qumran and the History of the Biblical Text* (F. M. Cross & S. Talmon, eds; Cambridge: Harvard University, 1975) 1−41; P. R. Ackroyd, "The Book of Jeremiah — Some Recent Studies," *JSOT* 28 (1984) 52 ff.

[17] For a partial list of passages, see note 8 above.

Concern for issues of restoration, specifically centered on Davidic rule, surface in Ezekiel and also in 2 Kings 25. As noted above, the merger of this final chapter with 2 Kings 24 was brought about in part in the context of emerging hopes for Davidic restoration (2 Kgs 25:27 — 30). The selectivity of 2 Kings 25 drives one important point home: with the events of 587 B. C. the final chapter in Judah's history was written. What report there is of the post-587 community under the twin leadership of Babylonian appointee Gedaliah and the prophet Jeremiah (2 Kgs 25:22 — 26) is only summarized (see Jeremiah 40 — 43) to the degree that a picture of its inevitable failure might emerge. In fact, Jeremiah is himself never depicted nor mentioned.

Many have argued that minimal use of Jeremiah traditions at this point in the DtrH stems from the desire to downplay the possibility of ongoing life in the land and any hopes which may have been associated with the leadership of Gedaliah.[18] Though not of the royal family, Gedaliah is an important figure at this juncture in history. He is the grandson of the influential Shaphan (2 Kings 22), who was secretary (*hassōpēr*) at the time of Josiah, and son of the same Ahikam who rescued Jeremiah from Jehoiachin years earlier (Jer 26:24). His uncle Gemariah held an influential position at Jehoiakim's court (36:10,25). Jeremiah's scroll was read by the scribe Baruch in Gemariah's chamber; there was a "secretary's chamber" (*liškat hassōpēr*) in the king's house (36:12), probably belonging to Elishama the scribe (36:12). It was Gedaliah's cousin Micaiah who reported the contents of the scroll to Elishama and other influential leaders in the royal court (36:11). Gemariah was among those who urged Jehoiakim not to burn the scroll (36:25). In sum, there are significant links between members of scribal families in Jerusalem at this period.[19]

The frequent appearance of these families in the background of the Book of Jeremiah suggests that they occupied significant positions of

---

[18] Baltzer, "Messias-Frage," 37 ff.; Dietrich, *Prophetie,* 143; Zenger, "Rehabilitierung," 29. Pohlmann ("Schlußkapitel," 107 ff.) extends the discussion in an attempt to account for the non-appearance of Jeremiah.

[19] See the stimulating suggestions of Norbert Lohfink, "Die Gattung der »Historischen Kurzgeschichte«," 335 ff. The fullest treatment remains that of S. Yeivin, "Families and Parties in the Kingdom of Judah," *Tarbiz* 12 (1941/42) 241 ff. [Hebrew]. Of related interest, see H. Cazelles remarks concerning the role of the "Shapanides" during the early years of Jeremiah, in "La Vie de Jérémie," *Le Livre de Jérémie,* 29 ff.

power, second only to the monarchy.[20] They probably played a significant role in the preservation and formulation of the Jeremiah traditions, as well as so-called deuteronomic traditions.[21] In this sense, the early and persistent attention paid to the figure of Baruch in the composition of the Book of Jeremiah is not completely off the mark. The specific question of the role of scribal families in the development of Jeremiah tradition, especially Chs. 27—29, 33—36, 37—43, will be taken up below.

In this context it should be noted that though Gedaliah was not of the royal family, there is no evidence to suggest that this fact was of any particular importance to Jeremiah. When given the option by Nebuzaradan to accompany the deportees to Babylon, Jeremiah opts to remain in Judah in support of Gedaliah: "Then Jeremiah went to Gedaliah ben Ahikam, at Mizpah, and dwelt with him among the people who were left in the land" (40:6). In the present Jeremiah narrative chronicling post-587 events, when a member of the royal family puts in an appearance (40:8,14,15), it is the assassin Ishmael (*mizzera' hammělûkāh,* 41:1).[22] His depiction in Jeremiah far from enhances broader claims to leadership made on the basis of royal lineage. 2 Kings 25 notes this lineage at one point, but is careful to imply that he was among "all the people, great and small, and the captains of the forces" who fled to Egypt, evacuating Judah and leaving behind an empty land (2 Kgs 25:26). Ishmael escapes to the Ammonites in the Jeremiah narrative (Jer 41:15), and his flight to Egypt cannot be established without considerable strain on the narrative. As a matter of fact, 2 Kgs 25:25 indicates that the reason there was a flight to Egypt was because Ishmael killed certain Babylonians who were with Gedaliah at Mizpah, and the whole community was afraid of reprisals. This particular connection is never made in Jeremiah. There the people are afraid because Gedaliah, the man appointed by the Babylonians, had been killed by a member of the royal family. For this reason they flee to Geruth Chimham (41:17).

---

[20] A seal with the exact inscription "Belonging to Baruch, son of Neriah, the scribe" (*lbrkyhw ben nryhw hspr*) has recently been found, raising the question of the status of royal scribes (Nahman Avigad, "Baruch the Scribe and Jerahmeel the King's Son," *IEJ* 28 [1978] 52—6). It is frequently held that Baruch was simply a private secretary of Jeremiah. In this regard, Avigad's conclusion is worth quoting: "The presence of Baruch's bulla in an archive amidst bullae of royal officers seems to indicate that at some time Baruch belonged to the category of royal scribes, as did his contemporaries Gemariah ben Shaphan the scribe, and Elishama the scribe (Jer 36:10—12)" (55).

[21] See: James Muilenburg, "Baruch the Scribe," *Proclamation and Presence: OT Essays in Honour of Gwynne Henton Davies* (John J. Durham & J. R. Porter; London: SCM, 1970) 215—38; Moshe Weinfeld, "The Scribal Role in the Crystallization of Deuteronomy," *Deuteronomy and the Deuteronomic School* (Oxford: At the Clarendon, 1972) 158 ff.; Kurt Galling, "Die Halle des Schreibers," *PJB* 27 (1931) 51—57.

[22] Recall that the same expression is used of Zedekiah in Ezekiel (17:13).

Though it is a more complex depiction, the Jeremiah narrative contains a subtle truth that argues for its essential accuracy.[23] The murder of a Babylonian appointee by a member of the royal house (as well as the murder of Babylonian soldiers, Jer 41:3) would have been viewed by the Babylonians as an act of treason, as the Judahite community recognized. After the events of 597 B. C., the Babylonians had appointed a member of the royal family, Zedekiah, to act as monarch in place of his nephew Jehoiachin. Though the motivation behind such a decision remains a matter of conjecture, it is clear what happened: he rebelled (2 Kgs 24:20). The appointment of Gedaliah (from a scribal rather than a royal family) after the deportation of Zedekiah, was doubtless designed to stave off further rebellion. As if to drive the point home, the Babylonians blinded Zedekiah and executed his sons at Riblah. Yet due to the ruthless action of Ishmael, continued existence for the remnant in Judah was again threatened. Moreover, 2 Kings 25 fails to mention the fact recorded in the Jeremiah narrative that the assassination plot involved Baalis, king of the Ammonites.[24] In other words, the treasonous activity was initiated by others beyond the contingent from Judah. There was every reason to expect that, this time, reprisals would be even more severe. At least in 42:16 ff., the decision to flee to Egypt is made on this basis. Moreover, based upon information in Jer 52:30, the Babylonians intervened to make yet further deportations following this assassination by Ishmael and his followers.[25]

Whatever one can conclude about the particular narrative presentation of 2 Kings 25, it is clear that the fullest possible story has not been made available. This was probably due to the desire to downplay the potential rule of Gedaliah. When a king emerges in the narrative of 2 Kings 25, it is Jehoiachin, who is graciously pardoned by a new Babylonian monarch (25:27−30). The logic of the narrative movement is clear. Various possi-

---

[23] The conclusion of G. Wanke that 2 Kgs 25:22−26 has the "better" and "geschlossenere Darstellung" follows from the fact that it is a summary of the original Jeremiah narrative, not that it is the original narrative (*Baruchschrift*, 115). This holds true as well for the reason given for the flight to Egypt, the clearer version of which he argues is found in 2 Kings 25. The "clarity" of 2 Kgs 25:26 is the result of secondary simplification: all Judah fled from the land because Babylonians were killed. The far more complex, and original, reason for the remnant's fear is given in Jeremiah: "for they were afraid of [the Babylonians] because Ishmael had slain Gedaliah, whom the king of Babylon made governor over the land" (41:18). See also Pohlmann, "Schlußkapitel," 97 ff.

[24] This explains Ishmael's flight to the Ammonites after the assassination (41:15).

[25] Consistent with the logic of 2 Kgs 25:22−26, this notice is lacking. If all fled to Egypt (25:26), then there would be no third deportation in 583/2. Jeremiah 52, on the other hand, presupposes the fuller Jeremiah narrative in Chs. 40−42, in which all details of the revolt by Ishmael are given. Consequently, the brief summary of Jeremiah in 2 Kgs 25:22−26 does not appear in Jeremiah 52, while Jeremiah 52 does tell of the third deportation.

bilities for future rule emerge (Gedaliah, Ishmael, Johanan, Seraiah, Jaa-zaniah). But in the tragic confusion of post-587 circumstances, Gedaliah is killed along with certain Judahites and Babylonians, and the rest of the community is forced to flee to Egypt, both great (leaders) and small (people who remained, 25:22). At this moment in the narrative, the exiled King Jehoiachin makes an appearance. The movement to this unit is so abrupt that its positioning must be motivated by the desire to focus, at the end of the history, on Jehoiachin's restoration.

There is one other important matter to note about the selectivity of 2 Kings 25. Not only is the narrative absolutely silent about Jeremiah and relatively silent about Gedaliah; it is unusually reserved about the 11-year tenure of Zedekiah. As noted above, 9 full years of his reign which receive ample attention in the Jeremiah traditions are summarized with the words at 20b: "And Zedekiah rebelled against the King of Babylon." The rest of the narrative (25:1—7) describes a rapid disintegration of his monarchial line. He flees during a severe famine (v. 4), makes it as far as the plains of Jericho (v. 5) where his army scatters from him; he is captured (v. 6), taken to Riblah for sentencing, and his sons are killed before his eyes (v. 7) before he is himself blinded and taken prisoner to Babylon. In other words, what now exists at 2 Kings 25, from all traditions available, is a compressed 7-verse example of what happens when a king does not "give himself up to the King of Babylon" together with his royal family, as did Jehoiachin (2 Kgs 24:12). In the present juxtaposition of the final chapters of Kings, a clear and consistent message to the monarchy emerges, spanning both chapters. Jehoiakim's submission leads to his eventual pardon; Zedekiah's failure to submit leads to his capture and the death of his sons; other leadership possibilities never materialize. The message to the community is clear: only the line of Jehoiachin — not that of Zedekiah, nor his sons, nor Gedaliah, nor Ishmael — survives to present possible leadership in the future, beyond exile.

This particular 2-chapter conclusion to the history of Israel/Judah only operates once Ch. 25 has been brought into play following Ch. 24. Taken by itself, Ch. 24's depiction of the monarchy, in the persons of Jehoiakim and Jehoiachin, is fairly negative in the former's case and relatively neutral in the latter's. The potential exists for seeing in the figure of Jehoiachin something of the proper stance toward Babylonian authority, especially when his depiction in 2 Kings 24 is set over against the unilaterally negative portrayal in the Jeremiah traditions. This potential has been exploited by the editor of Ch. 25 in his composite, 2-chapter evaluation of the monarchy. Again, theological proximity clearly exists between the editor of 2 Kings 25 and the developing Ezekiel traditions. It is in the latter that some movement appears toward the resuscitation of Jehoiachin and his line (e. g., Ezek 17). In fact, resuscitation may be the wrong term if in Ezekiel's view he remained the true king of Judah even as a deportee. Nevertheless, it is a correct term in the context of the conclusion of Kings, where we see Judah's monarch deported (Ch. 24), the city and temple destroyed (Ch. 25), and all other leadership possibilities disintegrate. For after all this, in the 37th year of his exile (note a chronological scheme familiar from the Book of Ezekiel),[26] Jehoiachin is restored by the Babylonian monarch and "given a seat above the seats of the kings who were with him in Babylon" (v. 29). Moreover, he dined at the king's table and was attended to all the days of his life (v. 30).[27]

The theological proximity between 2 Kings 25 and Ezekiel accounts for one other fact: the failure to mention Jeremiah the prophet in the summary of vv. 22—26, or anywhere else in the chapter. Though arguments from silence bear limited weight, the failure to mention Jeremiah here is striking enough to demand explanation. Compare, for example, the extensive Isaiah presentation at 2 Kings 19—20. Pohlmann is surely on the right track when he argues that Jeremiah's omission here involves more than an editor's access or non-access to sources.[28] The non-mention of the figure of Jeremiah is to be explained in any other instance as due to factors beyond our knowledge. But at a point where the author is making specific use of narratives drawn from the Jeremiah tradition itself, the non-appearance of their central character is extremely odd. With Pohlmann, it appears that the figure of Jeremiah was avoided at this point in the narrative because of the clear solidarity he demonstrated in the original Jeremiah source-material (39:14; 40:6; 42:10) with those who remained in the land under Gedaliah's leadership.[29] Alongside the many trials of the post-587 years, the Jeremiah narrative also described the successes of the remnant community (esp. 40:7—12).[30] This material likewise fails to find a place in the narrative of 2 Kings 25.

---

[26] Does the 37th year of the exile of Jehoiachin, plus the 30th year of Ezekiel (1:1), bring us toward the end of Jeremiah's 70-years? By the time of the Chronicler, concern with this 70-year term and its fulfillment are evidenced (2 Chr 36:22 ff.; Ezra 1:1). See also, Lev 26:34 ff. and Dan 9:2 ff.

[27] For an examination of the precise range of these terms, see Zenger, "Rehabilitierung," 19 ff. Incidentally, Zenger demonstrates points of contact between these terms and certain Akkadian expressions — another argument for the Babylonian provenance of 2 Kings 25. In this specific context, see also the arguments of Pohlmann, "Schlußkapitel," 101—108.

[28] This was Mowinckel's explanation for the silence: the Jeremiah tradition (at this point, "source B") was unavailable to the author of 2 Kings 25 (*Komposition,* 30). See also Wanke, *Baruchschrift,* 115. The theory of a common source below both Kings and Jeremiah is untenable due to the existence of slight but significant divergences in their respective presentations (viz, the reason for the flight to Egypt), when this "common source" was theologically tapped. Moreover, what kind of common source would fail to mention Jeremiah?

[29] "Schlußkapitel," 108—9.

[30] See Ackroyd, *Exile and Restoration,* 57; "Historians and Prophets," 52; Seitz, "Crisis," 92 ff.

On the basis of these observations, the following conclusions can be reached: what was selected from Jeremiah tradition for inclusion in 2 Kings 25 was any material which contributed to the theme now uniting Chs. 24 and 25, pointing beyond the history to a new future. This is the theme of Jehoiachin's obedience before Babylonian authority. It is for this reason that after the narrative takes such a dark turn in the events of 587 now recorded in 2 Kings 25, there is a sudden return to the deported King Jehoiachin. The narrative seeks to stress that his original act of submission in 597 (24:12) ultimately found its true purpose (25:27 — 30). It is to be stressed that in this submission he was joined by the wider Judahite community.[31] The clear implication is that they too, or their descendents, have received the pardon that follows obedience before Nebuchadnezzar or Evil-Merodach. At this point, the future existence of Israel, king and people, is again a possibility.

By contrast, within the Jeremiah tradition (esp. 37 — 43*) narratives were preserved regarding the post-587 community which indicated that obedient submission to Babylonian authority was possible in Judah, under the leadership of Gedaliah. In the detailed analysis to follow, it will be shown that this tradition presents the kind of uneven, theologically complex chronicle most logically attributable to one who shared the fate of the post-587 community. This firsthand chronicle does not hide the fact of disobedience before Jeremiah, or the tragic circumstances surrounding the death of Gedaliah, who ruled under Babylonian appointment and imprimatur. But it also narrates complex circumstances surrounding continued life in the land, and the many factors which contributed to its gradual disintegration. It relates that successes were possible as well, under the leadership of both Gedaliah and Jeremiah.

As it now appears in the present text of Jeremiah, this complex depiction has been edited in such a way that a more unilateral description of impending punishment might emerge. In the final form of the narrative, the complete disobedience of king and people is anticipated from the opening scene (37:1 — 2) and the disintegration of the community is tied more to this disobedience (flight of Zedekiah; decision to flee to Egypt) than to circumstantial factors (the assassination of Gedaliah; the general hardships following massive deportations; the destruction of Jerusalem and loss of temple). This editorial activity is similar to the work of the Exilic Redaction described above — especially in Jeremiah 27 — 29, where the validity of life in Judah in the post-597 period is questioned. With its larger theological perspective, this redactional activity stands close to the final perspective of 2 Kings 25. But while in 2 Kings 25 it was possible

---

[31] The post-597 community of 2 Kings 25 does not receive much attention (v. 11) in the overall narrative. The focus remains on the rebellion of Zedekiah, the death of his sons, and the execution of other important officials (vv. 18 — 21).

to make certain specific theological statements (regarding the exiles and exiled King) through selective handling of pre-existent (Jeremiah) traditions, this was not so easily accomplished within the Book of Jeremiah. As mentioned above, such editorial work would have to proceed by way of anticipating supplement, rearrangement, or concluding remark. In the section which follows, editorial work on this Jeremiah narrative (chs. 37—45*) will be more closely evaluated. It is to be noted at this juncture that the same basic editorial activity can be identified in post-597 and post-587 sections of Jeremiah tradition. Moreover, this editorial activity has much in common with the theological perspective of Ezekiel and 2 Kings 25.

Noth and Cross concluded that the finale of Kings was nothing but a terse validation of Yahweh's absolute judgment over Israel. In so doing, they failed to appreciate its importance precisely as the last word of the History.[32] One has a sense in the passage that all is not being said; or, more accurately, that all has not been said and that one will have to read further at a later point (see Ezra/Nehemiah; Haggai and Zechariah). The finale opens onto the future, and in that sense is as much a first as a last word. Negative assessment of the passage tends to perceive in the larger history such an inexorable decline that no final commentary could reverse its downward spiral. But the analysis of this study has suggested that the passage really functions in the more restricted context of Chs. 24 and 25. This is not to say that as the history now operates, these three final verses are only to be seen in relationship to the events of 597 and 587. But it is to suggest that one can best appreciate the movement into 25:27—30 when the nuances peculiar to Chs. 24 and 25, related to monarchial obedience in Judah's last days, are allowed to move to the forefront. Then the restoration of Jehoiachin has the impact it was intended to convey, as a final word to the whole history and as an answer to the question of future Davidic rule and the community's existence beyond the events of 597 and 587 B. C.

---

[32] Noth, *Dtr History,* 12. Cross agrees with Noth that 2 Kgs 25:27—30 is a "thin thread upon which to hang the expectation of the fulfilment of the promises to David" (*Canaanite Myth,* 277). Cf. G. von Rad, *Old Testament Theology,* 1.334—7; H. W. Wolff, "Das Kerygma," 171 ff.; J. D. Levenson, "The Last Four Verses in Kings," *JBL* 103 (1984) 353 ff.

III. THE EFFECT OF THE EXILIC REDACTION
ON THE FINAL FORM OF JEREMIAH

A. General Observations

The manner in which the conclusion to the DtrH was redacted, through the merger of Chs. 24 and 25, is intriguing beyond what it says concerning the theological movement of Kings. If the analysis undertaken of Ch. 24 is correct, then 597 events had a major impact on a significant portion of the population, at a crucial moment in history. This impact was experienced directly by those who were deported, but it also affected those who remained in Judah (see section A above). Ch. 24 provides an important testimony to the "final" significance of these events, at a point outside the Jeremiah traditions themselves. The impact of 597 is difficult to assess within so complex a prophetic collection as the Book of Jeremiah, which in its final 52-chapter form moves well beyond the events of 597 B. C. Moreover, the book has already undergone extensive editorial supplementation which may affect the way one perceives the significance of these events in the present text. As noted above, the poetic material which seems most directly tied to the impending catastrophe of 597 (Chs. 9—15*) remains only a slice of extremely forceful imagery in an otherwise broad and far-ranging collection. Fortunately, 2 Kings 24 represents a coherent, tightly constructed theological evaluation and historical chronicle, composed by one who experienced the 597 events, including deportation to Babylon. From this author's perspective, the events of 597 were as final as they now appear in this one section of Jeremiah (Chs. 9—15*).

In the final form of Kings, the Ch. 24 depiction looks like a foreshadowing or anticipatory enactment of the true finale of 587 B. C. Indeed, many critics argue that while this was not originally the case, Ch. 24 was edited to serve precisely this (proleptic) purpose. The logic behind such an editorial move ("anachronistic supplementation") was questioned above. It seems far more likely that the "anticipatory" rule the chapter plays is due to the fact that a second "conclusion" to the history was subsequently added (e. g., Ch. 25).

There is another place where a similar type of sequencing — such as appears in Chs. 24 and 25 of Kings — can be detected. That is the Book of Jeremiah, in its final form. Here language originally intended to describe the specific catastrophe of 597 now functions to anticipate a yet greater finale. Put another way, the pre-597 language of Jeremiah, by virtue of its present location in the larger book, applies now to historical circumstances reaching well beyond 597. This language cannot be tied to the more restricted literary environment of Chs. 1—15* in the present, fuller shape of the book.

The reason for this is complex. The larger prophetic books (especially Isaiah and Jeremiah) offer little by way of direct instruction as to how the reader should organize broad collections of material into more comprehensible blocks. Moreover, prophetic collections like Jeremiah and Isaiah have moved well beyond the period and provenance of their original prophetic figure, developing new tradition and new overall organization. If the thesis is correct that significant transformation occurred in the historical Jeremiah's vision of the future due to the realized experience of the 597 catastrophe, then one might have expected clearer structural evidence of this is the arrangement of sections in the final form of the book. But this evidence is not given in as direct a manner as the reader might expect.[33] It must be inferred on the basis of a careful reading, with an eye toward shifts in emphasis across levels of the text generally taken to be authentic to the prophet.

On the basis of specific Jeremiah material appearing in the central section of the book (Chs. 21—36), one can detect a particular post-597 emphasis on: (1) hopes for a continued existence of the remnant community in the land (Jer 27:1—18; 28:1—17; 29:1—9,15,20—32; 31:1—22; 32:1—15); (2) the necessity of submission to Babylon (27:12—13,17; 38:2,17—20), (3) irrespective of the specific fate of exile (27:16; 28; 29:1—9; 31:1—22; 32:1—15).[34] There are no strong literary or theological grounds for de-

---

[33] There is even no mention of the 597 catastrophe in the superscription — only the 587 events.

[34] On this last point, see especially Jer 29:27 ff. Here Jeremiah's words to the exiles ("Your exile will be long; build houses and live in them . . .", 29:28, cf. 29:4 ff.) are taken as a rebuke. From Shemaiah's standpoint, these words justify Jeremiah's harsh rebuke by Zephaniah the priest. We can get a limited sense of perspective by looking at the situation from the exiles' standpoint. Ezek 11:14 ff. suggests that more than theological factors may have been involved in the statement, made by the post-597 remnant in Judah, "to us is this land given as a possession." Here is a claim to property. As Greenberg puts it: "The Jerusalemites' arrogation to themselves of all the exiles' property (11:14 f.) on the ground that the latter had been removed from YHWH belongs to this vision as another aspect of the central issue of YHWH's nearness and distance" (*Ezekiel 1—20*, 203 f.). It is difficult to objectively judge a situation when the information is so scant, when it emerges from misunderstanding, or when it borders on polemic. Were Jeremiah's words "build houses, plant gardens" meant to imply that the exiles had forfeited property rights in Judah? Probably not in the first instance, for Jeremiah utters these words in the context of his call for submission to Babylon (Ch. 27). The main thrust of our argument has been that such submission could take place in Judah or in Babylon. That his words could be taken in a more restricted sense, by either those greedy in the land or those powerless to defend their property rights in Babylon, is not to be ruled out. The overriding concern of Jeremiah is the call for submission to Nebuchadnezzar, whom Yahweh has placed in authority — all property now belongs to him: "Now I have given these lands into the hand of Nebuchadnezzar . . ." (27:6 ff.).

nying this tradition to Jeremiah. Nothing in this material stands at odds with pre-597 language, beyond a greater sensitivity to the possibility of continued life in Judah, once the catastrophe of 597 had passed. However, when this level of tradition is set alongside another level, critically isolated on the basis of literary analysis, the contrast between the two is striking. In this new level of tradition, termed the Exilic Redaction, theological emphases quite distinct from Jeremiah's own post-597 statements appear. This level of tradition consistently (1) questions the validity of continued life in the land (20:1−6; 24:8−10; 27:19−22; 29:16−19; 32:26−29; 37:8−10); (2) presses for the inevitability of further disobedience and the necessity of a judgment which will bring about the final elimination of the post-597 remnant (21:3−7; 25:8−11; 32:30−35; 37:1−2; 38:21−23; 42:13−22; 44; 45); and (3) focuses on a future involving the return of exiles (23:1−8; 24:4−7; 27:22; 30:1−4,10−24; 31:27−34,38−40; 32:36−44; 33).

The reason that language calling for final judgment in 597 events is capable of application beyond the more restricted section in which it now appears is due to the presence of the Exilic Redaction in the central section of the book (Chs. 21−36). The presence of this supplementary level, interwoven with authentic post-597 tradition, considerably blunts whatever sense of contrast might have emerged due to the passing of the 597 catastrophe. It was a central conviction of the Exilic Redaction that the harsh judgment called for in pre-597 sections of the present text (Chs. 1−15*) had not reached its fulfillment in 597 B. C. As such, the thrust of genuine pre-597 language, concerned with announcing the thoroughness of judgment (4:23−26; 5:10−11,17; 6:22 ff.; 9:10; 13:20 ff.; 15:5 ff.), is brought over and underscored in the supplementary traditions of the Exilic Redaction — even as this message is modified by the prophet Jeremiah after the historical events of 597 B. C. From the perspective of the Exilic Redaction, also clearly stated in the Ezekiel traditions, the future could begin only when a full judgment was carried out. From the perspective of the post-597 Jeremiah traditions, however, the king and community in Judah remained in a position to "submit and live" in the land. This was true after the events of 597, and later, following the destruction of the city in 587.

In the final form of the Book of Jeremiah, pre-597 language has the potential for remaining operative right up until the final chapter, at which point a limited glimpse at the future restoration, anticipated by the Exilic Redaction's focus on return from Exile, emerges (Jer 52:31−34 = 2 Kgs 25:27−30).[35] This potential remains for one very important reason. Though language envisioning a final judgment is scattered throughout Chs. 1−20, reaching a crescendo in Chs. 9−15, at this literary juncture

---

[35] See note 8 above for a listing.

there is no historical narrative which presents 597 events and evaluates their significance comparable to 2 Kings 24. The only narrative like this in the Book of Jeremiah appears at the end (Jer 52) and it concerns 587 events. In other words, 597 events are never depicted as accomplishing the judgment of Yahweh without a necessary, later judgment (i. e., 587 B. C.).[36]

A more nuanced perspective on Jeremiah's part is demonstrated by a new emphasis in his message: the demand for obedient submission to Babylon that life might continue, in the land or in exile. In this sense, the merger of 2 Kings 24 and 2 Kings 25 is similar to the merger of Jeremiah tradition and Exilic Redaction, with one important qualification. The pre-597 judgment language does not merely anticipate the final judgment, as in 2 Kings 24; in the final form of the book it remains the normative statement of that judgment. As such, it overshadows an integral level of tradition traceable to the prophet Jeremiah, which never foreclosed on the possibility of ongoing life in the land if Judah would submit to Yahweh's will as accomplished in Nebuchadnezzar. Both the Exilic Redaction of Jeremiah and the final chapter of Kings (which ignores the post-587 and post-597 community altogether) agree that the future will involve those who submitted through deportation to Babylon.

B. Chronological Presentation in Jeremiah[37]

At a period when complete chronological coherence in the arrangement of prophetic narrative is possible and evident in biblical texts (see Ezekiel), the unusual disregard for such coherence in the Book of Jeremiah is striking and demands explanation. Why, at the pivotal point of the book (Ch. 21) is one placed at a later temporal period, in a scene drawn from a later chapter (37), in which Zedekiah is pleading for divine aid prior to a Babylonian attack which took place around 587 B. C.? Up to this point (Chs. 1—20) the reader has moved through a familiar narrative arrangement which, though not as temporally anchored as the Ezekiel material, nevertheless fits well in the period from Josiah to the events of 597 B. C.

---

[36] The notices which do appear in redactional supplements, likely drawn from 2 Kings 24, are only brief, scene-setting, pieces (Jer 24:1; 29:1—2). The theological assessment of 597, or a fuller report of the significance of events, never appears. They are never even mentioned as such in the superscription of the book (Jer 1:1—3). The "captivity of Jerusalem" occurred at only one point, in the fifth month of the eleventh year of Zedekiah (1:3), in conformity with Jer 52:12.

[37] This section is not concerned with developing a new chronological framework out of which to understand the present text (see W. L. Holladay, "A Coherent Chronology," 1981; "The Years of Jeremiah's Preaching," 1983); rather, it is interested in why many of the chapters of the Book of Jeremiah are dated, but then not arranged chronologically (e. g., Chs. 21—36).

Actually, it may be the general avoidance of temporal indication that promotes this sense of logical arrangement.[38] This is familiar in other pre-exilic prophetic works, which show little interest in locating speeches chronologically, except on rare occasion and with interesting effect (Amos 1:1b: ". . . two years before the earthquake"). But precisely within those Jeremiah chapters which give indication of date and location (Chs. 21—36), the greatest confusion reigns. One moves from the final years of Zedekiah (21), to a collection of oracles concerning pre-597 kings Jehoahaz, Jehoiakim and Jehoiachin (22), to the immediate post-597 period (24), to the 4th year of Jehoiakim (25), to the first year of Jehoiakim (26). Then the reader returns to Zedekiah's reign (27—29), plunges back into arguably pre-597 chapters (30—31*), and is then placed in what look like Zedekiah's later years (32—34). Chs. 35—36 return to the reign of Jehoiakim. Only upon reaching 37—45* do chapters evidencing a coherent chronological movement and organization reappear.

There appear to be several reasons for this temporally-interested but temporally-disorganized arrangement within the Book of Jeremiah (Chs. 21—36). First, the final editors want the ultimate sentence over the post-597 community made clear early on. It is for this reason that Chs. 21 and 24 fall where they do.[39] Moreover, both chapters are specifically concerned to announce the sureness with which judgment over Zedekiah will be carried out (21:7; 24:8 ff.).[40] Since Ch. 22 is a compendium of pre-597 statements from Jeremiah concerning the Davidic rulers Jehoahaz, Jehoiakim, Jehoiachin (the latter two receiving particular sharp rebuke), Ch. 21 prefaces this rebuke with judgment over Zedekiah on the eve of 587 defeat — even as Ch. 24 restores us to the immediate post-597 period in which the verdict over Zedekiah and Judahite community is already delivered. The intervening chapter (23) presents a general judgment over the monarchial house, as well as a vision of the future Davidic Branch. The chapter also anticipates the approaching prophetic conflict (Chs. 27—29) by offering a brief discourse on the nature of the prophetic task

---

[38] There is no specific indication of date for any chapter of the first twenty. We can make inferences, due to the setting or content, but this distinguishes Chs. 1—20 from 21—45. In Chart Three above, compare these two sections of Jeremiah. Then note the similarity between Ezekiel and Jeremiah 21—52. Even Ch. 7, a rough duplicate of which is placed at "the beginning of the reign of Jehoiakim" in Ch. 26, is undated in its present location. Undated, it remains a "typical" sermon of Jeremiah, potentially applicable throughout his career.

[39] Thiel, *Redaktion 1—25*, 230—61; Pohlmann, *Studien*, 41—7; Seitz, "Crisis," 81—84.

[40] Chapter 21 even goes so far as to anticipate the survival of king and people in the 587 catastrophe (21:7), and then predicts their ultimate punishment (Seitz, "Crisis," 82). The passage may anticipate, and correct or foreclose on the alternative for survival offered Zedekiah at 38:17 f., in the same way that 37:21 predicts Zedekiah's capture (see Pohlmann, *Studien*, 44).

(23:9—40), which has itself received extensive overlay.[41] The second unusual feature to note in these chapters is the return to the reign of Jehoiakim (Chs. 25, 26, 35, 36). The notion of a "return" is, however, dependent in part upon taking Ch. 22 as providing the death notice over both him and his son Jehoiachin. One has moved in Chs. 21/24 to the reign of Zedekiah. Zedekiah's reign is also the clear temporal location of Chs. 27—29, 32—34, 37—39, so the intervening Jehoiakim chapters, in his fourth-year or otherwise, seem out of place.

There is one possibility for the motivation behind this present arrangement. It is to be observed that the temporal distinctions between the reign of Zedekiah and Jehoiakim are "blurred." They are not done away with, or precise dating references would not appear. From the perspective of the final editor, the interweaving of the reigns of Jehoiakim and Zedekiah is designed to stress that the same message was delivered from Yahweh, through prophet to community, in both historical periods. In other words, the effect achieved is that the message of Yahweh to the community in Judah never underwent significant change from the reign of Jehoiakim to the reign of Zedekiah. If the historical and literary analysis above is correct, the present arrangement seeks to blunt significant transformations which did in fact occur in the prophet's word to the community, once the events of 597 had been experienced. By bringing the reign of Zedekiah to the forefront (Ch. 21), while at the same time drawing the reign of Jehoiakim into the post-597 years (Chs. 25—26; 35—36), the final editors reverse the movements of history in favor of a uniform prophetic word to Judah.

If this view of the redactional history of the Book of Jeremiah is accurate, then the editors responsible for the final form of the book, including the arrangements noted above, are to be sought within the exilic community and in clear proximity to the Ezekiel traditions. It is to be emphasized that those deported in 597 were familiar in a direct way only with the pre-597 message of Jeremiah. As stated above, this tradition anticipated the wholesale deportation of Judah, as well as widespread destruction of capital and countryside. From the perspective of 2 Kings 24, Jeremiah's prophetic message had in a real sense reached its fulfillment in the events of 597 B. C. (2 Kgs 24:2—3a,20a). From the later exilic perspective of Ezekiel, this word of Yahweh spoken by Jeremiah still applied for the remnant in Judah — it was only postponed. A different line was adopted in the post-597 Jeremiah traditions, with an emphasis upon submission of king and community in the land. However, for the post-597 exilic community, the ongoing Jeremiah traditions were either

---

[41] Jer 23:23—44 is an extremely complex unit, which anticipates the kind of conflict we see in Chs. 28—29. But it is not clear how its "burden" is to affect the reading of subsequent Jeremiah narrative.

unavailable (in the same sense as the pre-597 material), irrelevant (due to their specific interest in life in Judah after 597), eclipsed (due to the prophetic activity of Ezekiel), or, most likely, open to gross misinterpretation (compare Jeremiah 27−29* and Ezek 11:14 ff.).

At the point at which the fuller Jeremiah material, with post-597 traditions, became available to the Exilic community (following the 587 and 582 deportations), the final historical verdict over Judah had been delivered. The conviction that the Fall of Jerusalem was an inevitable correlate of Jeremiah's pre-597 preaching gave rise to the internal redactional moves noted above, including the early placement of Chs. 21 and 24, as well as the merger of Jehoiakim (pre-597) and Zedekiah (post-597) material. The former enshrined the kind of pre-597 message with which the exiles had been familiar, in one case offering a dated duplicate of a chapter appearing early in the book (Chs. 7 and 26).

C. The Growth of Jeremiah Tradition: A, B, and C Revisited

With these general observations about the final form of Chs. 21−36 in place, the broader shape of the 52-chapter Jeremiah can now be examined. The difficult question to answer in Chs. 21−36 concerns the extent to which the exilic editors inherited authentic tradition from the reigns of Jehoiakim and Zedekiah, either from Jeremiah or closely related scribal circles. The alternative would be to posit extensive literary development within the redactional effort itself. This holds true for chapters claiming location in the period of Zedekiah as well as Jehoiakim (Chs. 21−43*). One must isolate primary tradition, explain how this material has been edited, and then account for its present arrangement.[42] The same kinds of questions, related to distinguishing primary and secondary levels of tradition and explaining the present shape of the text, also arise throughout the book (Chs. 1−20; 46−50).[43]

Discussion of the nature and extent of secondary tradition in the Book of Jeremiah divides modern scholarship. There are those who argue that much of the prose material critically traced on literary grounds to deuteronomistic circles (source C) ought to be re-assigned on those same grounds to Jeremiah himself.[44] Others maximalize the amount of prose

---

[42] For a technical discussion of the growth of the so-called Baruch material (esp. Chs. 19−20; 26−29/36; 37−44; 45 and 51:56−64), and its inclusion within the larger book, see G. Wanke, *Baruchschrift,* 144 ff.; W. L. Holladay, "A Fresh Look at 'Source B' and 'Source C' in Jeremiah." Interesting proposals are also made by N. Lohfink in "'Historische Kurzgeschichte'," 333 ff.

[43] For a discussion of this problem, see E. W. Nicholson's fine short work, *Preaching to the Exiles* (1970), 38 ff.

[44] This is stressed in the work of Helga Weippert (*Prosareden*) and William Holladay (for bibliography, see Chapter One above).

tradition traceable to deuteronomistic circles.[45] The latter group also blurs the distinction between prose material traditionally classified "biographical" and that termed "deuteronomic" (sources "B" and "C").[46] The former generally maintains the distinction, and may go so far as to urge the priority of "C" over "B" material, with respect to questions of historicity or proximity to the figure of Jeremiah.

Critical evaluation of Jeremiah has reached an impasse precisely because literary argumentation alone is not able to produce a coherent description of the growth of the book. There are two main problems with the customary literary investigation. First, the strong likelihood that deuteronomic thought and idiom influenced the historical Jeremiah, circles close to him, and secondary redactors, calls into question the adequacy of criteria primarily developed on this basis (comparisons of language from Deuteronomy with Jeremiah narrative; or, authenticity = non-Deuteronomic).

Second, while a distinction can be made in theoretical terms between "C" and "B" tradition, the historical provenance of these two types of tradition remains murky.[47] Those responsible for developing and preserving so broad a phenomenon as the theological traditions of deuteronomism cannot be easily pinned down to one historical period or sociological location. Especially at the period of the Exile, when the movement is nearing its apex, it is likely that scribal circles under the direct influence of deuteronomic thought were among those exiled in 597. The author of 2 Kings 24 and editor(s) of Kings/DtrH can be placed within their ranks. At the same time, sections of the Book of Jeremiah indicate the presence of key scribal families working in close proximity to the figure of Jeremiah at both pre-597 (esp. Jeremiah 36 and 26) and post-597 periods (Chs. 32; 37—40). These scribal families were surely familiar with the language and thought of deuteronomic traditions, at least in pre-literary form. In other words, the deportations of 597 do not permit clear distinctions between exilic redactors and Judahite redactors, much less those who worked under so-called deuteronomic influence. One must reckon with editorial activity — in terms of collecting, preserving, and shaping Jeremiah tradition — both in Judah throughout the entire career of Jeremiah, and in Exile after 597, 587, and even 582, when Jeremiah traditions doubtless made their way to Babylon. Any and all of this editorial activity would have come under the influence of deuteronomic thought.

---

[45] The studies of Thiel, Nicholson, and Carroll are representative.

[46] By comparison, see the work of Wanke, Pohlmann, and Lohfink.

[47] In part to divert attention from the figure of Baruch in the composition history of Jeremiah, Wanke identifies the author of his 10-part narrative cycle (Chs. 37—43*) as someone in Gedaliah's administration at Mizpah (*Baruchschrift,* 146). The "cycle" of 26—28/36, unusual in scope and placement, has greater potential for assignment to Baruch, but Wanke is also quite cautious here (147).

There are, however, good reasons for maintaining a form-critical distinction between three basic types of prophetic material within the Book of Jeremiah: (1) poetic speech, traceable in form and function to an oral provenance, similar to other pre-exilic prophetic speech-forms (Amos, Hosea, First Isaiah, Micah, Jeremiah 1—6*; cf. ʿEzekiel)[48]; (2) prose chronicle in which speech of God/prophet is overshadowed by activity of the prophet and/or historical circumstance (Jer 37:1—43:7*; 27—29*; 32:1—15; 35; 36); (3) prose chronicle in which speech of God, spoken either to or by the prophet predominates (Jer 3:6—12, 15—18; 7:1—8:3; 11:1—17; 13:1—14; 14:11—16; 16:1—21; 17:19—27; 18:1—12; 19:1—15; 21:1—10; 24:1—10; 25:1—29; 26:1—9; 32:16—44; 33; 34; 43:8—44:30). This third type may include directions involving an activity (Ch. 13: waistcloth in the Euphrates; Ch. 18: potter's vessel; Ch. 19: broken flask), but it is the speech or interpretation of the action that remains central.[49] The important distinction is that in the former, the activity of the prophet has its own integrity and is related in some detail; in the latter, activity only serves to introduce speech of Yahweh. Often in the second type details related to quite specific people and places appear, again in sharp contrast to the third type. In addition to these three types, brief prose supplements, generally in the form of direct speech of God, explanations, or confessions to the reader, can also appear throughout the book (1:1—3; 2:4; 3:24—25; 4:9—10, 11—12, 27; 5:18—19; 9:11—15,22—25; 10:11; 11:21—23; 12:14—17; 18:18). They are especially noteworthy within Chs. 1—20, that section of the book where poetic speech still predominates. These brief units have been supplied as guides for reading, offering transitional or concluding commentary on passages apparently already anchored in the tradition (note the way in which 3:24—25, for example, comments on the preceding poetic unit, 3:19—23). A pedagogical interest

---

[48] Characteristic of this material: short, parallel lines introduced, if at all, by brief superscriptions; topically or otherwise loosely arranged (Jer 1—6); framed and organized by the addition of secondary prose narrative (Jer 7—20; 22; 30—31; 46—51).

[49] These prose narratives are often introduced by the expression "The word which came to Jeremiah from YHWH" (7:1; 11:1; 18:1; 21:1; 25:1; 34:1), close variations thereof (24:4; 26:1; 32:26; 33:1; 44:1), or simply "YHWH said to me" (3:6; 13:1; 14:11). These introductory forms are far too general, however, to develop a rigid redactional theory. Moreover, they can appear in the second type (27:1; 32:1). The important point of difference involves the degree to which prophetic activity only serves as a pretext for Yahweh Speech. In Ch. 7, for example, the prophet is never even depicted as actually going to the temple (see as well 11:1 ff.; 17:19 ff.; 19:1 ff.; Yahweh talks directly to him (the word which was to Jeremiah from YHWH), and it is only due to the fact that we, as readers, are made privy to the conversation that the sermon is "delivered." That is, the reader simply conjurs up the temple scene on the basis of the instructions of 7:2; the redactor dispenses altogether with the need to describe Jeremiah's action. Even when some action by the prophet is narrated in these word-dominated units, it can be done quite quickly (13:2; 18:3). For comparison, note how central are the actions of prophet and others in 37:1—43:8*.

is also displayed in these units (3:24−25; 5:18−19; 9:11 ff.; 9:23 ff.), similar in tone to Deut 29:29; 30:1−10, in which the lesson of exile is held up to the reader.

A quick look at the final form of Jeremiah indicates that the most comprehensive editorial intervention occurs in Chs. 21−45. Here one sees the greatest interest in specific dating, similar to what is found in Ezekiel. However, because of the lack of steady chronological movement, the likelihood of secondary arrangement and re-arrangement is strong. Different LXX organization in part confirms this. Moreover, it was reasoned that the convergence of Jehoiakim and Zedekiah periods has been intentionally carried out; it is not the result of accidental or random placement. In Chs. 21−45, the greatest percentage of prose material also appears. There is a distinct movement in this direction in the present form of the book: Chs. 1−6 preserving poetic speech with only occasional prose commentary, on analogy with other pre-exilic material; Chs. 7−20 offering a balanced interweaving of prose and poetry, including the so-called lamentations and prose interpretations of the prophetic role; Chs. 21−36 predominately prosaic; Chs. 37−45, almost wholly prosaic. Even if one were to substitute "formal prose" and designate the author Jeremiah, a decided movement toward such formal expression is evidenced in the present text.[50]

In an attempt to avoid the designation "biographical" when discussing the second type of prose narrative in Jeremiah, it has become popular to isolate within such material an emphasis on the effective quality of the word of God and prophetic figure.[51] The abandoning of the term "biographical" is to be applauded, for it wrongly suggests three things: (1) the presence of a biographer/author, usually Baruch; (2) a concern with the "life of Jeremiah" or a special aspect of it (the passion of the prophet)[52]; (3) a focus and style of presentation fairly unique within the prophetic

---

[50] H. Weippert, *Prosareden*.

[51] Stressed by Lohfink in particular through his lumping together of Jer 37−43 with Jer 36/26 and 2 Kings 22 under the rubric "Historical Short-Story" ("'Historische Kurzgeschichte'," 320 ff.). An emphasis on the "Geschick des Jahwewortes als solchem" (323) is more easily detected in his latter examples than the former. See also, G. Wanke, who settles on the theme: "die Wirklichkeit der prophetischen Existenz Jeremias" (*Baruchschrift,* 155). In an inciteful quote, he also goes on to talk about the merger of prophet and Yahweh-word: ". . . in der Erfolglosigkeit seiner Verkündigung, in das vergebliche Werben um glaubendes Vertrauen in das durch den Propheten ergehende Jahwewort wird die persönliche Existenz des Propheten miteinbezogen" (155), following Ackroyd's view that Jeremiah "is here the expression of the divine word" ("Historians and Prophets," 52). Kessler says of 26−36 and 37−45, "Both complexes may be properly designated a 'history of the word'" ("Jeremiah Chapters 26−45 Reconsidered," *JNES* 27 [1968] 87). See the critique below, in Section V.A.

[52] Of Jer 28, Rietzschel says, "Was hat aber eine solche Erzählung mit einer Leidensgeschichte zu tun?" (*Urrolle,* 96 ff.).

traditions of this period (cf. Jonah). However, singular focus upon a theme such as "the truth of the prophetic proclamation" is also misleading.[53] While such a theme appears on occasion (Ch. 28), it is by no means the consistent feature of this narrative type. Furthermore, recent studies of Chs. 37—43 have questioned whether sections where such a theme does occur (37:1 ff.; 42:15 ff.) are integral to the original narrative, or only secondary attempts to give the episodes recorded a consistent theological thrust.[54] It cannot be coincidental that emphasis on the "effectiveness of the prophetic word" has also meant a collapsing of two originally distinct prose categories. If the event-character of the second type is overshadowed by focus on the word of the prophet/God, then its distinctive quality is soon lost. Without returning to the designation "biographical," other possibilities exist for understanding this unique form of expression in Jeremiah.

There is one characteristic of the second prose type that fundamentally resists merger with other speech-central prose narratives. This is its remarkable attention to detail. In speech-central narrative, the scene is often set artificially, or only in such a way as to move quickly to the focus of the narrative, the speech of God/prophet (see Chs. 7, 11, 16, 25, 26, 33, 34, 35*). As mentioned above, even when specific action is detailed (Chs. 13, 18, 19), the activity has a primarily metaphorical or allegorical significance. Compare, for example, the narrative cycle appearing in Chs. 37—43*. This narrative is people, place, and circumstance specific, to a degree unmatched in the Book of Jeremiah.[55] A scene is never "set" in the same manner described above, where episodes appear to be constructs and not descriptions of actual events. Such scene-setting actually has the effect of putting the author at some distance from his subject. More generously, some argue that the style results from an author's dependance upon memory for recollecting and constructing the narrative scene.[56] In Chs. 37—43* details of such specific, even incidental, nature appear, that composition from a distance, or stylized invention, is ruled out.

The specificity is of two main types. First, where the reader has come to expect generic figures in other prose formats (servants, priests, prophets, princes; "kings of Judah"; "men of Judah"; "inhabitants of Jerusalem"; "all the people"; "all the cities of Judah"), here the specific individuals are revealed (see Chart One, above). These individuals do not put in neutral appearances for posterity's sake. They entreat Jeremiah (37:3 ff.); they

---

[53] W. L. Holladay, " 'Source B' and 'Source C'," 401.

[54] For example, Pohlmann (*Studien,* 48 ff.) and Wanke (*Baruchschrift,* 95 ff.).

[55] On the relationship between speech and event in Jer 37—43*, Kremers accurately notes, "In diesem Erzählungszyklus ist . . . keine einzige Erzählung als Ergänzung oder Rahmen einem Gottesspruch untergeordnet . . . die Gottessprüche (haben) nur Bedeutung im Hinblick auf das Geschehen, in das sie eingebettet sind ("Leidensgemeinschaft," 130).

[56] John Bright, "Prophetic Reminiscence."

charge him with treason and beat him (37:11 ff.); they demand his death (38:1 ff.); they rescue Jeremiah (38:7 ff.). They attempt to govern (39:14 ff.); they conspire and carry out treachery (40:13 ff.); they seek revenge for hostility and consider flight to Egypt (41:11 ff.). Second and related to the focus on specific individuals, this narrative displays an interest in circumstances themselves, not just an extracted interpretation of events. Note for example the way specific information related to the location of circumstances is given:

> land of Benjamin (37:12); Benjamin Gate (37:13; 38:7); house of Jonathan the secretary (37:15); dungeon cells (37:16); the baker's street (37:21); the cistern of Malchiah the king's son (38:6 ff. + 41:7); the court of the guard (38:6,28; 39:14); the wardrobe of the storehouse (38:11); the middle gate (39:3); the king's garden (39:4); through the gate between the two walls (39:4); the house of the people (39:8); Mizpah (40:6,8,12,13,15; 41:1 ff.); Shechem, Shiloh, Samaria (41:5); the large cistern which King Asa had made for defense (41:9); the great pool which is in Gibeon (41:12); the "Inn of Chimham" (41:17)

Two things are striking about this list. First, the specificity is not isolated here and there but is evenly distributed throughout the narrative. Second, certain information is so incidental — and so specific — that the likelihood of the author's being in close proximity to the events he records is overwhelming.[57] Note the detail at 38:11 ff., where it is related that Ebed-Melek used "old rags and worn-out clothes" to pull Jeremiah from the pit; similarly, it is reported not only that Jeremiah was put into a cistern, but that it was full of mire (38:6).[58] In stylized narrative, such detail would be unnecessary and might distract attention from some larger point.[59]

Furthermore, at several points the author relates material that suggests a privilege of position or a private source: he knows what Zedekiah secretly asks Jeremiah (37:17 ff.) and what the king, in fear, confides to the prophet (38:24 ff.). He also gives information that implies a special awareness of motivation (who was behind the assassination, 40:13 ff.; why Ishmael did not kill ten men, 41:7 ff.; why the remnant wanted to flee, 41:17). This information is given in blunt, compressed form, with no further commentary. Again, this is the consistent style of the narrative. Events are recorded about which it would be helpful to have more interpretative comment. The narrator can describe circumstances which evoke a degree of compassion and interest on the part of the reader

---

[57] For this reason, the narrative has been tied to Baruch (Kremers, "Leidengemeindschaft," 131). Concerning the even style of the narrative, Kremers speaks of "die gleiche Art des Aufbaus in all ihren Erzählungen" (131); as for its attention to detail, he talks about the narrative's "Nüchternheit" (131).

[58] Apparently, this detail is mentioned to assure us that Jeremiah will not drown (no water, only mire).

[59] Kremers: "Legendarische Züge fehlen völlig" (131).

(Jeremiah's rough treatment; the rescue by Ebed-Melek; the murder of Zedekiah's sons and his blinding; the successes of the post-587 community at Mizpah, and the return of dispersed Judahites; the ruthless assassination of Gedaliah and the revenge of Johanan; the final flight to Egypt). But with few exceptions, the narrative resists further description.

In sum, the prose narrative in Chs. 37—43 is of a form that can be firmly distinguished from narratives of the third type. In this narrative, the focus remains on reporting the immediate circumstances leading up to the Fall of Jerusalem (Ch. 39), as they involve Jeremiah but also the king and other individuals. What a closer literary investigation reveals is that very little theological comment or overarching structure is integrated into the original chronicle. Unlike Chs. 21—36, there is relatively little interest in precise chronological organization (39:1; 41:1), though the movement in these chapters is more coherent than what was noted there. The temporal indicators are far more general. See, for example, 37:11 ("Now when the Chaldean army had withdrawn..."), 37:16 ("When Jeremiah had come to the dungeon cells..."), 38:7 ("When Ebed-Melek the Ethiopian ... heard that they had put Jeremiah into the cistern..."), 38:28c ("When Jerusalem was taken..."), 40:7 ("When all the captains of the forces ... heard that the king of Babylon had appointed"), 41:1 ("In the seventh month..."), 41:4 ("On the day after the murder of Gedaliah..."), 41:11 ("But when Johanan ben Kareah heard of all the evil..."), 42:7 ("At the end of ten days..."). As a matter of fact, this particular means of moving narrative along, through evenly-spaced, temporal clauses (waw-consecutive forms with following finite verb), is a standard feature running straight through this 7-chapter block of tradition. A certain loose structure is also maintained by repetition of the phrase, *wayyēšeb yirmĕyyāhû,* or something similar, as numerous scholars have pointed out.[60]

Before drawing specific conclusions about the larger purpose, the authorship, and the provenance of this tradition-complex, its original literary scope will have to be determined. This also involves a discussion of the relationship between Jeremiah 39 and 2 Kings 25. A survey of the general content of Jer 37—43* confirms the view that the form-critical distinction between the two basic types of prose narrative in the Book of Jeremiah is accurate. It remains to be seen how such a distinction operates at other points in Jeremiah, noteably Chs. 21—36. Moreover, there is a strong likelihood that traditions basic to this original chronicle

---

[60] Jer 37:16b,21b; 38:13b,28a; 39:14b; 40:6b. Kremers, "Leidensgemeinschaft mit Gott," 122—40; Wanke, *Baruchschrift,* 91 ff.; Lohfink, "'Historische Kurzgeschichte'," 331 ff. See also 40:9,10; 41:17; 42:10,12; 43:4 ff., where the same verb appears in relationship to the broader post-587 community.

served as sources for secondary prose elaborations of the third type. But before this hypothesis can be explored, the original document must be separated from secondary redaction and the purpose of both must be determined.[61]

---

[61] Kremers puts it this way: "Zwischen Kap. 36 und Kap. 45 liegt uns aber heute Baruchs "Leidensgeschichte" nicht mehr in ihrer ursprünglichen Form vor. Sie ist nämlich nicht während ihrer Tradierung in ihren einzelnen Erzählungen überarbeitet worden, sondern man hat auch ganze Legenden anderer Herkunft in sie hineingeschoben" ("Leidensgemeinschaft," 132).

IV. THE FALL AND THE REMNANT: A SCRIBAL CHRONICLE (JER 37−43*)

A. Critical Introduction

There is wide critical consensus for viewing Jeremiah 37−45 as a unified narrative describing Judah's last days, set forth in a series of separate but coherent episodes. This consensus remains regardless of how one relates the narrative to the historical Jeremiah, other prose sections of the book, or even the figure of Baruch and narratives frequently traced to him (27−29; 26/36). There is very little consensus, however, over the precise nature of secondary expansion and supplementation in the narrative. Those who ascribe the narrative to Baruch tend to envision a unified work with relatively little overlay.[62] Others emphasize the episodic nature of the narrative and argue that several units were added later for redactional purposes.[63] Even within the latter group, strong arguments have been advanced for an original unified narrative with a central theme and a location in close proximity to events recorded.[64] Only in the recent period has concern with the original unity been dropped, in order that certain redactional features in a basically redactional composition might be emphasized.[65] It should be noted at the outset that one's understanding of the purpose of Jeremiah 37−45 follows directly from a determination of the narrative's original literary scope.

Kremers set the lead for critical work on this section of Jeremiah in his dissertation, "Der leidende Prophet" (Göttingen, 1952). Though very few have adopted the genre designation proposed by him, Kremers' literary analysis has found a wide following. Unfortunately, this analysis is only sketched out in the article-length précis of his thesis ("Leidensgemeinschaft mit Gott," 1953), and one must extrapolate from the few specific literary decisions he makes there the broader critical method employed in the dissertation.[66] In his "Urtext" there are ten separate episodes (I: 37:11−16;

---

[62] Duhm, *Jeremia,* xiv ff.; Mowinckel, *Komposition,* 24 ff.; Rudolph, *Jeremia,* xiv-v; 201 ff.; Bright, *Jeremiah,* lxvii. Mowinckel doubted Baruch-authorship, but not the unity of the narrative.

[63] Kremers, "Leidensgemeindschaft," 120 ff.; Rietzschel, *Urrolle,* 95 ff.; Wanke, *Baruchschrift,* 144 ff.; Lohfink, "Kurzgeschichte," 331 ff.

[64] Kremers, for example, holds on to Baruch-authorship and a passion-narrative theme, even as he greatly reduces the literary scope of the original narrative. So also Lohfink and Wanke.

[65] Pohlmann, *Studien,* 48 ff. Very little effort is made to outline a reasonably coherent *Vorlage,* from which the redactors worked.

[66] In most cases, he appears to follow the critical lead of B. Duhm's 1901 commentary (KHAT: *Das Buch Jeremia*).

II: 37:17—21; III: 38:1—13; IV: 38:14—28a; V: 38:28b; 39:3,14; VI: 40:13—41:2; VII: 41:4—9; VIII: 41:10—15; IX: 41:16—43:6; X: 45) which make up the complete "cycle".[67] These episodes betray the same form and literary style, and point to a single author, who strung them together "fast wie Perlen an einer Schnur" (131). Often the closing statement (*Schlußbemerkung*) of each episode contains the identical words "and Jeremiah dwelt . . ." (131).

Kremers' literary analysis has been picked up and further modified. For example, Rietzschel made the important observation that the basic tradition block (Jer 37—43*) was anchored in its present place by a redactor who supplied both Jeremiah 36 and 44.[68] Few have followed Kremers in seeing Ch. 45 as the conclusion to the original narrative; like Chs. 36 and 44, most feel it owes its present placement to secondary redactional concerns.[69] But with respect to internal analysis of Chs. 37—43, Kremers' work has set an important precedent. In many of his critical decisions he is followed by Wanke, Pohlmann, and Lohfink.

Without going into great detail, it is possible to summarize this direction in critical analysis by examining Jeremiah 37—39, chapters concerned with events prior to the Fall of Jerusalem. Working from the observation that certain obvious tensions exist in the present form of the narrative, several passages are taken as secondary additions. For example, Jer 37:3—10 presupposes both the Babylonian siege and its interruption at the advance of the Egyptians, information given at 37:11 ff. The transition remarks at 37:1—2 are an obvious attempt to link Ch. 36 and 37. In its present position, Jer 37:3—10 intends to make clear what may not have been clear in the original narrative: that the Babylonian retreat is only temporary. The city will be destroyed (Jer 37:10).[70] This concern to anticipate full judgment recalls Jer 21:1—10. The placement of 37:3—10 at this point blunts whatever hopes for city and king existed in the original narrative (see 38:17 ff.). It also results in an uneven sequence with respect to the events of siege and Egyptian advance, as given in 37:11 ff.[71] Similarly, Jer 37:17—21 presents problems in transition from the original

---

[67] Minor additions can also be detected at 37:19; 38:2; 38:17b,18; 40:7—12; 41:3,10; 43:1. For a helpful chart of Kremers' overall schema, see Wanke, *Baruchschrift*, 94.

[68] *Urrolle*, 110.

[69] Thiel, *26—45*, 87; Wanke, *Baruchschrift*, 140 ff. (together with 51:59—64); J. P. Hyatt, "Deuteronomic Edition," 89. Pohlmann does not even treat Ch. 45 in his analysis. Compare, A. Weiser, "Das Gotteswort für Baruch Jer. 45 und die sogenannte Baruchbiographie," *Glaube und Geschichte im Alten Testament und andere ausgewählte Schriften* (Göttingen: Vandenhoeck & Ruprecht, 1961) 321—9. In his final remarks, Weiser is remarkably close to the tone and position of Kremers, calling Ch. 45 Baruch's "eigenhändige Unterschrift unter sein Werk . . . das persönliche Siegel seines Glaubens . . ." (329).

[70] Pohlmann, *Studien*, 57—58; Wanke, *Baruchschrift*, 100 ff.; Seitz, "Crisis," 85 ff.

[71] Wanke, *Baruchschrift*, 101.

unit at 37:11—16. Certain important details are not given, and the unit is primarily concerned with demonstrating the evil intent of Zedekiah. As such, Pohlmann considers it secondary.[72]

While most of Ch. 38 is retained by Duhm, Kremers, Thiel, and Wanke as original, Pohlmann is more cautious.[73] Jer 38:7—13, which tells of Jeremiah's rescue by Ebed-Melek, presupposes 37:16 but nothing which intervenes (37:17—38:6). In Pohlmann's analysis, the unit 38:14,17,19—20 enshrines Jeremiah's actual response to Zedekiah's questioning during the siege. Here the opportunity to "submit and live" is extended to king by prophet that the city might not be burned (38:17). In Pohlmann's view, this original material has been considerably overworked in order to drive home the sharpness of the upcoming judgment over king, city, and people. The option given to Zedekiah (38:17) is foreclosed, as the anticipated judgment overshadows the possibility for surrender.[74] Ch. 39 moves quickly to the events of the Fall and the capture of Zedekiah. There is remarkable agreement among the scholars cited that Ch. 39 has been drawn up on the basis of the prior report of 2 Kings 25.[75] In Kremers' treatment, less than three verses make up this 5th episode (38:28b; 39:3,14), which in its greatly reduced form he can only entitle: Jeremiah's Fate During the Capture of Jerusalem.[76] Similarly, the word to Ebed-Melek (39:15—18) is generally taken as secondary, since the movement from 39:14 to 40:1 ff. is interrupted.

In an overview of critical analysis of these three chapters (Chs. 37—39), one gets a sense of the nature of the discussion. In Jeremiah 40—45* many of the same critical questions arise. This important post-587 section will be examined shortly. It is not to be doubted that problems in narrative sequence are confronted in Chs. 37—39. Many of the critical proposals offered by Pohlmann and others go a long way toward satisfying the modern desire for logical presentation. There seem to be three major areas in which problems emerge: (1) in relating events during the siege; (2) in focusing the precise threat to Jeremiah (king or princes or both); and (3) in determining a consistent message from the prophet concerning the fate of the king, people, and city. The third area is most important, since it is possible to isolate in Chs. 27—29 Jeremiah's message to Judah: that in submitting to Babylon, the remnant community can continue to

---

[72] Pohlmann, *Studien,* 69. Kremers sees only 37:19 as secondary ("Leidensgemeinschaft," 124); so also Thiel, *26—45,* 52 ff.; Duhm, *Jeremia,* 301.

[73] *Studien,* 69 ff.

[74] See Seitz, "Crisis," 89—90.

[75] Or some common source below them both. Rudolph sees Jer 39 "nachträglich aufgefüllt" from Jer 52 (*Jeremia,* 277).

[76] Kremers, "Leidensgemeinschaft," 126. So also Duhm, *Jeremia,* 309 ff.; Wanke, *Baruchs-chrift,* 108 ff.; Pohlmann, *Studien,* 93 ff.; Rudolph, *Jeremia,* 209 ff.; Thiel, *26—45,* 54 ff. Compare Noth, *Dtr History,* 74.

live in the land. There need be no destruction of the city or countryside (27:1—18). Now clearly one would have to allow that Jeremiah could, over the course of time or in view of changed circumstances, alter his position.[77] But at the same time one must be able to reasonably account for these changes. When sharp transitions are noted within a compact literary context, and there is also broader critical evidence for secondary supplementation, the likelihood of redactional overlay is strengthened. It is curious, for example, how a "certain repetitiousness" (Bright, *Jeremiah*, 233) dominates Chs. 37—39. In the space of two chapters, word is given to Zedekiah regarding the fate of the city on three separate occasions (37:6—10; 37:17; 38:15 ff.). In the latter case, Jer 38:17 is completely consistent with Jeremiah's stance in Chs. 27—29; yet even as it forcefully holds out for the possibility of life in Judah, 38:23 pronounces an irreversable judgment. Jeremiah is in and out of a makeshift prison (37:15), dungeon cells (37:16), house arrest (37:21), and a cistern (38:7), so often as to bewilder the reader. More to the point, it is not clear if Zedekiah is on the prophet's side (37:21; 38:20,25), or in league with the princes (37:15; 38:5). Does he (37:18; 38:15,24) or do the princes (37:15,20; 38:4,16,25—26) represent the primary threat to Jeremiah?

A further problem frustrates even redactional explanations for these changes. After secondary overlay is isolated, it is not clear that all tensions in the present narrative are done away with. Many details remain unaccounted for. For example, most take Jer 37:11—15, which tells of the retreat of the siege troops, as original. Yet at no point is one told how or when the siege resumed; these are the circumstances presupposed in Ch. 38 ff. But the most problematic issue concerns the literary scope of the original narrative. Pohlmann's *Vorlage* is barely a torso. He recognizes that certain significant features of the narrative must be accounted for, but can only make vague suggestions. For example, where is the original beginning and introduction to the narrative, once Jer 37:1—10 is taken as redactional? He makes the plausible suggestion that 34:1—7, in some form, could serve this purpose, but this is only the beginning of the problem.[78]

Similar questions can be raised about the radical surgery performed on Ch. 39. Is one to believe that a narrative chronicling events in the specific manner of Chs. 37—38*, 40—43* would fail to tell of the fall and capture of the city? Following the scholarly consensus, one is left with a sparse and odd report mentioning the fall of Jerusalem in a dependent clause (38:28b), a catalogue of Babylonian officials (39:3) who sat in the middle gate, and a note that Jeremiah was released to Gedaliah (39:14).[79]

---

[77] See the commentary of John Bright (*Jeremiah*, 232 ff.).

[78] *Studien*, 62 ff.

[79] Pohlmann says: "Im ursprünglichen Text (Jer 38,28b; 39,3.14*) wird lediglich Jerusalems Einnahme sowie die durch babylonische שׂרים (ohne Nebusaradan) veranlaßte Freilassung

One gets the suspicion that this torso is tolerated merely because it represents a plus over above the report of 2 Kgs 25:1—12, which this group of critics takes as prior to Jeremiah 39. Moreover, at a literary level the report of the flight and arrest of Zedekiah (39:4—8) forms a crucial link to Jeremiah's original words in Ch. 38. Without this scene, even the minimally isolated words of the prophet at 38:17, 19—22 (so Pohlmann) have no final referent. The reader is left to wonder what happened to the king and why no report of the fall of the city is given. Pohlmann says these are of no interest to a narrative which wants quickly to move to details of post-587 life, but this is hardly convincing.[80] Rather, such a conclusion only follows once priority is given to 2 Kings 25, and Jeremiah 39 is taken as dependent upon it. Otherwise the movement to a report of the fall of Jerusalem and the capture of Zedekiah is precisely what the reader expects as the next logical sequence in the narrative.

The type of critical logic which informs analysis of Jeremiah 37—39 points up a fundamental problem redactional analysis of prophetic literature must constantly address. It is not enough to make sense out of the supplementary level supplied by secondary redactors, in terms of theological intent and literary integration with the original narrative. One must also be able to give a coherent explanation for the literary shape of the *original narrative*, before it was received and editorially supplemented.[81] For if such priority is given to the freedom of secondary redactors, one begins to wonder why seams, narrative tensions, and the like are obvious in the present form of the text at all. Put bluntly, if the *Vorlage* was such a torso, and at such odds with the redactional position secondarily supplied, why did secondary redactors not drop it altogether? This is nowhere more obvious than in Pohlmann's redaction-critical work, where second and third levels of the text far overshadow any original document.

In the analysis to follow, it remains an important task to account for the original form of the narrative, its provenance and purpose. It is clear that the original narrative has undergone redactional supplementation with the intent (1) to anticipate the full judgment over king, people, and city; (2) to depict Zedekiah as the primary example of unheeding and life-

---

Jeremias konstatiert. Der Verfasser legt also keinerlei Wert auf die Mitteilung weiterer Einzelheiten. Nicht das Schicksal derer, die in die Hände der Babylonier fielen, das Los der für die Verbannung Bestimmten, das Verhalten der Babylonier, die unmittelbaren Folgen für Jerusalem, usw. . . ." (*Studien*, 106).

[80] Lohfink also follows this logic. Though he denies a biographical intent to the "Kurzgeschichte," he feels the narrative is so selective that it can avoid even reporting the Fall of Jerusalem: "Der Fall Jerusalems wird überhaupt nicht erzählt . . . Diese Geschichte setzt eine allgemeine Kenntnis der Vorgänge voraus und ist in dem, was sie bringt, viel zu selektiv, als daß man sie als Geschichte Judas oder Jerusalems für diesen Zeitabschnitt betrachten könnte" ("Kurzgeschichte," 332).

[81] This remains the concern of Kremers, for example, in his search for the original cycle of episodes that formed the "Ur-text."

threatening disobedience, to prophet and larger populace; (3) to blunt any statements found in the original document which underscore the possibility of continued life in the land, either before or after 587. As such, this redactional layer is in coordination with editorial efforts identified earlier in the book (Chs. 21—24; 27—29). But that the original document was as spotty and undeveloped as Pohlmann maintains is unconvincing.

B. The Scope of the Original Chronicle

With Thiel, the conclusion to be reached is that there was available to secondary redactors, located in Babylonian exile and in proximity to Ezekiel traditions, ". . . offenbar schon eine relativ geschlossene Darstellung der Schicksale Jeremias in der Zeit vor, um und nach der Eroberung Jerusalems . . .".[82] This scribal document was, however, concerned with the fate of Zedekiah, various key figures in Jerusalem, and the broader remnant community before and after 587, as well as with the specific figure of the prophet. Its original introduction is not to be found in Ch. 37, but earlier in the central section of the book (Chs. 21—36), specifically within Chs. 27—29. The core of these chapters enshrines the major post-597 statements of Jeremiah regarding life in Judah and life in Exile (27:1—18; 28; 29:1—9,15,20—32). They were delivered by the prophet in the opening years of Zedekiah's rule (see 27:1; 28:1 and note 2 above), at a point in time when the distinct fate of the separate communities had become a reality. In the face of prophetic opposition in Judah and Babylon, Jeremiah takes the unpopular line that submission to Nebuchadnezzar, in Exile or in the land, overrides hopes in either district for swift reunification. Opposition does not end for Jeremiah in these first years, but follows him right up to the events of 587 and beyond. A major feature of the scribal document in its fullest form is the chronicling of conflict between Jeremiah and various śārîm in Jerusalem (27—29*; 20:1—6; 37:11—15; 38:1—6). In all cases the opposition comes as a result of Jeremiah's consistent message calling for submission to Babylon, which is taken in some quarters as high treason (38:1—6). Its author is to be sought among those scribal families that survived the 597 deportations to remain in the land along with Jeremiah. The narrator depicts events candidly and directly, though his alignment with Jeremiah is unmistakeable. The prophet, whose activity and message is at all points a source of interest, remains the central figure of the chronicle as it narrates significant episodes in the life of the remnant community before and after 587.

---

[82] Cited from Pohlmann, *Studien*, 49, n. 15 (the quote appears on p. 620 f. in Thiel's original dissertation [Humboldt-Universität Berlin, 1970]). See CHART EIGHT below for a synopsis.

In the present form of the Book of Jeremiah, episodes from the original scribal document have been separated from each other and moved to different locations in the book in order to serve as pre-texts for redactional elaboration.[83] Their original linkage within the scribal narrative will have to be demonstrated in some detail, but several initial observations can be made. It is to be noted, for example, how many chapters within the central section of the present book take their cue and setting from episodes apparently integral to Chs. 37—39*. Jer 20:1—6, which tells of the harsh treatment of Jeremiah at the hands of Pashur, priest and chief officer in the temple, could easily fit within Jer 37—38. The inquiry of Zedekiah's delegation, found at 21:1 ff., has some obvious relationship to the 37:3 ff. inquiry, however one determines the nature of this relationship.[84] Jer 32:1—5 seeks a setting during a term of Jeremiah's imprisonment (32:2 || 37:4,15,16,21), as does Jer 33:1 ff. Jer 34:1—7 not only fits well within the time frame set forth in Chs. 37—39, there are obvious language resonances from 32:3—5; 37:9—10; 38:23, suggesting a common editorial background. Moreover, Jer 34:1—7 has very little in common with 34:8 ff., and the two blocks appear only secondarily connected.[85]

With respect to the relationship with Chs. 37 ff., there are two distinct forms of editorial work within Jeremiah 20—36. In some cases, scenes appear to have been pulled from another literary setting (viz, the original scribal chronicle of the form described here) where they can be re-integrated with relative success (20:1—6*; 32:2,6—15; 34:1—7*). In other instances, a setting from the original narrative is simply evoked without direct literary borrowing (21:1 ff.; 24:1 ff.; 33:1 ff.). In either case, however, one can spot the redactional motivation behind these rearrangements.

---

[83] Though this is not stated outright, it is suggested at points by Thiel (*Redaktion, 26—45, 29—43*). Pohlmann also makes some important observations about the relationship between sections in Jer 21—36 (esp. 32:6—15; 34:1—7) and Jer 37—43* (*Studien, 46—7; 62—4*).

[84] This is the kind of topic that draws enormous critical attention. For a discussion and bibliography, see G. Wanke, *Baruchschrift,* 96 ff.; Pohlmann, *Studien,* 43 ff.; Thiel, *1—25,* 231 ff.; Duhm, *Jeremia,* 168; Hyatt, *Jeremiah,* 977; they basically argue that Jer 21:1—7(8—10) is the "Deuteronomic editor's rewriting of the event of 37:3—10" (Hyatt, 977). Weippert (*Prosareden,* 68 ff.) and Bright (*Jeremiah,* 217) defend the independence of the two units, noting different temporal settings and persons in each envoy. Kremers argues for a common source below both reports (Diss, 22); Wanke heads in this same direction (102).

[85] This is almost universally acknowledged. Note too that 34:8 ff. presupposes a Babylonian retreat (vv. 21—22), a fact clearly not of issue in 34:1—7. For this reason, Bright lumps 34:1—7 together with 21:1—10, and places 34:8—22 with 37:1—10. Compare Cornill's rearrangement (C. H. Cornill, *The Book of the Prophet Jeremiah: Critical Edition of the Hebrew Text Arranged in Chronological Order with Notes* [SBOT 11; Leipzig: J. C. Hinrichs'sche, 1895] 71—72) and see the discussion below. See also Duhm, *Jeremia,* 277 ff.; Rudolph, *Jeremia,* 187 ff.; Thiel, *26—45,* 38—39; Hyatt, *Jeremiah,* 1053—5; E. Lipinski, "Prose ou poésie en Jér XXXIV 1—7?" *VT* 24 (1974) 112 ff.

Specifically, the judgment against Zedekiah and the remnant community is anticipated early on (Chs. 21; 24; 33), even as the return of the Golah is envisioned (24:4—7; 30:1—3; 31:31—34; 32:36 ff.; 33). The opening pretexts of Chs. 32 and 34 have the potential for emphasizing (1) Jeremiah's solidarity with the remnant community (purchase of land at Anathoth), or (2) his message of assurance to Zedekiah, that he will die in peace and be mourned abroad — in stark contrast to Jehoiakim (22:18 ff.) or the exiled Jehoiachin (22:24 ff.). Accordingly, they have been pulled from their original literary context and extensively supplemented.

In its present location, Jeremiah's word to Zedekiah at especially 34:4—5 has been considerably blunted by the addition of Jer 34:8 ff. In this unit, Zedekiah and the Jerusalemites are depicted as reneging on an agreement to free slaves within the city. For this breach of faith, the city and king are to receive even stronger punishment: non-burial (v. 20), total desolation (v. 22), and the return of Babylonian troops, whose retreat is presupposed but not recorded.[86] Similarly, Jer 32:6—12 depicts a Jeremiah who in obedience to Yahweh's word returns to Anathoth to purchase land. There is again widespread agreement that this unit (vv. 6—15) represents the oldest core of the chapter, and has secondarily received a redactional setting (vv. 1—5) and elaboration (vv. 16—44).[87] The opening unit (32:1—5) draws upon a setting from Jeremiah 37/38 (Jeremiah in court of guard) and fills it out with a composite word to Zedekiah (vv. 3—5) familiar from other settings (34:2—3; 21:3 ff.; 37:4—10). It implies, like these other units, that hopes are strong in the capital for either a Babylonian retreat or a Judahite military victory.[88]

The core unit (32:6—15) fits remarkably well in the context suggested by Chs. 37/38.[89] There, too, one hears of an attempt by Jeremiah to return to the land of Benjamin (37:11—15), thwarted by a sentry who, on the charge of desertion, handed the prophet over to princes for a beating and imprisonment. But in the next episode, King Zedekiah puts Jeremiah in the court of the guard not with hostile intent, as is the case in 32:3 ff., but because the prophet requested protection from the princes (37:20). Moreover, Jer 38:1—6 details renewed opposition from the princes, including a call for the death sentence. The charge against the prophet is summarized in 38:2—3: Jeremiah has called for those in the city to "go out to the Chaldeans" and "have his life as a prize of war and live;" the city offers no defense, and it will be taken (38:2—3). The activity of 32:6—15, the

---

[86] See Cornill, *Jeremiah,* 71; Thiel, *26—45,* 42—3; Duhm, *Jeremiah,* 279—84; Hyatt, *Jeremiah,* 1055—6.

[87] Thiel, *26—45,* 31: "In 6b liegt der älteste Bestandteil des Kapitels vor, ein authentischer Selbstbericht"; he terms the opening unit a "Situationsskizze" and "Summarium." See also Duhm, *Jeremia,* 261 ff.; Rudolph, *Jeremia,* 176.

[88] See Thiel, *26—45,* 29—30.

[89] Pohlmann, *Studien,* 47.

purchase of land at Anathoth, not only brings the prophet out into public (a fact which is presupposed by 38:1 ff., but not by 37:21), it also provides a coherent explanation for the fierce opposition from the princes and their charge that he "is weakening the hands of the people" left to defend Jerusalem. In other words, Jer 32:6—15 fits quite well between the present end of Ch. 37 and beginning of Ch. 38. It provides an important linking episode, anticipated by 37:11—15, that helps clarify the sequence of events. In Jer 37:11—15 the prophet tried unsuccessfully to return to Anathoth. A new word emboldens him in 32:6—15 and purchase is made. Note the same interest in details (sealed deed, scales, cost, conditions, open copy) in 32:6—15 that runs throughout Jeremiah 37—43*, and the same setting (court of guard: 32:12) where Jeremiah was last seen in 37:21.

When the unit is placed after Ch. 37, it clarifies the charges of the princes in 38:1 ff. It also provides important insight into the prophet's stance in Judah's last days consistent with Chs. 27—29 — and the nature of opposition to it. Jeremiah's purchase of land in his home territory underscores his solidarity with those in Judah and his conviction that submission to Babylon can mean ongoing life in the land. This activity is not carried out in disregard for the fate of the exiles. The clear thrust of vv. 14—15 is that Jeremiah's present purchase opens the way for the possibility of future purchase.[90] But the act of return to Anathoth also maintains a crucial significance for the remnant community. This significance, not for the future but for the present, is underscored in the opposition from the princes, both in Jer 37:11—15 and — if this rearrangement is correct — in Jer 38:1—7. They interpret such action on the part of the prophet as desertion, not submission to Yahweh's servant Nebuchadnezzar.

In the lengthy concluding prayer and sermon (32:16—44) the significance of the Anathoth purchase has shifted entirely to the future, as the return to Judah of those scattered is envisioned (32:36 ff.) and land is purchased again (32:42 ff.). In language familiar from restoration passages of Ezekiel (11:17—21; 36:22—38), a new people will be gathered and a new relationship will be inaugurated. But also, consistent with Ezekiel, this will happen only when a full end has been accomplished (Jer 32:26—35). In other words, in the present form of Ch. 32 Jeremiah's purchase of land becomes a kind of symbolic act of faith at a point when all is doomed (32:25), and as such functions only with reference to future restoration. The possibility of continued life in Judah is absolutely fore-

---

[90] It is unnecessary to take 32:15 as secondary, as does Herrmann (*Heilserwartung,* 185, 7), who classifies it under "Kleinen Heilssprüche deuteronomistischer Bearbeitung." Herrmann is essentially correct, however, to stress that in the present form of Ch. 32 (i. e., with vv. 16—44), the thrust remains on the adverb "again" (*'ôd*) and the future repurchase by returnees, rather than on the original purchase by the prophet.

closed as the Babylonian onslaught is depicted (32:26—35). The field purchased by Jeremiah becomes only a field in a land of which the prophet has said "it is a desolation, without man or beast" (32:43). Here classic pre-597 language (see 9:10) is directly applied to the post-597 activity of the prophet in such a way that any original hopes associated with Jeremiah's return to Benjamin, at a point prior to the Fall of Jerusalem, now relate purely to the return and re-occupation of the land.[91]

Redactional analysis of Jeremiah 32 reveals a core unit (vv. 6—15) separable from its surrounding literary context. In this unit, following a word from Yahweh (vv. 6, 8) the prophet redeems the property of his uncle. As Bright puts it, ". . . one can well imagine that in disturbed times, such as Judah was undergoing in 588/7, few would be eager to invest in real estate."[92] The significance of the act lies as much in Jeremiah's bold investment in present life in Judah as in hopes for future restoration. The unit is significant for other reasons. Many have suggested that the passage (or all of 32:1—16) fits the circumstances of Chs. 37—39 better than its present location.[93] Original placement following Ch. 37 is quite likely, for the reasons given above.

There is another reason supporting an original placement following Ch. 37. The opening unit of Ch. 32 (vv. 1—5) sets the Anathoth purchase at a point in time when the siege had resumed. In other words, the Babylonian retreat mentioned in Jer 37:5,11 and implied at 34:21 is over, and the troops have returned. It is quite likely that when Jer 32:6—15 followed Ch. 37, a note something like we find at 32:2 prefaced the unit. It is clear, for example, that 32:2 picks up directly with the concluding note of 37:21.[94] More to the point, there is in the present form of the narrative in Chs. 37—38 no explicit mention of the siege resuming. The retreat is mentioned in Ch. 37 at several points, and its significance is debated (37:6—10). In Ch. 38, the obvious implication of the charge of the princes in 38:2 ff. is that the Babylonians have returned, as in fact they have (see Ch. 39). If the core unit of Ch. 32, together with a temporal notice supplied in 32:2*, was originally found between Chs. 37 and 38, the sequence of events is better portrayed.

C. Excursus: The Fate of King and City

In its present location, Jer 32:1—5 as a full unit does more than provide a temporal setting for vv. 6—15. It provides an introductory speech from Jeremiah to Zedekiah, which in form and content appears to

---

[91] Pohlmann, *Studien*, 46—7.

[92] *Jeremiah*, 239.

[93] See even the RSV notes; also Bright, *Jeremiah*, 236.

[94] Bright puts it well: "These verses (2—5) are an editorial parenthesis explaining the circumstances of Jeremiah's imprisonment. Had the passage been transmitted with chs. xxxvii-xxxviii, where it belongs chronologically, they would not have been necessary" (*Jeremiah*, 236).

be a kind of editorial compendium: (1) the city will be taken; (2) Zedekiah will not escape; (3) Zedekiah will be deported. A review of Jeremiah's pre-587 counsel to Zedekiah reveals that it is point (1) which most consistently appears (32:3; 34:2,22; 37:8,17; 38:3). At no point is it suggested that the city (or temple) offers any particular protection, theological or military (Ch. 7); in fact, the other consistent counsel ("submit and live") often takes the form "he who goes out (*hayyōṣē'*) to the Chaldeans shall live" (38:2). In editorial sections to be attributed to the Exilic Redaction, point (1) is often accompanied by a sharper note, ". . . and he (Nebuchadnezzar) will burn it with fire" (34:2,22; 37:8,10; 38:23) or some more pointed description (see 21:1 – 10; 32:26 ff.; 34:20 ff.).

The Exilic Redaction has not simply invented this forceful language. As noted, the imagery is imbedded in pre-597 sections of the book.[95] Moreover, the same language can be used by Jeremiah in contexts in which king and people are offered a choice for or against submission (27:8; 38:17).[96] Yet the language in these contexts functions *conditionally;* from the pre-587 standpoint, it is not a statement of fact or a prediction of the future. This is made clear even on the eve of the Fall of the city, in Jer 38:17 – 22.

> "If you surrender to the princes of the king of Babylon, then your life will be spared and this city will not be burned with fire, and you and your house shall live" (Jer 38:17).

Extreme judgment follows as a condition of disobedience. But Jeremiah can lay out the alternatives even as he pleads, in the immediate post-597 period, "Serve the king of Babylon and live; Why should this city become a desolation?" (27:17); or, on the eve of the Fall, "Obey now the voice of the LORD in what I say to you, and it shall be well with you, and your life shall be spared" (38:20).

From the perspective of the Exilic Redaction, the wrong choices were ultimately made, especially by King Zedekiah (39:1 – 7). Moreover, the precise circumstances are known to them regarding the Fall of the city and the extent and nature of the Babylonian assault. It is for this reason that point (1) is so often accompanied by the more extreme depiction of the fate of the city, *especially when this fate is discussed in the context of Zedekiah's fate.* A survey of passages in which the burning of the city and widespread desolation figures prominently in Jeremiah's language reveals this to be true (see 21:1 – 10; 24:8 – 10; 32:3 – 4; 34:2 – 3; 34:21 – 22; 37:6 – 10; 38:23). In the majority of cases, the imagery appears in the context of a word from Jeremiah to Zedekiah. More to the point, in these

---

[95] Or passages relating pre-597 events in redactionally constructed scenes (especially Ch. 26, see v. 9).

[96] Sword/pestilence/famine come when one seeks the defense of the city (38:2).

cases the extreme sentence of judgment cannot be avoided through obedient submission — it functions as an irreversable description of the fate in store for king and city.

Point (2), the notion that Zedekiah could escape, is closely linked with point (1) and the demand for submission. Like point (1) it involves an alternative: that Zedekiah could somehow escape the king of Babylon or avoid submission. Though it appears that the possibility of escape is dependent upon the final outcome of Ch. 39, in which report is given of an attempt to flee and the tragic consequences, there is no reason to assume that this language has been redactionally developed. As numerous commentators point out, the thrust of Jeremiah's counsel is found in the phrase "you shall speak to him face to face (lit., 'mouth to mouth,' *dibber-pîw 'im-pîw*) and see him eye to eye" (32:4; 34:3).[97] The main thrust remains on the sure transfer of King Zedekiah to Babylonian authority. If one was searching for a pure *vaticinium ex eventu,* developed with knowledge of the events of Ch. 39, far greater detail would be expected (see 39:5—7).[98] In view of Zedekiah's blinding (39:7), 32:4 would have to be taken as a harshly ironic half-prediction.

The same is not true of point (3), the prediction of deportation. Though it is clear that Jeremiah had firsthand knowledge of the deportation of Zedekiah's successor Jehoiachin, at no other point in the present text is the future deportation of Zedekiah emphasized. As in 32:4, Zedekiah, like the city, is to be given into the power of the Babylonians; he is to be "led out" (38:22) together with other members of the court. At this juncture, talk of deportation moves beyond the more immediate horizon of 32:4. Moreover, throughout the book if there is a consistent thrust to Jeremiah's post-597 word to community and king, it remains at the level of submission or direct punishment. It could be argued that deportation is too light a form of judgment.[99] Even in levels of the text viewed as redactional, the deportation of the community as punishment is not emphasized, but rather their thorough destruction (see, for example, 21:7; 24:8—10). In its present context, 32:5 interprets v. 4 as meaning Zedekiah will be deported, a notion that seems to go beyond the more restricted sense of the original verse. It was likely developed in view of Zedekiah's final deportation, as a more detailed interpretation of 32:4.

As stated above, 32:3—5 offers a paraphrase of Jeremiah's counsel to Zedekiah from the standpoint of the Exilic Redaction. Specific features

---

[97] Bright, for example, translates: "Zedekiah . . . will certainly be handed over to the king of Babylon and, confronted by him face to face, will be made to answer to him personally" (*Jeremia,* 235).

[98] See the comments of Duhm on the parallel verse in 34:3, *Jeremia,* 278.

[99] After all, Jeremiah knows well enough of the fate of the community in Babylon, lively enough to have prophets, correspondence and contact with Judah, etc. His picture of exilic life does not emphasize its harshness (see 29:4—7). *šālôm* is possible in Babylon.

of Jeremiah's full word to Zedekiah and post-597 community are included, and others have been added. The same editorial work is to be noted elsewhere. Jer 34:2−3 is almost a precise duplicate to Jer 32:3−5, with the added note, discussed above, that promises a burning of the city by Nebuchadnezzar. The odd thing about this paraphrase is its positioning. It abuts a word from Jeremiah to Zedekiah in 34:4−5, promising in some distinction to the content and tone of 32:2−3 a peaceful death for the king and proper funeral proceedings. It has already been noted how 34:8−22 forms a unified piece, only loosely connected to 34:1−7. In this sense, Ch. 34 has some of the same characteristics as Ch. 32.

Jer 34:1−7 is mentioned at this point because of the similarities between the counsel of the prophet in 34:2−3 and in 32:2b−5. Both units function redactionally, setting the scene for what follows, and they may be at least partial summaries of authentic Jeremiah counsel to Zedekiah.[100] There are also similar editorial characteristics in both chapters: specifically, the juxtaposing of long prose units (32:16−44; 34:8−22), in which the absolute judgment over Zedekiah and city is emphasized, with briefer units (32:2,6−15; 34:4−7*) in which the fate of city, king, or remnant community is not so negatively depicted. The original placement of Jer 32:2,6−15 preceded Jer 38 in the original Scribal Chronicle. In a similar manner, the circumstances of Jer 34:1−7 are related to the events portrayed in Jer 37:1−21. Moreover, in the final form of Ch. 34 mention is made of a Babylonian withdrawal in 34:21 that has not been prepared for in the context of Ch. 34 itself. In other words, Jer 34:21, a verse which occurs in a secondary prose section of Ch. 34, assumes information available in direct form only in Ch. 37 (vv. 5, 11). All this underscores the likelihood that at a point prior to redactional intervention, the opening unit Jer 34:1−7* circulated with Ch. 37, where a temporary Babylonian retreat was mentioned.[101] Yet to be determined is the extent of the unit as it first appeared in Ch. 37. The larger question is begged as to the original form of Ch. 37, a chapter which itself exhibits considerable unevenness in narrative presentation.[102]

D. Jeremiah 34:1−7 and 37:1−10: The Delegation from Zedekiah

Unfortunately, the opening unit of Ch. 34 (vv. 1−7) is more uneven than that of Ch. 32. There is a sort of double-superscription provided first in 34:1 and then in 34:6−7. In the present form of the text, 34:6−7

---

[100] This is particularly true of 34:2−3, which seems connected through the contrasting 'ak with what follows in vv. 3−4: the promise a peaceful death for Zedekiah. However, references to the burning of the city and the deportation are secondary (see below). Also, Rudolph, Jeremia, 186, 189.

[101] See below, 489 ff.; also, Pohlmann, Studien, 63, n. 90b.

[102] So Pohlmann, Wanke, Lohfink, Seitz, Rietzschel, Kremers, Ackroyd.

appears to function as an introductory note to 34:8 ff., setting this unit at a slightly later time period. In Jer 34:1, Nebuchadnezzar is fighting against all the cities around Jerusalem, while in 34:7, only Lachish and Azekah are left. The movement is, however, clumsy because 33:8—22 functions quite well as an independent unit, complete with its own superscription (34:8).

As a possible solution to this problem, many critics take vv. 6—7 as the original superscription and read Jer 34:1 as a secondary editorial unit.[103] Rudolph, for example, points out in the description of 34:1 the "etwas bombastische Bezeichnung" of Nebuchadnezzar's army.[104] The whole opening verse is unusually comprehensive in its depiction of the military threat to Judah.

> The word which came to Jeremiah from the LORD, when Nebuchadnezzar king of Babylon and all his army and all the kingdoms of the earth under his dominion and all the peoples were fighting against Jerusalem and all of its cities.

The personal appearance of Nebuchadnezzar is also striking; it is not mentioned in 34:7, nor is it required from a strictly historical standpoint.[105] In fact, during the later capture of Jerusalem, the Babylonian king is depicted as actively involved only from his headquarters at Riblah (Jer 39:5—7,11), in contrast to his military officers (39:3,13), siege troops, and Nebuzaradan, captain of the guard (rab-ṭabbāḥîm). The latter appears to be in complete charge of affairs (see Jer 39:9 ff.). That Nebuchadnezzar still put in appearances in military engagements in Judah is not to be doubted.[106] But the overall tone of the verse is far too sweeping ("all his army, all the kingdoms of the earth, all the peoples, all Jerusalem's cities"). It is a general summary verse which collapses a variety of Babylonian and contingent-troop maneuvers in order to depict a massive assault on Jerusalem and Judah.[107] It places the reader at some general moment prior to the events of 34:7, the original time-setting of the oracle of 34:2—5*. As such, Jer 34:6—7 in the present form of the chapter is awkwardly related to the long unit at Jer 34:8—22, as though two phases are being described. Mention of Nebuchadnezzar may have been specifically made in Jer 34:1 since he is referred to within 34:2—5*.

As Thiel and the older critics point out, in the present form of Jer 34:1—7 the double mention of Jeremiah speaking to Zedekiah (34:2,6) is

---

[103] Thiel, 26—45, 38 ff.; Duhm, Jeremia, 277; Rudolph, Jeremia, 187; Hyatt, Jeremiah, 1053—55.
[104] Jeremia, 187.
[105] For events leading up to 587, see Malamat, "Last Years," 214 ff. On Nebuchadnezzar's personal involvement in battles in Phoenicia and broader Hatti-land, see Katzenstein, Tyre, 318—9.
[106] We unfortunately have no entry from the Babylonian Chronicle for events after 594 B. C.
[107] For a description of these maneuvers, see Malamat, "Last Years," 215 ff.; Hayes & Miller, 472 ff.

redundant. While this is true, it is also to be noted that the "word to Zedekiah" in the core of the unit is only loosely linked to either setting (34:1−2a; 34:6−7). Jeremiah's word is motivated only by the historical reality of siege and attack, with no further explanation.[108] In his word to Zedekiah, there is the hint that the king may have hoped for escape. However, in this context and given this abrupt movement, the promise of a peaceful death for the king (34:4), juxtaposed with the dire vision of 34:2,3 and 34:21−22, is unusual.

In the original form of the unit, vv. 6−7 functioned to provide the temporal setting of Jeremiah's word to Zedekiah in vv. 2b−5. As such, vv. 1−2a are secondary, and function in the present chapter in its two-stage presentation. The original word to Zedekiah began with the second messenger formula.[109] Because of its unusual tone and content, the promise to the king in 34:4−5 is almost universally regarded as original. In the first place, though Zedekiah was not slain by the sword (v. 4), the promise of a peaceful death (*běšālôm tāmût*) and extensive lamentation ("as for your fathers, the former kings") are contradicted by the facts of Zedekiah's trial, blinding, and deportation to Babylon. Indeed, it is to be noted that the promise of funeral proceedings "like your fathers, the former kings," if taken literally, implies burial in Judah (i. e., like Josiah, Zedekiah's father; see 2 Kgs 22:20; 23:30).[110] Again, though it is a subtle reference, it is perfectly consistent with Jeremiah's perspective regarding the possibility of continued life in the land following submission to Nebuchadnezzar. Rudolph has argued that the words "in Jerusalem" in v. 6 are awkward and have been transposed from the preceding word to Zedekiah: "You will die in peace, in Jerusalem."[111] Though this is unconvincing, it is to be noted that the force of vv. 4−5, even without Rudolph's alteration, is undone by the promise of deportation in v. 3b.

The sense of contrast implied in the *'ak* of 34:4 was an original part of Jeremiah's word. But this contrast is pushed too far with the explicit reference to deportation in v. 3b. The same can be said of Jeremiah's insistence that the city will be burned (34:2b).[112] In the original form of the oracle, Jeremiah insists that the city "will be given into the hand of

---

[108] Duhm, *Jeremia,* 278.

[109] Note how overloaded v. 2 appears with the double messenger formula, the first providing a command to Jeremiah, the second providing the word to Zedekiah. See Thiel's discussion (*26−45,* 38).

[110] A peaceful death for Josiah is interpreted as meaning, "your eyes will not see all the evil which I will bring upon this place" (2 Kgs 22:20). This promise is not contradicted by even the tragic death of Josiah at Megiddo (see also the word to Hezekiah in 2 Kgs 20:19). The promise to Zedekiah goes beyond this (Jer 34:4).

[111] *Jeremia,* 186, 189.

[112] Rudolph correctly sees these sections as supplementary, made with the knowledge of Zedekiah's actual treatment and the fate of the city. (See also CHART EIGHT below).

the King of Babylon"; Zedekiah shall not escape, but will be delivered over to Nebuchadnezzar. *Yet,* he will not die by the sword but will die in peace, and be buried with funeral proceedings appropriate for Judahite kings. This is the sense of *'ak* at 34:4.

Of course the striking thing about Jeremiah's word to Zedekiah is the contrast it makes with his statements to Jehoiakim and Jehoiachin (22:18—19; 22:24—30), as well as Jehoahaz. Jeremiah enjoins Israel not to mourn for Josiah, who is dead, but for his son Jehoahaz, Zedekiah's brother, who was carried off (22:10). By contrast, no lament is to be raised for Jehoiakim, and though his death is not mentioned, his less than royal burial indicates no peaceful end (22:18—19). The word to Jehoiachin focuses on his being hurled off, in order to die in a country not his own (vv. 24—28). The sense of contrast with the word to Zedekiah in 34:2b—5*, including even the promise of Babylonian capture, is unmistakeable.[113] In fact, a comparison of Jer 34:4—5 and Jer 22:18—19 gives the distinct impression that the word to Zedekiah has been delivered in conscious contrast to Jehoiakim, his half-brother, if not also to Jehoiachin, his nephew.[114] The additions regarding deportation (v. 3) and the burning of the city (v. 2) bring the word to Zedekiah in closer proximity to these other prophetic statements to the royal house, but the sense of stark contrast is not done away with.[115]

If this analysis of the unit is correct, then Jeremiah delivered the oracle to the king "when the army of the king of Babylon was fighting against Jerusalem" and only Lachish and Azekah were left of the fortified cities of Judah (34:7). Ch. 32 provided a unified episode (32:2,6—15) only secondarily brought into its present location, having originally functioned in the context of Chs. 37 and 38. The word to Zedekiah in Ch. 34 has the same loose connection with its present literary context, prefacing a long piece on the (insincere) manumission of slaves (34:8—22). The present merger of these two originally separate units was discussed above. There

---

[113] In this context, the note at Lam 4:20 is striking. Apparently even after the destruction of Jerusalem, it can be said of Zedekiah, in a dirge, "The breath of our nostrils, the LORD's *mašiaḥ,* was taken in their pits, he of whom we said, 'Under his shadow we will live among the nations'." It hardly needs mentioning what a contrast this dirge over Zedekiah forms to Ezekiel's dirge (Ezek 19).

[114] Regarding Jehoiakim: "They shall not lament for him saying, 'Ah lord!'" (*lō'-yispĕdû lô hôy 'ādôn,* Jer 22:18. Regarding Zedekiah: "So men shall burn spices and lament for you, saying 'Ah lord'" (*wĕhôy 'ādôn yispĕdû-lāk*), Jer 34:5.

[115] The Exilic Redaction has attempted to dull this contrast even more consciously by framing oracles directed at Jehoiakim and Jehoiachin (Ch. 22) with Chs. 21 and 24. In these chapters, Zedekiah is explicitly singled out for harsh judgment as head of the disobedient remnant community (21:3—10; 24:8—10). Note a similar move within Ch. 34 (esp. 34:21—22). Lengthy reference has already been made to the Ezekiel traditions, which share much in common with the Exilic Redaction of Jeremiah, especially their evaluation of Judahite Kingship.

is good evidence that, like Jer 32:2,6—15, the word to Zedekiah (Jer 34:6—7,2b—5*) originally functioned in a different narrative context. This is the same narrative context from which Jer 32:2,6—15 was drawn: the Scribal Chronicle of Jer 37—39/40—43. Right at the beginning of Ch. 37, following the transition verses (37:1—2) linking Ch. 37 with Ch. 36, the reader learns that Zedekiah sent a delegation to the prophet. The precise historical circumstances are not given in 37:1—2, but are loosely supplied at 37:5.[116] There are several reasons why the setting proposed in 37:5 is secondary, while that introduced in Jer 34:6—7;2b—5 functions better with the delegation notice of 37:3.[117] In other words, the direct and sober word from Jeremiah in 32:2b—5* formed the original response to Zedekiah, after the king sent a delegation to him, as is reported in Jer 37:3. In order to establish this argument conclusively, another problem must first be faced.

Both Jeremiah 37 and 21 include reports of Zedekiah sending a delegation to the prophet. In Ch. 21, the verb $drš$ is used, and the inquiry is clarified as intending a Babylonian withdrawal (21:2). In Ch. 37, a different verb is used ($htpll$) but the circumstances are similar. In fact, the reader is told that the Chaldeans had *already* withdrawn, so that in this instance the "prayer" of Jeremiah is intended to keep the Babylonians away. In both chapters, the harshest possible response from the prophet is given (see 37:6—10). In Jer 21:3—7, Yahweh intends to do the fighting that will destroy Jerusalem, and calls upon Nebuchadnezzar to punish any survivors (21:7—8).

There have been many different attempts to clarify the relationship between these two chapters. Those who argue for the authenticity of both units, 21:1—7 and 37:3—10, also insist upon their independence from one another.[118] They note that the delegations are slightly different; they feel the circumstances are also quite distinct.[119] In short, they see them as two separate episodes that are similar for other than redactional reasons. By contrast, a more extreme position sees *both* episodes as secondary, created solely for redactional purposes.[120]

---

[116] Wanke puts it this way, "Im Gegensatz zu 42:2(4,20), wo die gleiche Formulierung ($htpll$) begegnet, fehlt hier jede Motivierung für das Ansinnen Zedekias, so daß die eigentliche Absicht der Gesandtschaft im Dunkeln bleibt" (*Baruchschrift,* 98).

[117] In broad strokes, a similar argument is mounted by Rudolph (*Jeremia,* 201) and Cornill (*Jeremia,* 71—2).

[118] This position is strenuously defended by Weippert, *Prosareden,* 67 ff. Earlier, Giesebrecht, *Jeremia,* 116 ff. Also, Bright, *Jeremiah,* 216 ff. For a thorough bibliography and discussion, see Thiel, *1—25,* 231 ff.

[119] Bright: "Whereas that incident, as we shall see (Ch. 37), took place somewhat later, while the siege had been temporarily lifted because of the approach of the Egyptians, this one clearly fell at the very beginning of the campaign . . ." (*Jeremiah,* 217). Also Weippert, *Prosareden,* 69.

[120] For a full discussion, see Pohlmann, *Studien,* 43—45 (+ note 144).

In the view of this study, Pohlmann is right to stress the literary relationship between Chs. 21 and 24, and to see 21:1—10 as a redactional piece meant to foreclose on the possibility of ongoing life in the land.[121] He is also correct to point out that such a possibility is firmly imbedded in Jeremiah tradition, notably in 38:17 ff. As such, the delegation-account of Ch. 21 has been developed redactionally, and has a literary relationship with accounts in Jeremiah 37/38. However, Pohlmann's position is that all of Ch. 37, with the exception of 37:11—15, has also been secondarily composed by redactors.[122] It is far more likely that there existed within the original scribal narrative an account of Zedekiah's sending a delegation to the prophet, at a time of military crisis, as is mentioned in 37:3. Jer 21:1—3/7—10 was developed on the basis of this authentic scribal report to serve a very different purpose in a different location.[123] So as not to form an exact duplicate, the figures who appear in the delegation are different in Ch. 21.[124] On the other hand, the minute temporal distinctions between Chs. 21 and 37 of the kind argued for by Bright and Weippert are unconvincing. In sum, it is unlikely that both episodes were created out of thin air. Jer 37:3 ff. contained the original report.[125] However, Jer 37:5—10 did not circulate with it originally. This unit is similar in form and thrust to 21:3—10, and was supplied by the same exilic redactor that edited the scribal narrative and shaped Jer 21:1—10 in its entirety.[126] The delegation received another word from Jeremiah, and it appears now at 34:2b—5*.

There are two chief reasons why the setting proposed for the delegation from Zedekiah at 37:5 is artificial. First of all, it is more reasonable to assume that a delegation was sent to the prophet at a time of military crisis, such as is described in Jer 34:6—7, rather than during a retreat.[127] However, in its present form, v. 5 functions as an introduction to the unit at 37:6—10, which gives a response from the prophet related to hopes for

---

[121] *Studien,* 44; Thiel, *1—25,* 237; Seitz, "Crisis," 81 ff.

[122] So also Kremers, who feels that both 21:1—7 and 37:3—10 were developed from a common source (citation provided by Wanke, *Baruchschrift,* 102, n. 33). Recourse to the theory of a "common-source" is unconvincing at a point when redactional analysis reveals other possibilities for the similarity between narratives. Wanke's position is similar, though more strained (*Baruchschrift,* 102).

[123] Rudolph, *Jeremia,* 116—7; Thiel, *1—25,* 232 ff.

[124] The figure of Pashur ben Malchiah in 21:1 (not Pashur ben Immer, the priest, 20:1) appears at another point in the Scribal Chronicle, at Jer 38:1. He is a "prince" (*śar*), not a priest (Zephaniah ben Maaseiah, 37:3; 29:25; 2 Kgs 25:18?), and can appear together with other *śārîm* (Shephatiah ben Mattan, 38:1; Jucal ben Shelemiah, 37:3; 38:1). See especially the comments of Thiel, *1—25,* 232; also Rudolph, *Jeremia,* 116—17.

[125] With Thiel and Rudolph; Wanke, Kremers, and Pohlmann take all of 37:1—10 as secondary.

[126] Pohlmann, *Studien,* 53 ff.; Wanke, *Baruchschrift,* 101—2; Duhm, *Jeremia,* 168.

[127] Note use of the verb *htpll* at 42:2 ff., also a time of crisis.

a permanent retreat. By introducing this as a major motif of the chapter, and the actual background for Jeremiah's word to Zedekiah, problems in narrative flow are also introduced. No notice of the return of Babylonian siege troops, equivalent in tone and impact, is supplied in the narrative. When 37:11−15 returns to the action, the reader hears again of a Babylonian withdrawal, but in this instance it merely provides an occasion for the prophet to go to the land of Benjamin. Moreover, as a result of this action the prophet is accused of desertion to the Babylonians, a fact which makes less sense if the retreat was as major an event as is implied in 37:5−10. Taken by itself, Jer 37:11 merely speaks of the withdrawal as permitting Jeremiah to set out from Jerusalem (37:12), an activity which would have been impossible with the siege in full swing. This leads to the second reason why 37:5 is intrusive. At a literary level, it simply reproduces the information provided at 37:11, with slight variation, in order to develop the theme of hopes for major Egyptian assistance.[128] This theme is fully developed (21:1−10) or merely alluded to (34:8−22) at other sections of Jeremiah under clear redactional influence.

From a purely historical standpoint, it is difficult to reconstruct events leading up to the Fall of Jerusalem. There are no Babylonian records comparable to what exists for the events of 597 B. C. Hopes for Egyptian aid, under the new leadership of Pharaoh Hophra, are undoubtably being referred to in Ch. 37. Mention of this is made at other points in the biblical record, though details are sorely lacking (Ezek 17:15; 29/30; Lam 4:17); Psammetichus II is the Pharaoh of consequence in Zedekiah's earlier years.[129] By most estimates, Egyptian aid at this point in time was at best a perfunctory, if not coincidental effort; the Egyptians may have simply been on their way to assist the Tyrians or consolidate their position on the maritime coast.[130] This would not rule out a measure of hope within the capital, realistic or otherwise. The Lachish Letters, for example, record the cryptic notice: "the commander of the army, Coniahu ben Elnathan, has come down in order to go to Egypt." It is not clear what rank Coniahu

---

[128] Duhm makes a similar observation, but sees v. 5 as the original notice, while v. 11 "gehört noch dem Bearbeiter an, der für den hier weggenommenen Satz v. 5 eine Vertretung schaffen mußte" (*Jeremia,* 299). The principle is similar. The interrupting unit Jer 37:6−10 causes duplication at 37:5 and 37:11. However, the stronger case can be made for seeing v. 11 as an integral part of 37:11−15. V. 5, together with v. 4, is redactionally linked to 37:6−10.

[129] For reconstructions, see Malamat, "Twilight," 140−1; "Last Years," 218−9; Freedy & Redford, "Dates in Ezekiel," 470−2; 480 ff.; Hayes & Miller, 472−3; Katzenstein, *Tyre,* 317 ff.; Spalinger, "Egypt and Babylonia," 232 ff. Further, M. Greenberg, "Ezekiel 17," 308 ff.

[130] So, Freedy & Redford, 482; cf. Katzenstein, *Tyre,* 318 ff. Malamat calls the Egyptian assistance "too frail to be of any real consequence," (Last Years, 219), an opinion based upon the biblical references. Spalinger says: "The feint by Egypt into Palestine in 588 B. C. was a small affair . . ." ("Egypt and Babylonia," 232).

held, and the entry is so brief that it is impossible to reconstruct the full importance of such a mission. It may testify to the hope for Egyptian aid. On the other hand, no details are given, and simple flight to Egypt cannot be ruled out. At a later point in time, out of fear of the Babylonians, it is to be recalled that the post-587 community, under military leadership, seeks to flee to Egypt (41:17) and eventually does just that (Chs. 42 and 43).

While the available historical data is difficult to evaluate in terms of the nature, timing, and intent of Egyptian movements in southern Palestine (and Phoenicia), something can be said about the literary report at Jer 37:5—10. In contrast to the detailed style of the scribal narrative at other points, surprisingly little factual information is provided concerning this Egyptian intervention, which is otherwise treated as an important event. Its importance lies chiefly in what it suggests in theological terms. Jer 37:5—10 is a highly rhetorical piece in which hopes for a permanent retreat are voiced and firmly rejected. In style, language and movement it has far more in common with Jer 21:1—10 than Jer 37—43*. Details of the kind one expects to see in the following chapters are missing. The who, where, and how of such interest to the narrator elsewhere are not to be found in Jer 37:5—10.

It is probable that the same editorial hand which concluded the scribal narrative with Jer 43:8—44:30 also supplied Jer 37:5—10. This editorial conclusion will be discussed below, but it is clear that the flight to Egypt is depicted as the most glaring example of the remnant's disobedience. Jer 37:5—10 simply fleshes out one additional side to such a decision at an earlier point in the story, by pursuing the fullest possible implications of the notice at 37:11, where it was mentioned that the Babylonian troops had temporarily withdrawn because of Egyptian presence in the area. With the inclusion of Jer 37:5—10, aid from Egypt prior to the Fall anticipates flight to Egypt after the Fall. As early as Jer 24:8—10 the reader is prepared to follow the evil remnant down into Egypt. From the perspective of the Exilic Redaction, flight to Egypt was like reversing the Exodus event. Hope for Egyptian assistance functions similarly.

Many critics see all of Jer 37:1—10 as secondary, and take 37:11—15 as the first original episode in the narrative.[131] This begs the question as to the original beginning of the narrative, since 37:11—18 presupposes a situation of siege. The unit Jer 34:6—7,2b—5 fits remarkably well as a word from the prophet in response to the sending of a delegation at Jer 37:3. The details of siege, as well as the notice that Babylonian forces were engaged in fighting in the Judahite countryside, given at Jer 34:6—7, provide important and plausible background for Zedekiah's action in Jer

---

[131] Kremers, Wanke, Pohlmann, Lohfink. Pohlmann entertains the possibility that Jer 34:1—7* formed an earlier introduction (*Studien,* 62—63).

37:3. The report that only Azekah and Lachish remained of the fortified cities (*'ārê mibĕṣār*) forms a perfect backdrop for the military situation suggested in Chs. 37—39. Indeed, it is more than coincidence that letters found at Lachish itself make mention of an army commander's intent to go to Egypt, at just this period. But more than this cannot be said. The narrative likely continued after Jer 34:2b—5 with the episode at Jer 37:11—15. The Babylonians have been forced to withdraw in order to engage the Egyptian forces in the region. On this occasion, Jeremiah seeks to go out to the land of Benjamin, territory virtually undisturbed by Babylonian incursions throughout this period and beyond.[132]

Jeremiah's intent, in the idiom of the MT, is somewhat obscure: "Jeremiah set out from Jerusalem to go to the land of Benjamin, in order to divide (from) there among the people" (*lahăliq miššām bĕtôk hā'ām*), Jer 37:12.[133] Bright is correct that the force of the expression is to be understood in light of circumstances recorded at 32:1—10.[134] Jer 32:2,6—15 is to be placed in the scribal narrative as the episode following Ch. 37. As such, Jer 37:11—15 records the initial attempt of Jeremiah to leave Jerusalem and make a property transaction in the midst of the *'am* who remain in Benjaminite territory, among whom were his kinsmen (32:7 ff.). The fact that this territory remained relatively undisturbed, while other major portions of Judahite territory, especially south of the capital, were overrun in the "exilic" period (599—586 B. C.), is to be explained on several grounds. Either Benjamin, as a territory distinct from Judah and the capital, had "submitted" to Babylonian authority even with the events of 597 B. C., or it did so at some point just prior to the events of 587 B. C. The Scribal Chronicle itself reports (Jer 40/41) that Mizpah, a Benjaminite city, was made the governor's seat by the Babylonians after the Fall of Jerusalem. It continued to function as such into the post-exilic period.[135] More to the point, Jeremiah is accused by Irijah, a sentry at the Benjamin gate, of "deserting" (*'attāh nōpēl*) to the Babylonians, merely by intending to set out to Benjamin.[136] In other words, Benjaminite territory had *already* come to terms with Babylonian sovereignty, as demanded by Jeremiah within the capital throughout this period. This point merits

---

[132] See the important remarks of Malamat, "Last Years," 215 ff.; also, the recent contribution of J. N. Graham, "'Vinedressers and Plowmen': 2 Kings 25:12 and Jeremiah 52:16," *BA* 47 (1984) 55—58.

[133] The LXX understands the expression as related to some sort of business transaction (see BHS).

[134] *Jeremiah,* 229.

[135] Malamat, "Last Years," 218. Neh 3:7 speaks of "the men of Gibeon and Mizpah who were under the jurisdiction of the governor of the province of Beyond the River" (*lĕkissē' pahat 'ēber hannāhār*). Also, Malamat points out that the first towns resettled by exile returnees were in Benjaminite territory (see Ezra 2:21—35; Neh 7:25—31), suggesting that these had escaped destruction.

[136] Irijah is the grandson of Hananiah (Jer 37:13).

emphasis. Jeremiah's post-597 counsel, recorded within the Scribal Chronicle as early as Chs. 27—29, is also his immediate pre-587 counsel (see Jer 38:1—6 as well as Jer 34:2b—5*). It appears therefore that the prophet defended a policy of submission already in force in Benjamin, his own tribal territory, in the post-597 period. Jerusalemite princes, on the other hand, held out for possible independence through military action — hence the siege and general assault on the region. Jeremiah repeated his counsel to the king (Jer 32:6—7,2b—5*), that neither he nor the city could avoid Babylonian rule. The princes, enraged at this counsel and at Jeremiah's loyalty to Benjamin, beat and imprison him (37:15).

E. Prophet, King, and Princes in Jerusalem's Last Days (Jer 37—39)

Several important editorial moves beyond those already noted can be detected within Chs. 37—39 by paying close attention to the treatment of Jeremiah.[137] In the present form of Chs. 37—39 Zedekiah is clearly depicted in league with the evil princes, with respect to Jeremiah's imprisonment and harsh treatment. But there is strong reason to suspect that direct harrassment by Zedekiah is a supplementary theme of the Exilic Redaction, and not part of the original narrative. In fact, close attention to redactional moves within these chapters indicates that the general indictment of "the king, his servants, and the people," whose chief transgression was failure to heed "the words of the LORD which he spoke through Jeremiah the prophet," serves to shift direct blame away from the princes. This general indictment (37:1—2) functions as the rubric under which the scribal narrative now unfolds.

Episodes which depict direct hostility toward Jeremiah pinpoint his antagonists as the evil princes. In Jer 37:11—15 it is these princes who beat Jeremiah and put him in the house of Jonathan the scribe (bêt yĕhônātān hassōpēr), which had been converted to a prison for the occasion (kî-'ōtô 'āśû lĕbêt hakkele'). This latter fact is intriguing in and of itself. Scribal quarters are mentioned at other places in Jeremiah, notably in Ch. 36: "the chamber of Gemariah," v. 10; "the scribal chamber," v. 12 (liškat hassōpēr); "the chamber of Elishama the scribe," v. 20. These "chambers" are apparently rooms within a larger structure, in the first instance the temple, in the latter cases within the house of the king. It is within the scribal chamber that the princes are gathered when Micaiah comes to report to them what he heard Baruch reading from Jeremiah's scroll. The scroll is actually left here until Jehoiakim sends Jehudi to get it for a first-hand

---

[137] In what follows, compare the analysis of Pohlmann, *Studien,* 49 ff. (Hebrew text and chart on 208 ff.). See also this author's analysis in "Crisis," 86—92. Several modifications are made, especially regarding Ch. 37, in this study. For example, Jer 38:5 and 38:22 are retained in the scribal narrative. See CHART EIGHT at the conclusion of this analysis.

reading (36:19). In the present episode, Jeremiah is not placed in this scribal chamber, but in an actual house. It is also to be noted that while Jonathan is named as the owner of the house, he is at no point mentioned in the crime against the prophet. What is striking is that a makeshift prison had to be set up. It is not clear why the prophet, on a charge of treason, was not placed directly into the main prison, which was presumably under direct royal administration. Bright conjectures: "Perhaps other places of detention were full; or perhaps the secretary's house was a 'maximum security prison' for dangerous political offenders."[138] This hunch is at least half-correct. There is no way of knowing whether other places of detention were full. What is indicated by the episode at Jer 37:11−16 is that a prison was set up and the prophet detained, apart from the royal house or Zedekiah's action, which is nowhere mentioned. The same is not as obvious in the following unit (37:17−21).

In the present narrative flow Jer 37:16 goes on to mention a more specific place of detention where the prophet was held.[139] This "vaulted chamber" (*haḥănuyôt*) was in the cistern-house (*bêt habbôr*), probably connected with the house of Jonathan first mentioned. After he had been there several days, Zedekiah "sent and took him and inquired privately of him" (*wayyišlaḥ . . . wayyiqqāḥēhû wayyiš'ālēhû bĕbêtô bassēter*) in his own house. The force of *bassēter,* stressing the private activity of the king (see also 38:24 ff.), is connected with this transfer from the prince's prison to his own house. That in Judah's final days the king was fearful of the power of the princes is made clear elsewhere in the Scribal Chronicle (38:5,24 ff.). By virtue of his rescue of the prophet, he asks for a further word from Jeremiah (37:17). The king may also have interpreted Jeremiah's attempt to return to Benjamin as implying some shift in the prophet's counsel to the royal house. But Jeremiah simply repeats his original word, as it has been reconstructed from Jer 34:2b−5*: the king will indeed be given over to Babylonian authority.[140]

Up to this point, the narrative is consistent in its presentation. In Jer 37:18−19, however, another element is picked up which changes the force of the presentation as followed up to this point. Jeremiah asks the king what was the nature of his wrongdoing toward "you, your servants, and this people" (*lĕkā wĕla'ăbādêkā wĕlā'ām*), that "you (pl) have put me in prison" (*kî-nĕtattem 'ôtî 'el-bêt hakkele'*). The problem is that, up to this point, neither the king, his servants, nor "this people" have been involved in the imprisoning of Jeremiah. As a matter of fact, the king has only been involved in taking the prophet *out* of prison; it is the princes, acting

---

[138] *Jeremiah,* 229.

[139] Read *wayyābō'* (LXX *kai ēlthen*) instead of *kî bā'*.

[140] It is to be noted that there is no mention at Jer 37:17 (or 38:3) of deportation or the burning of the city, features we view as supplementary in Jer 34:2−5.

independently of the king, who beat and imprison Jeremiah. The triad indicted at Jer 37:18 is the same triad that was introduced in 37:2 as not heeding the words of Yahweh (see as well 21:7; 22:2,4).[141] Jer 37:4 pursues this same logic: "Now Jeremiah was coming and going among the people for *they* (pl) had not yet put him in the prison." Apart from the fact that this verse is only loosely connected with the preceding delegation note, and merely anticipates (editorially) action to follow, it develops the notion that a broader group was responsible for Jeremiah's plight.[142] Jer 37:11—16 is, however, far more specific about those responsible; so too the details and place of imprisonment are supplied. Along with this question put to Zedekiah at 37:18, a general question unrelated to the narrative is brought in at v. 19.[143] Here the concept is developed that the king has prophets on his side who, in stark contrast to Jeremiah, promise that Babylon will stay away. While this is possible, they make no appearance in the Scribal Chronicle at this point, and the question appears unrelated to the more specific event of Zedekiah's inquiry.[144]

The original narrative is resumed at v. 20. After the prophet had responded to the king's request for a word (v. 17), he makes a request of the king that he not be sent back to the makeshift prison at the house of Jonathan, "lest I die there." Here the original logic of the presentation is resumed: Jeremiah's life is threatened by the princes (37:11—16); the king extricates Jeremiah and asks for a word, which he receives (37:17); the prophet asks that he not be sent back (37:20); the king complies by putting Jeremiah under the protection of the court of the guard, where he is cared for under royal command: "So King Zedekiah gave orders, and they committed Jeremiah to the court of the guard; and a loaf of bread was given him daily from the baker's street, until all the bread of the city was gone" (37:21). The notion of a hostile and life-threatening Zedekiah, his servants, and the people cannot be sustained by the evidence of Jer 37:21.[145]

---

[141] For a full list of places where the threesome appears, see Thiel (*26—45*, 52—3); Pohlmann, *Studien,* 50—1. Thiel correctly sees 37:1—2 as an *Überleitung* connecting Chs. 36 and 37, and understands the triad, as it appears there and in 21:7, 22:2,4 as a D-expression, but then takes 37:18 as the place where the expression originally appeared (*Das Vorbild*). Apart from the type of linguistic arguments Thiel generally mounts, it is to be observed that the king/servants/people are *not* involved in the imprisonment of the prophet in 37:11—17 and following. Even in Ch. 36, where we are told that Jehoiakim and his servants "did not hear" the scroll, the ones indicted are those who in fact did not listen — neither were they afraid nor did they rend their garments, in contrast to the earlier action of the princes and scribes (36:11—19; and people? 36:10). At the editorial level of the scribal narrative, the triad (king/servants/people) does not function in the same specific manner.

[142] See also Pohlmann, *Studien,* 51 ff.

[143] 37:19 is rightly judged by Thiel, who otherwise sees almost all of Ch. 37 as original (non-deuteronomic), as "ein redaktioneller Vers" (*26—45*, 54).

[144] Chs. 27—29 mention prophetic action of this kind, as much in Babylon as in Judah.

[145] Seitz, "Crisis," 87—9; Hyatt, *Jeremiah,* 1072—3; Duhm, *Jeremia,* 301.

This same logic is continued in the original scribal narrative. At this point, the episode now located at Jer 32:2,6—15 appeared. Jeremiah was at the court of the guard, as mentioned in Jer 32:2 (// 37:21). However, in its present form, Jer 32:1—5 develops the line of argumentation at work in the Exilic Redaction of Jer 37/38. Here Zedekiah is depicted as having put the prophet in the court of the guard not to protect him, as requested by Jeremiah himself (37:20), but because he resented Jeremiah's prophetic word (Jer 32:3—5). This is precisely the direction the editorial hand at 37:18—19 has moved. However, enough of the original narrative (37:11—17,20—21) remains that even in its redacted form the picture of Zedekiah is considerably less flat. And if the redactional analysis of this study is correct, the original depiction of the king was a far more complex, at times even supportive, portrayal than what now appears in Jer 32:1—5.

Jer 32:6—15 went on to record Jeremiah's successful purchase of land from his own Benjaminite territory, his attempt to actually return there having been thwarted earlier by the princes. Jeremiah's cousin, Hanamel ben Shallum, comes to the prophet while he is at the court of the guard (32:8), just as Jeremiah had been promised (32:6). The Babylonian siege had resumed (32:2a), but since his cousin came to him it was unnecessary for the prophet to make the purchase in Benjamin itself. The actual transaction is carried out in the court of the guard, with witnesses who sign the deed, in the presence of other Judahites. The deed (and a copy?) are then secured in a vessel that "they might last for a long time" (32:14).[146] Though "Jeremiah remained at the court of the guard" (37:21), all the necessary, and highly symbolic, elements of this business transaction were able to be carried out. This is certainly the force of Jer 32:6—15. The proceedings were, however, public and significant enough, involving numerous individuals (32:12), that word quickly reached the princes.[147] They reappear in Jer 38:1—6, the next episode in the scribal narrative.

In Jer 38:1—6, a précis of Jeremiah's message is given (vv. 2—3). It is perfectly consistent with his post-597 counsel as isolated elsewhere, in its insistence that the city is no defense against Babylonian authority. By contrast, "the one who goes out" (*hayyōṣēʾ ʾel-hakkaśdîm*) to the Babylonians can "preserve his life as a prize of war (*wĕhāyĕtāh-lô napšô lĕšālāl*) and live" (*wāḥāy*). Again this is consistent with Jeremiah's action with respect to his purchase of land in Benjaminite territory. This is all the more true if Benjamin, Jeremiah's original and now future home, had already submitted to Babylonian authority. Consistent with its depiction of the role of the princes, the narrative insists that it is they who call for the death-sentence for Jeremiah (38:4), charging him with weakening the hands of the defense

---

[146] See Bright for a description of the *realia* involved in this transaction (*Jeremiah*, 237—8).
[147] Compare Pohlmann, *Studien,* 70 ff.

troops and people in the city. [148] Zedekiah's chief fault is not overlooked: he sees himself as incapable of action against the princes (38:5). This time the princes put the prophet in the cistern of Malchiah (termed a *ben hammelek*) and the pit (*habbôr*) is described in more detail and in more threatening terms than that of the house of Jonathan (37:15—16).

The next episode (38:7—13) describes the rescue of Jeremiah by a foreigner in the king's service (38:7). The king himself, despite his statement made earlier in the immediate presence of the princes (38:5), now commands Ebel-Melek together with three men "from here" (i.e., royal servants) to go and rescue the prophet (38:10). [149] He is apparently moved to action on the basis of Ebed-Melek's report, for he is told that Jeremiah will die of hunger as a result of the evil action of the princes. Jeremiah is successfully rescued and returned to the court of the guard (38:13) where he was originally placed for protection by the king and given bread daily (37:21). One of the striking things about the episode is that it is literally a "Servant of the King" (*'ebed-melek*), commanded by Zedekiah together with other servants, who is responsible for the prophet's rescue. This stands in absolute contrast to the opening rubric, where it is stated that "neither he nor his servants, nor the people" responded obediently to "the words of Yahweh spoken through Jeremiah" (37:2), but rather were the very ones that put him in prison (37:4,18). The episodes examined thus far are in agreement that it is the princes who refuse to heed the words of Jeremiah. Instead, they beat and imprison him, and when he continues to call for submission to Babylon, they in turn call for his death.

In the final episode of Ch. 38 (38:14—28) the same movement can be detected toward attributing the chief threat to Jeremiah's life to Zedekiah, and only secondarily to the princes (38:15,24). In view of the analysis up to this point, such a direct threat from Zedekiah seems thoroughly inconsistent. At every point it is the princes who represent the greatest danger to the prophet. Zedekiah may admit his own impotence, warranted or not, in the face of the princes, but he remains the one force able to protect the prophet at this extremely difficult time (37:20—21; 38:10—13). When he sends yet again for Jeremiah and asks for prophetic counsel, the danger to himself as well as to the prophet is clear. As such, Jeremiah's opening words in v. 15 make no sense, in view of his rescue and safekeeping at the court of the guard reported in the previous

---

[148] The same expression (*hû'-mĕrappē' 'et-yĕdê 'anšê*) pops up in the Lachish correspondence; see Malamat ("Last Years," 216) for the citation.

[149] Pohlmann eliminates any problem by striking all of 38:1—6 as secondary. In other words, Jeremiah was only imprisoned once (at 37:11—16) and Zedekiah is only now hearing about it (*Studien*, 80—3). Again, Pohlmann's *Vorlage* is too sketchy to be convincing.

episode.[150] He is convinced that the king seeks to kill him: "If I tell you, will you not put me to death?" (38:15). This verse seeks to editorially develop the original response of v. 16, but in a different direction.[151] In Jer 38:16, the king takes it upon himself to privately swear that the prophet's life remains under his protection: he will not put Jeremiah to death, nor will he hand him over "to these men who seek your life" (38:16). This opening action of Zedekiah is consistent with the presentation which precedes — the chief threat remains the princes.

The response of Jeremiah is also consistent with his earlier statements, though the alternatives are now more pronounced (38:17 — 18/19 — 22). This is due to the seriousness of the decision facing Zedekiah at this advanced stage of the siege, as well as its implication for the prophet. Zedekiah reveals one major source of concern: if he surrenders at this point, will he not be dealt with harshly by those who have already gone over to the Babylonians (38:19)? This concern emerges presumably because Zedekiah had adopted a policy of military resistence, at odds with the prophet and more pointedly with those Judahites who had already submitted. Surrender now would mean retaliation from his own people for his decision to hold out against the Babylonians. Jeremiah repeats that his life can be spared *only* through submission (v. 20). If submission is refused, the vision of the prophet sees (38:22) is one of women from the royal court being led out to victorious Babylonian princes. Moreover, the very contingent he continues to trust in resistence is the one who turns against him — not those who have "fallen to the Chaldeans" (38:19). The redactional addition at v. 23 does away with the question of alternatives and the possibility of submission.[152] It simply describes as fact the capture of the royal court and the burning of the city.[153] Similarly, Jer 38:25, like 38:15, assumes that the king is out to kill the prophet, a fact inconsistent with what precedes and what follows.

By contrast, the original movement of the unit follows well into Jer 38:25 — 27. Zedekiah responds to Jeremiah's words with concern for the retaliation of the princes. In 38:22, Jeremiah's picture of the king's trusted friends, those who like the princes stand behind a policy of continued

---

[150] Pohlmann, *Studien,* 85: "Man fragt sich, warum der Verfasser durch diese Äußerung Jeremias den König so darstellt, daß der Prophet von ihm das Schlimmste befürchten muß, obgleich nach Jer 38,7 — 13 derselbe Zedekia Jeremias Rettung vor dem sicheren Tode angeordnet hatte." Pohlmann unnecessarily strikes v. 16 along with v. 15.

[151] Compare Pohlmann, *Studien,* 86.

[152] See especially Pohlmann, *Studien,* 89. The verse is taken as a gloss by most older commentators; see recently Wanke, *Baruchschrift,* 94; Kremers, "Leidensgemeinschaft," 125; Thiel, *26 — 45,* 54.

[153] The preceding verses emphasize "daß Yahweh bis zuletzt durch seinen Propheten die Möglichkeit angeboten hatte, der drohenden Katastrophe zu entgehen" (Pohlmann, *Studien,* 92).

resistence, reveals them as deceitful and untrustworthy. Zedekiah is concerned that the princes — who seek the prophet's life, if not his own — will hear this report from Jeremiah. They had forbidden the prophet to speak and had demanded the death sentence for his most recent prophetic word. It is not simply the content of Jeremiah's new word to Zedekiah that was of issue, but the fact that he was functioning in his prophetic capacity. Zedekiah is concerned that by promising not to kill the prophet (38:25), Jeremiah will reveal the nature of their exchange to the princes. Instead, he counsels Jeremiah to tell them that, as in 37:20, he had simply asked the king to allow him to remain in the court of the guard. Jeremiah does as Zedekiah instructed him, and the princes are satisfied. Apparently, they are concerned that the prophet utter no further divine word. A request of the king regarding his own fate is of no consequence to them. The narrator assures the reader that the "conversation had not been overheard" (38:27), thus allowing the prophet to remain in the court of the guard, "until the day Jerusalem was taken" (38:28). With this entry the next major episode in the Scribal Chronicle appears: Jer 39:1—10.

As noted in the analysis of 2 Kings 24/25, the majority of critics see Jer 39:1—10, the account of the Fall of Jerusalem, developed on the basis of 2 Kgs 25:1—12.[154] Variations on this approach involve Jer 52:4—16 or a common source below all three accounts, but the result is essentially the same: Jer 39:1—10, with the exception of 39:3, was developed secondarily.[155] Noth was the single major exception to this position, in arguing the reverse: Jer 39:1—10 formed the basis of the present account in 2 Kings.[156] One interesting fact to note in this regard is that almost all critics who argue for the priority of 2 Kgs 25:1—12 are in agreement that 2 Kgs 25:22—26 is "ein Excerpt aus Jer 40:5,7—9."[157] While the direction of dependence is clear in this instance (Jeremiah to Kings), the reverse is held with respect to 2 Kgs 25:1—12 (Kings to Jeremiah, perhaps via Jer 52:4—16). By itself, this is an inconsistent set of conclusions. One would expect the same general direction of influence throughout 2 Kings 25:1—26, as argued by Noth. But other strictly literary arguments can be mounted for the priority of the Jeremiah report of the Fall of Jerusalem.[158]

---

[154] See Chapter Three, Section III for a discussion.

[155] Mowinckel, Komposition, 29 ff.; Rudolph, Jeremia, 209; Wanke, Baruchschrift, 106 ff.

[156] Noth states: ". . . the account in (2 Kgs) 25:1—26 is obviously based on the Baruch narrative concerning the prophet Jeremiah in Jer 39—41 . . ." (Dtr History, 74). Substitute "Scribal Chronicle" for "Baruch narrative" and this study is in essential agreement with Noth.

[157] Quote following is from Thiel, 26—45, 54; Pohlmann, "Schlußkapitel," 96 ff.; Baltzer, "Messias-Frage," 37; Zenger, "Rehabilitierung," 17; Dietrich, Prophetie, 140. Also Noth: ". . . he must be depending upon the Baruch narrative when he inserts the section on the governor Gedaliah and his end (25:22—26)" (Dtr History, 74).

[158] The summary way in which the priority of the Jeremiah report is dismissed, especially within German circles, is astounding. Drawing upon the majority vote, Pohlmann feels

In his brief treatment Thiel remarks that Jer 39:1−2/4−10 appears only loosely anchored in its present context, in distinction to 2 Kgs 25:1−12.[159] The clearly composite nature of the final chapter of Kings has already been noted. The chapter has a complex redactional history, well beyond the opening unit (vv. 1−12). Critics who see the original core of Jer 39 as restricted to 38:28b + 39:3 + 39:14 must assume that the Scribal Chronicle, otherwise an important source of information for this period (see 2 Kgs 25:22−26), simply had nothing to report about the Fall of Jerusalem.[160] The Fall of Jerusalem is reported in a dependent clause (38:28b) and beyond that mention is only made of certain Babylonian officials who "came and sat in the middle gate" (39:3,14).[161] Given the kind of detailed reporting the reader has come to expect in the Chronicle, silence at so important a moment as the Fall of Jerusalem is inconsistent.

Close literary analysis suggests that within the larger report of Jer 39:1−10 only the opening verses (39:1−2) are intrusive. Such specific temporal indications are not expected in the Chronicle. Beyond this, the reader already knows about the beginning of the siege, since it forms the background for all that precedes in Chs. 37−38.[162] As such, Jer 39:1 is superfluous, and has simply been drawn from 2 Kgs 25:1//Jer 52:4. Likewise, the units 2 Kgs 25:2,3//Jer 52:5,6 supply a second date, when a breach was made in the wall (11th year, 4th month, 9th day), forming the basis for Jer 39:2.[163] These later reports, however, agree that the breach was made from the inside, because of a severe famine. These details are not given in Jeremiah 39, but are probably a later development of the "plague, pestilence, and famine" theme from Jeremiah.

In fact, in Jer 39:1−10 no mention is made of the famine in connection with the fall of the city, nor is a breach in the walls related in any way to flight by Zedekiah or troops, as in 2 Kgs 25:4 and Jer 52:7. Rather, the flight of the king "by way of the king's garden through the gate between

----

only required to say, "Daß 2. Kön 25/Jer 52 von Jer 39 abhängig sind, ist nicht denkbar," with no further discussion (*Studien,* 97). He only pursues the question as to how and why Jer 39:4−12 was worked into this scanty *Vorlage* (vv. 3, 14). See also Bright, *Jeremiah,* 240−6; Hyatt, *Jeremiah,* 1078−80.

[159] *26−45,* 54, n. 12. Compare Noth: "These sections are so deeply imbedded in Jer 39−41 that they must be original there" (*Dtr History,* 137, n. 69).

[160] Lohfink ("Kurzgeschichte," 332) makes this explicit. In stressing (wrongly) the narrator's overriding concern for prophet and word, to the exclusion of other important features, Lohfink states bluntly, "Der Fall Jerusalem wird überhaupt nicht erzählt." Also, Pohlmann, *Studien,* 106.

[161] Even this feature is not without problems. See Wanke, *Baruchschrift,* 104; Rudolph, *Jeremia,* 210.

[162] Pohlmann: ". . . (V. 1) berichtet an dieser Stelle viel zu spät über Zeit und Umstände der Belagerung Jerusalem (*Studien,* 93).

[163] There is little disagreement over the point of origin of these two verses, since the majority of scholars see *all* of Jer 39 composed from another source (2 Kgs 25; Jer 52).

the two walls" in Jer 39:4 is depicted independent of the famine or a breach, factors which play very little role in the scribal narrative. The reader learns in Jer 37:21 and 38:9 of diminishing supplies, but the king flees because of the presence of the Babylonian officers who have entered the city and who begin to set up military/judicial proceedings.[164] Finally, the most compelling evidence for the intrusive quality of vv. 1—2 is that the clause from the end of Ch. 38, "When Jerusalem was taken..." (wĕhāyāh ka'ăšer nilkĕdāh yĕrûšālāim) moves directly to 39:3, as most critics agree.[165] Jer 39:1—2 was supplied by the editorial hand at work elsewhere in the Scribal Chronicle, at the point at which the original report at Jer 39:3—10 was drafted to function at 2 Kings 25 and Jeremiah 52.

In contrast with the opening verses, there is no evidence of literary seams or sharp disjunctures in the verses that follow (Jer 39:3—10).[166] In fact the episode reports the capture of Zedekiah and his sentencing in precisely the same manner the reader expects in the Scribal Chronicle. Moreover, a report of Zedekiah's capture, in view of the preceding episode at Jer 38:17—22 — over whose authenticity there is no debate — is almost necessitated. The torso retained by Kremers at this point, especially as compared with the other episodes sketched out in his analysis, seems peculiarly brief.[167] Is one to believe the Chronicle continued reporting post-587 events (Chs. 40—43) with no mention of the fate of Zedekiah? Even the most minimalistic reading of the Scribal Chronicle would see the role Zedekiah plays as a crucial one.[168] In Kremer's treatment, he is forced to title this episode: "Jeremiah's Fate at the Capture of Jerusalem," thus ignoring the integral place of the king in the narrative in Chs.

---

[164] Against Bright, who uncharacteristically argues that the MT "saw them" (rā'ām) at 39:4 "represents an adjustment of the verse in its present context" (Jeremiah, 242). He goes on to say, "Vs. 4 did not originally follows vs. 3. Zedekiah did not wait to see the Babylonian officers seated before fleeing; he fled (vs. 2) when the wall was breached." Accordingly, at 39:4 he reads "saw this", i.e., the breaching of vs. 2. Bright's seems to be the "adjustment," necessitated by the elimination of v. 3 at this point, in order that it might function with 38:28b and 39:14 as the original narrative. A connection between the famine/breach and the flight is made in order to serve a different purpose in 2 Kgs 25/Jer 52. See below.

[165] Hyatt, Jeremiah, 1079; Duhm, Jeremia, 309; Pohlmann, Studien, 97; Thiel, 26—45, 55; Wanke, Baruchschrift, 108.

[166] Here Noth's observations are on target.

[167] Kremers, "Leidensgemeinschaft," 126; also, Pohlmann, Wanke, Lohfink, Thiel. Even Bright opts for this analysis (Jeremiah, 244).

[168] In the rather convoluted logic of Wanke (Baruchschrift, 107), this omission is striking — but moreso to the interpolator of Jer 39:1—2,4—10 than to the original narrator: "... das Geschick Zedekias und seines Volkes, das in den Erzählungen bis 38:28a eine so große Rolle spielte, wird im entscheidenden Augenblick nicht einmal erwähnt..." (my emphasis). Therefore, this "Mangel" is filled in with the aid of Jer 52 and 2 Kgs 25, chapters which somehow include this important information otherwise lacking in Jer 39. Also Pohlmann, Studien, 96—7.

37 – 39.[169] In addition, a narrative concerned with the prophetic word would hardly allow Jeremiah's counsel and vision to Zedekiah in 38:17 – 22 to stand without final comment.

In conclusion, the evidence indicates that the report of the Fall of Jeremiah forms an integral episode within the Scribal Chronicle. With the exception of 39:1 – 2, the account is consistent in its reporting. Here again is the kind of firsthand narrative the reader expects, which focuses on the flight, capture, and sentencing of Zedekiah. The clear implication from all that precedes in the Chronicle up to this point is that Zedekiah's disobedience led to his harsh treatment, if not the wider events of the Fall and deportation (39:8 – 10). When the city is actually taken, no reports of destruction or widespread hostility are included. Jerusalem is simply described as "captured" (*nilkĕdāh*). Then Babylonian officials enter the city and take up position at the middle gate, thus constituting a military government.[170] The report immediately moves to the reaction and flight of Zedekiah (vv. 4 – 7).[171] Until he is captured and sentenced, the report of the events of "the Fall" does not resume (vv. 8 – 10). Then it is reported that Zedekiah's house was burned, along with "house of the people."[172] The walls are torn down, and deportation proceedings commence under Nebuzaradan's authority. The notice at 39:9 also fits well with details given in the broader Scribal Chronicle: the Babylonian officer deports both those who had held out in the city, as well as those who had already

---

[169] Kremers, "Leidensgemeinschaft," 126; Wanke calls it and Jer 39:11 f./40:1 – 6 "Berichte über Freilassungen Jeremias" (*Baruchschrift*, 108). For 38:28b + 39:4 + 39:14 = "Jeremiah is Released to Gedaliah: First Account" and 39:11,12,13a = "Jeremiah is Released: A Second Account" see also Bright (*Jeremiah*, 241). This splintering of Ch. 39 alone speaks against the divisions and original units proposed.

[170] Bright explains: ". . . the Babylonian officers constituted themselves a court, or better, a military government" (*Jeremiah*, 243). Duhm speaks of the action by the officials: ". . . nämlich zum Gericht und Ordnung der Dinge . . ." (*Jeremia*, 309).

[171] The notion that v. 4 can be separated from v. 3 is one of the weakest links in Pohlmann's argument (*Studien*, 95). He states that the appearance of the officials in v. 3 is "völlig unmotiviert" without an immediate continuation at 39:14. This is simply not true. The flight of Zedekiah is integrally linked to the appearance of the officials (". . . when he saw them") in the present form of the narrative. Only in 2 Kgs 25/Jer 52 is the motivation altered slightly. There Zedekiah flees, along with others ("all the men of war"), when a breach is made because of famine. In fact, this later shift results in focusing attention on the army of Zedekiah (vv. 7 – 8) and the army of Nebuchadnezzar. Zedekiah's army scatters from him, as though there was a major engagement of the two forces outside Jerusalem (Jer 52:8b; 2 Kgs 25:5b). In the Scribal Chronicle, Zedekiah flees with his soldiers, but they play no major role in the narrative. The focus remains on Zedekiah's individual action and his trial. By contrast, Jer 52/2 Kgs 25 tell of the trial of princes as well as Zedekiah.

[172] This house is conjectured by some as related to the "people of the land", perhaps as an assembly hall or the like. It is a curiously specific phrase. See Hyatt (*Jeremiah*, 1080) for a brief discussion and references. Compare Bright, *Jeremiah*, 240.

gone over ("fallen") to him.[173] These two groups are already familiar from Ch. 38. The final reference to vineyards and fields being given over to Judahites outside the city also fits well with a later reference at Jer 40:12.

In sum, a succinct report appears here of a type already witnessed in the scribal narrative. On the basis of this report, fuller accountings have been made in Jer 52:4—16 and 2 Kgs 25:1—12. With Noth, these are developments made at a later point when the greater detail evidenced in them is possible. Moreover, as fuller reports they serve new purposes in new redactional contexts. Unclear information is glossed (see, for example, 2 Kgs 25:9—12). New information from the specific perspective of a deportee is included (actual deportation of Zedekiah carried through: 2 Kgs 25:7 and esp. Jer 52:11; catalogue of temple vessels: 2 Kgs 25:13—17; other leaders executed: 2 Kgs 25:18—21; cf. Jer 52:10 and 52:24—27). Other information from the Scribal Chronicle is drawn upon as well (2 Kgs 25:22—26) and new interpretations of certain events are already being supplied.[174] In short, this is a classic example where the shorter, more compressed account is no loose summary of events but the original report. Secondary elaborations, at the close of Kings and as a final word in Jeremiah, were drawn up on the basis of this first report, which formed an integral part of the original scribal narrative.

It is fairly easy to reconstruct the logic operative for those who see the core report of Jer 39 as consisting only of 38:28b + 39:3 + 39:(13)14. Once the priority of 2 Kgs 25/Jer 52 is posited, it is to be observed that these verses stand as a plus over and above the other ("original") reports.[175] It only requires a short leap to see some logical movement across these verses: when Jerusalem is captured (38:28b), Babylonian princes enter the city (39:3, with repeat at 39:13 in order to work in the "missing" Nebuzaradan), and free Jeremiah from the court of the guard (39:14). Suddenly a report centered on Zedekiah and the Fall of Jerusalem, such as might reasonably be expected following Ch. 38, has been transformed into a narrative essentially about Jeremiah's being freed from the court of the guard (39:14). In light of the circumstances surrounding Jeremiah's "remaining in the court of the guard" in the first place (38:25—28), as an alternative to death in the house of Jonathan, it is not clear what the significance of even this minimal report would be.[176]

---

[173] See Bright for possible emendations, made on the basis of Jer 52:4—16 (*Jeremiah,* 240). The final reference to "those remaining in the city" appears repetitive. See also Wanke, *Baruchschrift,* 105.

[174] See my remarks on 2 Kgs 25 above, Section II.

[175] As Bright puts it: "The material mentioned (i. e., verses from Jeremiah found in 2 Kgs 25/Jer 52) having been subtracted, there remain two accounts of Jeremiah's release . . ." (*Jeremiah,* 245).

[176] Pohlmann vigorously argues for a direct continuation in the *Vorlage* from the first imprisonment scene (37:7—13) to the conversation at 38:14 ff. (esp. the "House of

In order to argue for the priority of Jer 52/2 Kgs 25, a fundamental caesura must be seen between Jer 39:3 and 39:4.[177] But such a caesura cannot be found. The motivation for Zedekiah's flight is integrally — not redactionally — linked to the appearance of Babylonian officials about to begin trial proceedings. Pohlmann argues that the report of Zedekiah's flight is a digression, but again this stems more from his commitment to the priority of 2 Kgs 25/Jer 52 than to any obvious literary problem in the text. Ch. 38 made clear that Zedekiah has as much to fear from internal as well as external forces, and judicial or other proceedings would have brought his concerns to a head.

Commitment to the priority of the fuller reports of Jer 52/2 Kgs 25 creates further problems. Wanke expends enormous energy explaining why it was that when Jer 39:1−2,4−10 was interpolated, an exact duplicate from 2 Kgs 25/Jer 52 did not appear.[178] The question must of course be answered by those arguing this direction of influence. Why, for example, did Nebuzaradan not appear in Jer 39 in the very specific way he did in 2 Kgs 25:8//Jer 52:12? Wanke answers that it has something to do with wanting to avoid depicting Nebuzaradan in separate action (so 2 Kgs 25:8 ff.; Jer 52:12 ff.) since in the *Vorlage* of Jeremiah he appears in one and the same major phase of capture, together with other Babylonian officials mentioned in 39:3 (see also 39:11 ff. and 40:1−6).

It is far easier to assume that the differences between Jer 39:1−10 and 2 Kgs 25/Jer 52 are the result of secondary developments in the latter. This is why they are fuller reports. In 2 Kgs 25:1−7/Jer 52:4−11, the first episode in the capture of Jerusalem, there is a more general focus on military engagement between the armies of Zedekiah and Nebuchadnezzar outside Jerusalem. As such, report is given of a famine and a breach being made from within, and then all of the men of war (*kol-'anšê hammilḥāmāh*) flee. Initially, neither 2 Kings 25 nor Jeremiah 52 even stress the presence of Zedekiah among the troops (cf. Jer 39:4). There is a chase scene, and Zedekiah's army scatters. Only then is the king captured and sentenced. In Jer 39:4, the flight is initiated by the fearful Zedekiah familiar from Ch. 38. His men of war accompany him in his flight, but the action remains centered on the king, who is captured and sentenced.

The temporal perspective of Jeremiah 39 is also striking. In Jer 39:7 the blinding of Zedekiah is reported in the main clause, while the actual deportation appears in an infinitive expression which tells us nothing

---

Jonathan" concern in 38:24−28) to 39:3,14, where we are (only) told how Jeremiah was freed from the court of the guard (*Studien*, 92−3). Yet since he argues for a more positive relationship between King and prophet (p. 90), why would a "rescue" scene be the next to appear? Again, Pohlmann's *Vorlage* is so scanty that it is difficult to reconstruct its internal logic, not to mention its original provenance and larger purpose.

[177] Pohlmann, *Studien*, 95; Bright, *Jeremiah*, 242. Also see notes 166, 173 above.

[178] Wanke, *Baruchschrift*, 107−9. See even Pohlmann's criticisms, *Studien*, 95−8.

beyond intention: ". . . and they bound him to take him to Babylon" (*wayyaʾasĕrēhû banĕḥuštaim lābîʾ ʾōtô bābelāh*). Compare the reports of 2 Kings 25 and Jeremiah 52. In 2 Kgs 25:7, the finite verb makes clear the realised deportation of Zedekiah: ". . . and they bound him in fetters and brought him to Babylon" (*wayyaʾsērēhû banĕḥuštayim wayĕbiʾēhû bābel*). Jer 52:11 knows this much and more, *including Zedekiah's death in prison*: ". . . and the King of Babylon took him to Babylon, and put him in prison until the day of his death" (*wayĕbiʾēhû melek-bābel bābelāh wayyittĕnēhû bĕbêt-happĕquddōt ʿad-yôm môtô*).

It is now clear why, in the later reports of 2 Kings 25 and Jeremiah 52, the actual activity in the city must be depicted in a new scene, under the leadership of Nebuzaradan, "in the fifth month, on the tenth day of the month, which was the nineteenth year of Nebuchadnezzar" (Jer 52:12; cf. 7th day in 2 Kgs 25:8). In Jeremiah 52, Nebuchadnezzar had personally taken Zedekiah to Babylon after his trial (Jer 52:11; further 2 Kgs 25:7). Even in Kings, activities in the plains of Jericho and at Riblah are distinct enough that a new, temporally designated phase begins with Nebuzaradan's activity in the capital itself (2 Kgs 25:8—12; Jer 52:12—16). Such a distinction is nowhere recorded in Jeremiah 39. Even as events at Riblah are reported, the reader never fully leaves the scene in Jerusalem. Immediately after the blinding and fettering of Zedekiah, the text speaks of "Chaldeans" (Jer 39:8) in Jerusalem who have presumably remained there together with Babylonian officials, while the chase and trial at Riblah were going on. No break is portrayed as Nebuzaradan, the captain of the guard, begins deportation proceedings in the capital (39:9) and resettles population in "the land of Judah" (39:10). Nebuchadnezzar plays no direct role in affairs of the siege, or its aftermath, as recorded in the Scribal Chronicle. Nebuzaradan, and the chief officers mentioned in 39:3 and 39:13, are fully in charge.

F. The Fall of Jerusalem in Jeremiah 37—39*

As noted in the treatment of Jeremiah 52 and 2 Kings 25 above, there is every reason to assume that the wider reports of the Fall of Jerusalem, as found in these final chapters of their respective works, were developed on the basis of information provided in Jeremiah 37—43*, as well as other sources.[179] To argue the reverse with respect to 2 Kgs 25:1—2/Jer 52:4—16 or any other part of these reports demands an unnecessarily complicated chain of logic. Jer 39:3—10 brings to a close events associated with Zedekiah as they had unfolded in Chs. 37—38. Even on the eve of Jerusalem's capture, Jeremiah counselled the king to

---

[179] See Section II above.

surrender "that you and your house" might live (38:17). Zedekiah's fear of those who had already gone over to the Babylonians (Jer 38:19; 39:9) the prophet viewed as groundless (38:20). In addition, the threat from Jerusalemite princes is witnessed to both at this moment (38:25—27) and earlier in the Scribal Chronicle (37:11—15; 37:20—22; 38:1—5). It is a threat which principally affects Jeremiah. But to the degree to which Zedekiah follows the prophetic counsel or protects the prophet, it is a threat which affects him as well (38:25—28). Ch. 39 provides the account of how the king, unwilling to trust Jeremiah's prophetic counsel, fled. The results of that action are also given, both as they affect Zedekiah (39:5—8a) and also the wider populace (39:8b—10).

In distinction to reports of 2 Kings 25 and Jeremiah 52, however, these events are not seen as bringing life in Judah to a complete end. Property is destroyed and deportations are carried out (39:8—9). But there is clear evidence within the narrower scope of Ch. 39 that the Babylonians were interested in maintaining stability in the region. People are left to maintain the land (39:10)[180] and very quickly indigenous leadership is placed in power in the person of Gedaliah ben Ahikam ben Shaphan (39:14; 40:7). Concern is shown for the prophet Jeremiah at more than one point (39:11—14, also 40:1—6).[181] In other words, if Ch. 39 is read apart from 2 Kings 25 and Jeremiah 52, the impression is conveyed that the tragedy of 587 events centered primarily on Zedekiah and his house (39:6—8a). Civil leadership as it had been exercised within Jerusalem in the lineage of David was brought to an end. This is the only interpretation of the Babylonian decision to brutally execute Zedekiah's sons, and then blind Zedekiah himself, thus rendering him unfit for further rule.

Though it is not often noted, it is to be observed that within Jeremiah 39 *there are no reports of the destruction of the temple*.[182] Such a report is given in 2 Kgs 25:9 and Jer 52:13, along with a catalogue of religious objects carried off (2 Kgs 25:13—17//Jer 52:17—23), as well as a notice concerning

---

[180] In a recent article, J. N. Graham looks closely at the economic policy adopted by the Babylonians for vassal states ("Vinedressers and Plowmen," *BA* 47 [1984] 55—58). More specifically, he discusses the allocation of property within Judah after 597 and 587, and its function within broader Babylonian policy. Marshalling recent archeological findings, he argues that the leaving behind of lower classes mentioned in the biblical text (Jer and 2 Kgs) was not simply a testimony to Babylonian cruelty or the harshness of life within Judah after deportations had been carried out. Nor does it suggest "that the Babylonians merely left the remaining Jews to their own devices" (56). Rather, such population groups functioned within a "deliberate Babylonian economic and agricultural policy" (56), in this case directed toward Judah.

[181] Critical analysis of these two units follows shortly.

[182] Of the later notice at Jer 41:5, B. Oded (Hayes & Miller, 478) does say: "This passage raises the question of whether the Chaldeans really completely destroyed the temple and whether the cult fully came to an end."

the execution of certain religious leaders (2 Kgs 25:18//Jer 52:24).[183] It is not clear why such a notice is missing, but all we are told at Jer 39:9 is that the king's house and the "house of the people" are burned, and that the walls of the city are broken down. This is not to suggest that when the Babylonians broke the siege, the temple was left completely alone.[184] It is only to stress that *within the context of Jeremiah 39 and the chapters that follow* the focus falls elsewhere.

More than this can be said. The omission of even a brief statement about destruction to the temple is not inconsistent with the overall tone of the Scribal Chronicle at this point. Among other things, we hear of concern shown by Nebuzaradan, under command from Nebuchadnezzar (39:11), for the prophet Jeremiah, who is the religious leader of the remnant community. Moreover, one gets the impression from Chs. 39—43 that the Babylonians are not concerned to destroy whatever sense of religious continuity the remnant community was able to maintain after 587 B. C. They remove political leadership from the house of David, and the center of civil authority shifts from Jerusalem to Mizpah (40:6—12; 41:1—10). In this regard the unfortunately brief notice at Jer 41:5 is most significant. It tells of pilgrims from Shechem, Shiloh, and Samaria returning to the temple of Yahweh in Jerusalem to make grain and incense offerings.[185] Enough of a sense of continuity was maintained that Jerusalem and the temple itself never lost its religious significance for those who remained in Judah, or for those from more northern regions.[186]

---

[183] Incidentally, if Jer 39:1—2,4—10 was secondarily supplied from 2 Kgs 25/Jer 52, this gap would certainly have been filled in, Jer 41:5 notwithstanding. Put another way, would the "shortened report" of Jer 39:1—10 fail to mention so significant an event as the burning of the House of Yahweh? Bright, among others, emends Jer 39:8, on the basis of Jer 52:13, to read *bêt hammelek wĕʾet bêt yhwh wĕʾet bāttê hāʿām* (*Jeremiah*, 240). See also Rudolph (*Jeremia*, 209), who adds, "ein Volkshaus (Rathaus?) gab es nicht in Jerusalem." Emendation is one way to solve the problem.

[184] The Book of Lamentations stresses personal loss and affliction (esp. Chs. 3, 4 and 5), the general destruction of Zion (Ch. 1; 2:6 ff.; 4:22) and the "strongholds of Judah" (2:2), its "palaces" (2:5), and the walls and gates of the city (2:8 ff.; 4:12). The only specific reference to the temple appears at 2:4—7. Here we are told that Yahweh himself "scorned his altar/disowned his sanctuary" (2:7).

[185] As is now widely agreed, to use the term "Samaritan" at this point in time is anachronistic, and a misreading of the evidence. No historical material exists which would suggest the kind of deeply religious, geographically defined, split between "Samaritan" and "Judean" which emerges at a much later period. It is to be assumed that pilgrims from northern regions made offerings in this period, just as they had before the events of 597/587 B. C. See especially the treatment of R. J. Coggins in *Samaritans and Jews*.

[186] Adopting a chronology that puts the activity of Jer 41:5 at a later point (4 or 5 years after 587), Hyatt assumes that "by this time the temple in Jerusalem had been sufficiently restored" (*Jeremiah*, 1088). This does not square well, as he admits, with the obvious mourning state of the pilgrims (see 41:5). On the other hand, since these pilgrims have come specifically to make offerings in the temple in Jerusalem, another question must be answered. Is this mourning related specifically to the state of the temple, or more

Returning to the literary context of Jer 39:1−10 and the broader Scribal Chronicle, the tragedy of 587 falls primarily on the person of Zedekiah, his house, and those deported with him to Babylon. By contrast, in 2 Kings 25 and Jeremiah 52 the broader significance of 587 events is spelled out from an exilic, rather than a Judahite perspective. Along with this brutal termination of civil leadership under Zedekiah and his house, religious life is depicted as coming to a complete end. The prophet Jeremiah, representing religious leadership in the post-587 community, finds no place whatsoever in these narrative depictions of the Fall of Jerusalem and its aftermath. As post-587 events are briefly sketched (2 Kgs 25:22−26), Jeremiah is never mentioned. Mention is made of a wholesale evacuation to Egypt by the final remnant community (2 Kgs 25:26), before the focus returns and settles on the exiled King Jehoiachin (vv. 27−30).

As is ultimately made clear in 2 Chr 36:17−23 + Ezra 1:5−11, restoration of civil leadership serves an even greater purpose: it stresses the full restoration of religious life, symbolized by the return of the temple vessels (Ezra 1:7), along with the charge from Cyrus to rebuild the temple "razed" by the Babylonians (2 Chr 36:17 ff. + 22−23). Chronicles develops a portrayal of Babylonian destruction in 587 which emphasizes an absolute end to civil and religious life in Judah, followed by a thorough restoration. In essence, Judah − land and people − is a void during the exilic period that it "might enjoy its sabbaths" and be made ready for return and restoration (2 Chr 36:21). The seeds for this portrayal are found in the depiction of 2 Kings 25/Jeremiah 52. A prior portrayal of events is found in the Scribal Chronicle of Jeremiah 37−43*, as it continues to narrate circumstances, religious and civil, involving the prophet Jeremiah and the remnant community in Judah beyond 587 events.

Redaction-critical analysis of Jeremiah 37−39 (+ Jer 32:2,6−15; 34:6−7,2b−5) has exposed the contours of a supplementary level of tradition, made from an exilic perspective, which seeks to anticipate the absolute destruction of the city and link it to the primary disobedience of King Zedekiah (see CHART EIGHT below). In the original Scribal Chronicle, the chief threat to the prophet Jeremiah, if not Zedekiah himself, is represented by the Jerusalemite princes. Not only do they refuse to heed "the words of Yahweh which he spoke through the prophet Jeremiah,"

---

generally to the effect of 587 (+ 597) events on Zion/Jerusalem, the Judahite countryside, as well as the deportations from both areas (see Lamentations)? For discussion of the nature of religious life for Judahites during the exilic period, and its relationship to the temple itself, see Peter Ackroyd, *Exile and Restoration,* 20−31. Further: Douglas Jones, "The Cessation of Sacrifice after the Destruction of the Temple in 586 B. C." *JTS* n. s. 14 (1963). Jones lays a great deal of stress on destruction of the altar, but he also discusses aspects of both continuity and discontinuity in the religious life of Judahites during this period.

they also demand the death sentence, because of the prophet's words and actions. Because the Exilic Redaction works from the ultimate perspective of Ch. 39 and the fate of exile itself, that is, with knowledge of the disobedient flight of Zedekiah and his sentence, it anticipates this sentence by showing the king actively involved with the princes as a chief threat to the prophet. From this exilic perspective, it is Zedekiah's refusal to heed the words of Jeremiah which brings about the destruction of the city, not to mention his own punishment (Jer 32:1—5; 34:1,2b*,3b*,20—22; 37:6—10; 38:23). Moreover, the Exilic Redaction of Jeremiah adopts the same basic stance toward the post-597 remnant and their "prince" as does the Ezekiel material (see Chapter Three). This factor contributes to the comprehensive negative portrayal of "Zedekiah, his servants, and all the people" such as is found in Jer 37—39 and in other key sections of the present book (Jer 21,24,32*,34*).

It is interesting to note that the extreme language concerning the burning of the city and its destruction by the Babylonians (and Yahweh) is not reported in detail in Jer 39:1—10, when the actual account of the "Fall of Jerusalem" appears. Rather it functions primarily as a redactional level in the Scribal Chronicle, and only appears in a more integral way in the final reports of Jeremiah 52 and 2 Kings 25. As a redactional layer interwoven with a scribal narrative concerned with the remnant community in the pre-587 and post-587 years, it funtions not only to underscore the primary disobedience and responsibility of Zedekiah, but also to foreclose on the possibility of ongoing life in the land in either the immediate pre-587 or post-587 years. Neither of these themes is highlighted in the Scribal Chronicle itself. The Scribal Chronicle makes it clear that ongoing life in Judah was more than a possibility brought to a close with 587 events. Jeremiah 40—42 depicts ongoing life in Judah as a reality made possible through Babylonian support. In the religious, economic, and civil aspects of that existence, there was clear potential for the continuing welfare of the community.

G. The Post-587 Remnant (Jer 40:7—41:18; 42—45*)

Similar exegetical difficulties, such as exist in the immediate pre-587 chapters of Jeremiah (37:1—39:10), also confront the interpreter in chapters recording post-587 events (39:11—45:5).[187] These difficulties involve the determination of primary and redactional tradition in the present text, and here the critics are again divided. In some distinction to Jeremiah 37—39, however, the central core of the post-587 chapters (Jer 40:7—41:18) is

---

[187] For an analysis of Jer 39:11—40:6, see the section following.

generally regarded as original tradition.[188] This nearly seamless narrative tells of the establishment and then rapid disintegration of the remnant community at Mizpah, primarily due to the assassination of Gedaliah. Fear of further Babylonian intervention following Gedaliah's assassination and other atrocities, including the cold-blooded murder of northern pilgrims on their way to Jerusalem (41:4—8), causes the community under the leadership of Johanan ben Kareah to consider flight to Egypt (41:17).

It is to be stressed that at no point in this narrative account is the post-587 remnant, under Gedaliah's leadership, negatively portrayed. Nowhere is the establishment of the post-587 community in Judah interpreted as an act of disobedience, in and of itself. On the contrary, by submitting to Babylonian authority, the remnant has the right to expect Yahweh's blessing (Jer 40:9—12). Gedaliah's words at 40:9 ("serve the king of Babylon and it shall be well with you") echo Jeremiah's earlier statements to the post-597 remnant (27:11 ff.).

In the broader literary context of the present Scribal Chronicle (Chs. 42—44), the theme of disobedience is developed on the basis of the remnant's decision to flee to Egypt. In these concluding chapters, the post-587 community is depicted as blatantly refusing to hear the word of Yahweh spoken by Jeremiah the prophet (Jer 42:13—43:13).[189] Ch.44 provides a lengthy sermon summarizing Israel's persistent tendency toward idolatry, epitomized finally by the remnant community itself in its decision to go to Egypt (Jer 44:22—23). Whatever sense of appropriateness or legitimacy the reader might have gained regarding the formation of the post-587 community in the original Scribal Chronicle disappears entirely. The final episodes render the final judgment over life in the land: what has been built up, in Judah and now in Egypt, remains to be plucked up (Jer 45:4; cf. Jer 1:10). Ch. 45 links the oracles against the nations (Jeremiah 46—51) with the oracles against the Judahite remnant in Egypt (Jeremiah 42—43*, 44) in such a way as to stress a judgment common to them both. Add to this the depiction of a wholly evacuated Judah (43:5—7) or a wholly deported Judah (52:27),[190] and one is prepared for the only vision of restoration finally in force in the present canonical text: the future

---

[188] Thiel remarks: "Im ganzen Abschnitt 40,7—41,18 findet sich kein einziger sicherer Hinweis auf die Arbeit der Redaktion" (*26—45*, 61); similarly, Kremers, "Leidensgemeinschaft," 126 ff. Kremers, Wanke (*Baruchschrift*, 114—5) question the first unit (Jer 40:7—12) and again posit some common source below both Jeremiah and 2 Kgs 25:22 ff. at this point. Pohlmann upholds Jer 40:11—12 (*Studien*, 134; "Schlußkapitel," 97), but sees 40:7—9 as secondary in view of its stress on an empty land. While he does argue for redactional intervention at points in Chs. 40—41, it is of a far more minimal order than in Jer 37—39.

[189] See the discussion below, Section V.

[190] As noted above, Jeremiah 52 provides no narrative presentation of life in Judah after 587 B. C., deferring to Jeremiah 39—45. 2 Kgs 25:22—26 summarizes the pertinent details regarding the post-587 remnant as provided in the Scribal Chronicle.

return of the exiles, symbolized by Jehoiachin and his liberation in Babylon (52:31—34).

A far more complex set of circumstances regarding the post-587 remnant is to be found in the original Scribal Chronicle. This is particularly true in the core section (Jer 40:7—41:18) of the Chronicle, whose authenticity on strictly literary grounds is generally upheld. As noted, in the broader context of the present text it is the decision to flee to Egypt that forms the basis for the negative portrayal of the remnant now found at Jer 42:13—45:5. Within the narrower context of Jer 40:7—41:18, however, the option to go to Egypt is considered solely on the basis of external threat to the remnant's continued well-being.

> And they went and stayed at Chimham's Inn, near Bethlehem, intending to go to Egypt because of the Chaldeans; for they were afraid of them, because Ishmael ben Nethaniah had slain Gedaliah ben Ahikam, whom the king of Babylon had appointed governor over the land (41:17—18).

Here the reason for considering escape to Egypt is made specific. The remnant fears yet another Babylonian intervention, this time brought about by the treachery of Ishmael.

The rationale for the flight is perfectly consistent with events as recorded in Jer 40:7—41:18. With Ammonite support (40:14; 41:10,15) one Ishmael ben Nethaniah, a "chief officer" of the throne (rabbê hammelek) and member of the royal line (mizzera' hammĕlûkāh), sought to wrest power away from the Babylonian appointee Gedaliah. As mentioned above, it is quite likely that in selecting Gedaliah the Babylonians intentionally bypassed a ruler from the Davidic house. The only explanation for Ishmael's wanton acts of violence is that he saw himself as legitimate ruler, and was willing to take whatever steps necessary to seize power. During the assassination itself, in which Judahites with Gedaliah at Mizpah are also slain, a small military contingent is willing to go so far as to kill Chaldean soldiers in support of Ishmael's efforts (41:3). After these brutal events, Ishmael himself intercepts eighty pilgrims from regions to the north on their way to Jerusalem and, luring them into Mizpah in the name of Gedaliah, he and his men slay all but ten of them (41:4—8). No explanation for this atrocity is given. It is to be concluded that Ishmael treated these men as loyalists to Gedaliah, since they responded favorably to the invitation to enter the city in his name. Those spared are willing to disclose hidden stores of goods, which would assist Ishmael's efforts (41:8).

There are other possibilities. At a minimum, the journey of the pilgrims to Jerusalem could be viewed as an attempt to maintain religious continuity after the events of 587 B. C. As such, from the perspective of Ishmael and his supporters it would have been far too capitulative an action, and at odds with their own anti-Babylonian efforts. By taking captive the king's daughters (41:10), Ishmael demonstrates his claim to royal 'power'[191]; by fleeing to the Ammonites, he indicates his willingness to enlist local support in his cause. In sum, his disruptive actions vis-à-vis the post-587 remnant under Gedaliah are aimed at consolidating his own power in the region. In this sense, his staunchly anti-Babylonian campaign is an example of the nationalistic position of the Jerusalemite princes, as noted in Jer 37—39, being put into action.

With this background material in place, Johanan's concern for the remnant's existence in Jer 41:18 is brought into proper perspective. Though he is successful in driving Ishmael off (41:12) and reconstituting the post-587 community, Babylonian intervention is now necessitated because of Gedaliah's assassination. Chaldean soldiers were also among those slain during the incident at Mizpah. It is for this reason that Johanan, together with commanders of the remaining forces and the general populace, seek out Jeremiah's counsel (42:1—5). A decision to escape to Egypt need not be interpreted as an anti-Babylonian or a pro-Egyptian move, in strictly political terms. Based upon the information supplied in Ch. 41, there are no grounds for seeing in Johanan's flight any conscious alignment with Egypt. Hopes for Egyptian assistance, unreliable throughout this period, is nowhere evidenced at this point in the Scribal Chronicle. His retreat to Bethlehem indicates the general and well-founded fear within the remnant community under his charge of new Babylonian intervention. Though no details exist upon which to reconstruct events, the list at Jer 52:28—30 indicates a third wave of deportations in Nebuchadnezzar's twenty-third year (52:30). Five years after the 587 deportations, it comprised about the same number of individuals (745 Judahites; cf. 832 "from Jerusalem" in 587). The only reasonable explanation for this third wave is that new unrest in Judah, as described in Jer 41:1—18, necessitated further Babylonian intervention.[192]

Unfortunately, the scribal narrative provides no further information regarding the remnant in Judah beyond these events. This is due to the fact that as the narrative continues, redactional overlay is concerned to depict a wholesale (43:5—7) and disobedient (42:13—22) evacuation to Egypt of the remnant under Johanan. From the perspective of the exilic redactors, responsible for the final shape of the Scribal Chronicle and its placement within the broader Jeremiah tradition, the decision to flee to Egypt signaled the final end to life in the land. The fate of the contingent under Johanan becomes representative for the wider post-587 remnant in Judah. As such, broader accounting of life in Judah up to the third deportation and beyond is not provided.

The Scribal Chronicle made its way from Judah to Babylon at some point after Jeremiah and Baruch, along with a contingent under Johanan,

---

[191] K. Baltzer, "Messias-Frage," 35—36.
[192] Hyatt, *Jeremiah*, 1084; Hayes & Miller, 478 ff.

made their way to Egypt. The narratives recording life in Egypt (Jer 43:8—44:30) are altogether different from what is found in the Scribal Chronicle, and there is broad critical consensus for viewing them as redactional compositions.[193] Moreover, there is clear evidence of redactional kinship between secondary levels of tradition in Jer 42:10—22 and these concluding chapters (Jer 43—44).[194] Critics offer differing interpretations of the original shape of Jeremiah 42, but there is widespread agreement that Jeremiah's response to the delegation of Johanan and the remnant (42:1—3), as it exists in the present text (42:4—22), has been redactionally expanded to work in coordination with Chs. 43—44. The section of Jeremiah's response most clearly under the influence of the Exilic Redaction is found at 42:13—22.[195] It is this section which anticipates most fully the presentation of Chs. 43—44. In much the same way that Jer 38:23 anticipates the destruction of the city and forecloses on the actual possibility of obedient response from Zedekiah, so Jer 42:13—22 anticipates the response of Azariah ben Hoshaiah, Johanan, "and all the insolent men" at 43:1—3 as it sketches out Yahweh's judgment over a remnant that flees to Egypt.

Though redactional supplementation can be detected at points in Jer 42:1—12, the basic response of Jeremiah to the delegation can be isolated in vv. 9—12. The original context of the inquiry (fear of the king of Babylon, 41:18) is picked up at 42:11. Consistent with the prophet's counsel in the post-597 years (Jeremiah 27—29*), especially as recorded prior to the events of 587 (Jeremiah 37—38*), the leaders of the remnant community are exhorted not to fear the Babylonians. More than this, Jeremiah indicates that Yahweh has brought to an end the period for pulling down and plucking up, and will build and plant the remnant if they remain in Judah, in fulfillment of Jer 1:10 (cf. Jer 45:4). Developing the redactional motif at work in 21:7 and especially 24:8—10, Jer 42:13—22 reverses Jeremiah's words of promise as it anticipates a disobedient decision, made by the entire Judahite remnant, to flee to Egypt. Such a decision sets into motion the sword/famine/pestilence, "no remnant or survivor" (42:17) theme tied earlier to judgment over Jerusalem (42:18); together with

---

[193] Wanke (*Baruchschrift*, 119), for example, says of them: "Der letzte von Kremers zum Erzählungszyklus Kap. 37—43:7 gerechnete Abschnitt 41:16—43:7 ist nach hinten durch die neue Einleitung 43:8 und die darauf folgenden Stücke, die sich in Stil und Gattung ... deutlich von den vorausgehenden Erzählungen abheben, gut abgegrenzt."

[194] Wanke, *Baruchschrift*, 127 ff.; Thiel, *26—45*, 62 ff.; Pohlmann, *Studien*, 136 ff.; Hyatt, *Jeremiah*, 1088 ff.

[195] So Hyatt (*Jeremiah*, 1092), Kremers ("Leidensgemeinschaft," 128). For a concise listing of recent redaction-critical alternatives (Wanke, Pohlmann, Kremers) and his own proposal, see Thiel (*26—45*, 62). There is some disagreement over which verses in this section are to be retained. Pohlmann, for example, sees the original core as comprised of 42:1*,2—5,7*,8,9—10,13a,14,16 (*Studien*, esp. 140 ff.); Wanke's *Grundbestand* is equally complex (*Baruchschrift*, 116—131), and he also argues for three redactional reworkings.

execration/horror/curse/taunt (42:18) this theme focuses the judgment on the Judahite remnant in Egypt.[196]

As others have suggested, Jeremiah's words at 42:9−12 find their logical response at 43:1−3.[197] Again, the original context of the inquiry (fear of Babylonian reprisals for the treachery of Ishmael) is picked up in the objection of Azariah, Johanan, and the "insolent men" (*hāʾănāšîm hazzēdîm*) that

> ... Baruch ben Neriah has set you against us, to deliver us into the hand of the Chaldeans, that they may kill us or take us into exile in Babylon.

At a later point in time, the latter course of action is apparently taken against part of the wider Judahite remnant (see Jer 52:30). The important point to note is that the original context of the inquiry is maintained here. Moreover, we can see in the narrative as it continues in 43:4−6 a clear indication that the original scope of the objection, involving the specific contingent of Johanan and Azariah, has been broadened to include "all the commanders of the forces and all the people" who "did not obey the word of the LORD to remain in the land of Judah" (43:4; see 37:2).[198] That this is a redactional feature supplementing the original scribal narrative is shown by two factors. At the literary level, Jer 43:5−7 goes to great pains to portray the comprehensiveness of the contingent fleeing to Egypt, including all groups ever mentioned as part of the post-587 remnant up to this point:

> But Johanan ben Kareah and all the commanders of the forces took all the remnant of Judah who had returned to live in the land of Judah from all the nations to which they had been driven − the men, the women, the children, the princesses, and every person whom Nebuzaradan the captain of the guard had left with Gedaliah ben Ahikam ben Shaphan (43:5−6).

Jeremiah and Baruch are also included (43:6). This wholesale evacuation is coordinated with the theological and literary movement of the narrative at this point, which clearly presupposes the existence of the entire remnant in Egypt (43:8−44:30).[199] All Judah is there, and all are disobedient.[200] The second objection to this portrayal of the extent of the evacuation is more obvious. There is no historical evidence to suggest that "all the

---

[196] Thiel, *26−45*, 63; Wanke, *Baruchschrift*, 127−8.
[197] Kremers, "Leidensgemeinschaft," 128; Hyatt, *Jeremiah*, 1092−3.
[198] Wanke, *Baruchschrift*, 129.
[199] Pohlmann, *Studien*, 159.
[200] The single exception is Baruch who, despite his "groaning" (45:3), is to be exempted from "the evil Yahweh is bringing upon all flesh" (45:5); like Ebed-Melek at the fall of Jerusalem (39:15−18), Baruch will have his life as a prize of war (45:5) "in all the places to which you may go." See the section which follows.

remnant of Judah" fled to Egypt in the post-587 years.[201] The biblical evidence itself contradicts such a portrayal (Jer 52:30; Lamentations).

In sum, from what can be inferred about the original scope of the Scribal Chronicle, a group within the post-587 community, headed by Johanan and Azariah, disobeyed Jeremiah's counsel to "remain in the land" out of fear of the Babylonians (43:4). The extent of the evacuation to Egypt cannot be determined because of the tendency within the Exilic Redaction to broaden the scope of the disobedience, so that all the people are viewed as refusing to hear Yahweh's word (37:2—43:4). We can only speculate about the original ending of the Scribal Chronicle, since it concludes in its present form with narratives of a wholly different order and provenance. Presumably it told of the descent of a Judahite contingent to Egypt. If this contingent included the prophet, and Baruch, the author of the Chronicle probably ended his narrative on this note. In the present form of the Chronicle, the original conclusion is impossible to recover.

H. Excursus: Jer 39:11—40:6

In the interest of completeness, a brief word needs to be said about the one unit remaining in the Scribal Chronicle: Jer 39:11—40:6. This composite section bridges the account of the Fall of Jerusalem (39:3—10) and the reports concerning the post-587 remnant (40:7—41:18; 42:1—8a*,9—12; 43:1*,2—3,7*) we have just examined. It is comprised of three sub-units, each quite distinct: (a) 39:11—14: Jeremiah's Release to Gedaliah; (b) 39:15—18: Jeremiah's Word to Ebed-Melek; (c) 40:1—6: Jeremiah's Second Release at Ramah. Like other sections of the Scribal Chronicle, these units have been the object of detailed critical analysis. There is no clear consensus over the interpretation of units (a) and (c), which represent two separate accounts of Jeremiah's release. That there is some tension between the two is made clear by comparing the notice at Jer 39:14, in which Jeremiah is released to Gedaliah and "dwells among the people," with Jer 40:6.[202] The latter reference presupposes a trip to Ramah for a chained Jeremiah, together with captives from Judah and Jerusalem (40:1). After his second release he is offered a choice to accompany the other exiles to Babylon or to remain in Judah (40:4—5). Jer 40:6 informs the reader, in a manner similar to 39:14, that Jeremiah went to Gedaliah "at Mizpah, and dwelt among the people left in the land."

A solution to the apparent problem of the sequencing in Jer 39:11—40:6 lies in the interpretation of the intervening unit, Jer 39:15—18.

---

[201] For a discussion and bibliography, see Hayes & Miller, 477—9. Also: Ackroyd, *Exile*, 20—31; Janssen, *Exilszeit*, 39—42; Malamat, "Last Years," 215—8.

[202] Wanke, *Baruchschrift*, 106 ff.; Hyatt, *Jeremiah*, 1082; Pohlmann, *Studien*, 97 ff.; Kremers, "Leidensgemeinschaft," 126.

There is little critical disagreement over the secondary nature of this piece, in which Jeremiah promises the faithful Ebed-Melek that he will "have his life as a prize of war" (39:18). In form and placement, it resembles Jer 45:1—5.[203] Both pieces are concerned to single out exceptions to Yahweh's judgment: Ebed-Melek as distinct from the remnant at the Fall of Jerusalem; Baruch as distinct from the post-587 contingent in Egypt. Neither unit demonstrates strong concern for temporal logic. Though the obvious setting for the prose narratives of Jer 43:8—44:30 is Egypt in the post-587 period, the oracle to Baruch situates itself in the fourth year of Jehoiakim, in Judah "when he wrote these words in a book at the dictation of Jeremiah" (Jeremiah 36).

In terms of literary placement, the oracle to Ebed-Melek is closer to its point of delivery, "when Jeremiah was shut up in the court of the guard" (39:15). But even this temporal location contradicts the preceding notice at 39:14, where the reader is informed that Jeremiah was released from the court of the guard. Consequently, critics who regard Jer 39:15—18 as original tradition from the "Baruch Memoirs" place it at an earlier point in the Scribal Chronicle, following Jer 38:28[204] or Jer 38:13.[205] The ease with which temporal logic is made secondary to theological concerns indicates an intentional redactional placement, carried out so that a specific word might be delivered at these two key points in the narrative presentation.[206] As redactional pieces, both stress Yahweh's fundamental consistency in calling for and then accomplishing his judgment over Judah/Jerusalem (39:16) and the whole land (45:5), including Egypt (Jeremiah 44; 46) and all the nations of the earth (Chs. 47—51). At precisely these moments in the literary movement of the Scribal Chronicle, Ebed-Melek and Baruch are singled out as exceptions to the respective judgments, even though the word of promise, like the word of judgment, was delivered at an earlier point in time.

A similar freedom with temporal sequence is taken at Jer 40:1—6. Though Jeremiah is released from the court of the guard to "dwell among the people" at Jer 39:14, in this unit he is pictured as bound in chains by the same Babylonians who released him earlier.[207] Moreover, the reader is told of the deportation of Judahite and Jerusalemite populations at Jer 39:9, after which Nebuzaradan makes provision for those who will remain to tend the land (39:10). The events of deportation appear to be completed when Jeremiah is first released. As such, the episode at Ramah, as it

---

[203] Thiel, *26—45*, 88—89; Wanke, *Baruchschrift,* 111 ff.; Hyatt, *Jeremiah,* 1081—2.

[204] Bright, *Jeremiah,* 229 ff.

[205] Rudolph, *Jeremia,* 212; cf. Thiel, *26—45*, 57.

[206] The same kind of redactional tendency was charted in Chs. 21—36 of Jeremiah above.

[207] See Wanke's observations, *Baruchschrift,* 108 ff.; Hyatt, *Jeremiah,* 1082—3; Thiel, *26—45,* 57—58.

appears in Jer 40:1 ff., follows unexpectedly and rather abruptly on Jer 39:11—14. No explanation is given for the (new) captive-status of Jeremiah.

The speech of Nebuzaradan, termed by Wanke a "Predict" and by Thiel a "dogmatische korrekte Rede,"[208] seeks to establish the rationale for Jeremiah's non-deportation, viz, how it was that the prophet came to share the fate of those who stayed in Judah, rather than those who were deported. Since the fact of Jeremiah's return to the people of Judah was noted already in Jer 39:14, the purpose of Jer 40:1—6 must be to depict the prophet, *at least at the initial stages of deportation,* as one of those marked for exile. Only because the Babylonians offer him the opportunity to stay in Judah does he go to Gedaliah. Actually, no speech of the prophet (as would be expected from Jeremiah at this point) is provided in response to Nebuzaradan's offer. He is simply freed and given an allowance of food and a present. Then he makes his way to Mizpah "to dwell with Gedaliah among the people who were left in the land" (40:6). Much in the same way that Jer 37:5 and 37:11 function in order that a redactional unit might intervene at 37:6—10, so 39:14 and 40:6 facilitate the inclusion of 39:15—18 and 40:1—5.

The episode which told of Jeremiah's release in the Scribal Chronicle (Jer 39:11—14) said nothing about the intention of the Babylonians to deport Jeremiah. On the contrary, he is to be released and treated well, according to Babylonian command (39:11—12). As such, he is taken from the court of the guard (40:13—14). If consulted as to his wish, consistent with Nebuchadnezzar's charge, his choice was to remain with the people (39:14). The Exilic Redaction is concerned in 40:1—6 to portray Jeremiah sharing the fate of the exiles. Since in the Scribal Chronicle it is recorded that Nebuzaradan was "to deal with [Jeremiah] as he tells you," the same motif is maintained in the Exilic Redaction. As such, the speech of Nebuzaradan functions in 40:2—5 in reference to the command of 39:11—12 (esp. 40:5//39:12). Only now it is the theme of Jeremiah's decision not to be deported with "all the captives of Jerusalem and Judah" (40:1) that is developed. Jer 39:11—14 was concerned only with Jeremiah's removal from the court of the guard, after the deportations were already underway (39:9—10).

---

[208] Wanke, *Baruchschrift,* 108; Thiel, *26—45,* 58.

V. CONCLUSIONS: THE SCRIBAL CHRONICLE IN THE BOOK OF JEREMIAH

A. Author, Theme, and Purpose

For the purpose of analysis, a division has been made between the pre- and post-587 sections of the Scribal Chronicle (Chs. 37—39//40—45). However, a quick look at CHART EIGHT shows this to be an artificial dividing point. Ch. 39 reports both the Fall of Jerusalem and the Release of Jeremiah to Gedaliah, the governor appointed by the Babylonians (Episodes VIII and IX). More to the point, there is no essential break in the narrative presentation with the events of 587 B. C. As noted above, though deportations are carried out and buildings are burned, the tragedy of 587 centers on the royal house and the figure of Zedekiah. Life for the post-587 remnant as described in Jeremiah 40—41 continues beyond the deportations to Babylon and the destruction in Jerusalem and the Judahite countryside. Under Gedaliah's leadership, the post-587 community finds its administrative center at Mizpah and a measure of continuity with pre-587 life is established. In fact, there is more general continuity between circumstances facing the post-597 remnant and life for the post-587 remnant than is often pointed out. It is the events of 597 that drive home the fact of Babylonian presence in the region. After this point, Judah's existence as an independent state is less and less possible. The Scribal Chronicle consistently reports Jeremiah's counsel to submit to Babylon, in the post-597 (Chs. 27—29), pre-587 (Chs. 37—39), and post-587 years (Chs. 40—42), for Zedekiah, Gedaliah, Johanan, and the broader Judahite remnant.

With a clearer sense of the broader scope and thrust of the Scribal Chronicle, it is possible to draw several conclusions as to its larger purpose and provenance. Though there is a decided interest in the activity and speech of Jeremiah, it is difficult to agree with the conclusion that the narrative's main concern is with "the reality of the prophetic existence of Jeremiah."[209] This description lacks a degree of focus and appears to be an attempt to distill from the many diverse episodes some general statement. If the thrust of Wanke's term (*Wirklichkeit*) is on the effectiveness of prophet and Yahweh-word, as it seems to be, this is relatively more precise. But in either instance, one might look for far greater elaboration of these two foci in the narrative.

---

[209] Wanke, *Baruchschrift*, 155.

Chart Eight

The Scribal Chronicle in the Book of Jeremiah

[EXILIC REDACTION]

27:1—18

28:1—17
29:1—9/15,20—32   Post-597 Tradition   27:19—22
                                                                     29:10—14,16—19

I. 37:3/34:1—3*,4—5   Prophetic Word to Zedekiah   37:1—2,4—10   36:1—32
                                                                     [34:1—3*,4—5 ← [34:1—22]
II. 37:11—15   Anathoth #1: Jeremiah Imprisoned
III. 37:16—17,20—21   Rescue & Prophetic Word to Zedekiah   37:18—19
IV. 32:1—2*,6—15   [Anathoth #2: Land Purchase   32:1—44]
V. 38:1—6   Jeremiah Imprisoned
VI. 38:7—13   Rescue by Ebed-Melek/Zedekiah
VII. 38:14,16—22,24a*—28   Prophetic Word to Zedekiah   38:23/24b
VIII. 39:3—10   Fall and Deportation   39:1—2   39:15—18
IX. 39:11—14   Jeremiah to Gedaliah   40:1—6
X. 40:7—41:18   The Remnant
XI. 42:1a*,2a*,3—5,7—8a*,9—12   Prophetic Word to Johanan Contingent   42:1b,2b,6,8b,13—22
XII. 43:1a*,2—3,7   Flight to Egypt   43:1b,4—6,8—13   45:1—5
                                                                     44:1—30

By contrast, it can be argued that the prophet Jeremiah, and to a degree his word, are really only two elements in a much broader narrative. Admittedly, the word of the prophet plays an important role at several points in the narrative presentation. But Ch. 39 describes the fall of the city with no need to directly link this important event with word of God or prophet, as one might expect. Only the capture of Zedekiah is tied to Jeremiah's prior word (Ch. 38), and at least part of the linking is secondary elaboration (38:23) based upon the report of Ch. 39 itself. After the fall of the city, the emphasis rests on the figure of Gedaliah (Episodes IX and X) around whom the remnant gathers, under whose authority the community prospers (40:7—12), and to whom the prophet Jeremiah is entrusted (39:14). Having returned to his people, the prophet recedes in these episodes, and the action centers on the assassination plot, its execution, and retaliation. After the murder of Gedaliah, it is Johanan ben Kareah who moves to the foreground (41:11—42:1 ff.). The prophet, and his word, only reappear when sought out by this fractured leadership (42:1—5*). In sum, nothing related to the 2-chapter saga of the foreshortened tenure of Gedaliah is directly linked to the word of the prophet. He is appointed by the Babylonians, only endorsed indirectly by prophetic presence (the word belongs to Gedaliah: 40:9 ff.), and his tragic death goes without prophetic comment.

Answers to the question of purpose, provenance, and authorship of the Scribal Chronicle are interrelated. As mentioned above, the narrative provides the kind of information available only to an eyewitness, who has experienced at close range the variety of circumstances reported in these episodes. This is the only plausible explanation for its specificity.[210] The Chronicle answers the question: "What happened to the remnant in Judah, prior to the Fall of Jerusalem, and in the days following?" As such, its answer is an historical as well as a theological one, the balance never tipping entirely in one direction. The few direct theological statements the narrative makes remain integrated at the level of historical circumstance (the rescue by Ebed-Melek; the capture of Zedekiah; the flight to Egypt). Because the question of the remnant's existence concerned the broader post-597 community (king, princes, officials, people), the focus of the Chronicle does not remain with the prophet. Jeremiah is depicted as a member of the remnant community with a decisive and central role, especially in the days before the Fall. His message to king and community continues the post-597 thrust isolated above: submit and live (37:17; 38:17—20; 39:18; 42:10—12), both before and after the 587 intervention.

But he is not the only figure of interest to the narrative. There is arguably as much concern with the activity (and speech) of Zedekiah, Gedaliah, Ishmael, Johanan, numerous other leaders (37:3; 37:11 ff.;

---

[210] Noted above, Section III/C (esp. 454 ff.).

38:1 ff.; 38:7 ff.; 38:25 ff.; 40—42*), and the broader community itself, as with the person of Jeremiah. In this regard, one of the striking silences of the entire Book of Jeremiah, which throughout demonstrates a measure of interest in Jeremiah the person, concerns the failure to tell of his ultimate end. The Exilic Redaction includes summarizing reference to the faithful Ebed-Melek (39:15 ff.) and Baruch (45:1—5), and it maintains the persona of the prophet in Egypt (43:8—44:32). But the historical Jeremiah disappears behind Yahweh's oracles against the nations (Chs. 46 ff.). The final reference to him "Thus far the words of Jeremiah" (51:64) illustrates the ultimate priority given to Jeremiah tradition and not Jeremiah the prophet.

The even focus and specific detail of the Chronicle at the levels described is due to the fact that its author was a member of the post-597 community that survived in Judah, under the leadership of Gedaliah, at Mizpah, after the Fall of Jerusalem.[211] He must have occupied a prominent position to have access to the information he relates. Because of the role Baruch plays in the Ch. 36 portrayal of the movement from prophetic word to prophetic tradition, there is a strong likelihood that the author of the Chronicle was also from one of the scribal families active in Jerusalem at this period. More specifically, it has been conjectured that the author was from the Shaphan family.[212] The probability of this is underscored when one observes how specifically named scribes, beyond Baruch himself, function as key *dramatis personae* in narrative episodes within the book (Chs. 26/36), particularly scribes from the Shaphan family. Moreover, when it is observed that the appointment and tenure of Gedaliah, with scribal background (ben Ahikam ben Shaphan), is not pejoratively but sympathetically related — in stark contrast to Ishmael, of the royal house — it can be concluded that the author of the Chronicle fully supported this Babylonian appointee and probably had similar scribal background.

Though it cannot be established with absolute certainty, there are strong grounds for arguing that the author of the Chronicle is to be sought from among the same Shaphan family whose members include Ahikam (26:24), Gedaliah (39:14), and Shaphan himself (2 Kgs 22:12—14). This Scribal Chronicle was drawn up as events unfolded, by one who experienced them firsthand. If this hypothesis is correct, then the author was probably deported when the Babylonians made reprisals for the death

---

[211] So also, Wanke, *Baruchschrift,* 146.

[212] Lohfink, "Kurzgeschichte," 333 ff.; Moshe Weinfeld, *Deuteronomy,* 158 ff.; More generally: James Muilenburg, "Baruch the Scribe," 215—38; K. Galling, "Die Halle des Schreibers," *PJB* 27 (1931) 51—57; Nahman Avigad, "Baruch the Scribe and Jerahmeel the King's Son," *IEJ* 28 (1978) 52—6. On the role of the "Shaphanides" during the reform of Josiah, see now H. Cazelles, "La Vie de Jérémie," 29 ff.

of Gedaliah (41:18; 52:30). Through whatever agency, the Chronicle made its way to Babylon in the third wave of deportations. This explains the Chronicle's silence over the ultimate fate of Jeremiah, as well as the sharp distinction now apparent between narratives set in Egypt and those in Judah. In the third wave of deportations, the Chronicle made its way to Babylon where together with fuller Jeremiah traditions, the present book was given its final shape.

Though it cannot be fully developed at this juncture, it would be intriguing to pursue the sociological and theological relationship between Jeremiah, the people of the land, and key scribal families within Jerusalem. Especially in terms of their assessment of Judahite kingship, its perogatives, dynastic claims, and general function within Israel, several areas of commonality might emerge.[213] What can be inferred is that Jeremiah and the author of the Chronicle shared a similar view over the possibility of legitimate existence for a remnant community and king, in the land, after the events of 597 and 587. From the perspective of the developing Ezekiel traditions and the final form of the Deuteronomistic History (Ch. 25), this possibility is ruled out. A similar stance is taken in the Exilic Redaction of Jeremiah, which likewise offers a final word in Jeremiah 52, focusing on the finality of judgment over remnant and king. No mention of the post-587 community or its leadership is made. Consistent with the Ezekiel traditions, the text concludes with a return to the exiled king Jehoiachin. In his favorable treatment, the restoration of the wider exilic community is symbolized, in distinction to Judahite remnant and king.

By contrast, the author of the Chronicle in its original form offered very little in the way of unilaterally negative judgment directed at the remnant community, either before or after 587. The ambiguity with which certain key figures (Zedekiah in Chs. 37–38) are portrayed, or the way other episodes (the tragedy of Gedaliah) are tersely but not unsympathetically depicted, also points to the author's having had direct exposure to the figures and events recorded; and he relates the kind of complications one might anticipate in this period. His solidarity with the post-597 community is nowhere an emphatic theme of the narration. But such solidarity can be sensed in the narrative's straightforward and empathetic presentation of the difficulties attending life in Judah, at the Fall of Jerusalem and in the years immediately thereafter.

The depiction of Zedekiah in the Chronicle, for example, does not hide the fact that despite assurances from the prophet Jeremiah that surrender would mean survival (38:17–20), the king disobeys and attempts to flee (39:1–9). This action costs him his own sons and brings about a sentence for the city and himself that could have been avoided. On the

---

[213] A number of interesting remarks along these lines are made by H. Cazelles in the article referenced above ("La Vie de Jérémie," 29 ff.).

other hand, Zedekiah can be depicted as taking the prophetic word of Jeremiah seriously (37:3 ff.; 37:17 ff.; 38:14 ff.). His failure to obey results not from arrogant disregard for the word, in stark contrast to Jehoiakim (36:23 ff.), but from his anxiety before his own princes (38:5; 38:25 ff.), Judahites who have gone over to the Babylonians (38:19), and the siege troops themselves (39:4 ff.). However, the narrative also records that he is able to stand against his princes, and actually intervene to protect the life of Jeremiah at a time when such action was perceived as treasonous (37:16—21; 38:1—6). He places Jeremiah in house arrest (37:21) and sees to his care — again in stark contrast to Jehoiakim (26:20 ff.; 36:26). During this period, Jeremiah is summoned on numerous occasions to provide private counsel to Zedekiah. Though the prophet's word is forceful (37:17,18), it emphasizes that the king, people, and city can be spared through submission to Babylon (38:17—20).

In the present form of the Chronicle, the ultimate decision of Zedekiah is anticipated at several points (37:1—2; 38:21—23), as if to flatten the complexity of the presentation. The same holds true for the depiction of the post-587 community under Gedaliah. Chs. 40—41 present a profile of this community that is not unsympathetic. Even after the catastrophe of 597 and 587, the prophet remains allied with the Judahite remnant (40:6). Following the assassination of Gedaliah and Johanan's retaliation, the reason given for considering a flight to Egypt is clear. The remnant is fearful of yet further Babylonian intervention (41:18). In the final form of the narrative, however, the decision to go to Egypt is evaluated strictly as an act of disobedience against the prophetic counsel of Jeremiah (42:13—22). The judgment litany (sword, famine, pestilence, execration, horror, curse, taunt), familiar from Ezekiel and sections of the Exilic Redaction, is invoked here, anticipating the disobedient decision (43:1—7) in a tone and force completely disproportionate to circumstances as they have unfolded.

B. Final Word from the Exilic Redaction

In order to demonstrate the sureness of the promise that evil days lay ahead (42:15 ff.), Chs. 43—44 describe the wholesale evacuation of a stiff-necked remnant (43:1—7) and envision the final judgment over this wholly disobedient people and their Egyptian host (44:1—30). The evil foreseen as early as Chs. 21 and 24, for those who survived the 587 catastrophe as well as "those who dwell in the land of Egypt" (24:8), remains in full force:

> Behold, I am watching over them for evil and not for good; all the men of Judah who are in the land of Egypt shall be consumed by the sword and famine, until there is an end of them (Jer 44:27; see also 44:11 ff.).

But just as in Chs. 21/24, where the reality of potential survival, beyond the judgment of 587, was acknowledged, so too the potential for survival, beyond even the hyperbolic vision of judgment in Egypt, is addressed in this final chapter (44:27—29). The horizon of Ch. 44 includes those who ultimately make their way back to Judah, having escaped the sword (44:28; 44:14). Though the precise sequence and the groups involved (remnant in Judah/Egypt) are not clear, Yahweh's word is to stand against them for evil:

> And those who escape the sword shall return from the land of Egypt to the land of Judah, few in number; and all the remnant of Judah, who came to the land of Egypt to live, shall know whose word will stand, mine or theirs (Jer 44:28).

Though it may anticipate (accurately) a return to Judah for "a few fugitives" (44:14), the remnant in Egypt are to witness the truth of Yahweh's word of judgment, even as they themselves are punished "in this place" (44:29). As in Ezekiel's vision of judgment, the sword must reach even to the last survivor, that all might acknowledge Yahweh's sovereign and righteous will:

> A third part of you shall die of pestilence and be consumed with famine in the midst of you; a third part shall fall by the sword round about you; and a third part I will scatter to all the winds and will unsheathe the sword after them. . . . Moreover I will make you an object of reproach among all the nations round about and in the sight of all that pass by. You shall be a reproach and a taunt, a warning and a horror, to the nations round about you, when I execute my judgments on you in anger and fury (Ezek 5:12 ff.).

and further:

> Yet I will leave some of you alive. When you escape the sword, and when you are scattered through the countries, then those of you who escape will remember me among the nations where they are carried captive, when I have broken their wanton heart which has departed from me . . . and they shall know that I am Yahweh; I have not said in vain that I would do this evil to them (Ezek 6:8 ff.).

Not only is the judgment imagery identical (Jer 44:11—14; 44:27—30), and the relationship between cultic abomination/idolatry and the judgment spelled out (Jer 44:1—10,15—23//Ezek 6:1—14), traditions from Ezekiel and Jeremiah at this juncture show identical concern with the vindication of Yahweh's word:

> This will be a sign to you, says Yahweh, that I punish you in this place, in order that you may know that my words will surely stand against you for evil (Jer 44:29).

These resemblances cannot be coincidental. Many of the concerns of Ch. 44 go well beyond the context and interests of pre- or post-597 Jeremiah traditions, and fit much better into Ezekiel's theological programme. Continued survival after the flight to Egypt, and return to Judah, is even anticipated. The particularity of the original Scribal Chronicle (Chs. 37—43*) vanishes, as Jeremiah and the remnant community recede in favor of a stock depiction of disobedient/idolatrous Israel before the word of prophetic judgment.[214]

The conclusion to be reached is that the Scribal Chronicle of Jeremiah 37—43* has received extensive editorial reworking from the Exilic Redaction, under the influence of the Ezekiel traditions. In its present form, the ultimate disobedience of king and remnant community is underscored from the very beginning (37:1—2). At its conclusion, a lengthy sermon has been constructed which provides a final statement of judgment over the remnant, who typify idolatrous, pre-exilic Israel in its entirety (see Ezekiel). Yet at the same time, the specific fact is not lost sight of that this is the Egyptian remnant. In order to focus the judgment of Yahweh, all survivors of the Fall of Jerusalem become the single remnant community "who did not obey the word of Yahweh ... and arrived in Tahpanhes" (43:7). In the final depiction of the Exilic Redaction, the land is completely emptied of inhabitants:

> But Johanan ben Kareah and all the commanders of the forces took all the remnant of Judah who had returned to live in the land of Judah from all the nations to which they had been driven — the men, the women, the children, the princesses, and every person whom Nebuzaradan had left with Gedaliah ben Ahikam ben Shaphan; also Jeremiah the prophet and Baruch ben Neriah. And they came into the land of Egypt, for they did not obey the voice of Yahweh (43:5—7).

The link to Jer 37:2 is clear. At other points, the biblical record has wrestled with how to stress the finality of the punishment and still acknowledge the reality of survivors (2 Kgs 24:14, "except the poorest people"; 2 Kgs 25:12, ". . . but left some of the poorest people of the land . . ."). At this point, the concern is dropped in favor of a picture of wholesale evacuation and judgment for the remnant in Egypt.

C. Redactional Placement of the Scribal Chronicle

This brings the redactional analysis of the Scribal Chronicle to a close. It is appropriate at this point to make several concluding remarks about the placement of Jer 45:1—5 and the significance of this placement for the overall organization of the Book of Jeremiah, including the Scribal Chronicle. The explicit reference to the dictation of the scroll in the "fourth year of Jehoiakim" at 45:1 is most certainly meant to direct attention to Ch. 36. Here the process by which Jeremiah's oral speech from the past ("from the days of Josiah until today" 36:2) becomes Jeremiah tradition for the present and future (36:32) is sketched out. By pointing to the fourth year of Jehoiakim at this post-587 juncture of the book, Chs. 36 and 45 are made to function together as frame units to the

---

[214] Kremers, "Leidensgemeinschaft," 132 ff.

original Scribal Chronicle, which now appears with redactional overlay in Chs. 37—44.

The final reference of Ch. 36, ". . . and many similar words were added to them" (36:32), indicates to the reader that two basic levels of tradition exist in the Book of Jeremiah, both originating with the prophet. The notion of the burned and reconstituted scroll (36:28—31) is meant to represent in the presentation of Ch. 36 the strong judgment tradition from the pre-597 period, such as is found in Jeremiah 9—15*.[215] The exact nature of the pre-597 tradition is emphasized at Jer 36:29. Placement of Ch. 36 in the reign of Jehoiakim underscores this fact. The pre-597 Jeremiah tradition was discussed above in Section I. The intent of Jer 36:32 is to make explicit the similarity between tradition which supplements the "scroll" (the *děbārîm rabbîm kāhēmmāh*) and the pre-597 tradition itself. Again, this intention is perfectly consistent with the kinds of redactional moves we noted at work in Chs. 21—36. In this section of the book, redactional arrangement has maximized the sense of continuity between the pre-597 tradition of Jeremiah and post-597 tradition by interweaving chapters dated in the reigns of Jehoiakim and Zedekiah. By stating at 36:32 that "many similar words were added" the reader is made to expect that the chapters which follow (37—45) will conform throughout with the kind of tradition that exists in the "first scroll." They will be *děbārîm rabbîm kāhēmmāh*.

Because the Scribal Chronicle as it existed in original form included prophetic traditions which expressed hope for the ongoing existence of the post-597 remnant community under Zedekiah in Judah, continuity with the "first scroll" tradition would not be obvious.[216] Consequently, the Exilic Redaction has sought to bring the Scribal Chronicle into coordination with the pre-597 traditions of Jeremiah. Externally, this was carried out by prefacing the main block of its narrative presentation (Jer 37—43*) with Jer 36, a chapter set in the fourth year of Jehoiakim, and then placing Jer 45 at its conclusion. At the same time, narrative segments, or general situations (delegation to prophet; prophet in court of guard)

---

[215] Specific assignment of material from Jeremiah to the "first scroll" is to be avoided because of the highly stylized nature of Ch. 36 (see also 2 Kgs 22—24). This chapter does not so much provide specific data about the contents and concrete growth of the book as it does point to some general directions for understanding how the tradition developed. Jer 36 finds more critical attention than any other section of Jeremiah, if not of the Old Testament. This is not the place to pursue a thorough internal analysis of the chapter (among many others, see Martin Kessler, "Form-Critical Suggestions on Jer 36," *CBQ* 28 [1966] 389—401) or try to identify the specific contents of the "two scrolls" (see, for example: W. L. Holladay, "The Identification of Two Scrolls of Jeremiah," *VT* 30 [1980] 452—67; *Architecture,* esp. 169 ff.; Rietzschel, *Urrolle*). On the latter task, see the cautious remarks of P. R. Ackroyd, "Jeremiah — Some Recent Studies," 48 ff.

[216] See for example the précis of this tradition at Jer 36:29, ". . . the king of Babylon will cut off from it [Judah] man and beast."

within the Chronicle have been extracted to serve redactional purposes earlier in the Jeremiah presentation (Chs. 21; 32—34) [See CHART EIGHT above]. These chapters emphasize the thoroughness of the coming judgment for king and remnant. By providing Ch. 45 with a temporal location in the same "fourth year," and an editorial location at the conclusion of the Scribal Chronicle traditions (+ 43:8—44:30), it is made clear that Yahweh's judgment as spoken by Jeremiah in the "fourth year of Jehoiakim" remains in force, in Egypt and over all flesh (45:5).

The many internal editorial moves brought about by the introduction of the Exilic Redaction into the Scribal Chronicle have been noted in the sections above. These involve the similar concern with anticipating the full judgment of Zedekiah at the Fall of Jerusalem (Ch. 39) and the ultimate punishment of the remnant community in Egypt (Ch. 44). In its redacted form, the Scribal Chronicle is made to fulfill the judgment proclaimed in the "first scroll," directed to Jehoiakim and "all the inhabitants of Jerusalem and men of Judah" who "would not hear" (36:31// 37:1—2). At Jer 39:15—18 and Jer 45:1—5 exceptions are made to Yahweh's judgment over king/servants/people (37:2) at the fall of the city, in the descent to Egypt, and in his judgment over "all flesh" (45:5). By situating itself in the "fourth year of Jehoiakim" Jeremiah 45 directs our attention back to Ch. 36. In this way, the sense of continuity the Exilic Redaction seeks to establish between all levels of Jeremiah tradition, regardless of provenance or temporal circumstances (pre-597, post-597, post-587), is underscored. Yahweh's judgment, as proclaimed by Jeremiah the prophet, is consistent throughout all periods, and is to extend even beyond Judah to include the nations themselves (Jeremiah 46—51). Put another way, though it may appear in the Scribal Chronicle that Yahweh can "build and plant" when the post-597 (27:1—11) and post-587 remnant (40:9—12; 42:10—12) submits to Babylonian rule, leaving Judah on its own land "to till it and dwell there" (27:11), the Exilic Redaction anticipates a greater judgment awaiting both Judah and "the whole land" (45:4—5). Only after this judgment is accomplished can restoration be considered (Jer 52:31—34). Throughout the Book of Jeremiah, the Exilic Redaction makes clear that the restoration of Israel involves Yahweh's returning of a deported people.

Chapter Five
Conclusions

The desire to describe the internal development and final form of the Book of Jeremiah has taken us down several different roads. We began with the thesis that a conflict over interpretation of the Exile stimulated the growth of primary and secondary levels of tradition, and accounted for the 52-chapter form the Book of Jeremiah (MT) finally took. We concluded that the best way to test this thesis was to broaden the scope of inquiry to include a full-scale socio/historical analysis of the exilic period, as well as an investigation of other biblical traditions emerging at this time. A thorough examination of the role of conflict in the exilic period, and in the formation of the Book of Jeremiah, demanded attention to sources beyond the Jeremiah traditions themselves. Our analysis of the history of critical research into the Book of Jeremiah pointed out the limitations of literary approaches adopted in the past century. The order of investigation was reversed, with literary analysis of Jeremiah material taken up only after the relevant historical and sociological factors were clarified.

Our socio/historical analysis sketched out a detailed profile of Judahite society in the years leading up to the Exile. During this period a decided shift was detected away from the internal stability typical of Judahite monarchy and society at an earlier time. After the death of Josiah, and with increased military and political pressure in the region, Judahite monarchy underwent certain fundamental changes. But by far the most significant strain on Judahite society, and the role of kingship within that society, was brought about by the Babylonian incursions and deportations of 597 B. C.

Analysis of the Ezekiel traditions provided an important testimony to 597 events. These traditions indicate how 597 events were interpreted by a prophet who along with King Jehoiachin and various other groups was exiled to Babylon. Recognizing the impact of 597 events, the Book of Ezekiel develops a normative statement of judgment and restoration related to the separate communities of Israelites in Judah and in Babylon. Ezekiel looks well beyond 597 events. Ezekiel's evaluation of Judahite monarchy, as represented in King Jehoiachin and ruler Zedekiah, is intimately related to his evaluation of the post-597 Judahite remnant. 597 events mark the initial phase of a season of judgment to be visited upon the remnant community in Judah. Neither "ruler" nor wider Judahite community have any legitimate future existence, apart from a sure confrontation with Yahweh's punishment at the hand of Nebuchadnezzar. Restoration ensues after Yahweh's fuller judgment, and involves the return and rehabilitation of a scattered people and their Davidic king.

Investigation of the conclusion to the Deuteronomistic History produced some surprising results. We began with the observation that a distinct level of Jeremiah tradition (Chs. 9—15) anticipates a thorough if not final punishment in the events of 597 B. C. Babylonian presence in Judah is interpreted by Jeremiah as a sign of Yahweh's judgment, about to be loosed upon a sinful nation and king. Literary analysis of 2 Kings 24 indicated that this concise report of 597 events was drawn up by one who experienced the breaking of the siege and actual deportation to Babylon. 2 Kings 24 took form very shortly after 597 and in complete independence of the later 2 Kings 25 account of 587 events. Moreover, 2 Kings 24 is perfectly coordinated with the picture of judgment found in the pre-597 Jeremiah traditions described above. It sees the events of 597 as bringing about Yahweh's judgment over a sinful nation in fulfillment of the message of the prophets. It interprets the deportation of king, treasures, royal house, and general population as signaling an end. There is no discussion of ongoing life for a remnant in Judah. There is no mention of a future beyond judgment for the exiles or for those in the land.

These topics are, however, fully addressed by the prophet Ezekiel. 597 events come to be seen as penultimate events. They anticipate a fuller judgment not just over the Judahite remnant and ruler but over all nations. In the final form of the Deuteronomistic History, 2 Kings 24 is given penultimate status by the inclusion of 2 Kings 25. This final word of the history coordinates the 597 judgment with the 587 judgment. At the same time a full judgment is being executed upon all inhabitants of Judah and Jerusalem, a new beginning for Israel is symbolized by the rehabilitation of Jehoiachin, the exiled king.

The coordination of 597 and 587 events developed gradually, as Israel formed a coherent presentation of Yahweh's judgment over the accumulated sins of nation and monarchy. In the course of time, the presentation of judgment was filled out with a vision focused on Yahweh's restoration of an exiled and scattered people. This comprehensive presentation of Israel's judgment and restoration forms an inextricable part of the biblical witness, as it takes shape in the prophetic and historical literature.

Investigation of the Jeremiah traditions underscored the *gradual* way in which Israel's presentation of judgment and restoration evolved. The observation was made that the Book of Jeremiah reached a crescendo of judgment with the events of 597. It was noted with what extreme, almost hyperbolic, language Jeremiah denounced the Judahite monarchy in the persons of Jehoiakim and Jehoiachin and called for the land to be emptied of man and beast. But then a clear shift in the prophet's message can be found. In post-597 Jeremiah traditions an emphasis develops on the necessity for Judah's submission to Nebuchadnezzar, people and king. This emphasis is maintained by the prophet right up to the eve of Jerusalem's Fall. After the 587 deportations, the prophet remains an integral part of the remnant community. He continues to press for submission to Babylon, and urges the community not to flee to Egypt. Against his counsel, this action is taken.

Through careful literary analysis, we were able to successfully isolate a major level of post-597 Jeremiah tradition, which we termed the Scribal Chronicle. This Chronicle forms an absolutely distinctive witness to the evolving presentation of exile, judgment and restoration found in Ezekiel and the final form of the Deuteronomistic History. It tends to lay more stress on the significance of 597 events as accomplishing Yahweh's judgment. After this point, Jeremiah's word to the Judahite community consistently urges submission in the land, for Zedekiah and the post-597 remnant. There is nothing in the Scribal Chronicle which insists a yet greater judgment awaits the remnant. Neither does the Chronicle place significant emphasis on the exilic community. In this sense, the Scribal Chronicle shows as much positive interest in Ezekiel, Jehoiachin, and the exilic community as the Ezekiel traditions show in Jeremiah, the post-597 remnant, and Zedekiah.

The final form of the Book of Jeremiah reflects significant redactional intervention carried out under the influence of Ezekiel traditions. The normative presentation of exile, judgment, and restoration which exists in Ezekiel and 2 Kings 24/25 gradually finds its place within the Book of Jeremiah. The Exilic Redaction coordinates primary Jeremiah traditions, the Scribal Chronicle, and its own redactional supplementation in such a way that a comprehensive perspective on 597 and 587 events emerges. The pre-597 judgment tradition from the prophet, such as is found in Jeremiah 9—15, becomes the normative word from prophet to Judahite community at all points in the present book: prior to 597, between the deportations, and beyond. Following a word of judgment to the Judahite remnant in Egypt, all the nations of the earth are brought before Yahweh, including Babylon. Then, like the final word of the Deuteronomistic History at 2 Kings 25, Jeremiah 52 provides a brief glimpse at the future. In the rehabilitation of Jehoiachin, exiled king, Yahweh's restoration of exiled Israel is foreshadowed.

Commitment to a broader base for literary analysis of Jeremiah traditions has meant a broader look at the role of conflict in the exilic period. This conflict evolved because 597 events fractured whatever sense of religious and sociological cohesion the Judahite community had been able to maintain, even during troubled pre-exilic times. Once the community was divided by events of 597, further charges of theological condemnation sharpened the conflict, and made the demand for normative statements regarding exile and restoration all the more pressing. These are quickly provided in Ezekiel and 2 Kings 25. Moreover, debate over the status of Zedekiah, remnant monarch, and Jehoiachin, exiled monarch, further complicated questions regarding Israel's exile and restoration — especially in light of significant disruptions in the Judahite dynastic enterprise, beginning with the death of Josiah at Megiddo.

Commitment to a broader base for literary analysis has meant less time and space to carry out detailed literary investigation of the entire canonical Book of Jeremiah. Specifically, the full extent of redactional supplementation in the earlier chapters has not received extensive comment, though general observations were made about the larger shape and movement of the present text. It remains a future task to coordinate the analysis of conflict in the exilic period with exegesis of the entire assortment of tradition in the Book of Jeremiah.

The same can be said with respect to another crucial exilic witness, from a slightly later period, which looks at the question of conflict between exiles and the Judahite remnant from a different perspective. This is the Isaiah material found in Chs. 40—55, commonly referred to as Second Isaiah. A thorough treatment of the role of theological conflict in the exilic period would move at this juncture to the prophetic traditions of Isaiah, a collection distinct in final form and internal development from Ezekiel, the Deuteronomistic History, and the Book of Jeremiah. Movement to Second Isaiah traditions would push the interpreter closer to the actual events of restoration and return from Exile, and a complex of biblical material generally treated within the context of Post-Exilic Israel. The present study has laid the essential groundwork for such a treatment.

Bibliography

Ackroyd, P. R., "The Vitality of the Prophetic Word." *Annual of the Swedish Theological Institute* 1 (1962): 7–23.

—, "History and Theology in the Writings of the Chronicler." *Concordia Theological Monthly* 38 (1967): 510–15.

—, *Exile and Restoration*. Philadelphia: Westminster, 1968.

—, "Historians and Prophets." *Svensk Exegetisk Årsbok* 33 (1968): 18–25.

—, "Aspects of the Jeremiah Tradition." *Indian Journal of Theology* 20 (1971): 1–12.

—, "The Temple Vessels — A Continuity Theme." *Supplements to Vetus Testamentum* 23 (1972): 166–81.

—, "Faith and its Reformulation in the Post-exilic Period: Sources." *Theology Digest* 27 (1979): 323–46.

—, "The History of Israel in the Exilic and Post-Exilic Periods." *Tradition and Interpretation*. Edited by G. W. Anderson. Oxford: University, 1979.

—, "The Jewish Community in Palestine in the Persian Period." *The Cambridge History of Judaism*. Edited by W. D. Davies and L. Finkelstein. Cambridge: University, 1984. Vol. 1, 130–61.

—, "The Book of Jeremiah — Some Recent Studies." *Journal for the Study of the Old Testament* 29 (1984): 47–59.

Aharoni, Y., "Excavations at Ramat Raḥel, 1954. Preliminary Report." *Israel Exploration Journal* 6 (1956): 102–11; 137–57.

—, "Excavations at Ramat Raḥel." *Biblical Archaeologist* 24 (1961): 98–118.

—, *Excavations at Ramat Raḥel, Seasons 1959 and 1960*. Rome: Centro di Studi Semitici, 1962.

—, "Hebrew Ostraca from Tel Arad." *Israel Exploration Journal* 16 (1966): 1–7.

—, "Beth-Haccherem." *Archaeology and Old Testament Study*. Edited by D. Winton Thomas. Oxford: At the Clarendon, 1967. 178–83.

—, "Arad: Its Inscriptions and Temple." *Biblical Archaeologist* 31 (1968): 2–32.

—, "Three Hebrew Ostraca from Arad." *Bulletin of the American Schools of Oriental Research* 197 (1970): 16–42.

Ahlström, G. W., *Aspects of Syncretism in Israelite Religion*. Lund: Gleerup, 1963.

—, *Royal Administration and National Religion in Ancient Palestine*. Leiden: E. J. Brill, 1982.

Albright, W. F., "The Seal of Eliakim and the Latest Preëxilic History of Judah." *Journal of Biblical Literature* 51 (1932): 77–106.

—, "King Joiachin in Exile." *Biblical Archaeologist* 5 (1942): 49–55.

—, *The Biblical Period from Abraham to Ezra*. New York: Harper Torchbooks, 1949.

Alt, A. "Judas Gaue unter Josia." *Palästinajahrbuch* 21 (1925): 100–16.

—, "Die Rolle Samarias bei der Entstehung des Judentums." *Kleine Schriften zur Geschichte des Volkes Israel*. München: C. H. Beck'sche, 1953. Vol. 2, 316–37.

—, "Die Heimat des Deuteronomium." *Kleine Schriften*. Vol. 2, 250–75.

—, "The Monarchy in the Kingdoms of Israel and Judah." *Essays on Old Testament History and Religion*. Oxford: Basil Blackwell, 1966.

Andreasen, N.-E., "The Role of the Queen Mother in Israelite Society." *Catholic Biblical Quarterly* 45 (1983): 179–94.

Avigad, N., "Excavations in the Jewish Quarter of the Old City of Jerusalem, 1970 (Second Preliminary Report)." *Israel Exploration Journal* 20 (1970): 129—40.

—, "New Light on the Naʿar Seals." *Magnalia Dei: The Mighty Acts of God*. Festschrift G. E. Wright. Edited by F. M. Cross, W. Lemke, and P. Miller. Garden City: Doubleday, 1976. 294—300.

—, "Baruch the Scribe and Jerahmeel the King's Son." *Israel Exploration Journal* 28 (1978): 52—6.

Bahat, D., "The Wall of Manasseh in Jerusalem." *Israel Exploration Journal* 31 (1981): 235—6.

Baltzer, D., *Ezechiel und Deuterojesaja. Berührungen in der Heilserwartung der beiden großen Exilspropheten*. Beiheft zur *Zeitschrift für die alttestamentliche Wissenschaft* 121. Berlin: Walter de Gruyter, 1971.

Baltzer, K., "Das Ende des Staates Juda und die Messias-Frage." *Studien zur alttestamentlichen Überlieferung*. Festschrift G. von Rad. Edited by R. Rendtorff and K. Koch. Neukirchen: Neukirchener, 1961. 33—43.

Barth, H., "Israel und die Assyrerreich in den Nichtjesajanischen Texten des Protojesajabuches. Eine Untersuchung zur produktiven Neuinterpretation der Jesajaüberlieferung." Dissertation, Hamburg, 1974.

—, *Die Jesaja-Worte in der Josiazeit. Israel und Assur als Thema einer produktiven Neuinterpretation der Jesajaüberlieferung*. Wissenschaftliche Monographien zum Alten und Neuen Testament 48. Neukirchen-Vluyn: Neukirchener, 1978.

Baudissin, W. W. Graf. *Einleitung in die Bücher des Alten Testaments*. Leipzig: S. Hirtel, 1901.

Bentzen, A., *Die Josianische Reform und ihre Voraussetzungen*. Copenhagen: P. Haase & Sons, 1926.

Bewer, J., "The Problem of Deuteronomy: A Symposium." *Journal of Biblical Literature* 47 (1928): 305—79.

Birkeland, H., *Zum hebräischen Traditionswesen. Die Komposition der prophetischen Bücher des Alten Testaments*. Oslo, 1938.

Bleek, J., *An Introduction to the Old Testament*. London: Bell and Daldy, 1869. Vol. 2.

Blenkinsopp, J., *A History of Israelite Prophecy*. Philadelphia: Fortress, 1984.

Bogaert, P.-M., Editor. *Le Livre de Jérémie. Le Prophète et son milieu. Les Oracles et leur transmission*. Leuven: University Press, 1981.

Borger, R., *Die Inschriften Asarhaddons König von Assyrien. Archiv für Orientforschung* 9. Graz: Weidner, 1956.

Bright, J., "A New Letter in Aramaic, Written to a Pharaoh of Egypt." *Biblical Archaeologist* 12 (1949): 46—52.

—, "The Date of the Prose Sermons of Jeremiah." *Journal of Biblical Literature* 70 (1951): 17.

—, *Jeremiah*. Anchor Bible 21. Garden City: Doubleday, 1965.

—, "The Prophetic Reminiscence: Its Place and Function in the Book of Jeremiah." *Biblical Essays*. Proceedings of the Ninth Meeting of "Die Ou-Testamentiese Werkgemeenskap in Suid-Afrika." Stellenbosch, 1966.

—, *A History of Israel*. Second Edition. Philadelphia: Westminster, 1972.

Broshi, M., "The Expansion of Jerusalem in the Reigns of Hezekiah and Manasseh." *Israel Exploration Journal* 24 (1974): 21—6.

—, "Estimating the Population of Ancient Israel." *Biblical Archaeology Review* 4 (1978): 10—15.

Brownlee, W. L., "Two Elegies on the Fall of Judah." *Studies in the History of Religions* 21.1. Leiden: Brill, 1972. 93—103.

Carroll, R. P., *From Chaos to Covenant. Prophecy in the Book of Jeremiah.* New York: Crossroad, 1981.

Cazelles, H., "Jérémie et Deutéronome." *Recherches de Science Religieuse* 38 (1951) 5—36. Reprinted in English translation as "Jeremiah and Deuteronomy" in *A Prophet to the Nations.* Edited by L. G. Perdue and B. W. Kovacs. Winona Lake, Indiana: Eisenbrauns, 1984. 89—111.

—, "Sophonie, Jérémie, et les Scythes en Palestine." *Revue Biblique* 74 (1967): 22—44. Reprinted in English translation in *A Prophet to the Nations.* 129—49.

—, "La vie de Jérémie dans son contexte national et international." *Le Livre de Jérémie.* Leuven: University Press, 1981. 21—39.

Childs, B. S., *Isaiah and the Assyrian Crisis.* Studies in Biblical Theology 2/3. Napierville, Illinois: A. R. Allenson, 1967.

—, *Introduction to the Old Testament as Scripture.* Philadelphia: Fortress, 1979.

Clements, R. E., "Deuteronomy and the Jerusalem Cult Tradition." *Vetus Testamentum* 15 (1965): 300—12.

—, *Isaiah and the Deliverance of Jerusalem.* Journal for the Study of the Old Testament Supplement Series 13. Sheffield: JSOT Press, 1980.

Cody, A., *A History of Old Testament Priesthood.* Analecta Biblica 35. Rome: Pontifical Biblical Institute, 1969.

Cogan, M., "A Technical Term for Exposure." *Journal of Near Eastern Studies* 27 (1968): 133—5.

—, "A Note on Disinternment in Jeremiah." *Gratz College Anniversary Volume.* Philadelphia: Gratz College, 1971. 29—34.

—, *Imperialism and Religion: Assyria, Judah and Israel in the Eighth and Seventh Centuries B. C. E.* Society of Biblical Literature Dissertation Series 19. Missoula: Scholars, 1974.

Coggins, R. J., *Samaritans and Jews: The Origins of Samaritanism Reconsidered.* Atlanta: John Knox, 1975.

Colenso, J. W., *The Pentateuch and the Book of Joshua Critically Examined.* London: Longmans, Green, 1866.

Cooke, G. A., *Ezekiel.* International Critical Commentary. Edinburgh: Clark, 1936.

Cornill, C. H., *The Book of the Prophet Jeremiah: Critical Edition of the Hebrew Text Arranged in Chronological Order with Notes.* The Sacred Books of the Old Testament 11. Leipzig: J. C. Hinrichs'sche, 1895.

—, *Einleitung in das Alte Testament.* Freiburg/Leipzig: J. C. B. Mohr, 1896.

—, *Das Buch Jeremia.* Leipzig: Chr. Herm. Tauchnitz, 1905.

Cross, F. M. and D. N. Freedman, "Josiah's Revolt Against Assyria." *Journal of Near Eastern Studies* 12 (1953): 56—8.

Cross, F. M., *Canaanite Myth and Hebrew Epic.* Cambridge: Harvard, 1973.

Curtis, E., *The Books of Chronicles.* International Critical Commentary. New York: Scribner's, 1910.

Daiches, S., "The Meaning of עם הארץ in the Old Testament." *Journal of Theological Studies* 30 (1929): 245—9.

Dietrich, W., *Prophetie und Geschichte.* Forschungen zur Religion und Literatur des Alten und Neuen Testaments 108. Göttingen: Vandenhoeck & Ruprecht, 1972.

—, "Josia und das Gesetzbuch (2 Reg. XXII)." *Vetus Testamentum* 27 (1977): 13—35.

Donner, H., "Art und Herkunft des Amtes der Königinmutter im Alten Testament." *Festschrift Johannes Friedrich zum 65. Geburtstag am 27. August Gewidmet.* Edited by R. von Kienle. Heidelberg: Carl Winter, 1959. 105—45.

—, "The Separate States of Israel and Judah." *Israelite and Judaean History*. Edited by J. H. Hayes and J. M. Miller. Philadelphia: Westminster, 1977.

Dothan, M., "Ashdod II—III." *'Atiqot* 9—10 (1971): 21 ff.

Driver, S. R., *An Introduction to the Literature of the Old Testament*. New York: Scribner's, 1897.

Duhm, B., *Das Buch Jeremia*. Kurzer Hand-Commentar zum Alten Testament 11. Tübingen: Verlag von J. C. B. Mohr (Paul Siebeck), 1901.

Eichhorn, J. G., *Einleitung in das Alte Testament*. Göttingen, 1824.

Eichrodt, W., *Ezekiel*. Translated by C. Quin. Old Testament Library. Philadelphia: Westminster, 1970.

Eissfeldt, O., *Einleitung in das Alte Testament*. Tübingen: J. C. B. Mohr, 1934.

—, "Silo und Jerusalem." *Supplements to Vetus Testamentum* 4 (1957): 138—47.

Elat, M., "The Political Status of the Kingdom of Judah within the Assyrian Empire in the 7th Century BCE." *Investigations at Lachish*. Tel Aviv: Gateway, 1975. Vol. 5.

Elgood, P. G., *Later Dynasties of Egypt*. Oxford: Basil Blackwell, 1951.

Emerton, J. A., "Some Difficult Words in Genesis 49." *Words and Meanings: Essays Presented to David Winton Thomas*. Edited by P. R. Ackroyd and B. Lindars. Cambridge: University, 1968. 81—92.

Eph'al, I., "Assyrian Dominion in Palestine." *The World History of the Jewish People*. Vol. IV/1, 276—80.

Erbt, W., *Jeremia und seine Zeit*. Göttingen: Vandenhoeck & Ruprecht, 1902.

Evans, C. D., "Judah's Foreign Policy from Hezekiah to Josiah." *Scripture in Context: Essays on the Comparative Method*. Edited by C. D. Evans, W. W. Hallo, and J. B. White. Pittsburgh Theological Seminary Monograph Series 34. Pittsburgh: Pickwick, 1980. 157—78.

Ewald, H., *Commentary on the Prophets of the Old Testament*. London/Edinburgh: William and Norgate, 1878. Vol. 3.

Finegan, J., "The Chronology of Ezekiel." *Journal of Biblical Literature* 69 (1950): 61—6.

Fitzmyer, J. "The Aramaic Letter of King Adon to the Egyptian Pharaoh." *Biblica* 46 (1965): 41—6.

Fohrer, G., *Ezechiel*. Handbuch zum Alten Testament 13. Tübingen: J. C. B. Mohr, 1955.

Frankena, R., "The Vassal Treaties of Esarhaddon and the Dating of Deuteronomy." *Oudtestamentische Studiën* 14 (1965): 122—54.

Freedman, D. N., "The Babylonian Chronicle." *Biblical Archaeologist* 19 (1956): 50—60.

Freedy, K. S. and D. B. Redford, "The Dates in Ezekiel in Relationship to Biblical, Babylonian and Egyptian Sources." *Journal of the American Oriental Society* 90 (1970): 462—79.

Friedman, R. E., *The Exile and Biblical Narrative*. Harvard Semitic Monographs 22. Chico, California: Scholars, 1981.

—, "From Egypt to Egypt: Dtr 1 and Dtr 2." *Traditions in Transformation*. Edited by B. Halpern and J. D. Levenson. Winona Lake, Indiana: Eisenbrauns, 1981.

Galling, K., "Die israelitische Staatsverfassung in ihrer vorderorientalischen Umwelt." *Der Alte Orient* 28 (1929): 5—64.

—, "Die Halle des Schreibers." *Palästinajahrbuch* 27 (1931): 51—7.

—, "Assyrische und persische Präfekten in Geser." *Palästinajahrbuch* 31 (1935): 75—93.

—, "Das Königsgesetz im Deuteronomium." *Theologische Literaturzeitung* 76 (1951): 134—8.

Gardiner, Sir Alan, *Egypt of the Pharaohs: An Introduction*. Oxford: At the Clarendon, 1961.

Gese, H., *Der Verfassungsentwurf des Ezechiel (Kap. 40—48) traditionsgeschichtlich untersucht*. Beiträge zur historischen Theologie 25. Tübingen: J. C. B. Mohr, 1957.

Geva, H., "Excavations in the Citadel of Jerusalem." *Israel Exploration Journal* 33 (1983): 52—60.

Giles, M., *Pharaonic Policies and Administration*. Chapel Hill, N. C.: The James Sprunt Studies in History and Political Science, 1959.

Ginsberg, H. L., "An Aramaic Contemporary of the Lachish Letters." *Bulletin of the American Schools of Oriental Research* 111 (1948): 204—8.

—, *The Israelian Heritage*. New York: The Jewish Theological Seminary of New York, 1982.

Good, E. M., "The 'Blessing' on Judah, Gen 49:8—12." *Journal of Biblical Literature* 82 (1963): 427—32.

Gordis, R., "Sectional Rivalry in the Kingdom of Judah." *Jewish Quarterly Review* 25 (1934/5): 237—59.

Graf, K. F., *Der Prophet Jeremia*. Leipzig: T. O. Weigel, 1862.

Graham, J. N., "'Vinedressers and Plowmen': 2 Kings 25:12 and Jeremiah 52:16." *Biblical Archaeologist* 47 (1984): 55—8.

Gray, J., *I & II Kings*. Second Edition. Old Testament Library. Philadelphia: Westminster, 1970.

Grayson, A. K., *Assyrian and Babylonian Chronicles*. Texts from Cuneiform Sources 5. Locust Valley, New York: J. J. Augustin, 1975.

Greenberg, M., "Ezekiel 17 and the Policy of Psammetichus II." *Journal of Biblical Literature* 76 (1957): 304—9.

—, *Ezekiel 1—20*. Anchor Bible 22. Garden City: Doubleday, 1983.

Greenwood, D. G., "On the Jewish Hope for a Restored Northern Kingdom." *Zeitschrift für die alttestamentliche Wissenschaft* 88 (1976): 376—85.

Gressmann, H., "Josia und das Deuteronomium." *Zeitschrift für die alttestamentliche Wissenschaft* 42 (1924): 313—37.

Gunneweg, A. H. J., *Leviten und Priester*. Göttingen: Vandenhoeck & Ruprecht, 1965.

Hammershaimb, E., "Ezekiel's View of the Monarchy." *Studia Orientalia, Ioanni Pedersen Septuagenario*. Copenhagen: Einar Munksgaard, 1953. 130—40.

Hanson, P. *The Dawn of Apocalyptic: The Historical and Sociological Roots of Jewish Apocalyptic Eschatology*. Philadelphia: Fortress, 1979.

Hartford-Battersby, J., *Studies in the Book of Ezekiel*. Cambridge: University, 1935.

Hävernick, H. A. Ch., *Handbuch der historisch-kritischen Einleitung in das Alte Testament*. Erlangen: Carl Heyder, 1839. Vol. 2.

Henshaw, R. A., "The Office of Šaknu in Neo-Assyrian Times." *Journal of the American Oriental Society* 87 (1967): 517—24 and *JAOS* 88 (1968): 461—82.

Herrmann, S., *Die prophetischen Heilserwartungen im Alten Testament: Ursprung und Gestaltswandel*. Beiträge zur Wissenschaft vom Alten und Neuen Testament 85. Stuttgart: W. Kohlhammer, 1965.

—, *A History of Israel in Old Testament Times*. London/Philadelphia: SCM/Fortress, 1975.

Hitzig, F., *Der Prophet Jeremia*. Leipzig: Weidmannsche Buchhandlung, 1841.

Holladay, W. L., "'Prototype' and 'Copies': A New Approach to the Poetry-Prose Problem in the Book of Jeremiah." *Journal of Biblical Literature* 79 (1960): 351—67.

—, "The Background of Jeremiah's Self-Understanding. Moses, Samuel, and Psalm 22." *Journal of Biblical Literature* 83 (1964): 153—64.

—, "Jeremiah and Moses. Further Observations." *Journal of Biblical Literature* 85 (1966): 17—27.

—, "A Fresh Look at 'Source B' and 'Source C' in Jeremiah." *Vetus Testamentum* 25 (1975): 394—412.

—, *The Architecture of Jeremiah 1—20*. Lewisburg/London: Bucknell University/Associated University, 1976.

—, "The Years of Jeremiah's Preaching." *Interpretation* 37 (1983): 146—59.

Hollenstein, H., "Literarkritische Erwägungen zum Bericht über die Reformmaßnahmen Josias in 2 Kön. XXIII 4 ff." *Vetus Testamentum* 27 (1977): 321—36.

Hölscher, G., *Die Propheten: Untersuchungen zur Religionsgeschichte Israels*. Leipzig: J. C. Hinrisch'sche, 1914.

—, "Komposition und Ursprung des Deuteronomiums." *Zeitschrift für die alttestamentliche Wissenschaft* 40 (1922): 161—225.

Honeymoon, A. M., "The Evidence for Regnal Names Among the Hebrews." *Journal of Biblical Literature* 67 (1948): 13—25.

Horn, S., "Where and When was the Aramaic Saqqara Papyrus Written?" *Andrews University Seminar Studies* 6 (1968): 29—45.

Horst, L., "Etudes sur les Deutéronome." *Revue de l'histoire des religions* 17 (1888): 1—22.

Hyatt, J. P., "Jeremiah and Deuteronomy." *Journal of Near Eastern Studies* 1 (1941): 156—73.

—, "The Deuteronomic Edition of Jeremiah." *Vanderbilt Studies in the Humanities* 1 (1951): 71—95.

—, *Jeremiah*. Interpreter's Bible 5. New York/Nashville: Abingdon, 1956.

Ihromi, "Die Königinmutter und der *'am ha'arez* im Reich Judah." *Vetus Testamentum* 24 (1974): 421—9.

Ishida, T., " 'The People of the Land' and the Political Crises in Judah." *Annual of the Japanese Biblical Institute* 1 (1975): 23—38.

—, *The Royal Dynasties in Ancient Israel*. Beiheft zur *Zeitschrift für die alttestamentliche Wissenschaft* 104. Berlin/New York: Walter de Gruyter, 1977.

Ittmann, N., *Die Konfessionen Jeremias: Ihre Bedeutung für die Verkündigung des Propheten*. Wissenschaftliche Monographien zum Alten und Neuen Testament 54. Neukirchen: Neukirchener, 1981.

Janssen, E., *Juda in der Exilszeit: Ein Beitrag zur Frage der Entstehung des Judenthums*. Göttingen: Vandenhoeck & Ruprecht, 1956.

Janzen, J. G., *Studies in the Text of Jeremiah*. Harvard Semitic Monographs 6. Cambridge: Harvard, 1973.

Jones, D. R., "The Traditio of the Oracles of Isaiah of Jerusalem." *Zeitschrift für die alttestamentliche Wissenschaft* 67 (1955): 226—46.

—, "The Cessation of Sacrifice After the Destruction of the Temple in 586 B. C." *Journal of Theological Studies* n. s. 14 (1963): 12—31.

Jones, G. H., *1 and 2 Kings*. New Century Bible. Grand Rapids: Eerdmans, 1984.

de Jong, C., "Deux oracles contre les Nations, reflets de la politique étrangère de Joaquim." *Le Livre de Jérémie*. Leuven: University, 1981. 369—79.

Junge, E., *Der Wiederaufbau des Heerwesens des Reiches Juda unter Josia*. Beiträge zur Wissenschaft vom Alten und Neuen Testament 23. Stuttgart: Kohlhammer, 1936.

Kaiser, O., *Das Buch des Propheten Jesaja 1—12*. Das Alte Testament Deutsch 17. Fifth Edition. Göttingen: Vandenhoeck & Ruprecht, 1981.

Kampman, A. A., "Tawannannas, der Title der hethietischen Königin." *Jaarbericht van het Vooraziatisch-Egyptisch Gezelschap 'Ex Oriente Lux'* 2 (1939—42): 432—42.

Katzenstein, H. J., *A History of Tyre*. The Schocken Institute for Jewish Research of the Jewish Theological Seminary of America. Jerusalem: Goldberg's, 1973.

Kennett, R. H., "The Date of Deuteronomy." *Journal of Theological Studies* 7 (1906): 481—500.

Kessler, M., "Form-Critical Suggestions on Jer 36." *Catholic Biblical Quarterly* 28 (1966): 389—401.

—, "Jeremiah Chapters 26—45 Reconsidered." *Journal of Near Eastern Studies* 27 (1968): 81—8.

Kienitz, F. K., *Die politische Geschichte Ägyptens vom 7. bis zum 4. Jahrhundert vor der Zeitwende.* Berlin: Akademie-Verlag, 1953.

—, *Fischer Weltgeschichte 4, Die Altorientalischen Reiche III.* München: Fischer Bücherei, 1967.

Kitchen, K. A., *The Third Intermediate Period in Egypt (1100—650 B. C.).* Warminster: Aris & Phillips, 1972.

—, "Late-Egyptian Chronology and the Hebrew Monarchy." *Journal of the Ancient Near Eastern Society of Columbia University* 5 (1973): 225—33.

Klamroth, E., *Die jüdischen Exulanten in Babylon.* Leipzig, 1912.

Klein, R., *Israel in Exile: A Theological Interpretation.* Overtures in Biblical Theology. Philadelphia: Fortress, 1979.

Knight, D., *Rediscovering the Traditions of Israel.* Society of Biblical Literature Dissertation Series 9. Missoula: Scholars, 1975.

Knobel, August, *Der Prophetismus der Hebräer.* Breslau: Josef Max, 1837. Vol. 2.

Koch, K., "Die Eigenart der priesterschriftlichen Sinaigesetzgebung." *Zeitschrift für Theologie und Kirche* 55 (1958): 36—51.

Kraetzschmar, R., *Das Buch Ezechiel.* Handkommentar zum Alten Testament. Göttingen: Vandenhoeck & Ruprecht, 1900.

Kremers, H., "Leidensgemeinschaft mit Gott im Alten Testament: Eine Untersuchung der 'biographischen' Berichte im Jeremiabuch." *Evangelische Theologie* 13 (1953): 122—45.

Kuenen, A., *Historisch-kritische Einleitung in die Bücher des Alten Testaments.* Leipzig: O. R. Reisland, 1892. Vol. 2.

Kugel, J., *The Idea of Biblical Poetry.* New Haven/London: Yale University Press, 1981.

LaCocque, A., *Daniel.* Atlanta: John Knox, 1979.

Lance, H. D., "The Royal Stamps and the Kingdom of Josiah." *Harvard Theological Review* 64 (1971): 315—32.

Larsson, G., "When did the Babylonian Captivity Begin?" *Journal of Theological Studies* 18 (1967): 417—23.

Levenson, J. D., *Theology of the Program of Restoration of Ezekiel 40—48.* Harvard Semitic Monographs 10. Missoula: Scholars, 1976.

—, "The Last Four Verses in Kings." *Journal of Biblical Literature* 103 (1984): 353—9.

Lindblom, J., "The Political Background of the Shilo Oracle." *Supplements to Vetus Testamentum* 1 (1953): 78—87.

Lipinski, E., "Prose ou poésie en Jér XXXIV 1—7?" *Vetus Testamentum* 24 (1974): 112 ff.

Lohfink, N., "Die Bundesurkunde des Königs Josias." *Biblica* 44 (1963): 261—88; 461—98.

—, "Die Gattung der »Historischen Kurzgeschichte« in den letzten Jahren von Juda und in der Zeit des Babylonischen Exils." *Zeitschrift für die alttestamentliche Wissenschaft* 90 (1978): 319—47.

—, "Der junge Jeremia als Propagandist und Poet: Zum Grundstock von Jer 30—31." *Le Livre de Jérémie.* Leuven: University, 1981. 351—68.

Luckenbill, D. D., *The Annals of Sennacherib.* Chicago: University of Chicago Press, 1924.

Lundbom, J., *Jeremiah: A Study of Ancient Hebrew Rhetoric.* Society of Biblical Literature Dissertation Series 18. Missoula: Scholars, 1975.

Malamat, A., "The Last Wars of the Kingdom of Judah." *Journal of Near Eastern Studies* 9 (1950): 218—27.

—, "Jeremiah and the Last Two Kings of Judah." *Palestine Exploration Quarterly* 83 (1951): 81—7.

—, "The Historical Background of the Assassination of Amon, King of Judah." *Israel Exploration Journal* 3 (1953): 26—9.

—, "The Last Kings of Judah and the Fall of Jerusalem: An Historical-Chronological Study." *Israel Exploration Journal* 18 (1968): 137—56.

—, "Josiah's Bid for Armageddon." *Journal of the Ancient Near Eastern Society of Columbia University* 5 (1973): 267—79.

—, "The Twilight of Judah in the Egyptian-Babylonian Maelstrom." *Supplements to Vetus Testamentum* 28 (1974): 123—45.

—, "The Last Years of the Kingdom of Judah." *The World History of the Jewish People.* Jerusalem: Massada, 1979. Vol. IV/1, 205—21.

May, H. G., "Three Hebrew Seals and the Status of Exiled Jehoiachin." *American Journal of Semitic Languages and Literature* (1939): 146—8.

—, "Towards an Objective Approach to the Book of Jeremiah: The Biographer." *Journal of Biblical Literature* 61 (1942): 139—55.

—, "Jeremiah's Biographer." *Journal of Bible and Religion* 10 (1942): 195—201.

Mayes, A. D. H., *Deuteronomy.* New Century Bible. London: Oliphants, 1979.

Mazar, B., "The Campaign of Pharoah Shishak to Palestine." *Supplements to Vetus Testamentum* 4 (1957): 57—66.

McKane, W., "Relations Between Poetry and Prose in the Book of Jeremiah with Special Reference to Jeremiah III 6—11 and XII 14—17." *Supplements to Vetus Testamentum* 28 (1980): 220—37.

McKay, J. W., *Religion in Judah under the Assyrians 732—609 BC.* Studies in Biblical Theology 26. Napierville, Illinois: Alec R. Allenson, 1973.

Melugin, R., *The Formation of Isaiah 40—55.* Beiheft zur *Zeitschrift für die alttestamentliche Wissenschaft* 141. Berlin/New York: Walter de Gruyter, 1976.

Menes, A., *Die vorexilischen Gesetze Israels im Zusammenhang seiner kulturgeschichtlichen Entwicklung.* Beiheft zur *Zeitschrift für die alttestamentliche Wissenschaft* 50. Berlin, 1928.

Milgrom, J., "The Date of Jeremiah, Chapter 2." *Journal of Near Eastern Studies* 14 (1955): 66—9.

Miller, J. W., *Das Verhältnis Jeremias sprachlich und theologisch untersucht mit besonderer Berücksichtigung der Prosareden Jeremias.* Assen: Royal VanGorcum, 1955.

Molin, G., "Die Stellung der Gebira im Staate Juda." *Theologische Zeitschrift* 10 (1954): 161—75.

Montgomery, J. A., *Kings.* International Critical Commentary. Edinburgh: Clark, 1951.

Moran, W., "Gen 49,10 and its Use in Ez 21,32." *Biblica* 39 (1958): 405—25.

Movers, F. G., *De utriusque recensionis Vaticinorum Ieremiae, graecae alexandrinae et hebraicae masorethicae, indole et origine commentatio critica.* Hamburg, 1837.

Mowinckel, S., *Zur Komposition des Buches Jeremias.* Kristiania: Jacob Dybwad, 1914.

—, *Prophecy and Tradition. The Prophetic Books in the Light of the Study of the Growth and History of the Tradition.* Oslo: Jacob Dybwad, 1946.

—, *He That Cometh.* Translated by G. W. Anderson. Nashville: Abingdon, 1956.

Muilenberg, J., "Baruch the Scribe." *Proclamation and Presence. Old Testament Essays in Honour of Gwynne Henton Davies.* Edited by J. I. Durham and J. R. Porter. London: SCM, 1970. 215—38.

Myers, J., "Edom and Judah in the Sixth-Fifth Centuries." *Near Eastern Studies in Honor of William Foxwell Albright.* Edited by H. Goedicke. Baltimore and London: Johns Hopkins, 1971. 377—92.

Naveh, J., "A Hebrew Letter from the Seventh Century BC." *Israel Exploration Journal* 10 (1960): 129—39; *IEJ* 12 (1962): 27—32; 88—99.

Nelson, R., *The Double Redaction of the Deuteronomistic History.* Journal for the Study of the Old Testament Supplement Series 18. Sheffield: JSOT Press, 1981.

—, *"Realpolitik* in Judah." *Scripture in Context II: More Essays on the Comparative Method.* Edited by W. W. Hallo, J. C. Moyer, and L. G. Perdue. Winona Lake, Indiana: Eisenbrauns, 1983. 177—89.

Nicholson, E. W., "The Centralisation of the Cult in Deuteronomy." *Vetus Testamentum* 13 (1963): 380—9.

—, "The Meaning of the Expression עם הארץ in the Old Testament." *Journal of Semitic Studies* 10 (1965): 59—66.

—, *Deuteronomy and Tradition.* Philadelphia: Fortress, 1967.

—, *Preaching to the Exiles: A Study of the Prose Tradition in the Book of Jeremiah.* New York: Schocken, 1970.

—, *The Book of the Prophet Jeremiah 26—52.* Cambridge Bible. Cambridge: University Press, 1975.

Nielsen, E., *Oral Tradition.* Studies in Biblical Theology 1/11. Chicago: Alec R. Allenson, 1954.

—, "Political Conditions and Cultural Developments in Israel and Judah during the Reign of Manasseh." *The Fourth World Congress of Jewish Studies, Papers* I (1967): 103—6.

Noth, M., *Das System der Zwölf Stämme Israels.* Beiträge zur Wissenschaft vom Alten und Neuen Testament IV/1. Stuttgart: Kohlhammer, 1930.

—, "Beiträge zur Geschichte der Ostjordanlande: I. Das Land Gilead als Siedlungsgebiet israelitischer Sippen." *Palästinajahrbuch* (1941): 98—9.

—, "Gott, König, Volk im Alten Testament." *Zeitschrift für Theologie und Kirche* 47 (1950): 157—91.

—, "Die Einnahme von Jerusalem im Jahre 597 v. Chr." *Zeitschrift des Deutschen Palästina-Vereins* 74 (1958): 133—57.

—, *The History of Israel.* New York/Evanston: Harper & Row, 1960.

—, *Exodus.* Old Testament Library. Philadelphia: Westminster, 1962.

—, "The Jerusalem Catastrophe of 587 B. C. and its Significance for Israel." *The Laws of the Pentateuch and Other Studies.* Translated by D. R. Ap-Thomas. Philadelphia: Fortress, 1967. 260—80.

—, *Numbers.* Old Testament Library. Philadelphia: Westminster, 1968.

—, *The Deuteronomistic History.* Journal for the Study of the Old Testament Supplement Series 15. Sheffield: JSOT Press, 1981.

Nötscher, F., "Gen 49,10: שׁי לה‎ = akkad. *šēlu."* *Zeitschrift für die alttestamentliche Wissenschaft* 47 (1929): 323—5.

Nyberg, H. S., *Studien zum Hoseabuch. Zugleich ein Beitrag zur Klärung des Problems der alttestamentlichen Textkritik.* Uppsala: A. B. Lundequistska, 1935.

Oded, B., "Observations on Methods of Assyrian Rule in Transjordan after the Palestinian Champaign of Tiglath-Pileser III." *Journal of Near Eastern Studies* 29 (1970): 177—86.

—, "Hezekiah's Rebellion and Sennacherib's Campaign against Judah." *Israelite and Judaean History.* Edited by J. H. Hayes and J. M. Miller. Philadelphia: Westminster, 1977. 446—51.

—, *Mass Deportations and Deportees in the Neo-Assyrian Empire.* Wiesbaden: Reichart, 1979.

Otzen, B., *Studien über Deuterosacharja.* Copenhagen: Prostant Apud Munksgaard, 1964.

—, "Israel under the Assyrians: Reflections on Imperial Policy in Palestine." *Annual of the Swedish Theological Institute* 11 (1977/78): 96—110.

Pardee, D., *Handbook of Ancient Hebrew Letters*. With S. D. Sperling, J. D. Whitehead, and P. E. Dion. Society of Biblical Literature Sources for Biblical Study 15. Chico, California: Scholars, 1982.

Pedersen, J., "Passahfest und Passahlegende." *Zeitschrift für die alttestamentliche Wissenschaft* 52 (1934): 161—75.

Pfeiffer, R., *Introduction to the Old Testament*. New York/London: Harper, 1941.

Plöger, O., *Theocracy and Eschatology*. Richmond: John Knox, 1968.

Pohlmann, K.-F., *Studien zum Jeremiabuch: Ein Beitrag zur Frage nach der Entstehung des Jeremiabuches*. Forschungen zur Religion und Literatur des Alten und Neuen Testaments. Göttingen: Vandenhoeck & Ruprecht, 1978.

—, "Erwägungen zum Schlußkapitel des deuteronomistischen Geschichtswerkes. Oder: Warum wird der Prophet Jeremia in 2. Kön. 22—25 nicht erwähnt?" *Textgemäß. Aufsätze und Beiträge zur Hermeneutik des Alten Testaments*. Festschrift E. Würthwein. Edited by A. H. J. Gunneweg and O. Kaiser. Göttingen: Vandenhoeck & Ruprecht, 1979. 94—109.

Polzin, R., *Moses and the Deuteronomist*. New York: Seabury, 1980.

Pope, M. H., "'Am Ha'Arez." *The Interpreters Dictionary of the Bible*. Edited by G. A. Buttrick. Nashville: Abingdon, 1962.

Procksch, O., "Fürst und Priester bei Hesekiel." *Zeitschrift für die alttestamentliche Wissenschaft* 58 (1940/1): 99—133.

Rad, G. von, *Studies in Deuteronomy*. Studies in Biblical Theology 9. London: SCM, 1953.

—, *Old Testament Theology*. New York: Harper & Row, 1965. Vol. 2.

—, *Genesis*. Old Testament Library. Philadelphia: Westminster, 1970.

Raitt, T., *A Theology of Exile: Judgement/Deliverance in Jeremiah and Ezekiel*. Philadelphia: Fortress, 1979.

Rendtorff, R., "Literaturkritik und Traditionsgeschichte." *Evangelische Theologie* 27 (1968): 138—53.

—, "Traditio-Historical Method and the Documentary Hypothesis." *Proceedings of the Fifth World Congress of Jewish Studies,* 1969, 5—11.

—, *Das überlieferungsgeschichtliche Problem des Pentateuch*. Beiheft zur *Zeitschrift für die alttestamentliche Wissenschaft* 147. Berlin/New York: Walter de Gruyter, 1977.

—, "The 'Yahwist' as Theologian? The Dilemma of Pentateuchal Criticism." *Journal for the Study of the Old Testament* 3 (1977): 2—10.

Reuss, E., *Die Geschichte der Heiligen Schriften des Alten Testaments*. Braunschweig: C. A. Schwetschke, 1890.

Reventlow, H. Graf, *Liturgie und prophetisches Ich bei Jeremia*. Gütersloh: Gerd Mohn, 1963.

Reviv, H., "The History of Judah from Hezekiah to Josiah." *The World History of the Jewish People*. Jerusalem: Massada, 1979. Vol. IV/1, 193—204.

Rietzschel, C., *Das Problem der Urrolle: Ein Beitrag zur Redaktionsgeschichte des Jeremiabuches*. Gütersloh: Gerd Mohn, 1966.

Robinson, T. H., "Baruch's Roll." *Zeitschrift für die alttestamentliche Wissenschaft* 42 (1924): 209—21.

Rose, M., "Bemerkungen zum historischen Fundament des Josia-Bildes in II Reg 22 f." *Zeitschrift für die alttestamentliche Wissenschaft* 89 (1977): 50—63.

Rost, L., "Sinaibund und Davidbund." *Theologische Literaturzeitung* 72 (1947): 129—34.

Rowley, H. H., "The Prophet Jeremiah and the Book of Deuteronomy." *Studies in Old Testament Prophecy Presented to T. H. Robinson*. New York: Scribner's, 1950. 157—74.

Rudolph, W., *Jeremia*. Handbuch zum Alten Testament 12. Tübingen: J. C. B. Mohr, 1947.

Saggs, H. W. F., *The Greatness that was Babylon*. London/New York: Sidgwick and Jackson/Hawthorn, 1962.

Šanda, A., *Die Bücher der Könige*. Exegetisches Handbuch. Münster, 1912. Vol. 2.

Scharbert, J., *Die Prophetie Israels um 600 v. Chr.* Köln: J. P. Bachem, 1967.

Scharff, A., *Ägypten und Vorderasien im Altertum*. München: F. Bruckmann, 1950.

Seebass, H., "Jeremias Konflikt mit Chananja. Bemerkungen zu Jer 27 und 28." *Zeitschrift für die alttestamentliche Wissenschaft* 82 (1970): 449–52.

Seitz, C. R., "The Crisis of Interpretation over the Meaning and Purpose of the Exile." *Vetus Testamentum* 35 (1985): 78–97.

Simons, J., *Jerusalem in the Old Testament*. Leiden: Brill, 1952.

Skinner, J., *Genesis*. International Critical Commentary. New York: Scribner's, 1917.

Smith, M., *Palestinian Parties and Politics that Shaped the Old Testament*. New York: Columbia University Press, 1971.

—, "Jewish Religious Life." *The Cambridge History of Judaism*. Edited by W. D. Davies and L. Finkelstein. Cambridge: University Press, 1984. Vol. 1, 219–78.

Snaith, J. G., "Literary Criticism and Historical Investigation in Jeremiah Chapter XLVI." *Journal of Semitic Studies* 46 (1972): 15–32.

Soggin, J. A., "Der Judäische 'am-ha'areṣ und das Königtum in Juda." *Vetus Testamentum* 13 (1963): 187–95.

—, *Das Königtum in Israel*. Beiheft zur *Zeitschrift für die alttestamentliche Wissenschaft* 104. Berlin: Alfred Töpelmann, 1967.

Spalinger, A., "Esarhaddon and Egypt: An Analysis of the First Invasion of Egypt." *Orientalia* 43 (1974): 295–326.

—, "Assurbanipal and Egypt: A Source Study." *Journal of the American Oriental Society* 94 (1974): 316–28.

—, "Psammetichus, King of Egypt: I." *The Journal of the American Research Center in Egypt* 13 (1976): 133–47.

—, "Egypt and Babylonia: A Survey c. 620 B. C.–550 B. C." *Studien zur altägyptischen Kultur* 5 (1977): 221–44.

—, "Psammetichus, King of Egypt: II." *The Journal of the American Research Center in Egypt* 15 (1978): 49–57.

Speiser, E. A., "The Background and Function of the Biblical Nāśî'." *Catholic Biblical Quarterly* 25 (1963): 111–7.

Spieckermann, H., *Juda in der Sargonidenzeit*. Göttingen: Vandenhoeck & Ruprecht, 1982.

Spohn, M. G. L., *Ieremias Vates e versiones Iudaeorum Alexandrinorum ac reliquorum us interpretum graecorum emendatus notisque criticis illustratus*. Leipzig, 1824.

Stager, L., "The Archaeology of the East Slope of Jerusalem." *Journal of Near Eastern Studies* 41 (1981): 16–22.

Stohlmann, S., "The Judaean Exile after 701 B. C. E." *Scripture in Context II: More Essays on the Comparative Method*. Edited by W. W. Hallo, J. C. Moyer, and L. G. Perdue. Winona Lake, Indiana: Eisenbrauns, 1983. 147–75.

Sulzberger, M., *The Am Ha-aretz: the Ancient Hebrew Parliament*. Philadelphia, 1909.

—, "The Polity of the Ancient Hebrews." *Jewish Quarterly Review* 25 (1912/13): 1–81.

Tadmor, H., "The Campaigns of Sargon II of Assur: A Chronological Historical Study." *Journal of Cuneiform Studies* 12 (1958): 22–40; 77–91.

—, "'The People' and the Kingship in Ancient Israel: The Role of Political Institutions in the Biblical Period." *Journal of World History* 11 (1968): 46–68.

—, "Assyria and the West: The Ninth Century and its Aftermath." *Unity and Diversity: Essays in the History, Literature, and Religion of the Ancient Near East*. Edited by H. Goedicke and J. J. M. Roberts. Baltimore and London: Johns Hopkins, 1975.

Talmon, S., "The Judaean 'am ha'areṣ in Historical Perspective." *Fourth World Congress of Jewish Studies, Papers.* Jerusalem, 1967. Vol. 1, 71—6.

—, "The Old Testament Text." *Qumran and the History of the Biblical Text.* Edited by F. M. Cross and S. Talmon. Cambridge: Harvard, 1975.

Terrien, S., "The Omphalos Myth and Hebrew Religion." *Vetus Testamentum* 20 (1970): 315—38.

Thiel, W., *Die deuteronomistische Redaktion von Jeremia 1—25.* Wissenschaftliche Monographien zum Alten und Neuen Testament 41. Neukirchen-Vluyn: Neukirchener, 1973.

—, *Die deuteronomistische Redaktion von Jeremia 26—45.* WMANT 52. Neukirchen-Vluyn: Neukirchener, 1981.

Thiele, E., "The Chronology of the Kings of Judah and Israel." *Journal of Near Eastern Studies* 3 (1944): 137—86.

—, *The Mysterious Numbers of the Hebrew Kings: A Reconstruction of the Chronology of the Kingdoms of Israel and Judah.* Grand Rapids: Eerdmans/Paternoster, 1965.

Thompson, J. A., *The Book of Jeremiah.* New International Critical Commentary on the Old Testament. Grand Rapids: Eerdmans, 1980.

Thornton, T. C. G., "Charismatic Kingship in Israel and Judah." *Journal of Theological Studies* 14 (1963): 1—11.

Torczyner, H., *The Lachish Letters.* London: Oxford, 1938.

Tov, I., "L'Incidence de la Critique Textuelle sur la Critique Littéraire dans le Livre de Jérémie." *Revue Biblique* 79 (1972): 189—99.

—, "Some Aspects of the Textual and Literary History of the Book of Jeremiah." *Le Livre de Jérémie.* Leuven: University Press, 1981.

Tromp, N. J., *Primitive Conceptions of Death and the Nether World in the Old Testament. Bibliotheca Orientalis* 21. Rome: Pontifical, 1969.

Tushingham, A. D., "A Royal Israelite Seal (?) and the Royal Jar Handle Stamps." *Bulletin of the American Schools of Oriental Research* 200 (1970): 71—8; *BASOR* 201 (1971): 23—35.

Umbreit, F. W. C., *Praktischer Commentar über den Jeremia.* Hamburg: Friedrich Perthes, 1842.

Ussishkin, D., "Royal Judean Stamp Handles and Private Seal Impressions." *Bulletin of the American Schools of Oriental Research* 223 (1976): 1—13.

Vatke, W., *Historisch-kritische Einleitung in das Alte Testament.* Bonn: Emil Strauss, 1886.

de Vaux, R., *Ancient Israel: Social Institutions.* New York: McGraw-Hill, 1965.

—, Review of Aharoni's *Excavations at Ramat Raḥel, Seasons 1959 and 1960. Revue Biblique* 73 (1966): 270—1.

Volz, P., *Der Prophet Jeremia.* Kommentar zum Alten Testament 10. Leipzig: A. Deichertsche Verlagsbuchhandlung D. Werner Scholl, 1928.

Wanke, G., *Untersuchungen zur sogenannten Baruchschrift.* Beiheft zur *Zeitschrift für die alttestamentliche Wissenschaft* 122. Berlin/New York: Walter de Gruyter, 1971.

Weber, M., *Das antike Judentum.* Tübingen, 1931.

Weidner, E., "Jojachin, König von Juda, in babylonischen Keilschrifttexten." *Mélanges Syriens offrets à Monsieur René Dussaud, II.* Paris: Paul Geuthner, 1939. 923—35.

Weinberg, S. S., "Post-Exilic Palestine: An Archeological Report." *Proceedings of the Israel Academy of Sciences and Humanities* IV/5 (1971): 78—97.

Weinfeld, M., "Deuteronomy — The Present State of the Inquiry." *Journal of Biblical Literature* 86 (1967): 249—62.

—, *Deuteronomy and the Deuteronomic School.* Oxford: University, 1972.

Weippert, Helga, *Die Prosareden des Jeremiabuches.* Beiheft zur *Zeitschrift für die alttestamentliche Wissenschaft* 132. Berlin/New York: Walter de Gruyter, 1973.

Weiser, A., "Das Gotteswort für Baruch. Jer. 45 und die sogenannte Baruchbiographie." *Glaube und Geschichte im Alten Testament und andere ausgewählte Schriften.* Göttingen: Vandenhoeck & Ruprecht, 1961. 321—9.

—, *The Old Testament. Its Formation and Development.* New York: Association, 1966.

Welch, A., *The Code of Deuteronomy.* New York: George H. Doran, 1924.

Wellhausen, J., *Prolegomena to the History of Israel.* Preface by W. Robertson Smith. Edinburgh: Adam and Charles Black, 1885.

Welten, P., *Die Königs-Stempel. Ein Beitrag zur Militärpolitik Judas unter Hiskia und Josia.* Wiesbaden: Abhandlungen des Deutschen Palästina-Vereins 4, 1969.

Westermann, C., *Genesis.* Biblischer Kommentar I/3. Neukirchen-Vluyn: Neukirchener, 1982.

de Wette, W. M. L., *Dissertatio critico-exegetica, qua Deuteronomium a prioribus Pentateuchi libris diversum, alius cuiusdam recentioris auctoris opus esse monstratur.* [Reprinted in his *Opuscula,* Berlin, 1833].

—, *Lehrbuch der historisch-kritischen Einleitung in die kanonischen und apokryphischen Bücher des Alten Testaments.* Berlin: Georg Reimer, 1869.

Wevers, J. W., *Ezekiel.* New Century Bible. Grand Rapids: Eerdmans, 1982.

Whitley, C. F., "The Date of Jeremiah's Call." *Vetus Testamentum* 14 (1963): 467—83.

Willi, T., *Der Chronik als Auslegung. Untersuchungen zur literarischen Gestaltung der historischen Überlieferung Israels.* Forschungen zur Religion und Literatur des Alten und Neuen Testaments 106. Göttingen: Vandenhoeck & Ruprecht, 1972.

Wilson, R., *Prophecy and Society in Ancient Israel.* Philadelphia: Fortress, 1980.

—, "Prophecy in Crisis: The Call of Ezekiel." *Interpretation* 38 (1984): 117—30.

Wiseman, D. J., "The Vassal Treaties of Esarhaddon." *Iraq* 20 (1958): 1—99.

—, *Chronicles of Chaldean Kings (626—556 B. C.) in the British Museum.* London: Trustees of the British Museum, 1961.

Wolff, H. W., "Das Kerygma des deuteronomistischen Geschichtswerks." *Zeitschrift für die alttestamentliche Wissenschaft* 73 (1961): 171—86. Reprinted in English as "The Kerygma of the Deuteronomistic Historical Work." *The Vitality of Old Testament Traditions.* Edited by W. Brueggemann and H. W. Wolff. Atlanta: John Knox, 1975. 83—100.

Würthwein, E., *Der ʿamm haʾarez im Alten Testament.* Beiträge zur Wissenschaft vom Alten und Neuen Testament 17. Stuttgart: Kohlhammer, 1936.

—, "Die Josianische Reform und das Deuteronomium." *Zeitschrift für Theologie und Kirche* 73 (1976): 395—423.

—, *Die Bücher der Könige: 1 Kön. 17 — 2 Kön. 25.* Das Alte Testament Deutsch 11,2. Göttingen: Vandenhoeck & Ruprecht, 1984.

Yadin, Y., Editor, *Jerusalem Revealed: Archeology in the Holy City, 1908—1974.* New Haven and London: Yale University Press and the Israel Exploration Society, 1976.

—, "The Historical Significance of Inscription 88 from Arad: A Suggestion." *Israel Exploration Journal* 26 (1976): 9—14.

Yeivin, S., "Families and Parties in the Kingdom of Judah." *Tarbiz* 12 (1941/2): 241 ff. [Hebrew].

—, "The Sepulchers of the Kings of the House of David." *Journal of Near Eastern Studies* 7 (1948): 30—48.

Zenger, E., "Die deuteronomistische Interpretation der Rehabilitierung Jojachins." *Biblische Zeitschrift* 12 (1968): 16—30.

Zimmerli, W., "The History of Israelite Religion." *Tradition and Interpretation: Essays by Members of the Society for Old Testament Study.* Edited by G. W. Anderson. Oxford: At the Clarendon, 1979. 351—9.

—, *Ezekiel 1.* Hermeneia. Translated by Ronald E. Clements. Philadelphia: Fortress, 1979.

—, *Ezekiel 2.* Hermeneia. Translated by James D. Martin. Philadelphia: Fortress, 1983.

Author Index

Würthwein, E. 2 n., 43, 43 n., 46, 46 n., 168 n., 169 n., 170, 173 n., 174, 175, 175 n., 178 n., 179 n., 181, 181 n., 199 n., 309

Yadin, Y. 63 n., 74 n., 309

Yeivin, S. 112, 112 n., 215 n., 309

Zenger, E. 19 n., 121 n., 196 n., 197 n., 199 n., 215 n., 219 n., 263 n., 309

Zimmerli, W. 21 n., 115 n., 121 n., 123 n., 124 n., 132 n., 134, 135, 136, 136 n., 137, 137 n., 140 n., 142, 148 n., 151 n., 153 n., 156 n., 159 n., 192 n., 309

Index of Biblical Texts

PAUL TILLICH
Main Works/Hauptwerke

6 Volumes. Large-octavo. Cloth

Edited by/Herausgegeben von Carl Heinz Ratschow
with the collaboration of/unter Mitwirkung von John Clayton,
Gert Hummel, Theodor Mahlmann, Michael Palmer,
Robert P. Scharlemann, Gunther Wenz

Already published

Volume 1/Band 1:

Philosophical Writings/Philosophische Schriften

Editor/Herausgber: Gunther Wenz
1989. XIV, 424 pages. DM 134, – ISBN 3 11 011533 6

Volume 4/Band 4:

**Writings in the Philosophy of Religion/
Religionsphilosophische Schriften**

Editor/Herausgeber: John Clayton
1987. IV, 422 pages. DM 118, – ISBN 3 11 011342 2

Volume 5/Band 5:

Writings on Religion/Religiöse Schriften

Editor/Herausgeber: Robert P. Scharlemann
1988. XVI, 325 pages. DM 98, – ISBN 3 11 011541 7

In press:

Volume 2/Band 2:

**Writings in the Philosophy of Culture/
Kulturphilosophische Schriften**

Editor/Herausgeber: Michael Palmer
1989. Approx. 384 pages. Approx. DM 118, – ISBN 3 11 011535 2

In preparation

Volume 3/Band 3:

**Writings in Social Philosophy and Ethics/
Sozialphilosophische und ethische Schriften**

Editor/Herausgeber: Theodor Mahlmann

Volume 6/Band 6:

Theological Writings/Theologische Schriften

Editor/Herausgeber: Gert Hummel

Prices are subject to change

Walter de Gruyter   **Berlin · New York**

SPÄTMITTELALTER UND REFORMATION

Texte und Untersuchungen

Edited by Heiko A. Oberman

Gregor von Rimini

Gregorii Ariminensis OESA
Lectura super Primum et Secundum Sententiarum
Ediderunt A. Damasus Trapp OSA, Venício Marcolino

Tomus I: Super Primum (Prologus, Dist 1—6)
Prologus: Edidit Willigis Eckermann OSA, collaborante Manfred Schulze.
Dist 1—6: Elaboraverunt Manuel Santos-Noya, Walter Simon, Wolfgang Urban
1981. Large-octavo. CIV, 522 pages. Cloth DM 234, —
ISBN 3 11 004950 3 (SuR, Volume 6)

Tomus II: Super Primum (Dist 7—17)
Elaboraverunt Venício Marcolino, Manuel Santos-Noya,
Walter Simon, Volker Wendland
1982. Large-octavo. VI, 491 pages. Cloth DM 228, —
ISBN 3 11 006517 7 (SuR, Volume 7)

Tomus III: Super Primum (Dist 19—48)
Elaboraverunt Venício Marcolino, Walter Simon, Wolfgang Urban, Volker Wendland
1984. Large-octavo. VII, 535 pages. Cloth DM 244, —
ISBN 3 11 006965 2 (SuR, Volume 8)

Tomus IV: Super Secundum (Dist 1—5)
Elaboraverunt A. Damasus Trapp OSA, Manuel Santos-Noya, Manfred Schulze
1978. Large-octavo. LXI, 396 pages. Cloth DM 198, —
ISBN 3 11 006516 9 (SuR, Volume 9)

Tomus V: Super Secundum (Dist 6—18)
Elaboraverunt A. Damasus Trapp OSA, Venício Marcolino, Manuel Santos-Noya
1979. Large-octavo. VI, 392 pages. Cloth DM 168, —
ISBN 3 11 004951 1 (SuR, Volume 10)

Tomus VI: Super Secundum (Dist 24—44)
Elaboraverunt Venício Marcolino, Walter Simon, Volker Wendland
1980. Large-octavo. VIII, 337 pages. Cloth DM 148, —
ISBN 3 11 006751 X (SuR, Volume 11)

Tomus VII: Indices
Index rerum: Elaboravit Manuel Santos-Noya, collaborante
Venício Marcolino. Index auctorum: Elaboravit Wolfgang Urban
1987. Large-octavo. X, 380 pages. Cloth DM 184, —
ISBN 3 11 007808 2 (SuR, Volume 12)

Prices are subject to change

Walter de Gruyter   **Berlin · New York**